GOD IS BACK

GOD IS BACK

How the Global Rise of Faith
Is Changing the World

JOHN MICKLETHWAIT
AND ADRIAN WOOLDRIDGE

ALLEN LANE
an imprint of
PENGUIN BOOKS

ALLEN LANE

Published by the Penguin Group
Penguin Books Ltd, 80 Strand, London WC2R 0RL, England
Penguin Group (USA) Inc., 375 Hudson Street, New York, New York 10014, USA
Penguin Group (Canada), 90 Eglinton Avenue East, Suite 700, Toronto, Ontario, Canada M4P 2Y3
(a division of Pearson Penguin Canada Inc.)
Penguin Ireland, 25 St Stephen's Green, Dublin 2, Ireland (a division of Penguin Books Ltd)
Penguin Group (Australia), 250 Camberwell Road, Camberwell, Victoria 3124, Australia
(a division of Pearson Australia Group Pty Ltd)
Penguin Books India Pvt Ltd, 11 Community Centre, Panchsheel Park, New Delhi – 110 017, India
Penguin Group (NZ), 67 Apollo Drive, Rosedale, North Shore 0632, New Zealand
(a division of Pearson New Zealand Ltd)
Penguin Books (South Africa) (Pty) Ltd, 24 Sturdee Avenue, Rosebank, Johannesburg 2196, South Africa

Penguin Books Ltd, Registered Offices: 80 Strand, London WC2R 0RL, England

www.penguin.com

First published in the United States of America by The Penguin Press,
a member of Penguin Group (USA) Inc. 2009
First published in Great Britain by Allen Lane 2009
1

Copyright © John Micklethwait and Adrian Wooldridge, 2009

The moral right of the authors has been asserted

Printed in Great Britain by Clays Ltd, St Ives plc

A CIP catalogue record for this book is available from the British Library

978-0-713-99902-0

www.greenpenguin.co.uk

Mixed Sources
Product group from well-managed
forests and other controlled sources
www.fsc.org Cert no. SA-COC-1592
© 1996 Forest Stewardship Council
FSC

Penguin Books is committed to a sustainable future
for our business, our readers and our planet.
The book in your hands is made from paper
certified by the Forest Stewardship Council.

For
Gus, Charlie, Hubert and Milanda Read
and Alexander and Penelope Privitera

CONTENTS

INTRODUCTION

IT WOULD BE HARD to find a better cross-section of the "new China" than the people gathered in the sitting room of this comfortable apartment in one of Shanghai's gated communities. The host for the day, Wang, is—right down to the BlackBerry on his belt—a prosperous, bespectacled management consultant, who once worked for Intel.[1] The guests, sitting on sofas and chairs brought in from the kitchen, or perched on the floor, include a pair of biotechnologists, a Chinese American doctor from Los Angeles, a prominent academic, a manager from a state-owned business, two ballet dancers and several successful entrepreneurs. A laptop adorns the coffee table, BMWs are parked in front of the building and advertisements for jewelry decorate the elevator. These people may not be Shanghai's super-rich, but they are well off and educated, men and women on their way up in life.

They are gathered in Wang's sitting room to worship God and interpret His ways to man. The proceedings are informal—as with most house churches, there is no pastor, just a group of Christians gathered together to discuss the Bible. The service is introduced by a chic young woman in a Che Guevara T-shirt. She apologizes for the late start, asking with a giggle why there are always technical problems when it is her turn. (Her husband is fiddling with the laptop.) She says a spontaneous prayer and the group sings the first hymn. The accompanying music is downloaded from the Internet and the words are beamed up on the apartment wall from the laptop with the help of a projector that Wang normally uses for corporate presentations. True to this karaoke format, the hymns are jaunty in a slightly overwrought way: the lead singer on the downloaded track sounds like a Chinese Céline Dion. The young fashionista follows on with four unscripted prayers, interspersed with four hymns, one with a smattering of English words. Then Wang takes over.

He starts by asking everybody to introduce themselves. There are a few absentees, including the owner of the apartment, who is away finishing a deal in Shenzhen, but Wang welcomes back a pharmaceuticals executive who has just returned from a visit to New Jersey. There are handshakes and a few hugs. Most of the children are ushered into a bedroom and bribed, not altogether successfully, to stay quiet with an assortment of sweets, videos and toy guns. It is time for the real business: Romans 1:18–32. The congregation reads the text together from heavily annotated Bibles. Then the discussion, led by Wang, begins. It lasts for almost two and a half hours.

Every sentence in the scripture is examined, beginning with the idea that God is wrathful. What exactly does this mean? Wang explains that the Lord's anger is triggered only by wickedness, which Wang defines as the opposite of righteousness (the topic of the previous week's meeting). The wicked are people who knew the right path—God had revealed Himself to them—but ignored it. This is the prompt for a long discussion about different forms of revelation and their relation to nature. Various passages of scripture are scrutinized, with a striking number of corporate allusions: the meteorologist cites research by Enron into predicting the weather; Wang argues that Adam was the first chief executive—everybody flips back through their Bibles to read the passage—because he was given dominion over nature. But gradually, the discussion of revelation gives way to a passionate attack on Darwinism. Evolutionary theory, argues Wang, breaking into English to reiterate the words, is "the biggest lie," because it pretends to be rigorous science. This is immediately confirmed by a biotechnologist who works on stem cells. Every day she looks at them, admiring their beauty and complexity: stem cells must be divine. If you trust evolution, you distrust God, rejoins the surgeon. Evolution is another false idol—not unlike Buddhism, Taoism, Confucianism or any of the other mock religions that China's Communists are trying to promote, now that they have discovered that they cannot kill God.

The second part of Romans 1:18–32 includes the New Testament's denunciation of homosexuality and other "shameful passions." ("Even the women pervert the natural use of their sex by unnatural acts. In the same way the men give up natural sexual relations with women and burn with passion for each other. Men do shameful things with each other, and as a result they bring upon themselves the punishment they deserve for their wrongdoing.") At first, Wang does not want to go there: he would rather concentrate on revelation. But he gets drawn in by one of the scientists, who asks about transsexual operations. These are not natural, advises Wang; like euthanasia, they are invading God's domain. As for homosexuality, it is plainly a sin—the text could not be clearer. But aren't homosexual urges natural in some people? The doctor backs up this observation by citing a paper from the American Psychological Association, and the group agrees that homosexual sinners should not be punished any differently from heterosexual sinners. The real problem is general immorality, which is on the increase all over Shanghai. Somebody mentions Sodom and Gomorrah. The passage is read—and one of the English speakers, perhaps wanting to show his translation skills, explains at some length how the word "sodomization" was derived. There is some awkward shuffling, relieved only when somebody else condemns gambling, citing a Royal Caribbean Cruise as evidence.

The most remarkable part of the Bible study comes at the very end. In his summary, Wang brings many of the evening's themes together—revelation, righteousness and false idols—and links them in a nationalist call to arms. Countries with lots of Christians become more powerful. America grew strong because it was Christian. The more Christian China becomes, the mightier it will be. If you want China to be a truly prosperous country, you must spread the Word to nonbelievers. If you are a patriotic Chinese, you have to be a Christian.

The service finishes with a couple of personal prayers. The worshippers wriggle out of the sofas and chairs. A few are going to a formal service that afternoon at one of Shanghai's government-recognized churches (largely for the children's sake, one person says). Most, however, seem to have something to do. There are meetings to attend, flights to catch, offices, hospitals and laboratories to run. They will once again be Chinese on the make—and now they have a patriotic duty to spread the Word as well.

ONWARD CHINESE SOLDIERS

The Chinese still regard the militantly atheist Mao Zedong as a national hero. Mao put religion second only to capitalism in his list of reactionary evils: he killed clergy, expelled foreign missionaries and destroyed temples and churches. Now China is rethinking.

The economic liberalization that followed Mao's death brought the "Great Leap Forward" that Marxist orthodoxy had singularly failed to deliver. But it also brought a disorientating whirlwind of change. The pell-mell pace of economic progress—the Chinese economy has doubled in size every eight years since the 1970s—is supersizing cities and decanting millions of people from the countryside. China is building skyscrapers and highways, suburban subdivisions and gated communities, shopping centers and theme parks, on a scale unprecedented in human history. The construction industry employs a workforce the size of California's population. And the advance of the new civilization inevitably means taking a wrecking ball to the old.[2]

This whirlwind is boosting demand for the consolations of religion. Wang's house church is part of what may well be the biggest advance of Christianity ever. The Chinese government's own figures show the number of Christians rising from fourteen million in 1997 to twenty-one million in 2006, with an estimated fifty-five thousand official Protestant churches and forty-six hundred Catholic churches.[3] (The government made religious freedom part of the constitution in 1982, though it limited worship to five official religions—Buddhism, Taoism, Islam, Protestantism and Catholicism—each overseen by a "patriotic association."[4]) But these figures exclude both house churches and the underground Catholic Church, which is bigger than the official one. A conservative guess is that there are at least sixty-five million Protestants in China and twelve million Catholics—more believers than there are members of the Communist Party. Some local Christians think the flock is well over one hundred million.[5]

Whatever the true numbers, the world's major religions are currently engaged in a "scramble for China." According to a survey by the Pew Global Attitudes Project in 2006, 31 percent of Chinese people regard religion as very or somewhat important in their lives, while only 11 percent toe the Maoist line that religion is not at all important. A poll in 2005, asking a slightly different question, put the proportion of people who deem religion important at 56 percent.[6]

That said, for most Chinese people religion is still a vague affair, mixing folklore with ancestor worship. Only about a fifth of Chinese name a particular religion as their creed, and most of them plump for some form of Buddhism, Taoism on Confucianism, plainly the varieties the state prefers.[7] Xinhua, the distinctly secular state news agency, recently proudly announced that there were approximately one hundred million Chinese Buddhists. The Olympics began at exactly 8 p.m. on the eighth day of the eighth month in 2008—because many Chinese people regard the number eight as lucky. It is no longer frowned on to wear prayer beads in the cities. In the countryside Buddhist temples are fast becoming part of the local economy. Every summer some two hundred thousand people visit the Black Dragon Temple in Yulin, a city in Guangxi Province, for its ten-day fair; local state officials and policemen are cut into the deal through taxes and gifts.[8] Despite the clashes with Buddhist monks in Tibet, the government tolerates an ornate, private Tibetan shrine in the heart of Beijing, and a few members of China's new commercial and political elite have followed the imperial tradition of seeking out confessor-gurus in Tibetan monasteries.[9]

Meanwhile, Islam is also surging, especially among the Hui and Uighur peoples in Ningxia and Xinjiang Provinces. Official numbers indicate that there are about twenty million Muslims. Again, that is probably an underestimate, but the Pew researchers point out that even using that number, China has almost as many Muslims as Saudi Arabia and nearly twice as many as the European Union's twenty-seven countries. By 2050, China could well be the world's biggest Muslim nation as well as its biggest Christian one.

The growth of Christianity is nevertheless the most startling religious development. Catholicism is vigorous in parts of Beijing and especially in poor rural areas. The Virgin Mary has a particular attraction: fishermen have started dedicating their boats to her, and every May thousands of Catholics descend on Donglu, a village in Hebei Province where the Virgin is said to have appeared in 1900 to rescue local Catholics during the Boxer Rebellion. A decade ago, the authorities imprisoned an underground Catholic bishop who led the festivities there—but he was quietly released in 2007. Nowadays police cordon off the village each May.[10]

Yet the core of Christianity in China is urban and Protestant. Evangelical churches took off at the same time as China itself did in the 1990s, drawing heavily on American and South Korean Protestantism. China has been a fixation for American missionaries since the nineteenth century. Nowadays the South Koreans, Asia's most enthusiastic Christians (who were mostly converted by the Americans), are even more numerous. One ruse is to set up trading companies in China that are really missionary outposts. Close to the North Korean border, there is even a full-scale Protestant university, which has now wangled permission to operate in Pyongyang too.[11]

Still, most Chinese churches are homegrown. They come in all shapes and sizes. The Fengcheng Fellowship (of house churches), which is based in Henan Province and headed by Zhang Rongliang, China's most prominent Protestant, claims to have ten million members.[12] But most house churches are like Wang's outfit: autonomous and reasonably small. Chinese Christians are inveterate downloaders. Many pastors find their stiffest competition not in the sermons of their local rivals around the corner, but in the weekly Web offerings from Asian megapreachers, such as Stephen Tong, who is based in Indonesia. Another notable characteristic, shared by both the South Koreans next door and the early Christians, is the importance of women as evangelizers: one Protestant jokes that the most popular silent prayer in house churches is for a husband, and the second most popular one is for a better husband.

House churches offer a remarkable formula for growth. They can be started by anybody: one prominent house church in Beijing was established by a foreign ministry official. Wang started his church in September 2006 with five or six friends. Now it has sprouted two offshoots: one is a specialist church for migrants; the other, which brings together a group similar to Wang's, uses the local office of a well-known American multinational as its base (a popular strategy, since offices are closed on Sundays). Now that the three churches attract about a hundred people, the worshippers will soon have to start another one. The Chinese government has set an informal limit of twenty-five people for an unauthorized religious gathering. Nowadays, most local authorities enforce this rule sporadically (there were twenty-eight people at Wang's Sunday service, not including the children) or not at all (in Wuhan, the capital city of Hubei Province, the congregation can run into the hundreds, reports one of Wang's flock). The danger for most house churches is not a police raid, but the possibility that a neighbor will complain about the noisy singing or, more likely still in China's overcrowded cities, about parking spaces being taken up. Yet as Wang's fast-growing flock illustrates, the twenty-five-person rule is a formula for growth, uncommonly close to that enforced on early Christians by similar demands for secrecy. It is the same cell model pioneered by John Wesley, the founder of Methodism, and by South Korean Protestants. It is almost as if the government secretly wants us to take over, muses Wang.

In fact, the Chinese government seems to have mixed feelings about religion. Hardliners still associate religious faith, particularly Christianity, with insurrection. The famous Taiping Rebellion (of Great Peace) in the nineteenth century was led by a Christian who claimed to be Christ's brother—and only put down at the cost of more than twenty million lives. The authorities think that John Paul II had an outsized role in bringing down the Soviet Union. Many of the student leaders at the Tiananmen Square protests in 1989 have become Christians. Zhang Rongliang, the head of the Fengcheng Fellowship, has been in and out of jail since the 1970s. China's relentless persecution of the Falun Gong cult shows how nervous it is about independent thought and organization.

Such worries are exacerbated by the fact that the growing religious organizations are becoming political actors in their own right. House churches have begun to add pastors, schools, libraries, even a few unofficial seminaries. One enthusiast boasts that house churches "are already the largest NGO in the country." Many churches teach the sanctity of life, a lively issue in a country where abortions have been routine. In Donglu, the Catholic nuns run a small clinic.[13] At the Black Dragon Temple, there is a thriving boarding school. In Xinjiang Province, the mosques control so much that the state government is worried about Muslim separatism; a scatter of terrorist incidents before the 2008 Olympics provided an excuse for a clampdown, but the problem remains. Even ancestor worship is having an unsettling effect on politics in the countryside, making it more likely that the village leader will be elected to that role because of his position in the clan hierarchy, rather than his loyalty to the party.

Yet on the other hand the regime increasingly accepts that some kind of moral code is useful to build a "harmonious society." Indeed, some of China's younger technocrats now openly welcome Confucianism, which Mao condemned as "feudal," as a form of social glue in their fast-changing country. The state has sponsored several Buddhist gatherings and is building Confucian institutes around the world. In October 2007 the Communist Party added an amendment to its constitution, with the personal imprimatur of President Hu, urging its members to "rally religious believers in making contributions to economic and social development."[14] At the local level, especially in the countryside, Buddhism and communism have fused: temple chiefs are often party bosses as well. The Chinese authorities are edging toward the conclusion that God and modernization can go hand in hand.

That case has been made most explicitly by a Chinese government economist, Zhao Xiao, in a widely read essay, "Market Economies with Churches and Market Economies Without Churches." Based on his travels around America, the paper, published in 2002, argues that the key to America's commercial success is not its natural resources, its financial system or its technology but its churches, "the very core that binds Americans together." The market economy, argues Zhao, is efficient because it discourages idleness, but it can also encourage people to lie and injure others. It thus needs a moral underpinning. At the end of the essay, as he travels from Boston to Indiana, "through North America's vast lands, the serene sounds of church bells ringing in every church," Zhao recalls an angry poem:

> *Be in awe of the invincible might,*
> *Be in awe of the lightning,*
> *And be in awe of the thunder in the sky.*

Without that awe, argues Zhao, China will not succeed. "Only through awe can we be saved. Only through faith can the market economy have a soul."

The people in Wang's church share Zhao's belief that worshipping God is the go-ahead thing to do. Asked why people become Christians, one man describes it as the sense of having joined the winner's circle. Every city has some form of club or network for Christian businesspeople. As he sips a cup of water after the service, Wang puts it simply. "In Europe the church is old. Here it is modern. Religion is a sign of higher ideals and progress. Spiritual wealth and material wealth go together. That is why we will win."

THE BATTLE FOR MODERNITY

Ever since the Enlightenment there has been a schism in Western thought over the relationship between religion and modernity. Europeans, on the whole, have assumed that modernity would marginalize religion; Americans, in the main, have assumed that the two things can thrive together.

This schism goes back to the modern world's two founding revolutions. The French and American Revolutions were both the offspring of the Enlightenment, but with very different views of the role that religion should play in reason's glorious republic. In France the *révolutionnaires* despised religion as a tool of the ancien régime. By contrast, America's Founding Fathers took a more benign view of religion. They divided church from state not least to protect the former from the latter.

These two versions of modernity have marched in different directions ever since. In Europe established churches sided with the old regime against the new world of democracy and liberty. In America, where there was no national established church, faiths embraced both democracy and the market: the only way they could survive was to attract customers. In Europe, "religion" meant war or oppression, Edmund Burke once observed; in America, it turned out to be a source of freedom.[15]

For most of the past two hundred years the European view of modernity has been in the ascendant. Europe gave birth to a succession of sages who explained, in compelling detail, why God was doomed. Karl Marx denounced religion as the "opium of the masses." Émile Durkheim and Max Weber argued that an iron law of history was leading to "secularization" (or "the disenchantment of the world," in Weber's rather more poetic phrase). Friedrich Nietzsche remarked, "I find it necessary to wash my hands after I have come into contact with religious people."[16] Sigmund Freud dismissed religion as a neurosis that was designed to divert attention from man's real interest, sex. A few intellectuals deplored God's disappearance, worrying that a godless world would also be a barbaric one. "When people stop believing in God," G. K. Chesterton argued, "they don't believe in nothing, they believe in anything." "If you will not have God (and He is a jealous God)", T. S. Eliot warned, "you should pay your respects to Hitler or Stalin."[17] Others welcomed the disappearance of an instrument of oppression and bigotry. A few tried to have it both ways: Jean-Paul Sartre railed against God's absence ("God doesn't exist—the bastard!"), yet celebrated the freedom that His departure provided. "Lord I disbelieve," E. M. Forster confessed, "help thou my unbelief."[18] Still, everyone who was anyone in European public life agreed that religion was dying—and that its effect on politics was ebbing.

The European idea, that you cannot become modern without throwing off religion's yoke, had a massive influence all around the world. It is hardly surprising that Marxist dictators such as Lenin and Mao tried to impose atheism by force. But a striking number of less dogmatic leaders in the developing world were also bent on enforcing secularization. In Turkey, Kemal Atatürk imposed a strict separation between mosque and state. ("The fez," he once complained, "sat upon our heads as a sign of ignorance, fanaticism, an obstacle to progress and to attaining a contemporary level of civilization.") In India, Jawaharlal Nehru tried to make "a clean sweep" of organized religion: "Almost always it seems to stand for blind belief and reaction, dogma and bigotry, superstition and exploitation and the preservation of vested interests." In the Middle East, Gamal Abdel Nasser and the Pahlavi shahs of Iran argued that their countries faced a choice between the mosque and mechanization; superstition and fanaticism had to be left behind.

America has always posed a problem for progressive secularists. Here was *the* quintessentially modern country. In his "Second Treatise" John Locke famously observed that "in the beginning all the world was America." The new republic was conceived as a *"novus ordo seculorum,"* as every dollar bill reminds us, a conscious antithesis to the European world of feudalism, the divine right of kings and state religion.

Still, as long as Europe remained the cultural arbiter of the world, America could be dismissed as an oddity. Perhaps America was nothing more than an evolutionary freak—the sociological equivalent of the duck-billed platypus. Americans might continue to worship God, but the rest of the world, as it modernized, would follow the European rather than the American example. Or perhaps the young country was just a little slow growing up: give it a bit more time and it would become as secular as Europe. The people you met on the cocktail circuit in New York and San Francisco seemed like sensible sorts. Surely the rubes would eventually catch up?

There were indeed signs that this was happening in the mid-twentieth century. American Evangelicals had retreated from the public square, embarrassed by the combination of Prohibition and the Scopes Monkey Trial, in 1925, where their views on evolution were mocked. Meanwhile, a growing army of American intellectuals argued that their country was becoming less exceptional. In 1959 C. Wright Mills, an influential sociologist at Columbia University, penned a self-confident summary of the modernization thesis in *The Sociological Imagination:* "After the Reformation and the Renaissance, the forces of modernization swept across the globe and secularization, a corollary historical process, loosened the dominance of the sacred. In due course, the sacred shall disappear altogether, except, possibly, in the private realm." In 1960, the same year that Jack Kennedy reassured worried Americans that his Catholic faith would not affect his politics, Daniel Bell argued in *The End of Ideology* that modern politics was no longer about the meaning of life but about who gets what—about how you distribute the largesse of an affluent society among various interest groups. In 1966, in its Easter issue, *Time* magazine asked "Is God Dead?" on its cover, and in the same year Thomas Altizer, a theologian, published to much acclaim *The Gospel of Christian Atheism.*[19] In 1968 Gallup found that sixty-seven percent of Americans believed that religion was losing its impact on society. A year later, an American reached the moon, meta-phorically conquering the heavens.

By the end of the twentieth century the intelligentsia had little doubt that modern man had outgrown God. Most trend-setting books in the 1990s saw the world through secular lenses.[20] Francis Fukuyama's *The End of History and the Last Man* predicted the triumph of secularization as well as liberalism. The word "religion" does not appear in the index of *Diplomacy,* Henry Kissinger's nine-hundred-page masterpiece on statesmanship, published in 1994. In 1980–99 only half a dozen of the articles in America's four main international-relations journals dealt with religion.[21] *The Economist* was so confident of the Almighty's demise that we published His obituary in our millennium issue.

Today an unsettling worry nags at Western liberals: what if secular Europe (and for that matter secular Harvard and secular Manhattan) is the odd one out? They are right to be worried. It now seems that it is the American model that is spreading around the world: religion and modernity are going hand in hand, not just in China but throughout much of Asia, Africa, Arabia and Latin America. It is not just that religion is thriving in many modernizing countries; it is also that religion is succeeding in harnessing the tools of modernity to propagate its message. The very things that were supposed to destroy religion—democracy and markets, technology and reason—are combining to make it stronger.

GOD IS BACK

Almost everywhere you look, from the suburbs of Dallas to the slums of São Paulo to the back streets of Bradford, you can see religion returning to public life. Most dramatically, Americans and their allies would not be dying in Iraq and Afghanistan had nineteen young Muslims not attacked the United States on September 11, 2001. America's next war could be against the Islamic Republic of Iran—or it could be dragged into a spat in Pakistan, where religious fanatics are determined to seize the country's nuclear weapons, or perhaps in West Africa, where there is a monumental clash between Evangelical Christianity surging northward and fundamentalist Islam heading south. Indeed, there are potential battlegrounds all around Islam's southern perimeter, along the tenth parallel, stretching through Sudan to the Philippines. Nor is it just a matter of Christians and Muslims. In Myanmar (Burma) Buddhist monks nearly brought down an evil regime; in Sri Lanka they have prolonged a bloody conflict with Hindu Tamils.

Meanwhile, many older conflicts have acquired a religious edge. The poisonous sixty-year war over Palestine began as a largely secular affair. Many of the pioneering Zionists in the early twentieth century saw the Middle East as an escape from the suffocating religiosity of Eastern European village life. Even after the Holocaust, the new "Jewish state" at first deemed religion a distraction: after Israel's founding in 1948 the secular David Ben-Gurion agreed that rabbinical law would prevail in matters such as marriage and divorce partly because he assumed the Orthodox would melt away. On the Palestinian side, many of the leaders of the PLO were Christian socialists; in Egypt, the spiritual champion of Arab nationalism, Nasser, clamped down on the radical Muslim Brotherhood. Nowadays, in the era of Hamas, Jewish settlers and Christian Zionists, the Israeli-Palestinian dispute has become a much more polarized, sectarian battle, with ever more people claiming that God is on their side.

As for the old Communist regimes, China is not the only country to have renewed its addiction to the opium of the masses. Vladimir Putin, that hardheaded product of the Soviet security apparatus, decks himself in symbols of religion in much the same way as Russian czars once did: he never takes off his baptismal cross, maintains a small chapel next door to his office in the Kremlin and has made regular visits to churches.[22] The KGB's successor, the FSB, has its own Orthodox church opposite its headquarters, complete with rare icons presented by the Patriarch. One poll in 2006— fifteen years after the fall of the Soviet regime—discovered that 84 percent of the Russian population believed in God while only 16 percent considered themselves atheists.[23] Meanwhile, Mikhail Gorbachev has shown signs that he is a Christian: after spending half an hour with his daughter Irina praying at the tomb of St. Francis of Assisi, the last Soviet leader confessed that "St. Francis is, for me, the *alter Christus,* the other Christ. His story fascinates me and has played a fundamental role in my life."

Atatürk's Turkey is now in the hands of an avowedly Islamist party. The president's wife, like many cosmopolitan women, wears a headscarf, once regarded as a symbol of backwardness. For most of the past decade India has been controlled by the Hindu nationalist BJP Party, which owed its ascendancy partly to the issue of the Ayodhya Temple, a fiercely contested place of worship for both Hindus and Muslims. And it is not just the familiar, bloody Hindu-Muslim divide. Two of the most touchy issues in modern Indian politics are the legality of Christian conversions of untouchables and an underwater "bridge" to Sri Lanka supposedly built by a team of monkeys for the Lord Rama, which the more secularist Congress Party wants to tamper with so that shipping can get through.

In America, the Evangelicals have long since reemerged from their caves. The religious right is an established part of politics in almost every state, and America has had a succession of "born again" presidents. The man it has just waved goodbye to was its most soul-on-the-sleeve religious leader since the nineteenth century: George Bush began each day on his knees and each cabinet meeting with a prayer, but he was a relatively moderate figure compared with Sarah Palin, the Pentecostal selected by John McCain to be his vice presidential candidate, who has undergone rites to protect her from witchcraft. The single most frequently used noun in the 2008 Republican Convention in St. Paul, Minnesota, was "God." But the left is not immune from the influence of religion either: Barack Obama borrowed the title of his autobiography, *The Audacity of Hope,* from a sermon delivered by Jeremiah Wright, the man who "brought him to God" when he was a young man (and later almost doomed his presidential campaign).

Religion is even (re-)emerging as a force in the very heartland of secularization. Europe is still a long way behind America: for instance, only one in ten French people say that religion plays an important role in their lives.[24] But nevertheless there are signs that the same forces that are reviving religion in America—the quest for community in an increasingly atomized world, the desire to counterbalance choice with a sense of moral certainty—are making headway in Europe. Across the Continent the loosening of the ties between church and state is opening the religious market. In France, the fastest growing creed is the most American of all, Pentecostalism. Some two million Britons have taken the so-called

Alpha Course, run by an Anglican church, Holy Trinity Brompton. After embracing modernism in the 1960s with Vatican II, the Catholic Church has now returned to a more traditional version of the faith, first under John Paul II and now under his successor, Benedict XVI. The aim is to Catholicize modernity rather than to modernize Catholicism.

The principle that European politicians do not "do God," as Alastair Campbell, Tony Blair's former spokesman, once angrily told an American magazine, looks out of date. Tony Blair was always a "praying person," and converted to Catholicism shortly after leaving office. His successor, Gordon Brown, claims that he learned his socialism listening to his preacher father's sermons. Before becoming president of France, Nicolas Sarkozy published *La République, les religions, l'espérance,* in which he called for a greater role for religion in public life. Poland's Law and Justice Party was elected on the promise of a "moral revolution," based on the social teachings of the Roman Catholic Church.

The arrival of millions of Muslims in Europe is also turbocharging religious debates. Growing Muslim minorities are plainly having a remarkable effect on European politics. At the most extreme end, this includes the bombings in Madrid and London, the killing of a Dutch filmmaker, Theo van Gogh, the riots in the Paris *banlieues* and the brouhaha about the Danish cartoons of Muhammad. More peacefully, the growth of Islam is also forcing secular people to reexamine the importance of religion. This applies both in working-class neighborhoods, where whites, confronted by immigration, are increasingly likely to identify themselves as Christian, and also in politics, where a striking number of the Continent's leaders, casting around for a reason not to admit Turkey to the European Union, have rediscovered Europe's Christian origins.

THE END OF ATHEISM

Another indication of religion's reappearance in the public sphere has been the outcry among secular intellectuals, many of whom hold that the real "clash of civilizations" is not between different religions but between superstition and modernity. A hit parade of recent books has torn into religion—Sam Harris's *The End of Faith,* Richard Dawkins's *The God Delusion* and Christopher Hitchens's *God Is Not Great—How Religion Poisons Everything.* The authors have crisscrossed the United States, debating religious leaders, even in the Bible Belt, in front of megachurch-sized audiences. Dawkins has set up an organization to empower atheists.

Part of that secular fury, especially in Europe, comes from exasperation. What if a central tenet of the French Enlightenment—that modernity would kill religion—is proving to be an *ancien canard*? Statistics about religious observance are notoriously untrustworthy, but most of them seem to indicate that the global drift toward secularism has been halted, and quite a few show religion to be on the increase. One estimate suggests that the proportion of people attached to the world's four biggest religions—Christianity, Islam, Buddhism and Hinduism—rose from 67 percent in 1900 to 73 percent in 2005 and may reach 80 percent by 2050.[25] Even if this number is padded by people moving from tribal religions to bigger ones, we are hardly seeing decline; and in terms of intensity—a harder-to-measure phenomenon—there seems to have been a considerable increase in most places outside Europe over the past half century.

For most casual observers the revival of religion means the revival of Islam. But Christianity is also growing rapidly, particularly across the developing world. In 1900 there were roughly ten million Christians in Africa. Today, thanks to waves of evangelization, there are four hundred million, almost half the population. And it is worth considering the intensity again. For instance, Latin America has been nominally Christian since the days of the conquistadores; but now the region is a much more competitive religious marketplace, with Evangelical faiths battling it out with Catholicism.

In most of these places, the growth in faith has coincided with a growth in prosperity. People are choosing to be Christians, or choosing which sort of Christians they want to be. Man, whether the neo-atheists like it or not, is a theotropic beast: given the option, he is inclined to believe in a God, not least because, as studies show, religion can increase his well-being in material as well as spiritual ways. (If one group of intellectuals is lamenting the rise of religion, another is trying to measure why it works.)

And it gets worse for the neo-atheists. There are two particularly upsetting things about the way that religion is prospering. The first is that the "wrong sorts" of religion are flourishing. In the 1960s most thinkers imagined that, if religion was to survive at all, it would be in its most reasonable and ecumenical guise—mild Anglicanism, say, or Graham Greene's doubting Catholicism. In fact, certainty has proved much easier to market: the sort of religions that claim Adam and Eve met exactly 6,005 years ago or that take a particularly strict interpretation of jihad. In America the tolerant-to-a-fault Episcopal Church has been in relentless decline. By contrast, the Southern Baptists have prospered. Altogether conservative Christians now make up a quarter of America's population, according to Pew, significantly more than fifty years ago. People who seek liberation from liberation do not turn to liberation theology.

The most remarkable religious success story of the past century has been the most emotional religion of all. Pentecostalism was founded just over a century ago in a scruffy part of Los Angeles by a one-eyed black preacher, convinced that God would send a new Pentecost if only people would pray hard enough. Today there are at least five hundred million renewalists around the world.[26] Their beliefs are not for the fainthearted. Most adherents have witnessed divine healing, exorcisms or speaking in tongues.

The hotter bits of Islam have also gained ground. As American neoconservatives never tire of pointing out, this is partly a matter of Saudi money: petrodollars have flowed into fundamentalist madrassas around the world and paid for millions of copies of the Koran with Wahhabi interpretations (for instance, stressing jihad, in the warlike sense, not just as personal striving, as an extra pillar of Islam). But it is also a matter of choice. In the Arab heartlands fundamentalism has become a refuge for anyone worried by the spread of Western culture and power. In overseas communities where Muslims are in a minority, notably Europe, it has had more to do with a search for identity. Scholars such as Olivier Roy have shown that extremism has become a form of generational warfare, with Western-born Muslim girls choosing to wear the headscarf that their mothers jettisoned on their arrival from Pakistan and Morocco.

There are all sorts of long-term reasons why hotter, more combative religions will gain. Demography is one. From Salt Lake City to Jerusalem, religious people marry younger and reproduce more prodigiously than nonreligious ones. An Ultra-Orthodox Jewish woman in Israel will produce nearly three times as many children as her secular counterpart. By some counts, three-quarters of the growth in the more ardent varieties of American Protestantism is the result of demography. Over the past half century the Church of Jesus Christ of Latter-Day Saints has grown sevenfold, with half the world's thirteen million Mormons living outside the United States. Another long-term trend that could stir up religion is climate change. Philip Jenkins, one of America's most distinguished students of religion, points out that by 2050 most of the largest Christian countries, other than the United States, will be located in the global south. He thinks that environmental change could spark intercommunal rivalry, recalling the "Little Ice Age" at the end of the thirteenth century that caused starvation and pogroms, with Christians turning on Jews in Europe and Muslims turning on Christians in Africa and Asia.[27]

If these religious sorts sound angry and poor, that gives the wrong impression. For the second, arguably still more frustrating thing for the neo-atheists involves the sort of people who are embracing religion. According to the secularist hymnbook, those drawn to religion should be the weak, the ignorant and the fearful. That is certainly true in some cases. Pentecostalism has spread rapidly in the favelas of Brazil; go to Gaza, and it is not hard to see why radical Islam offers a form of hope for so many Palestinians. But that is not the whole picture.

In much of the world it is exactly the sort of upwardly mobile, educated middle classes that Marx and Weber presumed would shed such superstitions who are driving the explosion of faith. In both Turkey and India, modernization has helped to create the up-and-coming bourgeoisie that Atatürk and Nehru prayed for; but these people are the most fervent supporters of the religious parties. In urban China the link between commercial prosperity and religion can be strikingly explicit. For instance Zhao, the economist who wrote the paper on market economies and churches, has since converted to Christianity (slightly to his surprise—"I thought I could never be a believer in God, because I was an economist"). He was recently asked to apply his skills as an economist to reorganizing his house church—a much bigger affair than Wang's, with six hundred members, a full-time pastor and five part-time ones. He promptly turned to the corporate world. His church now has five super-elders (or board members) to oversee the elders. Every year it has a congregational gathering (or shareholders meeting), and around two hundred people come to it. "Nobody reports us," explains Zhao, "as long as we don't sing."

The United States provides an even better case study. Many American Evangelicals are well educated and well off. For prosperous suburbanites, faith has become a lifestyle coach. Far from looking backward, American Evangelicals claim they are ahead of the curve in grappling with the question of how you preserve virtue in a consumer society. How do you keep yourself on the straight and narrow when you are constantly beset by temptations? How do you raise your children in a world where an Abercrombie & Fitch clothing catalogue looks like something that ought to be kept on the top shelf? The answer, they argue, is simple: turn to the eternal truths captured in the Bible. For them, far from being a quaint relic, religion is the only way that you can navigate the torrents of modernity. It is no accident that America's best-selling religious book is called *The Purpose Driven Life: What on Earth Am I Here For?* [28]

THE TRUTH AND THE CHANGE

What is driving this great upheaval? The answer, to use two religious phrases, is a combination of revealed truth (something that we should have recognized years ago) and genuine transubstantiation (real change).

From one angle, little of substance has changed. The only thing that has happened is that the political classes in the West are waking up, rather late, to the enduring power of religion. This "revealed truth" argument is, needless to say, popular with believers: God's power was bound to be recognized sooner or later. But it is also popular with some people who study religion for a living. Peter Berger, the dean of sociologists of religion, argues that outside Europe most people have always been religious— and chides journalists for investigating the religious rule, not the secular exception: "Rather than studying American Evangelicals and Islamic mullahs, you should look at Swedes and New England college professors."

On the other hand, there is also, plainly, an element of transubstantiation. To begin with, the change in the commentariat's perception of religious power may be overdue, but it is fairly gigantic. (Even Berger, who used to be one of the leading proponents of the secularization theory, realized that religion was not going to wither away only two decades ago—and it caused a furor in his discipline when he did so.) And, more important, there have been genuine changes of substance—both to do with religion itself and with its effect on politics.

In retrospect, religion's reemergence as a political force came long before Osama bin Laden declared his jihad on Jews and Crusaders. Timothy Shah, a scholar at the Council on Foreign Relations, has argued that the great turning point was the Six-Day War of 1967. The Arab world's crushing defeat persuaded many embittered Arabs to turn from Nasser's secular pan-Arabism to radical Islam. (In 1967, under Nasser, the Egyptian army went into battle crying, "Land! Sea! Air!"; six years later, under Anwar El Sadat, their new battle cry was, "Allahu Akhbar."[29]) At the same time, Israel's "miraculous" triumph gave God a stronger voice in its politics, emboldening the settler movement. In the same year a Hindu nationalist party won 9.4 percent of the vote in India. Faith gathered pace in politics in the 1970s. By the end of that decade, America had elected its first proudly born-again Christian, Jimmy Carter; Jerry Falwell had founded the Moral Majority; Iran had replaced the worldly shah with Ayatollah Khomeini; Zia-ul-Haq was busy Islamizing Pakistan; Buddhism had been formally granted the foremost place in Sri Lanka's constitution; and an anti-Communist Pole had become head of the Catholic Church.

What caused this shift in the 1970s? Believers see a populist revolt against the overreach of elitist secularism—be it America's Supreme Court legalizing abortion or Indira Gandhi harrying Hindus. From a more secular viewpoint, John Lewis Gaddis, a Yale historian, points out that the religious revival in the 1970s coincided with the collapse of secular "isms." By then the Soviet Union's evils had made a mockery of Marxism, and capitalism had also hit some buffers (the oil shocks, hyperinflation). More generally, politicians' ability to solve problems such as crime or unemployment was thrown into doubt: faith in government tumbled just about everywhere in the 1970s—and has stayed low since.

And why has religion's power continued to increase? Most obviously, there has been a series of reactions and counterreactions. Fundamentalist Islam, for instance, has helped to spur radical Judaism and Hinduism, which in turn have reinforced the mullahs' fervor. Hamas owes much to Israel's settlers. Without Falwell, there would have been slimmer royalties for Hitchens and Dawkins. But there is also something deeper going on: globalization. The biggest problem for the prophets of secularization is that the surge of religion is being driven by the same two things that have driven the success of market capitalism: competition and choice.

THE GOSPEL OF PLURALISM

To understand the competitive mechanism behind religion's revival, you need to consult only two sacred texts. The first is *The Wealth of Nations*, in which Adam Smith argues that the free market works with God as well as Mammon. Nonestablished clergy, who rely on the collection plate, show greater "zeal" in proselytizing "the inferior ranks of people" than established clerical salarymen, who are more interested in sucking up to their patrons. (Europe has been a textbook illustration of this.) The second text is the American Constitution. The First Amendment—"that Congress shall make no law respecting an establishment of religion, or prohibiting the free exercise thereof"—was actually a compromise between dissenters (who wanted to keep the state away from religion) and more anticlerical sorts like Thomas Jefferson (who wanted the church out of politics). Yet it became the great engine of American religiosity, creating a new sort of country where membership in a church was a purely voluntary activity.

Look back at the first great success in this free market, Methodism, and it is not difficult to spot where the growth formula for China's house churches came from. When Francis Asbury arrived in America in 1771, there were just 550 Methodists in the country. By the time he died in 1861, a million people, one-eighth of the entire population, were attending Methodist camp meetings, the nineteenth century equivalent of megachurches. The Methodists paid their preachers only a nominal stipend, gave them no job security and told them to avoid arid theology: "Always suit your subjects to your audience," went the instruction, and "choose the plainest texts you can."[30]

The competitive spirit is also infecting other religions. Buddhism, the major religion whose market share has shrunk most over the past century,[31] remains fairly passive: its adherents believe that people should discover faith for themselves rather than be energetically introduced to it. But even here there are signs of awakening. In South Korea Buddhist monks, often hidden away in inaccessible rural shrines, have set up meditation areas in cities to fight off the Protestants. Buddhist monks were to the fore in the rescue efforts after China's devastating earthquake in 2008.

Hinduism is more turf-conscious. Some states in India have passed "anticonversion" laws banning evangelists from using force or "allurement"—code for Christians and Muslims converting Hindu untouchables, who get a raw deal under the caste system. (In the eastern state of Orissa, where this has spilled over into violence, Hindutva politicians have even accused "fraudulent Christians" of burning their own churches.[32]) Still, when it comes to marketing, the trendier Hindu ashrams are more than a match for America's pastorpreneurs. The Art of Living, a Bangalore-based ashram that "is committed to making life a celebration on this planet," has offshoots in 141 countries.

This spirit of competition also helps to explain some of Islam's success. That may sound odd. Saudi Arabia enforces religious orthodoxy with police and prisons, punishing apostasy with death. In many Islamic countries mosques get a degree of financial help and direction from the state that would have scandalized Adam Smith. Islam is not as evangelical as Christianity. Its followers are less intent on spreading the good news than on stiffening the resolve of traditional Muslims. Yet there is more competition within Islam than at first appears.

Like Pentecostalism, Islam is a religion without much hierarchy: most mosques claim to be following the teachings of one preacher or another, but their real authority comes from the Koran. This helps new imams to start preaching and allows them to do pretty much what they like. Nor have they neglected marketing. There are megamosques (one in east London, planned by missionaries, will hold twelve thousand people, five times as many as St. Paul's Cathedral)[33] and televangelists, such as Amr Khaled, an engaging former accountant from Egypt, whose sermons are watched by millions in Europe and the Middle East. If you want a fatwa (ruling), you do not have to go to a mosque: you can get it online (and in English) from eFatwa.com, MuftiSays.com or Askimam.com.

Competition entails choice. In many parts of the world, though not crucially America, religion used to operate under the system of *cuius regio, eius religio* (whoever rules sets the religious norm—an idea from the Peace of Augsburg of 1555, which divided up a lot of what is now Germany between Protestant and Catholic princes). Now religion is becoming a much more bottom-up affair. People are increasingly likely to profess a religion out of choice rather than just because they are born into the faith. And they have far more choice about what sort of religion (or nonreligion) they will adopt.

Often the spur for pluralism is immigration. Richard Chartres, the Anglican Bishop of London, calls his city "a test case," pointing to the sprawling number of mosques, Sikh temples, synagogues, African and West Indian churches, even the Church of Scientology. In Latin America, Evangelical churches now offer a vigorous alternative to Catholicism, and in the United States, mainstream Protestants will soon account for less than half the population.[34] Although the country remains predominantly Christian, nearly 5 percent belong to other religions (such as Judaism, Islam, Buddhism or Hinduism) and 16 percent are unaffiliated (of whom 9 percent claim to be atheist or agnostic).[35]

Of course, pluralism has existed before, but never to the extent that it does now. "We made a category mistake," admits Peter Berger. "We thought that the relationship was between modernization and secularization. In fact it was between modernization and pluralism." For a growing number of people, religion is no longer taken for granted or inherited; it is based on adults making a choice, going to a synagogue, temple, church or mosque. Deciding not to go at all—a category that stretches from lazy stay-in-bed agnosticism to passionate atheism—is part of this pluralism, because it involves people making decisions about their relationship to God.

Zhao, the Chinese economist, also supports pluralism. Part of his argument to the Chinese government is that the way to solve its religion problem and to prevent cults like Falun Gong is to open up the market. "Thirsty people need to drink. If there is no good-quality water, people will go to bad-quality water. We need a free market so that good-quality religions can compete." Even Confucianism, he argues, gets corrupted when it is linked to the state. "It is much better if religion is free and separate."

Religious choice has a profound effect on public life. The more that people choose their religion, rather than just inherit it, the more likely they are to make a noise about it. If you have made a commitment to your faith, why would you leave it in the closet at home, or outside the voting booth? At its most basic, that commitment can be violent. Since 2000, 43 percent of civil wars have been religious. (The figure in the 1940s and 1950s was only about a quarter.)[36] But the main weapon is often the ballot box. Around the world, people have repeatedly chosen to exercise their new freedoms by increasing, not decreasing, the role of religion in politics. The newly democratized, from Moscow to Cairo to Beijing, have reinserted God back into the public square—and the profoundly secular foreign policy establishment in the West has struggled to deal with it.

THE RETURN OF THEOLOGY

However you look at it, faith is more likely to impinge on you than it once did, either because it is part of your life or because it is part of the lives of some of those around you—neighbors, colleagues at work, even your rulers or people seeking to topple them. This book is an attempt to explain this phenomenon—to understand how and why God has fought His way back into the modern world.

At its most basic, it is a book about politics and religion, but its underlying theme is the battle for modernity. That struggle is a global one, so this book travels the world—to look at persecuted Muslims in India, megachurches in Guatemala and the religious front line in northern Nigeria. In many cases our experience has been similar to the one we had with our last book, on American conservatism: reporting on a huge, hidden world that most outsiders barely know exists and that many insiders view through a highly personal lens. Repeatedly, we have been asked in a surprised, somewhat flattered way, "Why are you interested?"—and the question usually comes from people who have just insisted that religion was the most important thing in their lives. A young mother who has earlier collapsed howling to the floor in São Paulo, as a devil is cast out, can be shrugging her shoulders a few minutes later, worrying about the time it must have taken you to get there. A passionate Hindu nationalist who has survived several assassination attempts is so amazed by your interest that he dives into the Delhi traffic to find you a taxi, to the horror of his bodyguards.

Indeed, in trying to describe this phenomenon, we have been greatly helped by one thing: the amazing number of people, around the world, prepared to give their time freely. Many of the more extreme views catalogued in this book have been delivered calmly over cups of tea. Two journalists from a secular magazine have been evangelized, prayed for and pitied. Only very occasionally have we been prevented from going into places, and then often for good reasons—Israeli soldiers, for instance, worried that letting us near the al-Aqsa Mosque in Jerusalem at a troubled moment would be provocative.

If this book travels the world, it focuses more on America than anywhere else for a simple reason: because, perhaps for the first time since the dawn of the modern era, the world seems to be moving decisively in the American rather than the European direction. The American model of religion—one that is based on choice rather than state fiat—is winning. America has succeeded in putting God back into modernity partly because it put modernity, or at least choice and competition, back into God. In many parts of the world, it is American missionaries and products you find to the fore: *The Jesus Film,* put out by Campus Crusade for Christ, has supposedly been seen by more than a billion people in eighty languages. And America is the pioneer in religious politics too. If it has given the world megachurches and megapreachers, it has also exported its culture wars. Meanwhile, as the battered superpower, it is fated to deal with most of the world's new wars of religion.

If America plays an outsized role in our story, so does Christianity. Again the reason for this is straightforward: Christianity has spent longer grappling with modernity than other religions, notably Islam. There are plenty of modern Muslims; and there are also plenty of places, from Dubai to Detroit and the Dardanelles, where Islam sits quite comfortably with modernity. But in its Arab heartland, it plainly does not. And, overall, it remains the world religion that has found pluralism hardest to cope with. Islam has not been through a Reformation, let alone an Enlightenment. Look at every debate, from the relationship between the mosque and the state to the ethics of stem cells, and you tend to discover that Christian culture has got there first. Islam is still relevant to our argument—especially when it comes to the competition between religions. But, for all its power, we believe it is less of a harbinger of the future than Christianity.

The first part of the book tries to explain why Europe and America have evolved in such different ways over the past two hundred or so years. The second part examines the way that religion (and especially pluralism) is thriving in today's America—as an economic force, an intellectual catalyst and a political influence. The third part examines how America is exporting its version of religion. The fourth part examines the spread of wars of religion, in various guises, from the battles for people's souls to culture wars to terrorism and violence. In the conclusion we look for the best formulas for avoiding future explosions.

This book comes with two health warnings. The first is that it is not a book about whether religion is good or bad. If you want polemic about religion, either for or against, there are plenty of other books available. It neither praises nor damns believers, except when they do obviously magnificent or malignant things. For the record, it is written by a Roman Catholic and an atheist: no doubt some of the holy warriors on both sides will uncover examples of "bias." Our hope, however, is that whatever biases we bring have canceled each other out.

The second health warning concerns numbers. Statistics on religion are fraught with ambiguities. For instance, figures on church attendance are often collected by churches—organizations with a strong interest in promoting themselves. As for surveys about faith, people may not be telling the truth when they say they are believers (would you confess to atheism in Texas, let alone Jeddah?); and even if they are telling the truth, do they really believe what they are supposed to? Many pious Evangelicals and Muslims have peculiar ideas of what the Bible and Koran actually say.

Academics and polling organizations are struggling to catch up. For what it is worth, we have tried to stick to figures from the Pew organization as much as possible.

Yet there is also a danger of missing the forest for the trees. Even if the number of true believers is exaggerated, at least by the believers themselves, it is clear, to us at least, that God is back. The most important development is not quantitative but qualitative: the fact that religion is playing a much more important role in public and intellectual life. We might not go as far as Philip Jenkins, who claims that when historians look back at this century, they will probably see religion as "the prime animating and destructive force in human affairs, guiding attitudes to political liberty and obligation, concepts of nationhood and, of course, conflicts and wars."[37] But God will pose practical problems for politicians, be they in Berlin, Baltimore or Beijing.

In that, at least, Wang is surely right: religion is part of the modern world. Which brings us back to an important reason for putting America at the heart of this book. The Founding Fathers' clever compromise over religion not only allowed God to survive and prosper in America, it also provided a way of living with religion—of ensuring that different faiths can coexist, and of taming a passion that so often turns the religious beast to savagery. This was one of the Founders' greatest gifts to man: getting rid of the established church, establishing a firm distinction between public reason and private faith, and consigning theocracy to the past along with monarchy and aristocracy. Our instinct is that this is a lesson that people the world over—believers, atheists and agnostics—need now more than ever.

PART ONE

TWO ROADS TO MODERNITY

CHAPTER ONE

THE EUROPEAN WAY:

THE NECESSITY OF ATHEISM

❧❧

IN 1811, a troublesome undergraduate at University College, Oxford, published a short pamphlet titled *The Necessity of Atheism*. Percy Bysshe Shelley dismissed the idea that we have an obligation to believe in God—and a concomitant obligation to attend tedious chapel services—on the grounds that there is no solid proof of God's existence. He challenged readers to give him proof, if they had any. Shelley was ordered to appear before the college court, but he refused to answer their questions, so the dons expelled him. Shelley had to make his way in the world without the benefit of an Oxford degree.

Nearly two centuries later, Shelley is having the last laugh. Not only does his old college boast a statue of its most lauded poet, but the views for which he was expelled are common in the intellectual world. Richard Dawkins has made a fortune by expounding his own version of *The Necessity of Atheism* from the comfort of an Oxford professorial chair. He is just the most voluble of what Friedrich Schleiermacher once dubbed, in a different context, "Cultured Despisers" of religion. And for every cultured despiser, there are thousands who have a vague sense that religion is past it, incompatible with reason and science. Only about 6 percent of Britons attend church on an average Sunday.[1]

How did secularism triumph?

LOSING THEIR RELIGION

Prophets have been predicting the death of God for generations. One sociologist of religion, Rodney Stark, of Baylor University in Texas, claims that Thomas Woolston, an English Deist, was the first person to set an exact date for His last rites. In the early eighteenth century Woolston predicted, with the self-confidence that seems to be God's gift to certain types of English polemicists, that Christianity would be entirely expunged by 1900. Half a century later, Frederick the Great wrote to his friend Voltaire to say that Woolston had been too pessimistic: religion "is crumbling of itself, and its fall will be but the more rapid." Voltaire replied that its end would come in the next fifty years."[2] In 1882 Friedrich Nietzsche insisted that God was already done for. "God is dead. God remains dead. And we have killed him."[3]

For the most part, however, the prophets of secularization have been reluctant to put an exact date on religion's "inevitable" demise. Bertrand Russell's father, Viscount Amberley, announced that religion was going to disappear "shortly." (He tried to hasten the process by decreeing in his will that his son should be raised by atheists, a provision that did not survive the courts' scrutiny.) C. Wright Mills chose "in due course" rather than "shortly" in 1959. One of Tom Stoppard's characters in *Jumpers* (1972) observes that there came "a calendar date—a moment—when the onus of proof passed from the atheist to the believer, when, quite suddenly, the noes had it."[4]

THE "NOES" HAVE IT

The movement that began all this was the Enlightenment. In 1762 David Hume had dinner with Baron d'Holbach at his home in Paris. The Scottish philosopher said that he doubted that there were any real atheists in the world. "Look around you," the French *philosophe* replied, "and count the guests." There were eighteen at the table. "I can show you fifteen atheists right off. The other three haven't yet made up their minds."[5]

D'Holbach and his friends in Paris made a business out of helping people make up their minds about religion. Voltaire littered his letters with the battle cry, *"Écrasez l'infâme."* And there was no shortage of French thinkers, hanging around the coffeehouses and writing in the magazines, encyclopedias and dictionaries that poured from the presses, who were willing to engage in the intellectual struggle. The *philosophes* deployed every weapon they could against *"L'infâme"*—from classical learning to modern science. But in the end their critique rested on two foundations.

The first was confidence in human reason. Human reason allows men to produce peace and prosperity, they argued; by contrast, "unreasonable" superstition and fanaticism produce war and misery. In 1784 Immanuel Kant defined the Enlightenment with a simple motto: *Sapere aude, or* "Dare to know."[6] Cast off the fetters of the past. Take your fate in your own hands. Dare to exercise your own talents. Above all, reject the superstition and fanaticism that conspired to kill reason and spread bloodiness. Every Enlightenment thinker had his favorite example of Christianity's blood-soaked past: Voltaire claimed that he awoke from his sleep in a sweat every year on the anniversary of the St. Bartholomew's Day Massacre.

The second foundation was confidence in human goodness. The rejection of original sin has been described as the "key that secularizes the world."[7] It set men fighting against obscurantism in thought and repression in government. It transformed education from rooting out evil in God's garden to tending to young shoots. And it freed people to pursue real virtues such as human sympathy rather than false ones such as saintly self-mortification. ("A gloomy, hare-brained enthusiast, after his death, may have a place in a calendar," David Hume scoffed, "but [he] will scarcely ever be admitted, when alive, into intimacy and society, except by those who are as delirious and dismal as himself."[8]) This was a key that the *philosophes* turned whenever they could.

The *philosophes* did more than just argue with religion. They mocked it.[9] Edward Gibbon was never happier than when chronicling the absurd activities of the likes of St. Simeon Stylites, who for over thirty years lived on top of a seventy-foot-high and four-foot-square pillar. Voltaire was at his most waspish when ridiculing primitive superstitions like baptism: "What a strange idea, inspired by the wash-pot, that a jug of water washes away all crimes!"[10] In his novel *La Religieuse*, Denis Diderot mocked the religious for their psychological oddities and deviant pastimes, not least flagellation.

William Blake argued, at the beginning of the nineteenth century, that all this sarcasm was in vain.

> Mock on. Mock on. Voltaire, Rousseau;
> Mock on. Mock on: 'tis all in vain!
> You throw the sand against the wind,
> And the wind blows it back again.

But as Blake well knew, the wind did not throw all the sand back, at least in France. Religion became an object of ridicule and contempt. The number of full-blooded atheists who wanted to destroy both the church and Christianity multiplied in the eighteenth century. And eventually the French Revolution was unleashed upon the world in 1789.

END OF A *RÉGIME*

For the *révolutionnaires,* attacking religion was more than just dinner-party chitchat. The Catholic Church was one of the three pillars of the ancien régime, along with the aristocracy (which provided the church with many of its leading figures) and the monarchy. The church was one of the country's wealthiest institutions, fattened on both tithes and its clerical estates. Religious functionaries were omnipresent at royal occasions. Religious orders all but controlled education. At their coronations French kings were girded with the sword of Charlemagne, with which they were supposed to protect the church as well as widows and orphans.[11]

The French Revolution became more anticlerical as it gathered strength. The *révolutionnaires* started off by attacking the church's abuses, particularly its habit of siding with the monarch. Then they turned on the religious establishment and church functionaries. (Diderot rhapsodized that "man shall not be free until the last king is strangled with the entrails of the last priest.") In 1790 the *révolutionnaires* dissolved the monasteries and convents that weren't engaged in useful work, consolidating the remaining monks in fewer orders and sending the surplus priests out into the world. Barbers and tailors did a roaring trade turning ex-monks into presentable citizens. In 1792–93, three-quarters of France's bishops and a third of its lower clergy—some 30,000 people in all—fled the country.[12] By 1794 only about 150 of what had been 40,000 French parishes in pre-revolutionary days openly celebrated the mass.

But there was always a tension in the revolutionaries' attitude toward religion: as much as they disliked traditional Christianity in general, and Roman Catholicism in particular, some of them also recognized that religion, stripped of superstition, might serve a valuable social function. Maximilien Robespierre devised a new religion, the Cult of the Supreme Being, which was based on a combination of Deism and "civic religion," and which tried to provide the principles of the French Revolution with divine sanction. Robespierre claimed that his new "rational" religion had all the benefits of traditional religion without the vices. Many devout revolutionaries baptized their children in the name not of "the Father, Son and Holy Ghost," but "of Liberty, Equality and Fraternity."

Robespierre's decision, in 1794, to make the Cult of the Supreme Being the official state religion, complete with an official festival of the Supreme Being on June 8, helped to inspire the Thermidorian Reaction. Why bother to overthrow one official religion only to have another one imposed upon you from above? Napoleon was much more pragmatic about religion than the first wave of revolutionaries. He once boasted the he had conquered the Vendée by making himself a Catholic, and established himself in Egypt by making himself a Muslim. But he was really only happy when religion was subordinated to the state, by which he meant himself.

The *révolutionnaires* set the fashion for all subsequent assault on religion—replacing the worship of God with the worship of man. Alexis de Tocqueville complained that they turned the revolution itself into a "new kind of religion": "an incomplete religion, it is true, without God, without ritual, and without a life after death, but one which nevertheless, like Islam, flooded the earth with its soldiers, apostles and martyrs."[13] This actually understates the comparison. There was plenty of ritual. The *révolutionnaires* deliberately created secular saints: the remains of Voltaire and Jean-Jacques Rousseau were transferred to the Panthéon with elaborate processions and ceremonies. They created a secular calendar, with the revolution taking the place of Christ's death. They transformed Notre Dame into a temple of reason. "The only true religion is that which ennobles man by giving him a sublime idea of the dignity of his being," one revolutionary proclaimed, "and of the great destinies to which he is called by the human orderer."[14]

This tradition was picked up by many others. Henri de Saint-Simon, the godfather of French socialism, christened his philosophy the "New Christianity"—what was new about it being the substitution of man for God. "The throne of the absolute could not remain untenanted," he argued.[15] Auguste Comte, who drew on Saint-Simon's ideas, created an even more elaborate Religion of Humanity complete with a priesthood and secular saints. (British wits dubbed his weird creation "Catholicism minus Christianity."[16]) Robert Owen, one of the founders of British socialism, came to the conclusion, while still a child, that theologies were nothing more than tissues of lies, and subsequently set about replacing religion with a "spirit of universal charity toward the human race." But when he established his model communities in New Lanark and then New Harmony he found himself borrowing from religious rituals. Owen presided over "naming" ceremonies for children and delivered "ethical lectures" to his workers on Sundays. Owenites pored over *The Book of the New Moral World* and sang secular hymns that maintained that communal labor offered "redemption from the fall."[17] Owen was convinced that the "Old Immoral World" would soon be replaced by the "New Moral World" and that universal love and happiness would prevail. He inscribed the letters CM, meaning "Commencement of the Millennium," on the main hall of his last model community, Queenswood, in Hampshire; he also built "Halls of Science" across the country, which were supposed to offer people a foretaste of the rational world to come, once religion and exploitation had been done away with.

The French Revolution cemented the link between European radicalism and European anticlericalism. The European ancien régimes responded to the revolution by embracing the religious establishment even tighter, creating a synthesis between religion and reaction. Conservatives rejected the Enlightenment faith in reason and progress—a faith that several eighteenth

century monarchs had endorsed—on the grounds that it had led to anarchy, bloodshed and dictatorship. Instead, they reembraced ideas such as the
divine right of kings, the harmony between social hierarchy and celestial
hierarchy and the virtues of the Middle Ages. European conservatives not
only celebrated the church as a prop of the old order, they turned religion
into a backward-looking ideology that was thoroughly opposed to liberal
modernity.

For their part, European radicals responded by celebrating the revolution's assault on religion. France remained a hotbed of popular anticlericalism. During the Paris Commune in 1870–1 the rebels shot the
Archbishop of Paris and dozens of lesser clergymen. France was not
alone: across Europe, radicals of various hues dreamt of overthrowing the
corrupt church along with the corrupt state—sometimes because they
wanted to see "real Christianity" flourish but often because they wanted
to replace superstition with reason.[18] Leading Social Democrats in Germany regarded religion as "the main bastion of antisocialism" and "of
reaction."[19] Popular anticlericalism drew on deep wells of emotion: on the
belief that priests were props of an unjust social order; on the belief that
they were hypocrites, preaching religion while pursuing personal advantage; and on the belief that they were somehow unnatural. A striking proportion of eighteenth and nineteenth century pornography, at least as far
as we can judge, is devoted to the hypocritical indulgences, real or imagined, of monks, priests and nuns. Even today, in French slang, *abbaye* is a
synonym for a "whorehouse."[20]

WHEN GIANTS WALKED THE EARTH

The decline of religion was certainly not smooth. The Enlightenment
begat the Counter-Enlightenment. The German Romantics emphasized the importance of cultural traditions—including religious ones—as
opposed to Enlightenment abstractions about faith and reason. Thomas
Carlyle raged that secular capitalism was producing an ugly and atomized
society held together only by the cash nexus. Arthur Schopenhauer and
Nietzsche mocked the Enlightenment's naïve belief in reason.

European churches fought a rearguard action against the forces of secularism. The Catholic Church in France tried to recover lost ground after
the Bourbon Restoration in 1814–30. Victorian England saw a resurgence
of piety—first in the form of Evangelicalism and then also in the form of
High Church enthusiasm within the Church of England. British Evangelicals led most of the great British social reforms of the nineteenth century,
from abolishing slavery to combating drunkenness and dissolution. The
Duke of Devonshire, for example, celebrated the civilizing role of the
Evangelical movement in a passage that is worth contemplating by anyone
who has braved a modern British city late at night:

> Can you imagine for one moment what England would have been like
> today without those churches and all that those churches mean? . . . Cer-
> tainly it would not have been safe to walk the streets. All respect, decency,
> all those things which tend to make modern civilization what it is would
> not have been in existence. You can imagine what we should have had to
> pay for our police, for lunatic asylums, for criminal asylums . . . the charges
> would have been increased hundredfold if it had not been for the work the
> church has done and is doing today.[21]

Britain eventually produced a flourishing Christian socialist movement,
with early Labor MPs boasting that their party owed more to Methodism
than to Marxism. But these would prove to be exceptions. Religion was
more often than not allied to the old order. And the successive religious
revivals were too weak to overcome the most powerful intellectual tides of
the era. The nineteenth and early twentieth centuries saw a succession of
intellectual giants taking sledgehammers to the very foundations of faith.

Ironically, the man who did as much as anybody to start the sledge-
hammering was one of religion's most subtle defenders. G. W. F. Hegel's
deification of history—his conviction that it was the march of God on
earth—had the paradoxical effect of opening the way to secular arguments.
Ludwig Feuerbach, the most radical of Hegel's followers, branded himself as a second Luther.[22] He argued that history was a tale of progressive
disenchantment: the Christian God had displaced the parochial deities of
earlier men with a universal abstraction; now the job of philosophers was

to replace theology with anthropology, and put man in God's place. Man had invented God as both a consolation and distraction from the sorrows of the world.[23] For Feuerbach, God was a pretty thin consolation: religion distracts us from the real joys of the world and persuades us to focus on an illusion. Man is thus oppressed by the creation of his own mind—and the only way that he can end that oppression is to destroy his creation. Feuerbach wanted to produce nothing less than a new Copernican Revolution—instead of man revolving around God, God would revolve around man.

Feuerbach provided the raw materials for the most influential assault on religion of the past couple of centuries. Karl Marx embraced two of Feuerbach's ideas: that religion was a consolation for life's miseries (the "opium of the people"); and that the answer to the riddle of theology was to substitute God for man ("the criticism of religion," Marx once said, "ends with the precept that the Supreme Being for man is man"[24]). But he added two new arguments. The first was the materialist interpretation of history: religion, like all forms of intellectual life, is simply a superstructure that sits on top of the material "base." There is thus little to be gained in demonstrating that religion is intellectually empty or contradictory: the point instead is to demonstrate what material interests it advances.

The second addition was his revolutionary teleology: the only way for man to free himself from the illusions of religion was to free himself from a ruling class—and the only way to rid himself of the ruling class was to rid himself of the illusions of religion. "The struggle against religion is therefore indirectly a struggle against *that world* whose spiritual aroma is religion."[25] This is not only because the ruling class uses religion to dupe the workers into accepting their swinish lot; it is because class societies are by their nature alienated societies. End alienation and you kill the demand for religion.

Marx's critique of religion was all the more powerful because it was a critique with a chaser: it provided a substitute, an alternative solution to many of the longings that religion tried to satisfy. The descendant of a long line of rabbis, Marx found it impossible not to think in terms of grand eschatologies. He offered an end to the problem of alienation, a word taken directly from the Christian vocabulary, and one redolent of emptiness and despair. He argued that history has a meaning and a

destination—the meaning lies in the class struggle and the destination
lies in communism, a world in which contradictions are overcome and
paradise is created on earth. He employed numerous religious tropes—
Communists are latter-day Gnostics, communism is heaven on earth, the
revolution is the last judgment, workers are the saved and capitalists the
damned. Having first punched a "God-shaped hole" in the heart of modern man by deconstructing religion, Marx then offered to fill the hole by
revealing the meaning of history.

GOD VERSUS GALÁPAGOS

The most powerful challenge to religion, however, came not from
philosophy—whether in the manicured hands of the French philosophes
or the heavy hands of German scholars—but from science. Since the mid-
nineteenth century, a growing number of people have come to think that
the "scientific" attitude and the "religious" attitude are incompatible. Religion might provide consolation in bereavement. It might express wonder
at the grandeur of the universe. But it no longer offers a coherent explanation of the origin of life.

The most devastating questions were posed by a mild-mannered
English gentleman who was intensely worried about upsetting his pious
wife, Charles Darwin. *The Origin of Species* (1859) ignited a passionate public debate not just about giant lizards in the Galápagos Islands but also
about the validity of the Christian faith. Benjamin Disraeli famously
quipped that if it was a choice between apes and angels, he was "on the
side of the angels." In fact the controversial thing about Darwin was not
natural descent—even the Catholic Church jumped onto the apes' side
fairly quickly—but two other ideas. The first was survival of the fittest.
This implied that evolution was an amoral or even an immoral process:
"Nature, red in tooth and claw," as Tennyson had it.[26] The second was the
idea of random variation and natural selection—again this was immensely
hard to reconcile with belief in an all-knowing, benevolent Creator. The
recent fuss about intelligent design reflects a deep Christian unease about
the notion of a blind and purposeless universe.

Some of Darwin's followers were less restrained than their gentlemanly master when it came to doing battle with the religious establishment. T. H. Huxley, known as Darwin's bulldog, believed that the battle to advance science was also a battle to diminish the influence of Christianity. "Extinguished theologians lie about the cradle of every science as the strangled snakes beside that of Hercules," he wrote in 1860, "and history records that whenever science and orthodoxy have been fairly opposed, the latter have been forced to retire from the lists, bleeding and crushed, if not annihilated; scotched, if not slain."[27] Note the reference to Hercules: Huxley believed in science's ability to empower and liberate mankind. And note the phrase "fairly opposed": Huxley also believed that the only way religion could survive was by using the power of repression. These two themes—science's Herculean powers and religion's propensity to resort to oppression—were the stock in trade of other scientific bulldogs who yapped at the heels of a retreating Christian faith over the coming decades. In the 1890s a priggish Harrow schoolboy, George Macaulay Trevelyan, spoke for educated opinion when he informed his teacher that "Darwin refuted the Bible."[28]

Another blow came from a new school of biblical criticism. Gibbon and Voltaire had perturbed the pious by casting doubts on the authenticity of miracles, such as the virgin birth or Jesus walking on water. In the early nineteenth century, a school of German theologians, based at the Tübingen School, went further by treating the Bible as a historical document, subjecting it to close textual reading and testing its claims against historical and archaeological evidence.

Christianity is a historical religion, based on the claim that the divine world once intersected with the human world. Jesus was born at a particular time and place—in the town of Bethlehem to a woman called Mary in the reign of Herod. But as a historical religion it is open to historical inquiry, and the historical inquiry of the nineteenth century shook Bible-believing Christians to their core. The Germans argued persuasively that the first five books of the Old Testament, traditionally attributed to Moses, were in fact written much later and by a number of different authors; and that the book of Isaiah had at least two different authors. They also argued that many biblical events had no historical basis, and dismissed biblical miracles as literary tropes rather than real events.

The work of the Tübingen scholars—summarized in newspapers and reviewed and popularized in books such as David Friedrich Strauss's *The Life of Jesus* (1835)—acted like acid on the Christian faith. It seeped into popular intellectual culture. And it unmoored many distinguished minds from their simple Christian faith. Jacob Burckhardt, the great Swiss historian, read *The Life of Jesus* and became convinced that the history of the New Testament could not bear the weight that faith imposed upon it; T. H. Green, an Oxford philosopher and disciple of Hegel, embarked upon a quest to free Christian morality from its historical foundations.[29]

A Shared Neurosis

As if that were not enough, a further attack on religion came from a new discipline that hovered somewhere between science and pseudoscience. If Marx tried to bring God down to earth by digging into the material infrastructure of society, Sigmund Freud tried to bring Him down to earth by digging into the unconscious mind.

Freud thought religion was the manifestation of an immature personality. "The more the fruits of knowledge become accessible to men," argued Freud, "the more widespread is the decline of religious belief." His biographer, Peter Gay, called Freud "the last of the *philosophes*," but if he was a *philosophe,* he was a bad-tempered one, with a personal ax to grind.[30]

A Jew who was used to being looked down upon by the local Christians, Freud was at his most coruscating about Christianity in general and Catholicism in particular. For the author of *The Future of an Illusion,* religion was merely a shared neurosis, a personal malady made public and communal. Freud compared the obsessive behavior of religious people—repeating prayers, performing rituals and so on—to the obsessive behavior of neurotics. He insisted that the belief in God was just another manifestation of the "father complex": religious people cling to the idea of God because they haven't managed to escape from their infantile belief in the almighty father.[31] To be religious is to be trapped in childhood—taking comfort in an illusory protector and refusing to grow up. And, as if being childish is not bad enough, religious people are also female children: they want to be possessed by a masculine god. (Many of Freud's most religious male patients fantasized about changing their sex.) He argued that losing faith in religion is part of growing up: once we realize that our parents are not all-mighty and all-knowing, once we come to terms with our human limitations, we lose our belief in God.

Huxley, Freud and their kind had a tally-ho approach to the fight against religion. Others only abandoned their faith reluctantly. Many of the Enlightenment *philosophes* were of two minds about religion—educated in Christian schools, attached to Christian families and happy with the social order.[32] Voltaire refused to let people talk about atheism in front of the maids. "I want my lawyer, my tailor, my servants, even my wife to believe in God, and I think that then I shall be robbed and cuckolded less often."[33] He didn't stop at hoodwinking servants with religion: "An atheist king," he wrote, "is more dangerous than a fanatical Ravaillac." Gibbon admitted that religion might have its uses, though he much preferred the manly ancient Roman kind to the hysterical modern Christian variety: "The various modes of worship, which prevailed in the Roman world, were all considered by the people as equally true; by the philosopher as equally false; and by the magistrate as equally useful."[34]

For many Victorian men of letters the loss of faith was the most painful drama of their lives. Leslie Stephen sank into depression when he lost his faith and with it his career as a clergyman. In his "Stanzas from the Grande Chartreuse" (1855), Matthew Arnold, convinced that faith was at once impossible and essential, wrote of "Wandering between two worlds, one dead / The other powerless to be born / With nowhere yet to lay my head." Thomas Hardy envisioned "God's Funeral" as a time of mourning, not liberation. "I did not forget / That what was mourned for, I, too / Once had prized." Thomas Carlyle lamented that he and his friends "have quietly closed our eyes to the eternal Substance of things, and opened them only to the Shews and Shams of things. . . . There is no religion; there is no God; man has lost his soul, and vainly seeks antiseptic salt."[35]

"BELIEVERS WITHOUT GOD"[36]

One solution to the loss of faith was to find an alternative in secular ideology. These ideologies were at once substitutes and antidotes: substitutes because they helped to satisfy the yearning for meaning; antidotes because for the most part they tried to marginalize religion still further. Four secular faiths sprung to the fore in the nineteenth century: science, culture, the nation-state and socialism.

The most powerful was the cult of science. It is hard to recapture the force of this cult now that we have seen the dark side of science in the atomic bomb and Dr. Mengele. But for many Victorians and Edwardians science was an object of unqualified veneration. Science was explaining the world through such intellectual achievements as *The Origin of Species*. It was forcing men to give up their childish illusions and deal with the world as it actually is. (Science's appeal to John Stuart Mill was precisely that of "good down-right hard logic, with the minimum of sentimentalism," logic that enables you to "look facts in the face."[37]) It was also improving the world with a cascade of technological breakthroughs. Turn scientists into philosopher kings and war would be a thing of the past. Apply science to reproduction and you could bid farewell to stupidity and illness. H. G. Wells and many of his fellow Fabians believed that the world should be ruled by a scientific elite. Pablo Neruda, a Chilean writer and politician, summed up these feelings in his memoirs: "I shall never forget my visit to that hydroelectric plant overlooking the lake, whose pure waters mirror Armenia's unforgettable blue sky. When the journalists asked me for my impressions of Armenia's ancient churches and monasteries, I answered them, stretching things a little: 'The church I like best is the hydroelectric plant, the temple beside the lake.' "[38]

One of the most instructive products of this cult was social Darwinism. Its most illustrious advocate, Francis Galton, one of Darwin's cousins, wanted scientists to become a "new priesthood"—charged not just with officiating over wedding ceremonies but with preventing the unfit from getting married in the first place. A striking number of people believed that man was divided into distinct races that could be ranked according to their virtue and ability—and that the best way to produce progress (or social evolution) was to purify the race through selective breeding (or worse). The epicenter of racism was Germany: the Gobineau Library at the University of Strasbourg contained six thousand volumes on race. But it was not just a German phenomenon: Gobineau was French, and many of the movement's main proponents were English (Houston Stewart Chamberlain, Karl Pearson) or American (Madison Grant). Almost every advanced country in the world had flourishing eugenics societies, attracting the support of the left as well as the right. Sidney and Beatrice Webb, the founders of the Fabian movement, believed in population planning. George Bernard Shaw thought, "The only fundamental and possible socialism is the socialization of the selective breeding of man."[39]

Shaw points to another religion substitute that flourished in the nineteenth century: the cult of culture. Many people in that Age of Innocence—before modernism and postmodernism blurred the distinction between the sublime and the ridiculous—spelled culture with a capital C. They worshipped great artists, particularly Goethe and Beethoven, with the same reverence that religious people reserved for the prophets. They regarded great art as something that could forge a link between man and God—or, as Goethe put it, "He who possesses art and science has religion; he who does not possess them, needs religion." They treated great books as religious objects and concert halls as temples of worship. "One goes to the Conservatoire with religious devotion as the pious go to the temple of the Lord," one French writer put it in 1846. And they believed that Culture could civilize and redeem mankind—spreading "sweetness and light" among a vulgar and materialistic people and binding together a fractured nation. As Matthew Arnold argued, "Culture, disinterestedly seeking in its aim at perfection to see things as they really are, shows us how worthy and divine a thing is the religious side in man, though it is not the whole man."[40]

For many of its votaries, Culture wasn't just a substitute for religion but was superior to it. Culture wasn't contaminated with barbarism or superstition. Culture didn't generate wars or persecution. Culture—and particularly music—provided the distilled essence of religion free from the stains of dogmatism and warfare.[41] And the cult of culture was not restricted to a self-regarding aesthetic elite. Byron, Charles Dickens and Anthony Trollope enjoyed John Grisham—like sales. Mark Twain raked in a fortune traveling the country on the lecture circuit. More than two million people turned out to watch Victor Hugo's hearse pass through the boulevards of Paris—and the government gave him a twenty-one-gun salute.[42]

The third secular ideology was the ideology of the nation-state. Jules Michelet hoped that his "noble country," France, would "take the place of the God who escapes us" and "fill within us the immeasurable abyss which extinct Christianity has left there." Nationalists nationalized religious icons, such as St. George or St. Joan of Arc, and turned secular politicians, such as Giuseppe Garibaldi and Victor Emmanuel, into quasi-religious figures. Nationalism, in its triumphant nineteenth century form, drew much of its strength from the near-deification of two things—the "folk" and the state.

Cultural nationalists such as Johann Gottfried Herder believed that various peoples have a "creative soul" whose destiny is to fulfill themselves in a self-aware nation-state.[43] Thus Russia and Germany discovered their identities by rebuffing Bonapartism, and Italy realized its identity through the Risorgimento. Other nationalists spoke more simply of "chosen people" who had a quasireligious identity and purpose.

Hegel regarded the state as "the Divine Idea as it exists on earth" and, more famously, as "the march of God in the world."[44] The state is more than just a system of law and government. It is the embodiment of ethical principle and rational purpose—all-knowing and all-providing. The essence of human freedom lies in surrendering your will to the higher will of the state. "The Nation State is mind in its substantive rationality and immediate actuality," mused Hegel, "and is therefore the absolute power on earth."[45] These ideas naturally appealed to politicians keen to increase their power, especially ones who found the church in their way.

The nation-state marginalized religion as well as providing a substitute for it—sometimes consciously so (Otto von Bismarck presented his Kulturkampf as a cultural struggle between enlightened nationalism and obscurantist religion) but more often unconsciously. Bismarck decried the

"Black International" of Catholic priests as a threat to the Prussian state, and demanded that candidates for ordination must be German citizens and graduates of German theology faculties. An Italian newspaper celebrated Garibaldi's march on Rome in 1870 by declaring that "the medieval world has fallen: the modern age stands resplendent on the ruins of the theocracy."[46] In 1902 France witnessed the vigorous expulsion of the church from the public square, complete with the further expropriation of church property and the establishment of a state school system with a hard-edged state ideology. But you did not have to have an animus against the church to end up unintentionally squeezing it out of public life. Merely by providing public education, Victorians began the process of edging the church out of the business of education; merely by creating the first bits of a welfare bureaucracy, they began to perform functions that had previously been associated most with the church.

The fourth ideology—unsurprising, given Marx's views—was socialism. Socialists were divided over religion. Many, particularly on the European Continent, wanted to sweep it away as an illusion that legitimized an unjust social order. Others, particularly in England, argued that socialism was nothing less than Christianity in practice: indeed, only eight of the 249 Labor MPs in the House of Commons in 1929–31 described themselves as atheist or agnostic.[47] But, whatever their ideas about the hereafter, most socialists believed in some version of building Jerusalem first on earth.

THE GODLESS EXPRESS

In the twentieth century, many of these new secular faiths came together in a poisonous totalitarian cocktail. Communism didn't just draw on Marx's ideas. It also drew on Russian nationalism ("socialism in one country") and on the cults of science and culture. Stalin was keen on using science to solve man's problems and on exploiting culture to burnish Russian nationalism. Likewise, Nazism didn't just draw on "scientific" racism. It also drew on German nationalism and German cultural chauvinism, worshipping German gods such as Thor and German artists such as Goethe and (particularly) Richard Wagner. Both Hitler and Stalin owed a debt to Hegel's idea that freedom lies in the "realm of necessity"—submerging the individual's will into the will of the collective—and that history's purposes justify the crushing of individual rights.

On the totalitarian left, religion was simply unacceptable. The Soviet Union was an officially atheist state, just as Saudi Arabia is an officially Muslim state. "All modern religions and churches," Lenin wrote, "every kind of religious organization are always considered by Marxism as the organs of bourgeois reaction, used for the protection of the exploitation and the stupefaction of the working class." Communists expropriated church land, closed churches, shuttered seminaries, banned religious publications, erected museums of atheism and killed, purged or imprisoned priests. Symbolically enough, the first Soviet Gulag was opened in a former monastery in the Arctic region.[48] Communists also replaced Christian ceremonies with Red Weddings, Red Funerals and Red Christenings. Members of the League of the Militant Godless, which was established in 1925, wandered around the country mocking religion or took the "Godless Express" to the far corners of the Russian vastness. Alas, this enthusiasm for Godlessness did not prevent the Communists from embalming Lenin and erecting thousands of statues to him and his even more violent successor.

Things were more complicated on the right: Fascist sympathizers made common cause with the religious right in Spain, France and elsewhere in order to defeat socialism. But the Nazis had a much more ambitious agenda than just forming alliances with reactionary clerics—they wanted to create their own religion out of a mishmash of Christianity and Teutonic mumbo jumbo and then use it to strengthen the power of the party. They presented Hitler as a semimessianic figure who would not only make the fatherland work again, but redeem the soul of the *volk*.[49] This vision swept up much of the country, converting intellectuals (including Martin Heidegger), Prussian aristocrats, unemployed workers and people of all religions and none. In the 1930–33 elections Hitler proved particularly appealing both to people who had drifted away from religion after the First World War, and to Lutherans, whose church had nearly gone bankrupt.

Hitler described Aryans as "the highest image of the Lord," the tools of human redemption, the bearers of pure Aryan blood that needed to be harbored by eugenic breeding. Goebbels dismissed "the Jew" as "the Antichrist of world history." The Nazis had their own liturgy: fires, wreaths, altars, the swastika, bloodstained relics and a special Nazi book of martyrs commemorated on November 9, the Day of Mourning to mark both the 1918 revolution and Hitler's failed beer-hall putsch of 1923. Initiates into the SS promised, "We believe in God, we believe in Germany, which He created . . . and in the Führer . . . whom He has sent us." But in all of this blather God was strictly subordinated to the Führer and the church to the state: as with Bonaparte, religion was acceptable only in so far as it was a tool of political power.

Hitler and Stalin were unusually brutal. But many other countries produced leaders who tried to marginalize religion in the name of national integration and top-down modernization. The trend was particularly powerful in the developing world. The forerunner in this was Kemal Atatürk, who established a strict separation of mosque and state in Turkey in the 1920s: abolishing the Caliphate, the central source of religious authority; getting rid of separate religious schools and colleges; establishing a secular system of public education; doing away with religious courts, which applied sharia law, and replacing them with a new legal system based on the Swiss civil code; and replacing Arabic with Roman script.

This was welcomed at the time. Our own magazine gushed, "The repudiation of the Caliphate by the Turks marks an epoch in the expansion of Western ideas over the non-Western world, for our Western principles of national sovereignty and self-government are the real forces to which the unfortunate [caliph] has fallen victim."[50] There was also a broadly positive reaction to Reza Shah, an army officer who seized power in Iran in 1925 with Western help. He used an iron fist to enforce secular orthodoxy. Soldiers roamed the streets ordering women to strip off their veils, forcing clerics to remove their turbans and, on one occasion, gunning down religious students in the streets. Believers were forbidden to visit Mecca.

Such brutal tactics were not confined to the Islamic world. Across Latin America a weird assortment of populists and dictators attacked the Catholic Church in the name of progress. Plutarco Elías Calles, president of Mexico in 1924–8, shut down churches, convents and religious colleges, and established dozens of museums of atheism. One of his henchmen had the phrase "the personal enemy of God" inscribed on his calling cards.[51] In Argentina, Juan Perón crudely tried to replace the Catholic Church with his own nationalist iconography.

After the Second World War, many of the rulers of the developing world followed Atatürk in linking modernization with secularization. They not only imported Western technology and economics (often in the misguided form of socialist planning); they also imported Western ideas about the backward nature of religion. Mesmerized by European ideas, dressed in European clothes, surrounded by French- or English-speaking friends, they made war on the mullahs and priests and their primitive practices.

In the Arab world they eventually had a European sociological text to substantiate their beliefs, Daniel Lerner's *The Passing of Traditional Society: Modernizing the Middle East* (1958), which argued that Islam was "defenseless" in the face of rationalization and modernization. Reza Shah's son, Mohammad Reza Pahlavi, seized land controlled by the clergy as part of his "White Revolution." The shah, as he was known, substituted the term "holy book" for the Koran in Iran's constitution in order to prevent discrimination against religious minorities. He sent "mullahs of modernization" into the countryside to promote literacy and build infrastructure. When all this provoked a clerical backlash, he traveled to Qum, the seat of Shia learning, to denounce his critics as "lice-ridden mullahs." In Egypt, Gamal Abdel Nasser took a more middle-of-the-road position, trying to modernize Islam rather than marginalize it—though he all but crushed the Muslim Brotherhood in 1955 after a failed assassination attempt.

In India Jawaharlal Nehru replaced Gandhi's devout religiosity (the Mahatma once declared that "anyone who thinks that religion and politics can be kept apart, understands neither religion nor politics") with a Fabian commitment to reason and modernization. Secularization theory was not just an abstract concept: for many leaders throughout the developing world it was a (sometimes brutal) program for action.

THE LONG WITHDRAWING ROAR

Europe saw a brief revival of religion in the wake of the Second World War, as people tried to find a deeper meaning in the whirlwind of war-time events, and the West defined itself against Soviet tyranny. In 1954, for example, Billy Graham persuaded millions of Britons to turn up at greyhound tracks and football stadiums as part of his "sweep for God through Britain." In the same year seven out of ten Italians regularly attended mass.[52] But secularization soon resumed its long advance in the old Continent, gathering pace as the European economies heated up. For most people, the retreat of religion was not bloody and traumatic, but more gradual. For every hothead determined to fight a head-on battle with religion, there were countless people whose faith just seemed to ebb away. By the mid-twentieth century, fashionable intellectuals were presumed to be atheists. (The few who weren't—such as Graham Greene and Malcolm Muggeridge—found their writing defined by the mere fact that they believed, however doubtingly, in God.)

As for politics, the old establishment might still bow the knee in church and sniff at atheism (some even called themselves Christian Democrats), but the foundations were crumbling beneath their feet. Politicians mentioned God less and less, and even those who drew on religious principles seemed to trust the state more than churches. Clement Attlee, Britain's Labor prime minister in 1945–51, cut his teeth working in a Christian socialist mission in the East End of London; and Attlee's government happily described its new welfare state as nothing less than a New Jerusalem, but his creation left ever less room for churches.

We will take a snapshot of the current state of European religion in chapter four. But by most measures, the second half of the twentieth century saw the almost complete secularization of the British white working class—the estrangement of the indigenous population from the Anglican Church and other denominations. A century ago, Britain had the same level of religious faith as the United States. Respect for the general tenets of Christianity united the country. Half of under-fifteen-year-olds were enrolled in Sunday school. Soccer crowds regularly sang "Bread of Heaven" and "Abide with Me."[53] Today Britain is an "agnostic nation," in the words of Roy Hattersley, a Labor politician, and soccer crowds usually chant rather different fare.

In the Land of the Bald Knobbers

In the 1960s secularism seemed to be carrying all before it, with priests questioning God's existence, the young testing received boundaries, and leftists dreaming of building heaven on earth. In 1968 Peter Berger, then a prophet of secularization, assured *The New York Times* that by "the 21st century, religious believers are likely to be found only in small sects, huddled together to resist a worldwide secular culture."[54]

In the same year that Berger made his apocalyptic prediction, a hedonistic young American arrived at Shelley's old college in Oxford. But Bill Clinton shared none of the careless atheism of his British contemporaries or his Oxford tutors. He had joined the Southern Baptist Church at the tender age of nine—attending church every week even if it meant walking there alone—and, as he grew up, he refused to allow his success to dull his interest in religion. The most vivid parts of his autobiography concern religious faith—particularly the "hotter" forms of worship. "In 1955, I had absorbed enough of my church's teachings to know that I was a sinner and to want Jesus to save me," he wrote in one passage. "So I came down the aisle at the end of Sunday service, professed my faith in Christ, and asked to be baptized."[55] He recalled attending a Baptist service as governor in which one worshipper got so carried away that he had to be removed from the sanctuary and locked in a nearby room, where he continued to holler and bang about—and eventually tore the door off its hinges, returning into the church screaming.[56]

Clinton was particularly gripped by Pentecostalism. During the first Pentecostal service he attended he was reduced to tears at the sight of worshippers speaking in "tongues" and transported into religious ecstasy—and thereafter he made a point of attending Pentecostal summer camps every year from 1977 until he ran for president. He even sang with a Pentecostal quartet of balding ministers called the Bald Knobbers.[57] When he was defeated for reelection as governor of his home state in 1980, the Bald Knobbers were among the first people to visit him to offer their prayers.

As president, Clinton maintained an interest in religion that would have had him branded a dangerous Jesus freak in Europe. A few weeks after moving to the White House he hosted a private dinner for Billy Graham, whom he credited with bringing him to Jesus.[58] Unlike many of his predecessors, including Ronald Reagan, he regularly attended church in Washington, DC. Many members of Clinton's inner circle were devout Christians. Al Gore was a Southern Baptist who studied theology at Vanderbilt University in Nashville, Tennessee. George Stephanopoulos studied theology as a Rhodes Scholar at Balliol College, Oxford. Rahm Emanuel (who is now Obama's chief of staff) was an observant Jew. Mike McCurry was an active Methodist who helped out in his local Sunday school. Paul Begala was a pro-life Catholic who named his eldest son John Paul.[59] Clinton cultivated close relationships with several leading Evangelical preachers such as Billy Graham, Bill Hybels and Tony Campolo, a Baptist minister and academic. He cited Jesus Christ in public speeches more frequently than his successor: 5.1 times a year compared with 4.7 times for George Bush.[60] At the lowest point of his presidency, during the Lewinsky scandal, he turned to leading Evangelicals to ask for forgiveness, including Campolo and Gordon MacDonald. Evangelicals who encountered him casually were struck by the quality of his faith. Jack Hayford, the pastor of an eight-thousand-strong church in Los Angeles, said, "It may bewilder some to have it said that this man believes in the Bible and in Jesus Christ as God's son, the Savior." Compolo recalls that "I don't think I've met him where we both didn't pray."[61]

Clinton's enthusiasm for religion extended to a willingness to lower the wall of separation between church and state. He dealt heavily in religious symbols, talking in 1992 of a "New Covenant" between the federal government and the American people. He tried to welcome religious people into the public square. In August 1993, during a holiday in Martha's Vineyard, he strolled around the Bunch of Grapes Bookstore in Vineyard Haven and came across *The Culture of Disbelief*, a book by Stephen Carter, a Yale law professor. The book argued that America's high culture—the culture of the universities and law schools and liberal elites—did far too much to marginalize religious people. The Baptist from Arkansas strongly agreed. He told reporters, "Sometimes I think the environment in which we operate is entirely too secular. The fact that we have freedom of religions doesn't mean we need to try to have freedom from religion." *The Culture of Disbelief* became that summer's surprise best-seller.

In 1997 Clinton signed the most sweeping sanction for the expression of religious views in the federal workplace ever issued. Workers could discuss their religious views in the halls and cafeterias of federal workplaces just as freely as they could discuss the latest episode of *Sex and the City*. They could display religious messages such as "What Would Jesus Do?" just as easily as they could display football posters. And they could organize Bible studies and religious meetings. "The American workplace has not been the same since," argues Michael Lindsay, a prominent sociologist.[62] Clinton even flirted with faith-based social services: "You cannot change somebody's life from the outside in," he once said, "unless there is also some change from the inside out."[63]

In short, Bill Clinton—a man whom many Europeans regard as a kindred soul and whom many religious Americans regard as a godless fornicator—had very little in common with Shelley, at least when it came to the battle between modernity and religion.

Why did America evolve so differently from Europe?

CHAPTER TWO

THE AMERICAN WAY I:
THE CHOSEN NATION (1607–1900)

❧❧

THE IDEA THAT America was born religious is engrained in national mythology. Samuel Danforth talked of America's "errand into the wilderness." Samuel Sewall, one of Massachusetts' leading judges in the late seventeenth and early eighteenth centuries, dubbed America a "God City." Every American divine worth his salt had a sermon in his drawer about how America came into life as a "new Israel" with a special covenant from God. These days Evangelical publishers pump out books with titles such as *Faith, Stars and Stripes,* and conservative intellectuals revel in the contrast between God-fearing America, with its flexible economy and high birth rate, and secular Europe, with its empty maternity wards and sclerotic labor markets.

We do not pretend to know whether God has, indeed, chosen America for special blessings. But a dispassionate look at history quickly proves three things. First, America was not born religious. Church members never made up more than a third of the adult population of New England before the revolution, and may never have climbed as high as seventeen percent in the southern colonies.[1] Instead, America became religious. Second, religion and modernity have never been enemies in America in the way that they have in Europe. On the contrary, they were fraternal twins that grew up together: the more modern America became, the more likely

people were to go to church. And third, the key to America's religious life
was its "extreme division of sects," as Tocqueville had it. Evangelical historians make much of the Holy Spirit working in mysterious ways; the real
unseen presence in American religion, however, has been Adam Smith's
invisible hand.

THE NOT-SO-SHINING CITY

From the very beginning America was an unusual mixture of the religious
and the secular. Some of the first settlers were religious zealots, fleeing
from persecution; some were businessmen, bent on making money; and
still others were a combination of the two, worshipping God and Mammon at the same time (and, in Max Weber's view, worshipping Mammon
all the more successfully because they worshipped God).

The hundred or so settlers who alighted from the *Mayflower* at Plym-
outh Harbor were certainly zealots. They had fled England, first for the
Netherlands and then for America, because of theological quarrels; and
they worked hard to organize their lives according to scripture.[2] The
death penalty awaited not just murderers but also witches, heretics, adulterers and sodomites. Wigs were banned because they do not appear in
the Bible.[3]

Yet the colony failed to maintain its purity. By 1645 only 70 percent
of Boston's 421 families could claim some link to the church—a proportion that shrinks to less than half if you include servants. And 1645 was
in many ways a high-water mark: the proportion kept heading down for
decades after. The number was even lower in Salem, a town that Americans associated with their God-fearing past long before Arthur Miller
wrote *The Crucible*: by 1683 some 83 percent of the taxpayers confessed to
no religious identification.[4] New England's religiosity was diluted still
further by the fact that English judges were in the habit of sending their
most undesirable charges—thieves, rapists and murderers—to the colonies. Between 1718 and 1775 at least 66,000 felons were transported to
America by the British courts.[5]

And Massachusetts was a model of piety compared with Virginia.

The Virginia Company professed all sorts of highfalutin ideas about converting the heathen, who, according to the company's charter, lived "in darkness and miserable ignorance of the true knowledge and worship of God." Initially, the citizens of Jamestown had been legally obliged to attend church twice a day. Failure to observe the Sabbath was punishable by a whipping on the second offense and execution on the third. But the good intentions did not last. The Church of England had few resources to spare for the distant province. (In 1661, by one count, only ten of the colony's fifty parishes had ministers.[6]) The colonists made little effort to convert the ever-growing number of slaves they needed for the cultivation of tobacco.[7]

If America was not born religious, it was not born pluralistic either. The colonists sailed to America to establish the reign of truth, not a zone of tolerance. Perry Miller, the premier historian of the Puritans, described Massachusetts as a "dictatorship, not of a single tyrant, or of an economic class, or of a political faction, but of the holy and regenerate."[8] For one of the colony's religious leaders, John Cotton, "theocracy, or to make the Lord God our governor," was simply "the best form of government in a Christian commonwealth."[9] Increase Mather, Cotton's son-in-law and another leading divine, dismissed "the toleration of all Religions and Persuasions" as the "way to have no Religion at all."[10] And these theocrats enforced religious conformity with a terrifying range of punishments, including whipping, tongue-boring, ear-chopping and execution. Indeed, they were so zealous in stamping out dissidence that their British overlords were obliged to intervene: Charles II sent a missive to the Massachusetts authorities telling them to stop executing his subjects, and William and Mary issued an Act of Toleration that allowed all forms of Protestant worship, in the colonies as well as at home.[11]

The Puritans also began to think like members of a religious establishment. Pastors and governors all had to be members of the church in good standing. The franchise was restricted to church members. The state had the power to exact taxes to support the church and compel people to attend. Many of the bitterest religious disputes in New England had less to do with doctrine than with the benefits of church membership. In 1662 the Massachusetts General Court, or synod, decreed that there should be three levels of believer with accordant privileges. Solomon Stoddard's counterblast to this idea, *The Doctrine of Instituted Churches,* was so incendiary that it had to be printed in London.

America became a haven of tolerance not because the colonists left European habits of mind behind but because it was impossible to police such a huge country. From the mid-seventeenth century Rhode Island became a refuge for Baptists and Quakers, leading Cotton Mather to dismiss it as "the sewer of New England." William Penn, who gave his name to Pennsylvania, built his "holy experiment" on tolerance in Philadelphia, allowing in anybody who believed in Jesus Christ. Farther south, when the church authorities in Virginia clamped down on Protestant dissidents, the dissidents promptly fled across the border to more tolerant Maryland and then to the Carolinas, whose gentlemen investors used religious freedom to attract colonists. The result was a striking amount of religious diversity in a relatively small population.[12] The historian Sydney Ahlstrom points out that a traveler trekking from Massachusetts to the Carolinas in 1700 would run into several different varieties of Congregationalists and Baptists; Presbyterians and Quakers; Dutch, German and French Reformed; Swedish, Finnish and German Lutherans; Mennonites and radical pietists; Anglicans, Catholics, Jews and Rosicrucians.[13]

Awake for a While

The history of American religion under British rule is more than just a history of decay and decline. America experienced the first of its three (or perhaps four) Great Awakenings in the 1730s and 1740s. It was ignited by America's first significant theologian, Jonathan Edwards, who was "born again" in late adolescence—he said that he was seized with "so sweet a sense of the glorious majesty and grace of God that I know not how to express"[14]—and who later preached a series of sermons such as "Sinners in the Hands of an Angry God." The fire was reignited by America's first proper megapreacher, George Whitefield. "The reason why congregations have been so dead," Whitefield declared, "is because they have dead men preach them."[15] Whitefield was a tireless performer who preached on more than fifteen thousand occasions, and a highly skilled stirrer of souls who, in his own words, spoke with "Much Flame, Clearness and Power." Benjamin Franklin calculated that his voice was so resonant that he could make himself heard outdoors by as many as thirty thousand people. All he had to do was pronounce the single word "Mesopotamia," the legend went, and grown women would burst into tears.[16]

The Great Awakening had a lasting impact on American religion. Edwards remains a revered figure in Evangelical circles. He also had a great effect on John Wesley in England, who had started what became Methodism in the 1730s. The Great Awakening brought competition for souls, as some upstart sects began to poach members from established institutions. (In 1769–74, the number of Baptist churches in Virginia jumped from seven to 540.[17]) It also brought some modern marketing techniques. One of the main complaints among the Boston clergy against Whitefield was that he "used his utmost craft and cunning to stoke the passions and engage the affections of the people."[18]

But at the time it looked as if the Awakening had achieved little. The fires of enthusiasm guttered out. Church membership declined. Edwards spent most of his last years trying to convert the Native Americans (an Indian disciple translated his words into Mohican as he spoke) before finally being appointed to the presidency of the College of New Jersey (which became Princeton University) in 1757. His son and a few of his followers struggled to get his work published. Yale's president, Ezra Stiles, pronounced that his work would "pass into a transient notice perhaps scarce above oblivion."[19] The only church with a presence throughout the colonies was the Church of England, which was beholden to a clerical hierarchy that was based more than three thousand miles away and largely staffed by indolent duffers.

The smoldering row over America's relationship with the motherland also diverted attention from religion to the city of man. The great issues in 1780 were no longer man's relationship with God but America's relationship with Britain; and, increasingly, America's most illustrious intellectuals were no longer clergymen but statesmen. Political science took over from theology as the queen of the sciences.[20] The reason that there was no reference to God in the Constitution, Alexander Hamilton joked, was that the Founding Fathers had simply forgotten to put one in.

The truth was that religion in prerevolutionary America was not *that* exceptional. There was more tolerance and pluralism than in Europe. (In 1763 New York celebrated Britain's victory over France with a victory party at which the city's two Anglican clergymen were joined by ministers from Dutch, French, Presbyterian, Baptist and Moravian churches.[21]) But most colonists lived in a world of state-sponsored religion. Most lived by the code of *cuius regio, eius religio*; many paid church taxes. American ministers complained about the same things as European ones—that the common people were sunk in superstition and addicted to bestial pleasures. Moreover, American religion was still shackled to Europe. The Church of England answered to Canterbury; and some of the most vigorous preachers were European imports. Wesley was a British Tory who only spent a couple of (frustrating) years in the colonies, in 1735–37. Whitefield may have visited America thirteen times, but he was a minister in the Church of England, supported by the Countess of Huntingdon (to whom he generously bequeathed his American slaves who worked in the Georgia orphanage he founded). It took the American Revolution to set America on a different path from Europe.

A TALE OF TWO REVOLUTIONS

The American Revolution was a unique event in modern history—a revolution against an earthly regime that was not also an exercise in anticlericalism. As we have seen, in Europe the state and the church were so intertwined that it was impossible to attack one without attacking the other. In America the identification between the established regime and the established church was much less pronounced. Some clergymen supported the revolution (about a hundred chaplains, half Anglicans and half Presbyterians, served in the revolutionary army). Others preferred to keep their heads down in what they regarded as a secular conflict. The Philadelphia Presbyterian synod in 1775 insisted that "it is well known . . . that

we have not been instrumental in inflaming the minds of people, or urging them to acts of violence and disorder."[22]

Tocqueville's verdict on the revolution remains the best available.
"There is no country in the world where the boldest doctrines of the
philosophes of the eighteenth century in matters of politics were more
fully applied than in America," he argued. "It was only the anti-religious
doctrines that never were able to make headway." Almost alone in the
world, Americans saw no contradiction between embracing the values
of the Enlightenment and republicanism while at the same time cling-
ing to their religious principles. Revolutionary France defined itself by
its hostility to religion (no less a person than Tom Paine worried that
"the people of France were running headlong into atheism"); revolutionary America embraced religion alongside liberty, reason and popular
government.

There are plenty of historians who quibble with this argument. Evangelical historians like to stress their country's deep-rooted religiosity.
Didn't George Washington kneel in prayer at Valley Forge? Secular historians like to portray the Founding Fathers as Frenchified Deists. Didn't
Thomas Jefferson go through the Bible with a pair of scissors, removing
the bad bits? (The bad bits usually concerned resurrection and miracles
and other "deliria of crazy imaginations.") And wasn't Washington an
irregular churchgoer who never took communion and refused to display
religious symbols in his house at Mount Vernon?[23]

The truth is that Tocqueville got it just about right. The Founding
Fathers were certainly not enemies of religion in the French manner.
Some, like Patrick Henry, John Jay and John Witherspoon, were fervent
believers. (Witherspoon was a first-rate theologian.) Most of the Deists
would have agreed with Tocqueville's aperçu that "despotism can do without faith, but freedom cannot." Franklin and Jefferson regarded Jesus as
an important moral teacher. Washington declared in his farewell address,
"Reason and experience both forbid us to expect that national morality
can prevail in exclusion of religious principle." John Adams argued that
"no other institution" was as effective as "the Christian religion" in dis-
pensing moral education throughout the entire society."[24] Without their
Puritan faith, he argued, the original settlers would have been "rakes,

fops, sots, gamblers, starved with hunger, or frozen with cold, scalped by Indians."[25]

But the revolution they made was essentially a secular affair. There were no religious grievances among the long "history of repeated injuries and usurpations" in the Declaration of Independence. The Founders occasionally cited God in their various writings but as a great watchmaker rather than an intervening presence. There were no references to biblical texts in the Declaration of Independence, the Constitution or the new state charters, an astonishing fact for the time. Washington seldom referred to God except under vague titles like "the Great Disposer of events," and never mentioned Jesus Christ in his personal papers.[26]

The problem that the Founding Fathers were grappling with was political rather than theological. How can you prevent tyranny? How can you stop overmighty people—whether they are princes or priests—from imposing their will on ordinary folk? How can you preserve liberty? They consulted the Bible, but they also drew on other sources, classical historians and philosophers such as Thucydides and Aristotle, European theorists such as Montaigne, Locke and Smith. This points to the paradox at the heart of the revolution. If the Founders were intent on grappling with a secular problem, their solution to that problem—the separation of church and state and the division of power—allowed the survival of religion in the modern world.

THE FOUNDERS' GIFT TO GOD

The First Amendment—that Congress shall make no law respecting an establishment of religion, or prohibiting the free exercise thereof—did two remarkable things. It created tolerance in its fullest sense: not just the top-down tolerance involved in allowing dissent but the bottom-up tolerance that recognizes that individuals have a right to choose their own religious opinions. And it introduced competition: churches had to get people in through the door. Neither of these things happened immediately, but the result, in William Lee Miller's words, was that "Christianity, the great muddy Mississippi of Western civilization, was able almost uniquely in the American setting to flow unvexed to the sea of modern democratic life."[27]

Why did the Founding Fathers strike out in this radically new direction? Few questions in American constitutional history have produced so much heat. But the answer is surprisingly simple: because they did not want to see an established church on the European (and particularly the British) model. This did not mean driving religion out of the public square. (Seven years after the amendment was passed, John Adams saw nothing odd about calling for a day of fasting and prayer before God.) But it did mean making religion a matter of individual conscience rather than statecraft. Once you grant that principle, the entire edifice of established churches and religious compulsion comes tumbling down.

This was not only a radical break from established European practice. It was also a radical break from what was going on in America. Most of the state constitutions written immediately after the revolution supported Christianity in some way—for example, by declaring Christianity the true religion and imposing religious tests for office-holding. The Congregationalists would remain a de facto established church in Massachusetts for a long time. Congress proclaimed national days of prayer. Five of the new nation's thirteen states raised taxes to support ministers. Twelve imposed religious tests for office.

The turning point for the Founding Fathers came in Virginia. In 1784 the state legislature allowed the new Episcopal Church to take over its Anglican predecessor's property. But what about church taxes? Only about a third of the state's believers belonged to the Episcopal Church. Why should the other two-thirds be forced to pay taxes to support it? The Episcopalians and their allies initially proposed an ingenious compromise whereby Virginians would be taxed, but only to support the denomination of their choice.[28] This compromise had the support of Patrick Henry and most of the squirearchy. But it was eventually defeated by an odd coalition of Evangelical dissenters (who wanted to keep politics out of religion) and Deist revolutionaries (who wanted to keep religion out of politics). This strange coalition then rallied behind a very different solution to the problem—Jefferson's Act for Establishing Religious Freedom, a measure that was designed to disestablish the church and make religion a matter of individual conscience. Jefferson later described the debate over the measure as one of the "severest contests in which I have ever engaged."[29] But the measure eventually passed the Virginia Assembly—and provided the model for the First Amendment.

The two presiding geniuses of the act were Jefferson and Madison. Garry Wills has demonstrated that the two were not simply engaged in pragmatic politics. Nor were they engaged in a battle to sideline religion. They believed firmly that disestablishment was good for both religion and the state. Jefferson repeatedly emphasized that disestablishment was good for religion because it would promote competition and punish idleness.[30] Madison argued that disestablishment would be good for the state because it would free religion to promote public morality unencumbered by state patronage and corruption.[31]

The Constitutional Convention repeated many of the arguments that had already been rehearsed in Virginia. There was a sharp debate about church taxes. Constitutional politics sometimes trumped principle: some states, most notably Congregationalist New England, had to be bought off by allowing the northeastern states to continue to give state support for religion—hence the idea that the First Amendment would apply only to federal law. (It begins, "Congress shall . . .") But the Constitution nevertheless established the principle that religion is a matter of individual conscience. And Madison and Jefferson became increasingly determined to reinforce that principle as time went on. The decision to get government out of the religion business did as much as almost anything else to establish America's role as the most religious country in the advanced world.

Why is disestablishment a recipe for religious vigor? As we have already pointed out, Adam Smith gave the best answer to this question more than two centuries ago in *The Wealth of Nations:* a free market in religion forces clergymen to compete for market share. But English fiction is also an acerbic commentary on the way that an established clergy can sometimes behave: think of the obsequious Reverend Mr. Collins pursuing his patron Lady Catherine de Bourgh in *Pride and Prejudice* or the infighting over livings in Trollope. And the European clergy's close alliance with the political establishment meant that political dissidents had to turn against the church as well as the state. In Europe left-wing politics have been tinged with anticlericalism: many left-wing firebrands embraced atheism along with socialism, and even Christian Socialists were fiercely critical of established churches. In America—at least until the 1960s—left-wingers were as likely to be Christian as their conservative opponents were.

One of the things that most struck foreigners was the power of America's religious market. Francis Grund, an immigrant from Bohemia, noted in 1837, "In America every clergyman may be said to do business on his own account, and under his own firm. He alone is responsible for any deficiency in the discharge of his office, as he alone is entitled to all the credit due to his exertions. He always acts as principal, and is therefore more anxious, and will make greater efforts to obtain popularity, than one who serves for wages."[32] Karl Griesinger, a German liberal who personally disliked American religiosity, remarked in 1858, "Clergymen in America must . . . defend themselves to the last, like other businessmen; they must meet competition and build up a trade, and it's their own fault if their income is not large enough. Now is it clear why heaven and hell are moved to drive the people to the churches, and why attendance is more common here than anywhere else in the world."[33] A Swedish Lutheran noted, "In America the shepherd seeks the sheep and gathers them to his bosom, and does not conduct himself after the manner of Sweden, were the sheep must seek the shepherd and address him with high-sounding titles."[34]

Two modern scholars, Roger Finke and Rodney Stark, have used this insight to provide a compelling account of "the churching of America." The free market reduced the start-up costs of getting into the religion business. It boosted the supply of both sects and clergy. And it produced relentless innovation. The American religious market threw up new religious "products," some of them suspiciously well adapted to their local market. (The founder of Mormonism, Joseph Smith, said he had discovered a new book of the Bible that proved that Jesus had visited America.) It also put a premium on communication—colloquial sermons that offered "plain truth for plain people," revival meetings that encouraged audience participation, and a new form of popular religious music.

METHOD IN THEIR METHODISM

The organization that personified this direct approach was the Methodist church. The growth of American Methodism, especially the way that
it plugged into the religious energy of the people, was one of the wonders of the Age of Reason.[35] Francis Asbury, a preacher who arrived in the
country from Britain on the eve of the revolution, inevitably gets a lot of
credit for this. He traveled through every state in the union annually for
more than thirty years, covering around five thousand miles a year and
making himself the most widely recognized face in the new country.[36] He
was so much on the move that he did not have time to acquire any of the
trappings of normal life, such as a wife or a home, and when age and illness made it impossible for him to ride, he hauled his frail body around in
a buggy.[37]

Superhuman though Asbury's effort was, the genius of Methodism lay
in its system. It was centered on itinerant preachers like him, who brought
the Word to a scattered population (which was moving ever westward).
The preachers, who were plucked from the common folk, got a quick
training and a minimal salary. This ensured that their overheads were
low, that enthusiasm was high, and that they spoke to people's hearts.
Methodists were famous for using the language of ordinary people and for
focusing on preaching rather than engaging in arid theological debates.[38]
"Methodist preachers never converted the pulpit into a professor's chair,"
the Reverend C. C. Goss wrote in 1866, "but with earnestness have urged
and beseeched men to flee the wrath to come."[39]

Congregations were divided into classes of about a dozen members
that met once a week. These classes provided a mixture of social support
and religious reinforcement; they also offered ordinary people a chance
to lead others, putting the faith in line with the democratic spirit of the
country. Yet there was direction from above. National and regional organizations (which focused on record-keeping and publishing) provided the
movement with a spine: they also helped organize camp meetings. These
meetings exposed as many people as possible to Methodism's superstar

preachers, such as Asbury, and created a highly charged atmosphere in which people were particularly susceptible to being moved by the Holy Spirit.

The old established churches struggled to compete. By the mid-nineteenth century there were ten times as many Methodist preachers as Congregationalist ministers. The mainline churches had high fixed costs. Their clergy were educated in expensive seminaries and they expected job security: what self-respecting Harvard man would forsake the drawing rooms of New England for the shotgun shacks of the frontier? Inevitably, more attention went into holding on to their existing markets through gentlemen's agreements and what were in effect restrictive practices.[40]

By 1850 the Methodists were by far the biggest religious group in the country, with more than a third of the country's church members (up from just three percent in 1776).[41] But thereafter they began to suffer from many of the problems that plagued the mainline churches. They created a professional clergy—trained in formal seminaries, rather than in on-the-job-apprenticeship, and increasingly concerned with impressing polite society. These professional priests not only softened many of Methodism's once-austere rules and rituals, they also shifted their focus from preaching the Word to reforming society and doing good works.

The waning of Methodism created a marketing opportunity for the Baptists, who were even more "bottom-up" than the Methodists.[42] Local congregations jealously guarded their independence, hiring and firing their own preachers (most contracts only lasted a year), and vigorously resisting the emergence of Baptist seminaries. The result was that they preserved a much more fundamentalist approach to faith—and a much stronger commitment to winning souls. After the Civil War, the Southern Baptists had the added advantage of being the main vehicle for the preservation of the distinctive culture of the shattered South.

FORGING EVANGELICAL AMERICA

The result of all this religious energy was spectacular. Between the Revolution and the Civil War the proportion of churchgoing Americans rose

from 17 percent in 1776 to 34 percent in 1850[43]—and the number of clergymen rose three times as fast as the population as a whole. The ratio
of one minister per 1,500 Americans in colonial times became one per
500.[44] By 1830 the American Bible Society was producing over a million
copies of the Good Book every year (with an average of twenty-seven new
editions), and the American Tract Society was producing over six million
tracts.[45] There were some 605 distinct religious journals.

This period is best known for the Second Great Awakening—an awakening that started in New England but also spread to the frontier, where
week-long revival meetings had Americans weeping and falling to their
knees in prayer. It saw the birth of the black church as well as an explosion of Methodism and Baptism. The Second Great Awakening was even
more powerful than the first, but it was really a symptom of two more
fundamental developments.

The first might be described as the forging of Evangelical America.
Jefferson had predicted that the future lay with liberal Unitarianism—"I
trust that there is not a young man now living in the United States who
will not die a Unitarian," he once wrote. But in fact the religious market
that he did so much to establish hugely favored the "hot" form of religion
that he despised. By 1860 Evangelicals of one sort or another made up at
least 85 percent of America's churchgoing population.

The other development was the "Americanization" of religion. The
Puritans had brought over a European theology shaped by the Protestant Reformation. The Evangelicals created an American theology
shaped by the exigencies of revolutionary and postrevolutionary America—particularly by the rejection of hierarchy and tradition. Out went
the Calvinist emphasis on the spiritual elect and predestination; in came
the preoccupation with being born again. Out went the idea that salvation needed to be mediated through social institutions—the church, the
family, the covenant; in came the idea that all you needed was a Bible and
your own conscience. Out went the traditional clergy; in came a troupe of
charismatic leaders who had a gift for preaching. "Crazy" Lorenzo Dow
(1777–1834) would never have survived in Trollope's Barchester, with his
weird hair, harsh voice and disheveled clothes, but he was such a charismatic preacher that his autobiography became the country's best-selling

book after the Bible, and "Lorenzo" was one of the most popular names in the 1850 census.

By 1850 American Evangelicals were in effect on their own: far more emotional than the dour Calvinists of Scotland and Northern Ireland, far more committed to the Bible and the experience of conversion—or being born again—than Swiss and Danish Protestants, far less impressed by ecclesiastical tradition than the Anglicans in England or Canada, and much more democratic than Protestants or, of course, Catholics just about anywhere.[46] America's brand of Evangelicalism was as different from the religion of the Protestant Reformation as the religion of the Protestant Reformation was from medieval Catholicism.[47]

The more distinctive American religion became, the more successful it grew. "In no other part of the world," boasted Robert Baird, "do the inhabitants attend church in larger proportion than in the United States; certainly no part of the Continent of Europe can compare with them in that respect."[48] Philip Schaff, a Swiss theologian, stated in 1854 that "there are in America probably more awakened souls, and more individual effort and self-sacrifice for religious purposes, proportionately, than in any other country, Scotland alone perhaps excepted."[49]

Both these two trends—the emergence of Evangelical America and the Americanization of religion—took place during a time of rapid change. Two and a half million Americans in 1776 became twenty-three million in 1850. It also took place despite or because of the movement of millions of people into the dark corners of the land. In 1790 three-quarters of Americans lived in the thirteen former colonies; by 1850 only half of a much larger population did. The similarities between Dow's America and Wang's China are hard to ignore.

THE GLUE OF A NEW NATION

The Methodists and Baptists were the shock troops of what almost amounted to a second American revolution, one that was much more raw and populist than the gentlemanly revolution of 1776. The churches were the first effective national institutions in a country where the federal government was little more than a "midget institution in a giant land." Itinerant preachers saw more of America than anybody else: Asbury put in fifty visits to New York and eighty-four to Virginia.[50] "The ties which had held each denomination together," observed John Calhoun, a leading Southern politician, "formed a strong chord to hold the whole union together."[51] By 1850, the Evangelical churches, taken together, employed twice as many people as the post office, then the most important instrument of the federal government.[52] They even delivered more letters.

Evangelicals were compulsive institution builders. They formed societies of every kind—the American Bible Society, the American Sunday School Union, the American Temperance Society and so on. Indeed, there were so many societies with so many intricate connections that people talked of "the Evangelical United Front." And this front did have an effect: illegitimacy, drunkenness and various other unfortunate conditions declined under the relentless criticism of the Evangelicals. The front also provided a counterweight to the disorientating social mobility—the America where, as Tocqueville pointed out, there were "no traditions, or common habits, to forge links between their minds." The more people were uprooted from the moorings of family and community, the more they turned to religion to give their lives an anchor. New communities formed around churches and voluntary societies. And new immigrants discovered an enthusiasm for God that they had not felt back home.

The Evangelicals even provided an inspiration for America's emerging political system. Political campaigns borrowed liberally from revivalist meetings, with their torchlight parades, pitched tents, and emotional hullabaloo. Evangelicals formed the backbone of the Whig Party (which gave birth to the Republican Party). They also provided the nucleus for the country's first political convention. The Anti-Masonic Party, which held the first presidential nominating convention in 1831, was both an Evangelical reform movement and a political party.[53]

A FAITH THAT SPOKE AMERICAN

American religion also adapted itself to the governing assumptions of the new nation: assumptions that were—for the most part—republican, democratic, individualistic, optimistic. (We say "for the most part" because the South is always an exception to such cultural generalizations.) In Europe, Christianity was a creature of the old establishment; in America, it was a child of the revolution.

The idea of the free individual was at the heart of American Evangelicalism. The link between "freedom" and "religion" preceded the revolution. The rebels hung effigies of George III and his ministers on "liberty trees" alongside effigies of the Antichrist and the Pope. But it became far more pronounced as the years wore on. "In France, I had almost always seen the spirit of religion and the spirit of freedom marching in opposite directions," Tocqueville noted. "But in America I found they were intimately united and that they reigned in common over the same country."[54] By embracing the notion that conversion was a matter of individual choice for everybody, Americans also embraced the idea of equal opportunity. All a man needed was a clean heart and a good Bible—"a book dropped from the skies for all sorts of men to use in their own way."[55]

Evangelicals swept away the age-old distinction between the clergy and the laity. "I see no gospel law that authorizes any man, or set of men, to forbid, or put up bars to hinder or stop any man from preaching the gospel," Lorenzo Dow once wrote.[56] In the first quarter of the nineteenth century virtually every restriction to ordination was swept aside. The archetypal form of American religion—the Methodists' revival meeting—was religious democracy at its rawest. Revivalists pitched huge tents outside towns, conducted mass rallies and torchlight processions, employed gospel singers, and sent their audiences into paroxysms of emotion. Asbury estimated that revival meetings brought together three million to four million Americans every year—a third of the total population. He called camp meetings "the battle axe and weapon of war" that could "break down walls of wickedness" and "part of hell."[57]

Nineteenth century America did not see the open warfare between religion and the forces of progress that was common in Europe. The educated classes read Hegel and Darwin—but those thinkers did not strike the same chords. Indeed, many American Protestants thought that natural science would provide irrefutable proof of the existence of God. Benjamin Rush, an ardent Evangelical, was the first professor of chemistry in America. Charles Finney was fascinated by the possibility of applying practical science, particularly advanced planning, to the organization of revival meetings. Producing a revival was just as scientific as producing a crop of grain, he argued: both were God's handiwork but man could discover the principles of success.[58] William Miller, a New York farmer, proved, by dint of careful reading of the Bible and elaborate calculations, that the Second Coming would occur in 1843.[59] Theologians at Princeton University tried to use reason to prove that every word of the Bible was true. One of the reasons why so many Protestants rejected the advance of Darwinism was precisely because they clung to an older notion of scientific reasoning. As late as 1920, A. C. Dixon, the founder of fundamentalism, explained that he was a Christian "because I am a Thinker, a Rationalist, a Scientist."

MODERNITY AND RELIGION

So religion had a very different relationship to reason in America from the one it had in Europe: republicanism, liberalism and Protestantism were combined into a single God-flavored cocktail. It also had a different relationship to liberty.

Consider the different fates of Methodism in England and America. British Methodists faced a choice between religious purity and social respectability. Many of them chose to embrace the establishment even at the cost of losing their earlier fire. American Methodists faced no such choice. They could embrace their faith and social acceptance at the same time, saving them from the agonies of their British counterparts and cementing their support for the American experiment. Indeed, by the time Tocqueville visited the country in the 1830s there was a consensus that religion helped sustain the new republican order: "I do not know if all Americans have faith in their religion—for who can read to the bottom of hearts?—but I am sure that they believe it necessary to the maintenance of republican institutions. This opinion does not belong only to one class of citizens or to one party, but to the entire nation; one finds it in all ranks."

The identification of religious fervor with America was certainly not a smooth process. Witness the two great schisms of nineteenth century

America—the Civil War and the growing squabbles between Catholics and Protestants. These disputes simultaneously tore religious America apart and showed how different America had become.

The Civil War split religious America asunder: with slavery being denounced from some pulpits and defended in others, denominations that had done so much to bring the country together split between North and South even before a shot was fired.[60] Once the conflict began, two of the most religious armies in the world rode into battle to slaughter each other, each believing God was on their side. Evangelicals showered the soldiers with Bibles. Soldiers sang hymns and attended revivals. The South even invoked "the favor and guidance of Almighty God" in its Constitution. All this religious fervor contributed to the war's bloodiness—and, for the South, made the experience of defeat all the more dreadful.

The battle between Protestants and Catholics never reached the same bloody intensity as North against South, but it was a bitter war nonetheless. Protestant mobs rioted against Catholics and even burned churches to the ground. James Blaine, the Republican presidential candidate in 1884, denounced the Democrats as the party of "rum, Romanism and rebellion." But beneath these tensions, something rather intriguing was going on: Catholicism was becoming a very American faith.

Catholicism was arguably the most striking Evangelical success story of the second half of the nineteenth century. In much of Europe, Catholicism was the definitive state religion, relying on tradition and habit rather than on personal conversion. But in America the Catholic Church had to fight for every soul. A church that was in the habit of thinking of itself as an establishment rapidly became yet another religious entrepreneur. And a religion that, in Europe, emphasized tradition began to emphasize individual conversion and personal relations with God.

The American Catholic Church focused on two things—turning nominal Catholic immigrants into the real thing and then deepening their attachment to the church by building a parallel welfare state. Parish priests met new immigrants at the dock, welcoming them with open arms, and followed them westward.[61] (Even today Catholics make up 60 percent of churchgoers in San Francisco but only a quarter of the population.[62]) They abandoned Europe's formal sermons in favor of soul-stirring performances. They produced their own version of revivalist preachers, such as the Jesuit Francis Weninger, who traveled more than two hundred thousand miles across the country preaching to more than eight hundred Catholic parish missions.

The Catholic Church provided immigrants with a private welfare state offering a mind-boggling range of services: in one working-class parish in Chicago in the 1890s the church sponsored twenty-five societies that dealt with everything from charity to baseball.[63] But its greatest glory was its education system. The parish grammar schools equipped young Catholics to compete with the best that Protestant America had to offer (and absorbed a huge amount of the church's wealth and energy). The church also provided immigrants with a decompression chamber, allowing them to adapt to the rigors of the new country while helping them to preserve their ethnic identities. Immigrants couldn't think of their native food or language without also thinking of their local Catholic church. Being Catholic was not just a matter of *attending* church. It was a matter of *belonging* to a church.

A CONVENIENT CREED

Americans of all persuasions, Catholics as well as Protestants, commingled the Puritan sense of being God's chosen people with a quasireligious sense of their national identity. America was the first modern country to shift public veneration of the government from veneration of particular kings or princes to veneration of the nation and its principles. And in doing so it endowed the nation-state with a quasi-religious identity.

The United States developed a set of rituals and symbols that bore a striking resemblance to Christianity. The flag was a sacred object with elaborate rules about how it could be handled. The Founding Fathers played the role of patron saints. Americans made pilgrimages to national monuments, they celebrated the Republic with national holidays and they were taught that they were a chosen people—with a God-given duty to export the creed.

This much more aggressive version of American nationalism had in fact been building for a long time. Even bookish old Jonathan Edwards believed that God worked His will through favored nations and empires. In 1783 Ezra Stiles, the president of Yale College, celebrated independence by assuring his congregation that "God has still greater blessings in store for this vine which his own right hand hath planted." In his inaugural address as president in 1797, John Adams thanked an "overruling Providence which had so signally protected this country from the first." A generation later, his son, John Quincy Adams, the sixth president, remarked that "the Declaration of Independence was a leading event in the progress of the gospel dispensation."[64] Throughout the nineteenth century clergymen argued that "the cause of America" had become "the cause of Christ."

This Christian nationalism had huge consequences. From fairly early on, Americans justified expansion in religious terms. At first, America's religious leaders focused on the "errand" at home. Missionaries traveled to the "dark corners of the land" to try to convert the Indians and bring frontiersmen back to God. In 1798, the Congregationalists created the Missionary Society of Connecticut to take the Gospel to the "heathen lands" of Vermont and Ohio. The Congregationalists were soon outperformed by more muscular denominations, particularly Methodists and Baptists. Missionaries moved westward with the American population, first to the great Midwest and then to the West Coast. The land rushes and gold rushes were also soul rushes. In Cotton Mather's phrase, the aim was to turn American geography into "Christianography."[65]

The vision of "Manifest Destiny," which so perfectly summed up the mood of a nation that was expanding over a vast continent and pushing aside Native Americans and Mexicans as it did so, was a more grandiose version of the Puritan vision of America as a latter-day Zion. The man who coined the phrase, John O'Sullivan, the editor of the *Democratic Review*, captured the mood of exuberant expansionism:

> The far-reaching, the boundless future will be an era of American greatness. In its magnificent domain of space and time, the nation of many nations is destined to manifest to mankind the excellence of divine principles; to establish on earth the noblest temple ever dedicated to the

worship of the Most High—the Sacred and the True. Its floor shall be a hemisphere—its roof the firmament of the star-studded heavens, and its congregations a Union of many Republics, comprising hundreds of happy millions.[66]

This desire to improve the world soon pushed beyond the North American continent. Walter McDougall argues that religion inspired America's first attempt to "improve" a foreign society. In 1819, when the American Board of Commissioners for Foreign Missions decided to evangelize the Sandwich Islands (now Hawaii), it told its young missionaries to rebuild the feudal realm from the ground up. They were to "aim at nothing short of covering those islands with fruitful fields and pleasant dwellings, and schools and churches; of raising up the whole people to an elevated state of Christian civilization . . . to make them acquainted with letters; to give them the Bible with the skill to read it; to turn them from their barbarous courses and habits; to introduce . . . among them, the arts and institutions and usages of civilization and society."[67]

The links between evangelism, missionary work, diplomacy and imperialism became stronger as the century wore on. Missionaries helped to shape America's relations with other powers, great and small. Some of America's earliest treaties with China, Japan, Siam and the Ottoman Empire were designed to give missionaries the right to operate without persecution.[68] America was willing to use its military might to support its missionary sons. In 1844, for example, the USS *Independence* rescued endangered missionaries in Lebanon. By the end of the nineteenth century, the Manifest Destiny had become a pretty broad one. American Christians felt they were better missionaries than other nations: as Josiah Strong, one of the founders of the Social Gospel movement, argued in 1891, they had all the right qualities for evangelizing the world—"money-making power," a "genius for colonizing" and "persistent energy."[69] They also firmly placed their country at the center of the world—like the Israel of old. "Wherever on pagan shores the voice of the American missionary and teacher is heard," John Barrows, the leader of the World's Parliament of Religions, argued in 1898, "there is fulfilled the manifest destiny of the Christian Republic."[70]

It was a short step from this to celebrating what the Reverend Alexander Blackburn called "the imperialism of righteousness."[71] In 1898 President William McKinley formally annexed Hawaii and fought the Spanish-American War, which brought in Guam, Cuba and the Philippines. He said that America had a religious duty to bring God to the (Catholic) Filipinos. "There was nothing left for us to do but to take them all, and to educate the Filipinos, and uplift and civilize and Christianize them, and by God's grace do the very best we could by them, as our fellowmen for whom Christ also died."[72] American religiosity was too vigorous a force to be kept within the borders of even such a gigantic country.

MOODY BUT MAGNIFICENT

The forces that kept religion vital in nineteenth century America can all be seen at work in the career of a man who died in its last year. Dwight Moody built one of the great religious-cum-business empires of the Gilded Age. He started life as a successful shoe salesman in Chicago before turning to God full-time in 1860. He spent years working in Chicago slums. He preached to vast crowds about the "three Rs"—Ruin by sin, Redemption by Christ and Regeneration by the Holy Spirit—while his partner, Ira Sankey, set ancient hymns to hummable tunes.

Moody never lost his sense of what America was about. "As he stood on the platform," the Reverend Lyman Abbott remarked, "he looked like a businessman: he dressed like a businessman; he took the meeting in hand as a businessman would."[73] He applied the most meticulous business methods to his revival campaigns, preparing the ground for each city visit with an advance staff of a dozen and titillating the audience with carefully targeted advertising. Every moment of his audience's time was scripted— with ushers holding wands to show them to their places and huge choirs entertaining them between his sermons. He turned to business leaders for financial support—he needed huge tabernacles to be erected wherever he spoke, for example, because churches were too small to house his gigantic crowds. He eventually built a Bible-study empire, including Bible-centered schools and the Moody Bible Institute, which was a combination of a publishing-cum-broadcasting center and a training school for evangelists. And Moody did not stop at America's borders: he inspired the creation of the Student Volunteer Movement, which brought hundreds and then thousands of students into the missionary movement under the watchword "the Evangelization of the World in this generation." By the time Moody died it was estimated that he had spoken to a hundred million people. Moody represented something new. For all the myths about the country's religious origins America had clearly become a very different country, in matters of faith, by the late nineteenth century. For the most part people like Moody did not exist elsewhere. Nowhere else was religion so bound up with emotion, competition and big business. Europeans no doubt continue to view Moody as an example of American exceptionalism. But for the rest of the world he was a harbinger of the future.

CHAPTER THREE

THE AMERICAN WAY II:

SURVIVING THE ACIDS OF

MODERNITY (1880–2000)

❧

ROBERT INGERSOLL was the Christopher Hitchens of the Gilded Age—a voluble atheist who crisscrossed the country railing against Christianity. In 1880 he proudly announced that "the churches are dying out all over the land." To which Charles McCabe, the head of the Methodist Church Extension Society, immediately replied by telegram, "All hail the power of Jesus' name—we are building more than one Methodist Church for every day of the year, and propose to make it two a day."[1]

McCabe was right about the numbers. Churches were making converts to the "power of Jesus' name" at an astonishing pace. But Ingersoll also had a point. Even if America's religious free market ensured that it was never as deeply affected by secularization as Europe, it was affected nevertheless. What the great American journalist Walter Lippmann called the "acids of modernity" did their corrosive work in the United States just as they did in Europe. In the twentieth century American religion underwent three setbacks that reduced its ability to resist.

The first setback saw American Protestantism split between liberals (who wanted to compromise with secularism) and fundamentalists (who wanted to resist it). The hegemonic Protestant culture that had done so much to define America was forever split asunder. The second defeat saw

Protestantism—particularly fundamentalism—humiliated in its battles with two great demons, drink and Darwin. The hard-core Protestants were marginalized as well as divided from their more liberal colleagues. The third defeat was rather more complicated. After the Second World War, the political establishment embraced "the Judeo-Christian tradition" as a symbol of Americanism. But in the process it threatened to reduce religion to a mere civic bauble—a symbol of respectability that had little power to shake up people's lives or roil the public realm. That never happened: American religion returned in the final years of the twentieth century, as "hot" and as disruptive as it ever had been.

The Power of Jesus' Name

James Bryce, one of the intellectual giants of the British Liberal Party, remarked, upon visiting America in the 1880s, that clergymen were America's "first citizens," who exerted "an influence more powerful than that of any layman." These "first citizens" not only presided over a remarkable exercise in church building, they also presided over a moral reformation. One historian has calculated that 85 percent of social reformers of the era had some connection with Evangelical Protestantism.[2] Teddy Roosevelt's Bull Moose Party sang "Onward Christian Soldiers" at its great 1912 convention.[3]

The reason why America's Christian soldiers, old and new, kept marching on regardless of the prophets of secularization was one we are already familiar with—they embraced the free market with such enthusiasm. Nineteenth century America remained a petri dish of new religious movements, such as Phoebe Palmer's "holiness" movement (which taught that every believer should experience a "second blessing" leading to a holy life) and Mary Baker Eddy's Christian Science (which melded science, Christianity and health faddism). Millenarians wandered the country preaching that the Second Coming was at hand.

America also remained a breeding ground for charismatic preachers. In 1900 there were 650 full-time evangelists wandering the country and 2,200 part-timers.[4] For instance, Billy Sunday, a former baseball star, railed against humanism and alcoholism, and sang the praises of virility and muscles. "Lord save us," he implored, "from off-handed, flabby-cheeked, brittle-boned, weak-kneed, thin-skinned, pliable, plastic, spineless, effeminate, sissified, three-carat Christianity."[5] Sunday preached to more than a hundred million people, visited the White House as an honored guest and, in 1918, tied with Andrew Carnegie in a newspaper poll to find the greatest American.[6]

These charismatic preachers treated new technology as a God-given tool rather than a challenge. Preachers used new railway networks to reach the far-flung corners of the land. They even created special "chapel cars" or "cathedral cars," with names like *Glad Tidings* and elaborate interiors that included a pulpit, an altar, an organ and, on occasion, stained-glass windows. In 1922 a Chicago pastor, Paul Rader, created a radio station called WJBT—Where Jesus Blesses Thousands. R. R. Brown sent listeners certificates of membership of his "radio church" in return for donations.[7] Father Charles Coughlin, a voluble Detroit priest, who at different times supported FDR, Huey Long and Mussolini, was so popular that, according to legend, his broadcasts blared out of so many windows in ethnic neighborhoods that you could walk a dozen blocks in a big city without missing a word.

There is no better example of the creativity of American religion than Pentecostalism. In 1906 an itinerant black preacher arrived in Los Angeles and began to preach wherever he could. William Seymour had no formal theological training. He was also a forbidding-looking chap—"dishevelled in appearance," blind in one eye and scarred by smallpox. One woman who heard him pray wrote, "I felt that serpents and other slimy creatures were creeping around me. After he had left the room, a number of the students said they felt he was devil possessed. . . . In my evangelistic and missionary tours I had met all kinds of religious fakirs and tramps, but I felt he excelled them all."[8]

Yet this strange man, this untutored son of freed slaves, was also on fire with a vision—that Jesus was about to return and that God would send a new Pentecost if only people would pray hard enough. On April 9, 1906, he watched as one of his followers was overcome with the Holy Spirit and started speaking in tongues. Within days he founded a makeshift church in a run-down part of town—the Apostolic Faith Mission in Azusa Street—and soon thousands joined him. Most of his flock were poor and disappointed—domestic workers, itinerant laborers, janitors and no-hopers. "God sent this latter rain to gather up all the poor and outcast, and make us love everybody," D. W. Myland, one of Pentecostalism's earliest chroniclers, wrote in 1910. "He poured it out upon the little sons and daughters, and servants and handmaidens. . . . God is taking the despised things, the base things, and being glorified in them."[9]

Los Angeles was becoming the embodiment of the American dream of progress and prosperity. The city was the most modern bit of the most modern nation on earth—conjured up out of an inhospitable terrain by optimism and technology. But LA also had its dark side. The city was divided between a white overclass and the racial minorities who existed to serve them. It was also full of losers—people who failed to find their dreams, or people who were condemned to a life of thankless toil so that the golden people could frolic in the sun.

Many of these losers were spiritually hungry refugees from the South and the Midwest. They quickly filled the church and responded to Seymour's sermons. People spoke in tongues, floated six feet in the air, or so we are told, burst into tears, fell to the floor in trances, "slain by the Lord." The faithful prayed every day for three years, sometimes all night too, and dispatched hundreds of missionaries abroad. They began to refer to Los Angeles as the New Jerusalem.

This new religious movement derived its name from the biblical feast of the Pentecost, which takes place on the fiftieth day after Easter. According to scripture, a mighty wind blew through the house in Jerusalem where the Twelve Apostles were gathered and the Holy Spirit, taking the form of tongues "as of fire," baptized them with the supernatural ability to spread the Gospel to men "from every nation under heaven." The curse of Babel was lifted; people from different countries could understand each other; and three thousand souls were saved that very day by the Apostles' newfound eloquence. Doubters heard only gibberish and mocked that "these men are full of new wine."

Pentecostals are like Evangelicals in their emphasis on being born again and on spreading the Word. But they differ from Evangelicals, as well as other Christians, in their emphasis on the Holy Spirit. They not only believe that the Last Days are coming, but that the Spirit can enter ordinary mortals and give them extraordinary powers.

Respectable America had no time for the Azusa Street revival. The *Los Angeles Times* complained about a "weird Babel of tongues," a "new sect of fanatics" and "devotees of a weird doctrine" who "work themselves up into a state of mad excitement."[10] Respectable people were outraged that Seymour encouraged interracial worship, particularly given that the worship involved hugging and ululating. This was, after all, Jim Crow's America. They were also offended that the dregs of society had the audacity to claim that they had found a door to the New Jerusalem. Mainline churches were predictably hostile, but even fundamentalists condemned Seymour for focusing on the Spirit rather than the Letter. "The last vomit of Satan," was one preacher's verdict on the movement.[11]

But the revival continued to gather strength, throwing up charismatic preachers, establishing churches and sparking off fiery religious revivals. The year after Seymour's death in 1922, Los Angeles was the scene of yet another great Pentecostal crusade—this time led by a woman rather than a black man, and this time marketed with all the glitz of a Hollywood spectacle.

Like Seymour, Aimee Semple McPherson had no formal religious training. She grew up in a Methodist home, where she preached to her dolls, but seems to have lost her faith as a teenager.[12] Marriage to Robert Semple, a young Pentecostal, changed that: they set out to take God's word to the heathens of Europe and Asia, but Robert Semple died in Hong Kong in 1910, leaving her with a young daughter. Back in America, another marriage and another child resulted in postnatal depression. By all accounts extremely ill, she heard God's call and started driving around in her "mission car" from one revival meeting to another, children in tow, Aimee writing sermons in the backseat: she was an immediate hit. In 1923, two years after her second husband filed for divorce citing "abandonment," she established her own megachurch, the Angelus Temple in Los Angeles, and her own denomination, the International Church of the Foursquare Gospel.

The temple was one of the religious wonders of the era: a $1 million mammoth that could seat five thousand worshippers. On either side of the church sat two massive radio antennae—like huge electronic bookends—powerful enough to broadcast Aimee's words around the world. The nerve center of the complex was a prayer tower where volunteers equipped with telephones prayed in two-hour shifts. The church was topped off with a huge rotating cross that could be seen from fifty miles away.

Aimee was a master self-publicist. She flew around the Los Angeles Basin dropping prayer leaflets on the masses below. She ordered members of her orchestra to wander the streets playing hymns. (One player was the young Anthony Quinn.[13]) Charlie Chaplin was an admirer. Her sermons were everything that you could hope for from the Golden Age of Hollywood. Angels and devils did battle. Trumpeters played "Stars and Stripes Forever." The orchestra and choir worked the crowd into a frenzy while ushers passed around the collection plate. Then a staircase appeared from nowhere and Aimee, bathed in spotlights and cradling a bouquet of roses, descended as if from on high. Aimee held services seven days a week—three times on Sunday—but still people had to be turned away.

Perhaps setting a fashion for subsequent Pentecostal televangelists, Aimee's career was hardly free of controversy. There was a scandal when she disappeared in 1926. Many of her followers feared her dead, but she appeared out of the desert in Mexico with an elaborate story about how she had been abducted. The fact that a man who could have been her lover had vanished at the same time (and, some claimed, been seen with her) gave the press a field day; and she was charged with obstruction of justice. The charges were dropped—perhaps fairly—on grounds of lack of evidence.[14] Her publicity did not altogether improve when she moved to a huge garish mansion, an hour's drive from the city.[15] Yet she was soon back on the road again and married again (it didn't last), her mission reenforced by the Depression. She eventually died in 1944. The Foursquare Gospel church, which was then run by her son, Rolf, for four decades, still boasts a couple of million members, the vast majority outside the United States.

THE ACIDS OF MODERNITY

Yet for all the raw vitality of religious America, there was no escaping the acids of modernity. Indeed, they had been quietly seeping into American intellectual life throughout much of the late nineteenth century—especially in the universities.

The rise of America's colleges to global prominence coincided with the secularization of the campuses. In colonial America there had been an explicit link between intellect and religion. The Puritan oligarchy was one of the most highly educated in history. Most of the founding divines had been educated at Oxbridge—thirty-two at Oxford, a hundred at Cambridge. New England pastors were expected to know Hebrew and Greek as well as Latin. Many published learned works: Cotton Mather, for example, churned out an astonishing 458 books and pamphlets. One of the first things the Puritans did was to establish Harvard University. America's great seats of learning were originally factories for clergymen, very much like their English models. The universities taught Protestant theology and Christian ethics, required students to attend chapel, and had clergymen as presidents (in 1839, 51 out of 54 were men of the cloth). The book most highly regarded by the majority of American academics was the Bible.

All this changed in the second half of the nineteenth century. Academic reformers such as Harvard's Charles Eliot put forward a radically new model of university life. They not only argued that the purpose of universities was to advance knowledge and understanding rather than to inculcate eternal verities, they argued that the best way to do this was through a market in ideas—with scholars competing to advance knowledge and students picking and choosing from the resulting theories. If religion could flourish in this market of ideas, then bully for religion; but it was to be given no special privileges or protections. Cornell University, which was founded in 1865 as a seminary for technicians, avoided religious connections of any kind. Johns Hopkins University was founded in 1876 as a new sort of creature, a secular research institution. The university invited T. H. Huxley to give a speech during its opening ceremony and eschewed prayers completely. Ten years later, Harvard dropped compulsory chapel.

Thereafter, the priests were driven from the temples. Clergymen were replaced on governing boards by businessmen and bankers. The colleges increasingly measured themselves against purely academic standards. Few professors—particularly in the elite schools—would describe the Bible as the book that they most admired. Some members of the new academic elite were self-conscious enemies of religion. Andrew Dickson White, the first president of Cornell University, published a two-volume *History of the Warfare of Science with Theology in Christendom* (1896). The message was simple and extremely "European": science was on the side of progress and enlightenment, religion on the side of reaction and superstition, and one was bound to win.

The revolution in the universities both reflected and reinforced a wider revolution among America's intelligentsia. William Graham Sumner, a prominent Yale professor who had been trained for the ministry but later discovered that his real vocation was for social science, once remarked that he had put his religious beliefs in a drawer one day, and twenty years later he opened the drawer only to find that his beliefs had gone. A striking number of American intellectuals did something similar, sometimes finding their beliefs gone, sometimes finding them mouldering away under the influence of powerful intellectual tides.

One of the most powerful tides was social Darwinism. Sumner merrily applied the doctrine of the survival of the fittest to human society, dismissing Christianity as sentimental tripe and consigning great political principles to the realm of illusion. Man had "no more right to life than a rattlesnake," he proclaimed, "no more right to liberty than any wild beast." Sumner felt that man's "right to the pursuit of happiness, [was] nothing but license to maintain the struggle for existence." Sumner had legions of followers: so many that social Darwinism became a sort of unofficial creed of the intelligentsia and eugenics the de facto policy of a startling number of states.

Many intellectuals who balked at the harshness of social Darwinism accepted the Enlightenment idea that history was a battle between scientific light and superstitious darkness. John Dewey argued that education should replace religion as the foundation of moral life, and that schools should replace churches as agents of socialization. A few even queried America's conception of itself as a God-blessed nation. In 1913 the leader of the "progressive" school of historiography, Charles Beard, published a Marxist history of America's founding document, *An Economic Interpretation of the Constitution of the United States,* which argued that, far from being a semi-sacred embodiment of natural law, the American Constitution was an expression of economic interests. Oliver Wendell Holmes, a Supreme Court judge who had fought in the Civil War, took a similar approach to justice: for him the law was simply the product of social forces—an evolving social experiment that was created by the play of power and self-interest. Thus were the Founders' lofty certainties about "natural law" dissolved in the acids of social Darwinism and economic reductionism.

At the same time, some of the country's finest literary figures treated religion as an object of fun. In *The Gilded Age* (1873) Mark Twain and Charles Dudley Warner lampooned Senator Dilworthy, a Republican who was rancid with corruption but who nevertheless spent his election campaigns addressing Sunday schools and missionary societies. In 1906, the same year that Seymour started preaching in Los Angeles, Ambrose Bierce, one of America's finest satirists, published a wonderful guide to bullshit, *The Cynic's Word Book,* or, as it was later rechristened, *The Devil's Dictionary.* To pray, he said, is "to ask that the laws of the universe be annulled on behalf of a single petitioner confessedly unworthy." A Christian is "one who follows the teachings of Christ so long as they are not inconsistent with a life of sin." Religion is "a daughter of Hope and Fear, explaining to Ignorance the nature of the Unknowable." For Bierce, as for so many sophisticates of his generation, Christianity was an antiquated superstition. Sinclair Lewis cast *Elmer Gantry* (1927) as a self-rightous hypocrite. H. L. Mencken (to whom *Gantry* was dedicated) treated Evangelicals as hypocrites and nincompoops, even suggesting, to the delight of many of his readers, that American cities should build giant stadiums in which clergymen could be turned loose on each other while the public watched.

DIVIDED WE FALL

These advances by Ingersoll's forces of secularism coincided with a succession of setbacks for McCabe's army of Jesus. The first setback was a sharp division within American Protestantism. America started this period as an overwhelmingly Protestant nation—ruled by a self-confident WASP upper class and defined by a Protestant ethic of hard work and social respectability. "Surely, to be a Christian and an Anglo-Saxon and an American in this generation," the Reverend Josiah Strong wrote in 1893, "is to stand on the mountaintop of privilege."[16]

But this mountaintop was split asunder by a bitter struggle between traditionalists and reformers, which, in the 1920s, led to open competition for control of the Protestant denominations. The subject of the struggle was nothing less than modernity: How should Protestantism adjust itself to the rise of science? Should it revise faith in the light of reason or should it cling to the fundamentals? And should it use the expanding state to create a better society—or resist state intervention in the name of traditional charity?

Most mainline Protestants took a "progressive" stance. Forget about the earth being created in six days: this was just a poetic way of saying a jolly long time. Many of them also embraced a more activist state. Mainline Protestants were heavily influenced by the Social Gospel movement, which began in the 1880s and directed Christians to do as much as they could to help the poor. They read books such as Archibald McCowan's *Christ the Socialist* (1894), in which Jesus stood upon the steps of New York City Hall and denounced corporations as Pharisees, or *In His Steps* (1896) in which Charles Sheldon asked what life might be like in small-town America if people consistently asked themselves, "What would Jesus do?" They pored over the writings of Walter Rauschenbusch, who ran a church on the edge of New York's Hell's Kitchen and preached that Christians should do everything in their power to overcome the "social crisis." They flicked through *If Christ Came to Chicago* (1894) and shuddered at the stories of unChristlike neglect of poverty. They might even have listened sympathetically to Eugene Debs, the head of the American Socialist Party and railway union boss, who constantly invoked the name of "the supreme leader," Jesus Christ. But their real political home was in the progressive movement. The social gospellers were the progressive movement at prayer.

Most Evangelicals took a much more traditionalist position. They fought to preserve the "fundamentals" of Biblical Christianity. (The term "fundamentalist" came from a series of pamphlets in which Evangelical scholars, led by A. C. Dixon, argued against the modernist attempt to dilute the Bible.) They also accused the social gospellers of being unable to tell the difference between the Bible and what Billy Sunday called "godless social-service nonsense."[17] Traditionalists believed in personal responsibility rather than government welfare.

The modernists had the weight of respectable opinion on their side. But the traditionalists tapped into two rich wells. One was the growth of "hot" religions like Pentecostalism that emphasized the role of the supernatural in everyday life. People who were in the grip of these ideas regarded modern scientific thinking not so much as wrong but as irrelevant: they saw God intervening in the world on a daily basis to heal the sick and perform miracles; they also saw history hurtling toward the "Rapture," a series of dramatic events that included the transport of the faithful to heaven, seven years of wars on earth, the conversion of the Jews to Christianity and Jesus' victory over the Antichrist in the Battle of Armageddon. The other was southern culture. The South determined to rise again from the humiliation of the Civil War—and the southern religious denominations were crucial parts of southern cultural identity. The fight against "modernism" was bound up with the fight to preserve southern Christian civilization, with its belief in biblical literacy and its enthusiasm for revivals, against northern hegemony.

The traditionalists were also highly innovative in their own idiosyncratic way. They developed the notion of the "inerrancy" of the Bible as a counterblast to the modernists' insistence on the importance of context. (The notion of papal infallibility dates from the same era.) They also developed an elaborate theory of premillennial dispensationalism. This divided history into seven eras ("dispensations") and argued that a careful reading of the Bible revealed that man was living at the end of the sixth dispensation. At any moment Jesus would return to inaugurate the Rapture. Cyrus Scofield's 1909 edition of the Bible for Oxford University Press, which viewed the document entirely through a dispensationalist framework, was a fixture in every fundamentalist household.

So the traditionalists were strong. But they overreached in two dramatic ways.

A DRINKING PROBLEM

For a while Carrie Nation was one of the most famous women in America. She was an imposing figure (almost six feet tall and 180 pounds) as well as an angry one (her husband drank himself to death) and she regarded herself as "a bulldog running along at the feet of Jesus, barking at what He doesn't like." She wielded her Bible and her ax with equal enthusiasm as she burst into saloons to "preach, pray and smash." In the first decade of the twentieth century she was arrested some 30 times—but she wouldn't let things like the law get in the way of her campaign to produce a "liquor-free, tobacco-empty, sex-abstaining and decadence-rejecting America."[18]

The Prohibition movement was the last great hurrah of the United Evangelical Front. The movement drew progressives and traditionalists, and indeed northerners and southerners, into a great dry coalition. Protestant America saw all sorts of evils lurking in the bottom of a glass—not just drunkenness and loss of self-control, terrible though they were, not just loose women and debauchery, but also the new America that they feared, an America of polyglot immigrants and unassimilated Catholic crowds. "This battle is not a rose-water conflict," roared the *Anti-Saloon League Yearbook,* "it is war—continued, relentless war."[19]

The drys won the early battles, introducing some form of Prohibition in twenty-six states in 1906–17 and then getting the Eighteenth Amendment ratified in 1919. But they ended up losing the war, much as their latter-day descendants are losing the war against drugs. Speakeasies sprang up everywhere, from inner cities to politicians' mansions. Gangsters and Kennedys made fortunes out of illicit drink. The police were forced to waste their time trying to prosecute people for doing what people had done throughout history. Congress eventually repealed Prohibition in 1933—and Protestant America suffered a long-standing rebuff to its reputation for sense and moderation.

The second exercise in overreach was equally disastrous. The fundamentalists had long railed against Darwinism, for undermining the dignity of man, for robbing the universe of its purpose and design, for contradicting the Good Book, and for acting as a Trojan horse for godless socialism. They would rather trust the rock of ages than the age of rocks, they argued. Their railing became ever more strident as the Darwinists became more and more self-confident and, indeed, more and more arrogant, producing the pseudoscience of eugenics and the pseudotheory of social Darwinism.

The Evangelicals constructed a battering ram of organizations to advance their cause, such as the Research Science Bureau (1920), the Anti-Evolution League of America (1924) and the Defenders of the Christian Faith (1925). They also turned to the law, with a clutch of heartland states passing laws banning the teaching of evolution. Progressive forces, led by the newly formed American Civil Liberties Union, massed to challenge the most extreme of these laws, Tennessee's Butler Act. The pretext was provided by a young schoolteacher, John Scopes, who deliberately incriminated himself by teaching evolution in the small town of Dayton.

The result was the Scopes "Monkey" trial, a Jazz Age version of the O. J. Simpson trial.[20] The Evangelicals enlisted William Jennings Bryan, a former presidential candidate and cabinet member who was affectionately known as "the great commoner," to make their case. The defense enlisted a polished trial lawyer, Clarence Darrow. The *Baltimore Sun* sent five journalists, headed by the greatest newspaperman of the era, H. L. Mencken. The judge allowed radio lines to be brought into the courtroom, bent over backward to accommodate photographers and, when the court got too crowded, moved the events outside. A bizarre crowd of preachers and peddlers, local worthies and wild-eyed misfits marched up and down in the street outside, adding to the carnival atmosphere.

The result was a public relations disaster for Evangelical America. The Evangelicals scored a legal victory: the judge decreed that the Tennessee legislature had the right to decide what was taught in its schools, and anti-evolutionary ordinances stood across the country until the 1960s. But the victory was Pyrrhic. The fundamentalists were branded as numbskulls and know-nothings. People across the country chuckled at Mencken's descriptions of "the boobs" of Tennessee. They chuckle still. The "monkey trial" became a global example of backwardness and bigotry. *Inherit the Wind,* a

1950s play that lambastes Evangelicalism and McCarthyism in one fell swoop (and was made into a film in 1960), has been rerun ever since.

The Evangelicals responded to their humiliation by withdrawing into a private cave of their own making. Until Scopes, they had harbored dreams of conquering the wider culture. Now they detached themselves from public affairs, retreated into their own subculture and laboriously created a network of inward-looking Evangelical institutions—Christian schools and Bible institutes, Evangelical colleges, Evangelical support groups. The great imperative was self-preservation rather than cultural conquest.

Garry Wills has also identified a more subtle consequence of the Scopes overreach: the marginalization of progressive Evangelicalism. In the long term the biggest losers from the public relations catastrophe were not conservative Evangelicals, who were to reemerge after the war even stronger after their period of self-imposed isolation, but liberal Evangelicals. It is easy to forget that William Jennings Bryan was a liberal, not a conservative: a two-time Democratic presidential candidate who stood for the little guy—particularly western farmers—against the money power of the East Coast. The Scopes trial drove a wedge into progressive Evangelicalism. It created identification in the public mind between liberalism and secularism, and it drove Bible-believing Christians into the arms of people who were both culturally and economically conservative.

The Age of Equipoise

The next threat to American religion, which did not gather till the 1940s, was far subtler: a threat born of success rather than failure. This was that religion would degenerate into mere observance—its power diluted, reduced to a bland celebration of "Americanness."

The Second World War hugely reinforced American religiosity. One of the most widely quoted remarks of the era was, "There are no atheists in foxholes." And one of the most widely repeated stories was the story of how the Reverend Howell Maurice Forgy, a naval captain, told his tired troops, during Pearl Harbor, to "Praise the Lord and pass the ammunition," an exhortation that was later expanded and set to music.[21] God and Jesus were rooting for the good guys against the axis of evil.

The government did not have any ACLU-style worries about turning religion into a morale booster. Thousands of army chaplains distributed prayer books and Bibles. The U.S. Printing Office worked around the clock to produce religious publications. The government distributed small statues of Jesus and Mary. Crosses, crucifixes and Stars of David were standard army issue to anyone who wanted them. Six hundred interfaith chapels were built at military posts.

The religious revival continued after the war. Postwar polls revealed that Americans were significantly more religious than people in other industrial countries—nineteen out of twenty Americans believed in God, nine out of ten prayed, six out of seven regarded the Bible as the Word of God, and three out of four believed in life after death.[22] Church membership rose from 49 percent of the population in 1940 to 55 percent in 1950 to 69 percent in 1959.[23] Church construction became the fourth-largest building activity in the private sector. Religion saturated the popular culture. Books such as Fulton Oursler's *The Greatest Story Ever Told* and Norman Vincent Peale's *A Guide to Confident Living* reached the best-seller lists. Popular music hits included "I Believe," "It's No Secret What God Can Do" and "The Man Upstairs."[24] Hollywood celebrities dropped the Lord's name into their conversation, with the bodacious Jane Russell calling God a "livin' doll."[25]

At the same time, religion regained some of the intellectual prestige that it had lost in the Jazz Age. Religious books such as Thomas Merton's *Seven Storey Mountain* sold remarkably well. Sophisticates turned to Søren Kierkegaard, Paul Tillich, Reinhold Niebuhr and Simone Weil.[26] "There is evidence," Niebuhr mused, "that in the world of culture, there is at least receptivity toward the message of the historic faiths which is in marked contrast to the indifference or hostility of past decades."[27] Departments of religious study even began to spring up in academia. Will Herberg noted in 1955 that the old-time "village atheist" was a thing of the past, a folk curiosity like the town crier."[28] Most Americans simply could not understand what it meant to be "against religion."[29] "The *avant-garde* is becoming old-fashioned," quipped Herberg; "religion is now the latest thing."

Politicians reinforced the link between religion and patriotism. In the Cold War religion was "the shield of the nation," America's "secret weapon," a force "more powerful than the H-bomb."[30] And Soviet communism was, of course, "a great sinister anti-Christian movement masterminded by Satan." George Docherty, a pastor who was popular in Congress, preached that "an atheist American is a contradiction in terms."[31] Dwight Eisenhower turned himself into a spiritual as well as a political leader, declaring himself "the most intensely religious man I know." He publicly embraced religion before his inauguration, also making up for his parents' oversight by getting himself baptized, and began his inaugural speech with a prayer. After listening to a sermon by Docherty, he worked with Congress to ensure that the words "under God" were added to the pledge of allegiance. "Recognition of the Supreme Being is the first, the most basic, expression of Americanism," he declared in a speech launching the American Legion's "Back to God" campaign in 1955. "Without God, there could be no American form of government, nor an American way of life."[32] The Supreme Court lent its weight to the general fervor: in one case about religious instruction William Douglas, writing on behalf of the majority, argued that "we are a religious people whose institutions presuppose a Supreme Being."[33]

This period also saw a remarkable step forward in religious toleration. The flames of anti-Catholicism still burned in the immediate aftermath of the war. Paul Blanshard's polemic *American Freedom and Catholic Power* (1949), which argued that "neither Rome nor Moscow knows what tolerance means," remained on the best-seller list for six months; in 1951 Harry Truman was forced to abandon his attempt to appoint an ambassador to the Vatican. But the Pope seemed an ever less convincing target. After all, Catholics had proved their patriotism in the Second World War, and proved it again in the Cold War, sometimes going a little over the top, as with the McCarthy crusades. (Daniel Patrick Moynihan quipped that during the Cold War Fordham men checked the anti-Communist and patriotic credentials of Harvard men.) Catholics also moved into the American mainstream. The new universities turned "shanty Irish" into "lace-curtain Irish." Meanwhile, the local Catholic church became more determinedly American, adopting American views on both the separation of church and state and religious pluralism.

The growing prominence of American Jews also encouraged tolerance. The Jewish population was growing at a healthy clip, from 50,000 in 1850 to about 5.5 million in the mid-1950s, or 3.2 percent of the population.[34] Jews were producing spectacular intellectual successes, with the arrival of distinguished refugees and the success of the children of immigrants, and the Holocaust discredited the casual anti-Semitism that had been rife in American society. The publication of Herberg's *Protestant-Catholic-Jew* in 1955 marked the culmination of a broad trend: what Richard Fox, an academic at the University of Southern California, has called "pluralizing the symbolic sacred core of America."[35] Herberg summed up his thesis in a single sentence that elided his own view of the country into the view of the majority of Americans: "America today may be conceived, as it is indeed conceived by most Americans, as one great community divided into three big sub-communities religiously defined, all equally American in their identification with the 'American Way of Life.' "[36] America was a "community of religious communities," a "triple melting pot" into which various populations were poured before emerging not as Protestants, Catholics and Jews but as Protestant Americans, Catholic Americans and Jewish Americans, which was something else entirely.

There was something a little odd about this idea of equal status: Jews were a tiny proportion of the population, compared with Catholics or Protestants. But the contrast with earlier views of America as a basically Protestant nation is clear. Catholics and Jews were now fully eligible for membership in the religious club at the heart of America's national identity. They just had to demonstrate to the satisfaction of the existing members of the club that their primary loyalties were not to Rome or to Israel but to the United States. The Judeo-Christian nation was born.

Yet the identification of religiosity and Americanism carried dangers—not least the draining of religion of any of its distinctively religious content. Eisenhower embodied the danger perfectly (if unwittingly) when he urged people to practice their faith and then added, "And I don't care what it is." It is one thing to tolerate doctrinal differences and another to be indifferent to them.

Religion was not only reduced to a symbol of patriotism, it was reduced to a vehicle of upward mobility—a cheap ticket to the American dream machine. All you needed to do was believe in yourself and success would be yours. Norman Vincent Peale, a prominent minister at the Marble Collegiate Reformed Church on New York's Fifth Avenue, preached self-help with a thin religious veneer. His *Power of Positive Thinking* (1952) was not only an instant best-seller, it was also often blind to the real meaning of religion. Self-confidence and faith can work wonders, the book argued, particularly when it comes to getting on in life; self-doubt and defeatism are the road to ruin. Religion was reduced to a mere badge of commitment to the American creed of individualism, egalitarianism and upward mobility. Martin Marty, a prominent religious historian, has described it as "faith in faith itself."[37]

America could hardly be called a secular country during this period. Religion prospered in a wide variety of forms—from suburban piety to Peale's self-help. Politicians bent the knee to the Lord. America was not Europe, but religion was nevertheless in danger of what might be termed secularization from within. It was in danger not so much of marginalization as blandification—of religion becoming so all-embracing that it was almost a synonym for "Americanism." That changed dramatically in the next few decades.

The End of Equipoise

The apogee of Eisenhower's age of equipoise came with John F. Kennedy's speech to a convention of Evangelical preachers in Houston in September 1960. Kennedy told them that his Roman Catholicism was a strictly private affair: he would not allow the pope to tell him what to do in his public life (or, indeed, in his private life, cynics added). The issue, as far as Kennedy was concerned, was not what sort of church he believed in but what sort of America he believed in—and that was one where the separation of church and state was "absolute," where there was no state funding for church schools, where there was no discrimination for or against any particular church. "I am not the Catholic candidate for president," he told the ministers, "I am the Democratic Party's candidate for president who happens to be a Catholic. I do not speak for my church on public matters and the church does not speak for me." This was the high point of bland civic religion. Americans all warmed themselves around the hearth of "faith," even as they agreed to keep their theological positions to themselves.

But the next forty years saw the emergence of a very different religion—far less tame and far less unifying. By 2000, the country was split just as dramatically over religion as it had been in 1900—but this time the split was not between different denominations (Protestants for the Republican Party and Catholics for the Democrats) but between people who were hot for religion, whether they were Protestants, Catholics and Jews, and people who were cooler, whether they were atheists, modernists or infrequent church attendees. How did this happen?

The first blow to Eisenhower's religious settlement came from the left. The two great protest movements of the 1960s—the civil rights movement and the antiwar movement—both reinserted religious passions into politics. The anti–Vietnam War movement included large numbers of prominent religious figures such as Dorothy Day and William Sloane Coffin. (Richard John Neuhaus and Michael Novak, who went on to become leading theoconservatives, also cut their teeth in the movement.) A poll in 1968 found that 85 percent of Lutheran clergy felt that the church should support antiwar protests.

If religious people contributed to the antiwar movement, they were the soul of the civil rights movement. Its leadership was almost entirely composed of clergymen, many of them with highly traditional theological views: Martin Luther King (who was not christened Martin Luther by accident) was the son, grandson and great-grandson of Baptist preachers. Many of the activists were also religious, including some white mainstream Protestants who for once allowed themselves to be swept up by religious passion. More than five thousand church people were arrested in demonstrations leading up to the passage of the Civil Rights Act in 1964. Indeed, as Brink Lindsey has pointed out, civil rights marches were "redolent of religious ritual," with their beatings and jailings, water-cannon dousings and teargasings, sanctified protesters and evil billy-club-wielding police officers.[38] "Like a holy crusade," was the verdict of John Lewis, a leader of the Student Nonviolent Coordinating Committee, on the movement.

The second blow to Eisenhower's religious settlement came from legal secularists. If the religious wars of the early twentieth century were ignited by the overreach of America's Evangelicals over alcohol and evolution, the religious wars of the second half were ignited by the overreach of those bent on driving religion to the margins of American society. The most important overreacher was the Supreme Court. The Court issued two rulings in the early 1960s (*Engel v. Vitale* in 1962 and *School District of Abington Township v. Schempp* in 1963) that banned official prayers and Bible readings from public schools on First Amendment grounds. These decisions shocked even modernists such as Niebuhr, who complained that *Engel* "practically suppresses all religion, especially in the public schools."[39] They infuriated Evangelicals who thought that prayers and scripture were the foundation stones of all real education. Billy Graham called the rulings part of a "diabolical scheme" that was "taking God and moral teaching from the schools."[40] "They say God is dead," Ronald Reagan quipped during his campaign for the governorship of California. "Well, He isn't. We just can't talk about Him in the schoolroom."[41]

The Court's decision on school prayer was made all the more unholy to religious Americans by the fact that it was soon followed by a permissive decision on pornography. The very people who had tried to ban the Lord's Prayer from schools were making it easier to get your hands on dirty books! But the thing that drove religious Americans over the edge—that transformed a collection of angry individuals into an organized army— was a 1973 decision that legalized abortion throughout the country. *Roe v. Wade* not only left social conservatives feeling disenfranchised. (Even Ruth Bader Ginsburg, no friend of the right, argued, in her nomination hearings for her position on the Supreme Court, that it would have been better, for the social health of the nation, to allow the state legislatures to decide the subject.) It left them determined to capture the Supreme Court from the legal secularists.

And it was not just the Supreme Court that was driving religious America mad. They were infuriated too by the Democrats, the new class of leftish bureaucrats and the academics. (In 1972, thirty-four of thirty-eight Harvard Law School professors voted for George McGovern, a left-wing Democrat, a proportion not entirely in line with the feelings of the wider electorate, who gave Nixon a landslide victory.[42]) Cultural luminaries not only defined "deviancy down"—in Daniel Patrick Moynihan's phrase—but also mocked *Leave It to Beaver* America. And what did they have to be so snooty about? By the end of the 1960s, the ask-not optimism of the start of the decade had curdled into doubt, pessimism and violence. The inner cities exploded in fiery rebellion. The campuses were torn apart by protests. "Five serious crimes every minute," *U.S. News & World Report* noted in a typical article on August 8, 1965. "A murder every hour . . . a rape every 23 minutes . . . a burglary every 27 seconds . . . a car stolen every minute."[43] The rate of teenage pregnancies and illegitimate births soared.

Michael Novak, a Catholic intellectual who began his political career as a left-wing activist before moving steadily rightward, tells two anecdotes that highlight the growing tension between blue-collar America and the liberal elite. The first concerns a New York judge called Bruce who was so soft on crime that he earned the sobriquet "let 'em loose Bruce." Bruce was eventually mugged himself. Festooned in bandages, he told a meeting on crime about his pain and humiliation, but insisted that he would not allow the experience to change his views. The ensuing silence was broken by a voice from the crowd: "Mug him again." Novak's other anecdote concerns the 1972 McGovern campaign, in which he worked for the Democrat's vice presidential candidate, Sargent Shriver. Novak kept hearing that Shriver was doing badly with Pennsylvania steelworkers, a bedrock constituency. But why? He discovered the answer in the party's advance person in the area—"a young woman wearing a miniskirt, high white boots and a see-though blouse with a large pro-abortion button on her collar."[44]

BORN AGAIN

This liberal overreach coincided with a resurgence of Evangelical America. The person most identified with this was Billy Graham. Graham presided over an internal revolution—encouraging conservative scholars to muster more sophisticated arguments and founding first-class publications such as *Christianity Today*. He also became the public face of Evangelical religion for millions of Americans who had never visited the Bible Belt.

There was no doubt where Graham's sympathies lay. In 1949 he stated that "communism is inspired, directed and motivated by the Devil himself. America is at the crossroads. Will we turn to the left-wingers and atheists, or will we turn to the right and embrace the cross?" But he was also elegant and stylish—a man who dressed well and charmed Middle America with his smooth cadences and southern manner. He became a close spiritual adviser to every president from Eisenhower onward. His favorite Old Testament character was Daniel, a prophet who relished politics and politicians.

In the 1950s other Evangelicals followed Graham's example. They dropped the harder edges of their faith and began to venture into "enemy territory." Bill Bright and Stacey Woods brought evangelism to America's universities with, respectively, the Campus Crusade for Christ and the InterVarsity Christian Fellowship. They created national organizations such as the International Council of Christian Churches to act as counterweights to national mainline organizations.

This resurgence was driven by success. In 1940–60 the Southern Baptist Convention doubled its membership to ten million. But as the 1960s revolution gathered pace, conservative denominations continued to grow while the mainline denominations headed downward. In 1965 the Southern Baptists and the Methodists both claimed around 11 million souls; by 1985, the Southern Baptists had jumped to 14.5 million, while the number of Methodists had shrunk to 9 million. The largest Pentecostal church, the Assemblies of God, quadrupled to 2 million in 1985. And the Pentecostals' charismatic style was being copied by both Protestants and Catholics.

The next generation of prominent Evangelicals were more divisive figures than Graham. Jerry Falwell and Pat Robertson were born on the opposite sides of the tracks. Falwell was the son of a drunk who killed his own brother in a gunfight, and his higher education was limited to a humble Bible college. Robertson was the son of a U.S. senator (for Virginia) who studied law at Yale and joined the Marines. But they both demonstrated Evangelical America's talent for institution-building.

Robertson bought a ramshackle UHF station in Norfolk, Virginia, for a few thousand dollars and turned it into the giant Christian Broadcasting Network. By 1985, CBN enjoyed an annual budget of $230 million and broadcast on two hundred TV stations. Falwell began his ministry in 1956 in an unused soda-bottling plant in Lynchburg, Virginia, with just a handful of congregants. When he died in 2007, he bequeathed to his children a sprawling religious empire—a church with twenty-five thousand members, a house for alcoholics, a summer camp for children, and Liberty University. He may have preached the good old-time religion—insisting on the literal truth of the Bible and fulminating against smoking, drinking and short dresses—but he was also an enthusiastic user of the fruits of modernity. His "Sounds of Liberty" choir featured good-looking young women with *Charlie's Angels* haircuts.

Falwell and Robertson rediscovered Aimee McPherson's media savvy. They realized that radio and television stations were megaphones for Evangelical America to reach beyond the Bible Belt into greater America. The broadcasting establishment had been in the habit of handing free airtime to the mainstream churches while leaving Evangelicals to fend for themselves in the free market. This stood them in good stead when the Federal Communications Commission decreed an end to free handouts and technological innovation created new market niches. Other televangelists included Jim Bakker (whose empire also included a Christian amusement park and a luxury hotel) and Jimmy Swaggart (who perfected the art of weeping on air). By the end of the 1970s there were thirty religious TV stations and more than a thousand religious radio stations. "We have a better product than soap or automobiles," Bakker claimed. "We have eternal life."[45]

Evangelical culture was out of its cave. "Evangelical Christianity has finally emerged from its anti-cultural ghetto into the mainstream of American life," Richard Quebedeaux argued in *The Worldly Evangelicals* in 1973. "It is now a force to be reckoned with."[46] Evangelicals produced their own blockbusters, their own pop songs, their own cultural forms, their own version of Bible-infused modernity. They even produced their own sex guides, thanks to Tim and Beverly LaHaye. Miss America contestants and professional athletes, country-and-western singers and film stars, sex therapists and management writers, B-list celebrities and even academics—all started popping up and proclaiming that they had been born again. The loosening of the Bible Belt's buckles changed American politics too.

Behold, the Jesus Machine

Evangelicals had a long tradition of disdain for politics. Falwell condemned Martin Luther King's involvement in the civil rights movement on the grounds that "preachers are not called to be politicians but soul-winners." Robertson refused to campaign for his father because "active partisan politics is the wrong path for true Evangelicals." And insofar as they had any political allegiances, those were to the socially conservative southern wing of the Democratic Party.

The early relations between religious activists and political conservatives were tentative—clumsy gropings followed by frustration. Many religious Americans rallied to Barry Goldwater and even more to Richard Nixon, who captured 80 percent of the Evangelical vote in 1972. But Goldwater was a libertarian with little sympathy for social conservatism, and religious conservatives felt betrayed by Nixon's foulmouthed Machiavellianism. (Billy Graham confessed to vomiting when he read transcripts of the Nixon tapes.)[47] As for Gerald Ford, he seemed like a nice enough chap—a regular American if ever there was one—but he treated the born-agains as if they were creatures from another planet, and he was married to a woman who winked at premarital sex (it reduced the divorce rate), likened marijuana smoking to drinking "your first beer," and praised *Roe v. Wade* for taking abortion "out of the backwoods" and putting it "in the hospitals where it belongs."[48]

All this changed in 1976 when a proudly born-again Christian ran for the presidency. Jimmy Carter was a Democrat, but he was a southern Democrat—and rather than seeing his religion as a purely private affair, like Kennedy, Carter wore it like a badge of honor. The first Evangelical to run for the White House since William Jennings Bryan, Carter was a Southern Baptist who had memorized his first Bible verse ("God is love") at four, who had accepted Jesus as his savior at eleven, who had done missionary work "up north" in Massachusetts and Pennsylvania, and whose sister, Ruth Carter Stapleton, was a well-known faith healer (his brother, Billy, was a different matter).[49] Carter persuaded millions of Evangelicals who had hitherto been leery of politics to vote for him, including Robertson, who boasted that he had done everything short of violating FCC regulations to get him elected.

Alas, like many whirlwind romances, things soured on the honeymoon. Why would a born-again Evangelical give an interview to *Playboy*, as Carter did, famously confessing that he had committed adultery in his heart? And why would he climb into bed with pro-choice feminists? Carter's support among Evangelicals began to dissolve before the election, and fomented into furious hostility over the next four years. The biggest grievance was the IRS's decision to deny thousands of religious schools tax-exempt status, on the grounds that they were de facto racist institutions. Evangelicals departed en masse to the Republican Party.

Horrified by Carter, Falwell organized a series of "I love America" rallies in state capitols, and introduced a new ritual in his church services, asking the entire congregation to stand when the service was over and then telling the registered voters to sit down. The nonregistered voters had to continue to stand while he delivered a long soliloquy on the importance of voting.[50] "If you would like to know where I am politically," he said, "I am to the right of wherever you are. I thought Goldwater was too liberal."[51] James Dobson founded Focus on the Family in 1977. Beverly LaHaye formed Concerned Women of America, which agitated against abortion, no-fault divorce and the Equal Rights Amendment. CWA soon had a membership of five hundred thousand, significantly more than the left-leaning National Organization of Women.

All that was missing was a way to bring these disparate conservative groups into a coherent movement. This came in the shape of the Moral Majority, set up in the late 1970s by Falwell with three social conservatives from Washington, Paul Weyrich, Richard Viguerie and Howard Phillips. The new organization, which Falwell described as "pro-life, pro-family, pro-morality and pro-American," quickly set about meshing Evangelical organizations with the wider conservative movement. By 1981 its *Moral Majority Report* was circulated to 840,000 houses and its daily commentary appeared on 300 radio stations.[52]

The rise of the religious right bound Evangelical Protestants to "conservatives of the heart" from other religious traditions that they had previously disdained. A generation before, Nelson Bell, Billy Graham's father-in-law and the executive editor of *Christianity Today,* had dismissed the Catholic Church as "a political system that like an octopus covers the entire world and threatens those basic freedoms and those constitutional rights for which our forefathers died in generations past." Evangelicals were initially reluctant to get involved in the right-to-life movement, because they regarded it as a "Catholic affair." (The Southern Baptist Convention even passed a resolution supporting certain sorts of legalized abortion in 1974.) But the Moral Majority changed this. Viguerie was a Catholic, Phillips a Jew and Weyrich a Catholic Mennonite. In the budding culture wars the enemy of my enemy was my friend.

As for the Republicans, the GOP moved somewhat closer to becoming God's Own Party. Ronald Reagan told an adoring crowd of Evangelicals in Dallas in 1980, "I know you can't endorse me but I want you to know that I endorse you." At the close of his acceptance speech at the Republican National Convention he asked his audience to "begin our crusade joined together in a moment of silent prayer."[53] His successor, the preppie George Bush, Sr., also posed as a born-again Evangelical. In office neither man remotely delivered on his promises. In 1981 Reagan refused to throw his weight behind the Human Life Statute and the Family Protection Act, both of which would have outlawed abortion. But "values voters" relentlessly increased their influence in the party. White Evangelicals had split their vote almost evenly between Carter and Ford in 1976. Four years later they broke two to one for Reagan. On the morning after Reagan's election, Falwell marched into a rally at Liberty University to the tune of "Hail to the Chief," which is usually reserved for the president.[54]

From being merely vocal supporters, Evangelicals became players and organizers. In 1988 Robertson mounted a spirited run for the Republican nomination, beating George Bush, Sr., in the Iowa caucuses (and helping to persuade Bush to appoint a leading social conservative, Dan Quayle, as his running mate). The defeated Robertson then teamed up with Ralph Reed, a rising Republican operative, to form the Christian Coalition. Reed, a born-again Christian who had turned to God after a hard-drinking youth, wanted to build a mass religious-cum-political movement from the ground up. The religious right should focus on local races for parent-teacher associations and schools, rather than the big political prizes, he argued. Three years after its foundation in 1989, the Christian Coalition had 350,000 members, an annual budget in excess of $10 million and a vast network of state and local affiliates.[55] Twenty-two percent of the delegates attending the 1992 Republican convention identified themselves as fundamentalists and 52 percent as either members of the "Christian right" or sympathizers (though arguably Reed's greatest success came in 2008, when a Christian activist who had gone into politics through the PTA was nominated as vice president).

SAND IN THE GEARS

Life on the Christian right was never easy. Evangelical religion and radical politics are volatile enough forces in themselves without being mixed together. The history of the Christian right is a history of fissure and fallout. Combinations that seem to work magnificently fall apart; people who seem to be committed to political activism retreat into their caves; organizations that bestride the political landscape implode.

The religious right was unusually susceptible to scandal. Everybody likes to read about a preacher—or a preachy politician—who is caught with his trousers down or his hand in the till. In 1987 Jim Bakker was caught committing adultery with his church secretary and embezzling millions of dollars of church money, while Jimmy Swaggart was spotted with a roadside prostitute. The Republican Class of '94, which surfed to power on a wave of worry about "family values," was stuffed full of miscreants. Newt Gingrich was having an affair with a former member of his staff during the Clinton impeachment. The GOP's first choice to replace him as speaker, Bob Livingston, withdrew his name when he too was exposed as an adulterer.

A second problem was organizational decay. All pressure groups are difficult to sustain—they start with a burst of energy before being transformed from agencies of righteousness into administrative chores—and religious pressure groups are particularly prone to the contrast between their Godly ambitions and the mucky compromises of political life. The Moral Majority never quite lived up to Weyrich's vision—it was a mechanism for organizing pastors rather than galvanizing the masses—and Falwell finally wound it up in 1989. The Christian Coalition never succeeded in delivering votes with the machinelike efficiency of the big trade unions: in 1996, when Ralph Reed and Pat Robertson endorsed Bob Dole, nearly half the Christian Coalition voters in the Louisiana and Iowa caucuses supported the Catholic Pat Buchanan over the Protestant Bob Dole.[56] The Coalition imploded after Reed left, accumulating millions of dollars in debt and tangling with antidiscrimination laws.

A third problem was Christianity's otherworldly focus. Christians are always tempted to give up politics in favor of saving mankind one soul at a time, or preparing themselves for the next world. Christian activists have been perpetually disappointed by their political champions. Reagan was more interested in cutting taxes than ending abortion. George Bush, Sr., put the liberal Justice David Souter on the Supreme Court. Cal Thomas, a former secretary for the Moral Majority, worried that Christians were "blinded by the might," to quote the title of one of his books. Weyrich was so disgusted by the public's indifference to Bill Clinton's adultery that he urged conservative Christians to retreat from politics.

A final problem was faction fighting, both theological and political. Though a shadow of its former self, anti-Catholicism survived. Bob Jones University churned out anti-Catholic literature and awarded an honorary doctorate to the arch Ulster Protestant Ian Paisley. (His entourage affectionately call him "the doc.") Swaggart said that Catholics were destined to burn in hell because they simply weren't Christians.[57] Tim LaHaye denounced Catholicism as a "false religion."[58]

Christians also had an uneasy relationship with the wider Republican Party. Country club Republicans looked down on them as wild-eyed hicks. Libertarians dismissed them as killjoys with bad haircuts and dripdry shirts. In *Holidays in Hell* (1989), P. J. O'Rourke argued that holidaymakers would be better off joining the Ku Klux Klan than vacationing in Jim Bakker's Heritage USA. At least they would be able to smoke and drink again and "wear something halfway decent like an all-cotton bed sheet." For their part, Christian conservatives worried that business Republicans were more interested in making a fast buck than in protecting family values.

Still, for all these difficulties, the religious right succeeded, from the 1980s onward, in constructing a mighty political infrastructure. Religious conservatives created what Dan Gilgen has christened a "Beltway Bible Belt"—a network of organizations that were designed to bring the right's message to bear on Washington politics day in and day out. James Dobson founded the Family Research Council in 1981 to promote family values in the capital. (It now has 4.5 million members, revenues of more than $10 million a year, and an impressive office building that is the center of seminars, lectures and lobbying.) He also, to litigate on behalf of socially conservative issues, helped in 1994 to found the Alliance Defense Fund, which has notched up more than twenty-five victories before the U.S. Supreme Court and hundreds more before the lower court. The conservative churches and denominations all got into the habit of sending representatives to Washington, notably Richard Cizik, of the National Association of Evangelicals, and Richard Land, of the Southern Baptist Convention.

The religious right was even more successful in the states than in the nation's capital. Social conservatism is the opposite of neoconservatism— the product of the heartland rather than the East Coast Bos-Wash corridor, an army in search of generals rather than generals in search of an army. James Dobson created a network of Family Councils in states across the country. Louis Sheldon's Traditional Values Coalition embraced forty-three thousand churches from more than twelve denominations. And local churches across the country were the most important cogs in the Jesus machine.

A RELIGIOUS NATION

For all its problems, the religious right tapped into two powerful movements that kept propelling it ahead. The most obvious was the continuing growth of hot religion. The Southern Baptist Convention grew by an average of 5 percent a year during the 1990s. The other was the demographic shift toward the Sunbelt. Gallup's survey of religious practices in 1992–98 shows that 70 percent of people in the South said that they found religion "very important" in their lives compared with 52 percent in New England and the mid-Atlantic states.[59]

The rise of the religious right, the expansion of the Sunbelt and the success of hot religion: in 2000 all these things came to a head in the candidacy of George W. Bush. Bush was the first modern American president who was seen by the religious right as "one of us," an Evangelical of the heart. His administration contained a remarkable number of committed Christians; and he went further than any previous president in putting the religious right's agenda into practice. More clearly than any other president, he also signified the immense gap between Europe and America when it came to religion and politics.

CHAPTER FOUR

BUSH, BLAIR, OBAMA AND THE GOD GAP (2000–2008)

❧

TONY BLAIR and George Bush are so often lumped together that it is easy to forget that when they first met as leaders of their countries—at Camp David shortly after Bush's inauguration in 2001—the chemistry was hardly immediate. The new president associated the British prime minister with several things he disliked: worthy European politics, multilateral diplomacy and, above all, Bill Clinton. Asked by reporters how the special relationship was faring, Bush made a lame joke about them having something important in common: they both used the same brand of toothpaste. In fact, there was another rather obvious thing that the two men shared right from the beginning: religion.

Both men are sincere Christians. With Bush this was clear. He is an Evangelical Christian, who reached for God in his forties after a dissolute youth in which he drank too much and achieved very little. (One of the turning points was a walk on a beach with Billy Graham, who asked him if he was "right with God.") But Blair too is a deeply religious man—perhaps the most devout Christian to inhabit 10 Downing Street since William Gladstone. He was drawn to Christianity as a student, and the New Testament underpinned many of his views about both social justice and foreign policy. (He was unusually willing to use the word "evil," for example.) Cherie Blair says that one of the first things that struck her about her future husband was his religiosity: "Religion was more important to him than anyone I had ever met outside the priesthood."[1] Faith remained a large part of Blair's life when he was at Number 10. He slept with a Bible by his bed, promoted a surprising number of fellow believers, sent all four of his children to Catholic schools (his wife was a "cradle Catholic") and took instruction in Catholicism in his final year as prime minister.[2] He converted to Catholicism shortly after leaving office.

Yet the way the two men presented their beliefs to the electorate was very different—and spoke volumes about the transatlantic divide when it came to faith. Blair stuck firmly to the principle that European politicians do not "do God," as his own spokesman, Alastair Campbell, once angrily told an American magazine. His flunkies did their best to prevent the media from filming him going to church.[3] Even when delivering his preachiest and most passionate speeches (the two often intertwined), he never invoked the Almighty. He thought of ending his address to the nation when he sent the troops into Iraq with a phrase like "God bless you"; his advisers persuaded him that he might look like a hypocrite or an American-style fanatic.[4] Unlike Margaret Thatcher, who once ventured into a Scottish pulpit (and was roundly condemned for it even by the Conservative press), he never tried to present his social beliefs in a religious setting. The reason was simple: as Blair complained after leaving office, if a politician talks about God, people "think you're a nutter." True to that spirit, far from acknowledging that he and Bush shared a common Christian faith, Blair found himself having to deny, to a BBC interviewer, rumors that the two men had prayed together, and looking very embarrassed as he did so.[5] The fact that Blair did his best to keep his Christian faith under wraps while he was in office did not prevent the British from making fun of it: *Private Eye,* a satirical magazine, portrayed him as the self-satisfied "Vicar of St. Albion's."

For Bush, the opposite was true. He happily wore his religiosity on his sleeve from the beginning—and profited mightily from it. Before running for president, he summoned a group of prominent pastors to the governor's mansion in Austin to "lay hands" on him. During a presidential debate in Iowa in 2000 he named Jesus as his "favorite philosopher . . . because he changed my heart." Asked if he had consulted his father, the forty-first president, about his plans to invade Iraq, he replied that he had consulted his heavenly father. Bush's public rhetoric was saturated with religious references—to God's will, God's role in history and, especially, to the conflict between good and evil—a habit that sent shivers down the spines of European relativists.

Just as Blair's refusal to discuss faith was rooted in political pragmatism, Bush's flaunting of his religiosity also had an element of political calculation. Bush asked Billy Graham's son, Franklin, to give the invocation at his inaugural. He made a point of cultivating the Evangelical press. *The Faith of George W. Bush: Faith in the White House,* a hagiographical film, pulls no punches in presenting him as a Christian hero. One scene shows him speaking in church. The camera lingers for a while on a massive portrait of Jesus Christ draped in a yellow robe. It then pans down to reveal Bush on the podium with his face perfectly positioned beneath Jesus' body. "My faith has made a big difference in my personal life, and my public life as well," he says. "And I pray. I pray for guidance. I pray for patience. I firmly believe in the power of intercessory prayer. And I know I could not do my job without it."

David Kuo, who worked in the White House promoting faith-based solutions to social problems, noted that Karl Rove and his political shop were nothing less than "obsessed" with Evangelical voters.[6] There were weekly conference calls with Evangelical leaders, including Tom Minnery, Focus on the Family's head of public policy; Ted Haggard, the head of the National Association of Evangelicals; and Richard Land, president of the Southern Baptist Convention's Ethics & Religious Liberty Commission. The White House also had a functionary, Tim Goeglein, whose full-time job was to act as a liaison with Evangelical groups. Christian leaders such as Charles Colson and Rick Warren were invited to the White House. H. L. Mencken once wrote of Calvin Coolidge that "the president of the United States may be an ass, but he at least doesn't believe that the earth is square, and that witches should be put to death, and that the whale swallowed Jonah. The Golden Text is not painted weekly on the White House wall, and there is no need to keep ambassadors waiting while Pastor Simpson, of Smithville, prays for rain in the Blue Room."[7] In the Bush era ambassadors had to compete with pastors for the president's time.

In return, the religious right—Evangelicals in particular but also conservative Catholics—provided Bush with his most solid base. Evangelicals had been suspicious of George Bush, Sr., even when he was giving them everything they wanted; and they were initially nervous about his wayward son. (Rove thinks the late revelation of a long-ago drunk-driving charge against Bush persuaded several million Evangelicals to stay at home in 2000, setting the stage for the Florida fiasco.) But they soon came to recognize Bush as one of their own—disappointing and wrongheaded sometimes, but a member of the team. The bond intensified after September 11, 2001, when many Evangelicals saw Bush as God's chosen instrument in an unfolding war between good and evil. Ralph Reed said that he heard people say, "God knew something we didn't," about the president;[8] Bush often remarked about the number of people he met on rope lines who said they were praying for him.

In the five ABC News/*Washington Post* polls taken during the year after September 11, 2001, Bush's approval rating among white Evangelicals ranged from 98 to 100 percent. In the 2004 election self-identified Evangelicals provided roughly 40 percent of Bush's total vote; if you add in other theological conservatives, such as Mormons and traditional Catholics, that number rises closer to 60 percent.[9] And they remained loyal for longer. Evangelicals clung to Bush's original justifications for the war in Iraq (that Saddam possessed weapons of mass destruction and had close ties with Al Qaeda) long after most other people had abandoned them.

For many modern Menckens on both sides of the Atlantic, the gap between "rational" European politics and "faith-driven" American politics loomed larger than it ever had under Bush, Sr. Kevin Phillips, a renegade Republican, described America as "a high-technology, gospel-spreading superpower."[10] Jonathan Raban, a British writer who has lived in Seattle for years, declared that "the greatest military power in history had shackled its deadly hardware to the rhetoric of fundamentalist Christianity."[11] Bruce Bartlett, a domestic policy adviser to Ronald Reagan, complained that the second Bush "truly believes he's on a mission from God. Absolute faith like that overwhelms a need for analysis."[12] In private many former advisers to George Bush Sr. were much ruder.

From Europe the howls were even louder. Jacques Delors, perhaps the European Commission's most successful president, described "the clash between those who believe and those who don't believe" as the most important force shaping the transatlantic relationship.[13] Europeans associated God with ghosts in the attic such as nationalism and racism, argued Delors, ghosts that had done more than enough damage already. Jacques Derrida and Jürgen Habermas also weighed in: "In our latitudes it's hard to imagine a president who begins his daily business with public prayer and relates his momentous political decisions to a divine mission."[14]

Suspicion of American religiosity was not confined to the sort of European elites that assailed the Blairs at dinner parties. Polls showed that three in five French people and nearly as many Dutch people thought that Americans were too religious; and Europeans who thought that America was "too religious" were more inclined to anti-Americanism than their fellow countrymen. One survey showed that 38 percent of Britons had an unfavorable view of America, but that number rose to 50 percent among people who were hostile to American religiosity. It is not hard to see why Blair was wary of rumors that the two men prayed together.

Is the Bush-Blair divide a fair reflection of the faith gap? On closer examination, the gap between religious America and secular Europe in 2000–2008 is both overplayed and underappreciated. It is overplayed in the short term because the degree to which Bush actually adopted policies for purely religious reasons is exaggerated. It is underappreciated in the long term because, once you strip out the Bush factor, there is still a yawning gap between the two halves of the Western Alliance: the tensions between secular Europe and religious America are likely to persist in some form under Barack Obama.

A NUCLEAR-ARMED THEOCRACY?

Was the Bush presidency really as theocratic as secularists feared? Certainly his inner circle was strikingly religious. Condoleezza Rice is the daughter of a Presbyterian minister named John Wesley. Andrew Card, his White House chief of staff in 2001–6, is married to a Methodist minister. Karen Hughes, one of his closest advisers, is a Presbyterian elder nicknamed "the Prophet." Don Evans, his secretary of commerce in 2001–5, bonded with Bush during Bible study meetings in Midland in the 1970s. Michael Gerson, his chief speechwriter until 2006, is an Evangelical who was educated at Wheaton College, the Harvard of Evangelical America. The White House Office of Personnel was run by Kay Coles James, a former dean of Pat Robertson's Regent University and a former vice president of the Family Research Council, and she made sure that "people of faith" were not sidelined in the way that they had been in the past. Over half the White House staff attended Bible study meetings. John Ashcroft, Bush's first attorney general, held one in his office.

Bush's presidency also coincided with a surge in the influence of conservative Christians on Capitol Hill. All six top Republican leaders in the Senate before the 2006 midterms earned 100 percent ratings from the Christian Coalition.[15] The House Values Action Team—a group that tries to heighten the influence of religion on politics—included some seventy Republican congressmen. James Dobson, the founder of Focus on the Family, had a particular hold on lawmakers.[16] Senator Jim Talent, who was raised in a Jewish household, pulled over to the side of the road and gave his life to Christ after listening to one of Dobson's broadcasts. Tom DeLay gave up his hard-drinking ways—he claimed that he drank ten martinis a night as a young congressman—as a result of watching Dobson's film Where's Dad? in a colleague's office: He burst into tears and decided to rededicate his life to God.

Under Bush, American political life constantly threw up figures or events that shocked secularists at home and abroad. Consider just two out of many possible examples: General William (Jerry) Boykin and the 2006 Values Voter Summit in Washington, D.C.

Even amid the cacophony over America's decision to depose Saddam Hussein, Boykin was impossible to ignore. Dressed in full combat gear, he toured American Evangelical churches delivering fiery sermons. Bush was in the White House, explained the general, because "God put him there." Who was America fighting against? Hardly Osama bin Laden or Saddam Hussein. America was in "a battle for our soul"—and the enemy was "a guy called Satan." Boykin was hardly a marginal figure, a retired military man who had accidentally engaged in a mind-meld with Dr. Strangelove. He was deputy undersecretary of defense intelligence, one of the leaders of the hunt for bin Laden. Nor was this a momentary lapse. When he led the failed Black Hawk raid on Mogadishu in 1993, Boykin claimed that he "could feel the presence of evil . . . in a place that has rejected God." He frequently argued that America was destined for victory in the war against Islam because "our God" is bigger than "their God."[17] And when Boykin's speaking tour became a matter of controversy, the administration stuck by him. Bush said that Boykin didn't "reflect my point of view" but left him in place until after the 2006 elections. Why stand by such an extreme figure? Because even as allies fretted and liberals guffawed, the religious right rallied to Boykin.

Our second example, the Values Votes Summit at the Omni Shoreham hotel in late September 2006, showed the religious right in all its pomp. With the midterm elections fast approaching, two thousand religious conservatives gathered in Washington, DC, under the auspices of the Family Research Council. The meeting started with an invocation by Father Frank Pavone, the national director of Priests for Life, who delivered a fiery talk on the importance of giving "all the energy we can to advance the cause of righteous candidates." After the presentation of the colors and a tear-stained rendition of the national anthem, a parade of potential presidential candidates came to pledge their troth, including Mitt Romney, the governor of Massachusetts, Senator Sam Brownback of Kansas, Senator George Allen of Virginia and Newt Gingrich, a former speaker of the House. Thereafter various luminaries from the Christian right, including Dobson from Focus on the Family and Land from the Southern Baptists, expounded on the struggle against liberals at home and Islamists abroad.

The meeting was relentless—session after session, running without a break, on "getting church voters to the polls," "impacting the culture through the church," "training the next generation of pro-family leaders." Those delegates without iron buttocks found themselves wandering off into the exhibition center to buy T-shirts emblazoned with the slogan "One Nation Under God" or peruse pamphlets on the evils of the "homosexual lifestyle." *The Slippery Slope of Same-Sex Marriage* addressed the civilizational consequences of gay marriage. (The first section is entitled "A Man and His Horse.")

Throughout the whole event, the values voters engaged in an elaborate dissimulation concerning their political activism, because they were not legally allowed to endorse particular parties. Land, for instance, declared categorically that "God is not a Republican, God is not a Democrat. But He is pro-life. He is anti-homosexual values. . . ." But in practice the assembled values voters were not so much aligned with the Republican Party as intertwined with it. All the big-name politicians addressing the event were Republicans. Sean Hannity, from the "fair and balanced" Fox network, won a standing ovation when he defined a "Republican" as a "normal American." A car in the hotel parking lot had a license plate that read "PREACHN"; just above it was a Republican bumper sticker for "W '04."

BUT WHAT DID HE DO FOR HIM?

Anybody who saw Boykin in action or attended the Value Voter Summit would be hard-pressed to deny that faith was a large part of the Bush presidency: the level of religiosity in American politics was off the scale in comparison with other modern countries. But that did not mean policy was determined by it, or that Bush stepped wildly outside the historic mainstream; indeed, when the religious right appeared to go too far it was punished at the polls.

Take foreign policy first. America's view of the world under Bush was plainly more faith-driven than that of its main allies. But how unusual was that? General Boykin, remember, has plenty of antecedents—at least in believing that America has a special relationship with God. The Lord's vineyard, a shining city built upon a hill, an asylum for the oppressed from every corner of the earth: such phrases litter the earliest writings about the colonies. The American revolutionaries "called upon God to protect them because He—not George III—was their King."[18] Woodrow Wilson hoped the American-backed League of Nations would lead to nothing less than the "redemption of the world."[19] Harry Truman denounced the "terrible fanaticism" of communism that "denies the existence of God."[20] In his view the Almighty had brought America to power to defend spiritual values."[21] Reagan described the Soviet Empire as "evil" and introduced demands to stop religious persecution, backed up by specific examples, into the most sensitive negotiations with the Soviets.

So religion has always been part of the mix. Yet America seldom makes really big decisions—such as the decisions to invade the Philippines or Hawaii—for purely religious reasons. That is because American foreign policy, even more than those of other countries, has been a jumble of traditions and contradictions. As Eugene Rostow once remarked, "We embrace contradictory principles with equal fervor and cling to them with equal tenacity. Should our foreign policy be based on power or morality? Realism or idealism? Pragmatism or principle? Should its goal be the protection of interests or the promotion of values? Should we be nationalists or internationalists? Liberals or conservatives? We blithely answer, 'All of the above.' "[22]

There has also been much more to America's national hubris than the belief that the country has a special relationship with God. Other factors—imperialism, cultural superiority and plain old greed—are often at work. A contemporary historian, Walter Russell Mead, has divided American foreign policy into four main traditions: Jeffersonianism, Jacksonianism, Hamiltonianism and Wilsonianism. Of these only the last is based upon religiously infused moralism. And throughout America's history, an overdose of one tradition usually produces a lurch in another direction.

Bush fit this pattern. Take the two areas where foreigners most often spotted religion: the Iraq war and the administration's trenchant support for Israel. On Iraq, there was a lot of Manichaean rhetoric after September 11. Bush insisted that America had been "called" or given a "mission" by the "Maker of Heaven" and "Author of Liberty." The 2002 National Security Strategy boldly stated that "our responsibility to history is already clear: to answer these attacks and rid the world of evil." The religious right's leadership prominently supported the invasion of Iraq (though Robertson told Bush that he had foreseen an unfolding disaster in Mesopotamia in a dream). But for all the religious rhetoric and the cheerleading Boykins, the war was run by people like Dick Cheney and Donald Rumsfeld, who saw the world in terms of national rather than spiritual struggles. There was hardly a shortage of earthly reasons for America's intervention in Iraq, from worries about deadly weapons to concerns about oil supplies to the belief that democratization could provide a long-term salve for the region. And, not least, good old dynastic revenge.

In fact, when it came to its "war on terror," the supposedly faith-based Bush administration was often strangely blind to the centrality of religion. Very few people in the White House understood the difference between Shiites and Sunnis before the invasion of Iraq. In its obsession with state sponsors of terrorism, and in its assumption that the cure of democracy could wean people off radical Islam, the administration undervalued the importance of religion to devastating effect. Holy warriors, it turned out, had no need of state sponsors, and democratization played into the hands of popular religious movements. In the Iraqi elections of 2005, the Shiite alliance won almost half the seats in parliament. In the first Palestinian elections in a decade, Hamas defeated the secular Fatah Party. The administration managed to ignore religion even as Iraq was erupting in a religious war.

Religious America was also more divided over Iraq than Boykin and his amen-corner might suggest. Many leading religious figures—including the head of Bush's own Methodist church—opposed the invasion of Iraq. Jimmy Carter, one of Bush's fellow Evangelicals, was one of the war's most prominent and vituperative critics. And even the Evangelical base eventually got tired of the president's "heroic" foreign policy. In May 2008, 36 percent of the Evangelicals interviewed by Pew's researchers said that they favored an active approach in foreign affairs, with 54 percent preferring to concentrate on home, almost identical to the nation as a whole.[23] Bush's overreach in Iraq (combined with other disasters) meant that his support among young white Evangelical voters collapsed in his final years, dropping to around 45 percent.[24]

For most Europeans Israel is a more disturbing example of faith-flavored foreign policy than Iraq. Israel divides Europeans and Americans more powerfully than any other subject. Even Blair, who could hardly be described as anti-Israel (his support for its assault on Hezbollah in Lebanon in 2006 cost him his premiership), was deeply frustrated by Bush's failure to put any real pressure on Israel. It is also Europe's favorite example of how faith drives American foreign policy off the rails. Before Bush, outsiders blamed America's position on the fabled "Jewish lobby." Under Bush it was increasingly blamed also on Christian Zionists, who not only believed that God had given all the Holy Land to the Jews, but also that the full establishment of Israel was necessary for the Second Coming and Armageddon.

As with Boykin, there was history there. Israel has always figured large in the imagination of Christian America. The Pilgrim Fathers saw themselves as new Israelites.[25] John Adams said that he "really wish[ed] the Jews again in Judea an independent nation."[26] The first Protestant missionaries from America to the Middle East, in 1819, had the goal of restoring Palestine to Jewish sovereignty: America soon had more consular agents in Palestine than any other country did, largely to deal with the demands of American pilgrims and missionaries.[27] In 1844 a New York University professor of Hebrew wrote a treatise, *Valley of Vision: Or the Dry Bones of Israel Revived,* dismissing Muhammad as a "pseudo prophet" and calling for the "elevating" of the Jews by re-creating their state in Palestine, that was unremarkable apart from the author's name: the Reverend George Bush.[28] Indeed, by the end of the nineteenth century "restorationism" was a mass movement. In 1891, William Blackstone, an evangelist-cum-real-estate-magnate, delivered "the Blackstone Memorial" to the White House. Signed by more than four hundred people, including John D. Rockefeller, J. P. Morgan and William McKinley, it called for Palestine to be given back to the Jews: "According to God's distribution of nations it is their home, an inalienable possession from which they were expelled by force."

Once Israel was created, religious sympathies played a role in America's decision to recognize it. In presenting the case in May 1948, Clark Clifford, the White House chief counsel, quoted the Book of Deuteronomy ("Behold, I have set the land before you: go in and possess the land which the Lord swore unto your fathers, Abraham, Isaac, and Jacob, to give unto them and to their seed after them"[29]). Even when they were keeping out of politics, Evangelicals kept close relations with Israel, with Oral Roberts, a Pentecostal preacher, visiting Jerusalem to see David Ben-Gurion in 1959. Randall Balmer, a writer who was born into an Evangelical family, remembers being waked by his mother to celebrate the fact that "we" had just won the Six Day War in 1967. Billy Graham made a film in Israel in 1970 called *His Land,* and Golda Meir attended the premiere in the United States.[30] For years, transporting American Christians to the Holy Land has been a booming business.

True to this picture, American Evangelicals were pretty firmly on Israel's side under Bush: 55 percent sympathized with Israel, according to a Pew poll in 2003, while a mere 6 percent backed the Palestinians. And 46 percent of them said that this stemmed from their religious beliefs. Seventy-two percent believed that God gave the land of Israel to the Jews, while 63 percent stood by the passage in the Book of Revelations that states that the return of the Jews to their ancient homeland is a necessary precondition for the Second Coming.[31] In Evangelical circles there were plenty of strident supporters of Israel. The 2005 meeting of the National Religious Broadcasters featured an exhibit of the burned-out hull of a Jerusalem city bus that had been struck by a suicide bomber, and Kay Arthur, a popular radio evangelist, told one breakfast meeting audience that "if it came to a choice between Israel and America, I would stand with Israel."[32] John Hagee, a Texas televangelist who believes that supporting Israel is a "biblical imperative," has been particularly active in summoning Evangelicals to the Israeli cause. In July 2006, with Israeli bombs falling on Lebanon and Labor MPs massing against Blair in Britain, Hagee brought thirty-five hundred people from across the country to Washington, DC, to cheer on Israel.

So religious support for Israel runs deep in Christian America. But it is quite a big step to claim that Bush's policy was driven by it. To begin with, as with Iraq, support for Israel was not as universal among American Christians as Europeans imagine. From 2000 to 2003, 37 percent of the statements issued by the mainline Protestant churches on human rights focused on Israel.[33] In 2004, the Presbyterian Church even passed a resolution calling for limited divestment of companies doing business with Israel. As well as being a trenchant critic of the Iraq war, Jimmy Carter has also been a thorn in Israel's side, calling it an apartheid state.

And if Bush felt pressure from Evangelicals to stand by Israel, there were also plenty of secular reasons to do so—ones that European critics (though not Blair) are often rather slow to recognize. Solidarity with a nation of settlers; identification with a besieged democracy; the Palestinians' appalling knack for public relations (continuing suicide bombing after September 11, for instance); the neoconservatives' intellectual domination of foreign policy; and, yes, the extremely powerful Israeli lobby in Washington: it would have been a brave president, especially a conservative one, who ignored these things. Non-Evangelical Americans say they sympathize with Israelis by a ratio of more than three to one—an astonishingly high figure by European standards. Hagee was hardly unusual in rallying to Israel's side. With Hezbollah rockets falling indiscriminately on America's ally, a chorus of leading secular Democrats, including Nancy Pelosi, the House leader, and Harry Reid, the Senate leader, demanded that Iraq's prime minister, Nouri al-Maliki, recant his criticism of Israel or have his invitation to address Congress revoked. At the height of British pomp and power, Matthew Arnold attributed "the genius and history of us English, and of our American descendants across the Atlantic, to the genius and history of the Hebrew people." Many feel the same way in today's America.

On Israel, Bush himself seemed less influenced by faith than by political pragmatism and Texan stubbornness. He had no doubt where his base stood on the Middle East. Bush's main reflection on visiting Israel was not to do with the Second Coming, but how small and vulnerable it was: he famously pointed out that freeways back home seemed wider. He felt that Clinton had been sucked into a quagmire at the end of his presidency— and he refused to deal with Yasser Arafat after the Palestinian leader was caught lying to the administration about a weapons shipment. (Personal duplicity with Bush was always a fatal mistake, as Gerhard Schröder also discovered.) On the other hand, far from spurring on Evangelical dreams of Armageddon (or, for that matter, the neocons' more worldly ambitions), Bush never gave up his public commitment to a Palestinian state. In his own mind, he struck a reasonable balance.

Indeed, on the vexed issues of both Iraq and Israel the role of religion under Bush was similar: it helped push America into positions that much of the rest of the world disagreed with, but it was hardly the trump card. It reinforced decisions that also had secular justifications. Religious America generally believed the same things as many other Americans—only more strongly. That did not mean that religious Americans could not change their minds—Iraq showed that. Just that they tended to be more inflexible. Bush was a particularly extreme example of this inflexibility. He also dressed his foreign policy in unusually strong religious language. But it is hard to claim that he ran a theocratic foreign policy.

Red Meat at Home

At home, Bush certainly served the values voters some red meat. He clearly did much more for the religious right than Ronald Reagan, for example. While the Gipper appointed the pro-choice Sandra Day O'Connor to the Supreme Court, Bush named two solid social conservatives, John Roberts and Sam Alito, and made Roberts chief justice. Clever and politically savvy, these two men have a chance to shape the Court for decades to come. (Both, incidentally, are Catholics, illustrating the deepening ties between Evangelicals and Rome.) Bush also consistently pushed, with varying degrees of luck, for conservative candidates in the lower courts, shifting them to the right on social issues and building up a "farm team" for future conservative Supreme Court appointees.

On the core social issues of "life" and "family," Bush also did more than Reagan, but less than his rhetoric suggested. Officially, Bush backed constitutional amendments to outlaw abortion and to ban gay marriage. But he refused to spend much political capital on furthering either cause in the Senate (where they stood little chance of passing). He put more effort into specific measures to limit abortion that were popular even with some pro-choice supporters, such as the 2002 Born-Alive Infants Protection Act, the 2004 Unborn Victims of Violence Act (which made an assault on a pregnant woman two separate crimes) and, especially, a bill banning "partial-birth abortion," a gruesome practice that was unpopular with voters of all stripes. The only area where Bush clearly defied the popular will (and the business wing of the Republican Party) on the issue of life was over stem cells: he trenchantly opposed giving more federal funds to research.

The fate of compassionate conservatism, the core idea of his 2000 campaign, was more indicative of his priorities. Bush's plan to use faith-based organizations to deliver social services was popular with Evangelicals; it was also something he genuinely seemed to believe in. But once in office, Bush hit a wall. Congress refused to pass the main package of reforms, because of worries about the separation of church and state. Bush certainly did not abandon the idea completely—he issued executive orders setting up faith-based offices in ten federal agencies. But he lost focus on the subject amid the enthusiasm about tax cuts and deposing Saddam. Two of the people at the heart of the program resigned in disgust: John DiIulio, who complained about "Mayberry Machiavellis" in the White House; and David Kuo, who said the office had become little more than a "cross around the White House's neck."

Bush was a practical politician—a man constantly engaged in the trade-offs that are necessary for exercising power. Social conservatives rightly point out that, although they won on stem cells, Bush generally devoted more political capital to economic issues than to social ones, promoting tax cuts at the beginning of his first term, and Social Security reform in the second. Paradoxically, Bush's status as "one of us" gave him a surprising amount of leeway either to rebuke religious conservatives (he slapped down Franklin Graham's description of Islam as an "evil religion") or to dump them for other parts of the Republican coalition, especially business. For instance, he supported China's admission to the World Trade Organization over the protestations of Evangelicals. James Moore and Wayne Slater, two of the most dogged reporters on the Bush presidency, describe a visit Bush paid to a Boeing plant in Washington State during the 2000 election campaign. Bush stood in front of a wide-bodied aircraft bound for China and proclaimed his fealty to the principles of free trade. A Texan reporter from a hotbed of Christian activism north of Austin joked that the candidate's stand might cost him the religious vote. "Oh yeah," Bush replied. "You only think that because you live around all those whackos."[34]

Some of Bush's closest advisers took an even dimmer view of the "whackos." Dick Cheney and Donald Rumsfeld were far from heart-on-the-sleeve Evangelicals. Cheney, whose eldest daughter is a lesbian, was a voluble critic of the Federal Marriage Amendment. (Both Cheneys attended the ceremony where their daughter married her partner.) Rumsfeld attended an Episcopalian church in Georgetown, Christ Church, in much the same spirit that an eighteenth century squire attended his parish church. Karl Rove admitted that he had never received a religious calling: from his perspective Evangelicals were another regiment in a vast conservative army, stretching from antitax crusaders to gun nuts, that he tried to muster into a coherent fighting force. The Senate contained a handful of moderate or pro-abortion-rights Republicans who could block any initiative that they considered far-fetched.

Rove's instincts were right. The religious right had a habit of overreaching, running ahead not just of the nation as a whole but also of the rest of the conservative coalition—and it did so after Bush's reelection. Looking back, the vainglorious speeches at the gathering of the values voters in 2006 seem rather like sepiaed pictures of a British officers' mess dinner in 1913: in both cases slaughter was just around the corner. The congressional elections that followed were a disaster for the religious right. On "Bloody Tuesday," as one anti-abortion campaigner called it, the Republicans lost control of both Houses of Congress. Many of the luminaries of the Values Voters Summit, most notably Rick Santorum, were mowed down. A few days before the election, Ted Haggard, who had been a leading campaigner against same-sex marriage, was exposed in a gay-sex and drugs scandal.

The most disastrous example of the religious right's penchant for overreaching was the Terri Schiavo affair—the case of a brain-damaged woman who was caught in a battle between her husband, who wanted to remove her feeding tube, and her parents, who wanted to keep it in place. The religious right tried to use the full might of the federal government to keep Schiavo "alive." And a large majority of the general public—including 72 percent of Republicans in one poll—responded with a resounding boo. In 2006 more than twenty senators and representatives who supported the Schiavo intervention were defeated while all Republicans, and all but one Democrat, who opposed the intervention were reelected. But there were plenty of other examples of overreaching. The right's hard-line opposition to stem-cell research put it well beyond the mainstream: as even Bush has been known to point out privately, stem cells are a tricky subject for devout pro-lifers, because they can involve two lives, that of the sacrificed embryo and that of the potential beneficiary from the research. The right's preoccupation with "the homosexual agenda" also slid into the quirky. It is one thing to oppose gay marriage, another to argue that it might open the door to an epidemic of "man on dog" sex, as Santorum did. Dobson, who in 2004 had been able to do little wrong politically, had become a political liability by 2008, a grumpy old man, spluttering that *The Da Vinci Code* had been cooked up "in the fires of hell" (surely it would have been better written if it had been?) and comparing stem-cell research to Nazi experiments.

The religious right's political ineptitude was repeated in the 2008 presidential campaign. The right could not decide who to support, with fatal consequences. Mitt Romney made the right noises about "life" and "marriage"—but he was also a Mormon who had been a socially liberal governor of Massachusetts. Rudy Giuliani was a thrice-married lapsed Catholic who had also dressed up in drag and bunked with a homosexual couple after his second marriage collapsed. Fred Thompson claimed that he did not attend church in Washington because he could not find one nearby. Prominent social conservatives dithered between the front-runners (Robertson endorsed Giuliani, for example; several others opted for Romney) but in their dithering ignored the one candidate who lit up the Evangelical rank and file. Mike Huckabee, a former preacher turned governor of Arkansas who believed that the Constitution should be rewritten to make it a more Christian document, won the Iowa caucuses and some southern primaries on a tide of Evangelical votes. But he lacked institutional support and the nomination eventually went to a man whom the religious right's leaders liked least. John McCain was certainly sound on abortion, but he had denounced Falwell and Pat Robertson as "agents of intolerance."

As in most political disasters, there was one final heroic last stand. Sarah Palin wanted to be seen as the religious right's Margaret Thatcher. In fact, she was closer to being its Boudicca—a warrior queen who flashed across history, yet ended up in total annihilation.

Sarah Palin has the deepest roots in the Evangelical subculture of any candidate for high office during the past century. She attended a Pente-costal church while she was growing up and was rebaptized along with her mother. She led the Wasilla High School chapter of Christian Athletes. She has strong views against gay marriage and abortion. Her eldest son, Track, has a tattoo of the "Jesus fish" on his calf. During the campaign she celebrated the fact that her pregnant teenage daughter "chose life" (and a shotgun wedding).

During the presidential campaign videos emerged showing her at wor-ship. In one a preacher predicts that Alaska will become a "refuge state" in the Last Days, with thousands of people fleeing from "the Lower 48." In another a preacher asks Jesus "to bring finances her way, even in the politi-cal realm," and to free her from "every form of witchcraft." "I grew up in the Wasilla Assemblies of God," she remarks at one point, "nothing freaks me out about the worship service."

The trouble was that Palin's various worship services "freaked out" a lot of other people. There were plenty of reasons why the governor of Alaska proved to be a drag on the Republican ticket, not least her lack of experi-ence in global affairs. But she was also the personification of the limits of the religious right. She certainly showed its power: McCain tried to make a fuss about her maverick reformer qualities and there was also the appar-ent hope that through sheer hockey-momness she would draw some Hill-ary women to the Republican ticket, but Palin's main electoral asset for McCain was that she reconnected him to the Evangelical base of his party, especially on the issue of abortion. The right salivated about a woman who had told voters during her run for lieutenant governor in 2002 that she was "as pro-life as you can get." But the rest of the country saw her views as too extreme—and also wondered about the wisdom of choosing a vice presi-dent for her views on one social policy. She contributed to the impression that the American conservative movement had gone off the rails.

OBAMA'S INHERITANCE

The fact that the religious right ended up with a bloody nose does not mean that the country that Bush handed over to Barack Obama in January 2009 had somehow solved its culture wars or become a less religious place. If the influence of religion on American politics under Bush was sometimes exaggerated, it will continue to play a significant role under his successor. Regardless of which party is in the White House, American politics will be more faith driven than those of its main allies.

Abroad, America seems intent on pursuing a foreign policy that is much more infused with religious values than the foreign policies of other great powers. (We will return to this subject in our conclusion). At home, the past few years will probably not be seen as a period in which religion ceased to shape American politics, but rather as one in which a new religious politics was born, a politics driven by two new groups, the "new, new" religious right and a newly emergent religious left.

The right is seeing the emergence of a new generation of politicians who are much more in tune with the times than Jerry Falwell (who died in May 2007) and Pat Robertson (who had been kicked off the board of the National Religious Broadcasters after thirty years of service the previous year). These new activists are mixing familiar conservative concerns, such as abortion and gay marriage, with new worries about global warming, inequality, human trafficking and prison rape. They are also proving much cannier about getting their message across to mainstream America.

The pied piper of this group is Rick Warren—the Billy Graham of the new generation. Warren could hardly look less like Graham—he has a goatee rather than a clean-shaven lantern jaw and sports open-necked shirts, mostly of the open-necked variety, rather than a suit and tie. But he has a considerable amount in common with him including the Southern Baptist faith and a genius for adapting religion to his time. Just as Graham took the barbed-wire fundamentalism of his youth and reshaped it for the postwar era of two-car garages and upward mobility, Warren took postwar Evangelicalism and reshaped it, yet again, for the world of suburban anomie and the search for meaning. Warren has become a one-man dispenser of "purpose." More than four hundred thousand pastors have attended his seminars on the "purpose-driven church," and more than thirty million people have bought his book, *The Purpose Driven Life*. Warren's message is hardly unconservative: in 2004 he supported Bush behind the scenes, taking part in White House conference calls and informing thousands of pastors that they should regard issues such as abortion and stem-cell research as "nonnegotiable." But Warren is just as often to be found stressing issues such as poverty, HIV-AIDS, overseas aid and global warming.

The latter is particularly important. The old religious right was very skeptical of climate change, associating it with regulation-obsessed East Coasters and New Age weirdos. People like Warren and Richard Cizik, until late 2008 the chief Washington lobbyist for the National Association of Evangelicals, prefer to talk about "creation care," taking their inspiration from Genesis 2:15 ("The Lord God took the man and put him in the Garden of Eden to work it and take care of it"). Cizik even appeared in a photograph in *Vanity Fair*'s 2006 "green issue" that gave the impression that he was walking barefoot on water. Warren and Cizik were among the eighty-six luminaries who backed the Evangelical Climate Initiative in 2006, which argued that Christians had a moral responsibility to deal with global warming—and urged the Bush administration and Congress to get their act together on the subject. This was roundly condemned by Dobson and the old guard. But the rank and file was moving in Warren and Cizik's way. In 2006, 52 percent of Evangelicals told a Pew survey that they supported strict rules to protect the environment, even if it cost jobs or raised taxes.

Meanwhile, a religious left also gathered strength under Bush. One example was the "spiritual progressives," who are liberal in both theology and social policy. They belonged either to the modernist wings of various Judeo-Christian faiths or to the New Age movement. The most prominent spiritual progressive is Rabbi Michael Lerner, who once taught Hillary Clinton "the politics of meaning." His conference in Washington in May 2006 resembled nothing so much as a religious menagerie: the speakers included a wilderness-guide-cum-meditation-teacher and a shaman who specialized in helping activists to "access spiritual wisdom." More prominent were "Red-Letter Christians"—traditionalists in theology but activists in social policy. (They take their name from the practice of printing the Bible with all Jesus' words in red.) Their flag bearer is Jim Wallis, a preacher who believes in the inerrancy of the Bible, opposes gay marriage and abortion but nevertheless campaigns hard for the Democratic Party.[35] He points out that the Bible contains three thousand references to alleviating poverty and none to gay marriage.

The person who symbolized the religious left more than anyone else was Barack Obama. Even before he emerged as a political force, the Democrats were trying to take God seriously. After the 2004 debacle Nancy Pelosi, the minority leader, asked one of her colleagues, James Clyburn, a preacher's son, to put together a Faith Working Group to educate her caucus about religion. She even attended one of Joel Osteen's services to celebrate his church's move to the former Compaq Center in Houston. In 2005 Tim Kaine mounted a successful bid for the governorship of Virginia—generally a Republican stronghold—by emphasizing his religious credentials. He placed his first ads on Christian radio, defended his opposition to the death penalty on the grounds that "my faith teaches life is sacred" and talked about his missionary work in Honduras as a young man. In the 2006 election, several Democrat candidates hired Common Good, a consulting firm that specializes in teaching politicians how to appeal to religious voters, and obviously religious Democrats such as Ted Strickland in Ohio and Bob Casey in Pennsylvania did well. Hillary Clinton burnished her Christian credentials: she kept reminding her audiences that she is a "person of faith" who once contemplated becoming a Methodist minister herself. She even softened her line on abortion, telling a group of family-planning providers in 2005 that "abortion in many ways represents a sad, even tragic choice to many, many women." Another presidential candidate, John Edwards, carried a copy of Warren's *The Purpose Driven Life* around with him, bound in leather and with his name embossed on the cover.[36]

Yet one reason why Barack Obama beat Hillary Clinton was that he succeeded in out-Godding her. Here was a man who had not recently remembered his faith, but talked at length about his religiosity in his two autobiographies, detailing how he became a Christian after a largely secular childhood (his father was a Muslim turned atheist and his mother was a "nonpracticing Christian"), and talking about the ways in which religion influenced his life. "Kneeling beneath that cross on the South Side of Chicago," he wrote in *The Audacity of Hope*, "I felt God's spirit beckoning me. I submitted myself to His will, and dedicated myself to discovering His truth." Obama has forcefully argued that the "fear of getting preachy" may have led some people on the left to "discount the role that values and culture play in some of our most urgent social problems." In 2006 he visited Warren's Saddleback Church to address Evangelicals on fighting AIDS. Like Hillary, he hired a full-time staffer to work with Evangelical voters, Josh DuBois, a member of a church affiliated with the Pentecostal Assemblies of God.

Obama's relationship with God was not always helpful to him. The emergence of explosive videos of his preacher, Jeremiah Wright, crying "God damn America!" threatened to hand the party's nomination to Clinton. Sarah Palin certainly neutralized any possible God effect Obama might have had with the core Evangelical vote. But for the first time since Jimmy Carter, it was the Democrats who plainly fielded the more prayin' candidate. (Bill Clinton does not count, because his prayin', well intentioned though it was, so conspicuously failed to alter his livin'.) John McCain was unhappy talking about his faith, and at one point during the Republican primary he got confused as to whether he was a Baptist or an Episcopalian. Obama made a point of talking about how the Almighty had found him. Warren officiated at his inauguration.

None of this means that the Democratic Party is going to be as consistently pro-God as the Republicans. A fifth of Democratic votes in 2004 came from what Pew classified as "seculars, atheists and agnostics." Many mainstream Democrats are woefully ignorant about religion: Terry McAuliffe, a former head of the Democratic National Committee, drew a blank when Warren was introduced to him. Edwards, the "purpose driven" candidate, briefly hired a liberal blogger, Amanda Marcotte, who mocked pro-life Catholics by asking, "What if Mary had taken Plan B after the Lord filled her with his hot, white, sticky Holy Spirit?" But in 2008 the Democrats were a patently more Godly bunch than in 2004, when Howard Dean located the Book of Job in the New Testament and assured Pat Robertson that "Christians" and "Democrats" had a lot in common.

The most striking thing about the reconfiguration of the religious right and the emergence of a religious left is that it is likely to increase the role of religion in the American public square. Rather than being confined to a certain group (white Evangelicals) and to certain issues (abortion and gay marriage), religion is expanding its empire. Democrats as well as Republicans are repeatedly evoking religion to justify their actions. And they are addressing a wider range of issues in religious language, including some, such as climate change and distributive justice, that are likely to dominate the debate for years to come.

Two Religious Landscapes

Why would that be so? Because the politics of any country in the end reflect the voters, and the America that George Bush handed over to Barack Obama in 2009 remained a deeply religious place—a three-hundred-million-strong refutation of the secularization thesis that modernity was bound to destroy religiosity and push faith out of public life.

The most thorough study of American religious beliefs, the U.S. Religious Landscape Survey by the Pew Forum on Religion and Public Life, demonstrates clearly that the world's most powerful country is also one of the most religious. More than nine in ten Americans (92 percent) believe in the existence of God or a universal spirit. Seven in ten are absolutely certain of God's existence. Six in ten adults believe that God is a person with whom you can have a personal relationship. A majority of American adults (58 percent) say that they pray at least once a day, three-quarters say that they pray once a week, and nearly a third say that they receive definite answers to their prayers at least once a month. Nearly two-thirds of Americans (63 percent) believe that their faith's Holy Book is the Word of God.[37] Most Americans (74 percent) believe in life after death and a majority (59 percent) believe in a hell where the wicked are eternally punished. Nearly eight in ten adults (79 percent) believe that miracles still occur today as they did in ancient times.[38] A third (34 percent) say that they have experienced or witnessed a divine healing. Forty-five percent of Americans in general, and 70 percent of Evangelicals, reject the theory of evolution.[39]

This religiosity is institutionalized in collective worship and family habits. Six in ten Americans (61 percent) report that they or members of their family belong to their local church or house of worship.[40] Four in ten participate in prayer groups or Bible study groups at least once a week.[41] Most parents with children living at home do something religious with their children, with 63 percent praying or reading scripture with their children and sixty percent sending them to religious education programs.

You can see evidence of America's religiosity everywhere you look in the American landscape. America may not have produced anything to match medieval Europe's grand cathedrals, but its faith catches the eye everywhere—from the Crystal Cathedral in Orange County to the neon churches of Nevada to giant crosses that line many a highway in the Midwest. Every suburb has its Wal-Mart-style megachurch. Across the Bible Belt people build shrines in their gardens and arrange their flowers to spell "Jesus lives." In the outskirts of Monroe, Ohio, a sixty-foot-tall bust of Jesus made of plastic foam and fiberglass beseeches onlookers from the front of the Solid Rock Church. The Ridge Assembly of God in Davenport, Florida, boasts a cell-phone tower in the shape of a cross 175 feet tall and 80 feet across.

Americans have surprisingly little difficulty in reconciling their faith with their country's secular creed of individualism. More than one in four American adults (28 percent) have swapped the religious tradition in which they were raised for another tradition (e.g., Catholicism to Protestantism or Judaism to "no religion"). Add changes within religious traditions to the mix (e.g., from one type of Protestantism to another) and forty-four percent of Americans belong to a religious tradition other than the one in which they were raised. Nearly four in ten married Americans have spouses with a different religious affiliation. At first sight the Roman Catholic Church is an exception: about a quarter of Americans have consistently described themselves as Catholics over several decades. But in fact, the Catholic Church has lost more people to other denominations or to no religion at all than any other single religious group. About a third of Pew's respondents who were raised Catholic no longer describe themselves as such. These losses are being offset partly by conversion (2.6 percent of the adult population are Catholic converts) but largely by immigration. Latinos make up 12 percent of American Catholics age seventy and over but nearly half of all Catholics age eighteen to twenty-nine. For a striking number of Americans, faith is less a place where you root your life than a journey of discovery. It is about seeking rather than dwelling.

Some of the remaining advocates of the secularization thesis—call them the neosecularists—have tried to attach asterisks to the idea that America remains a strikingly religious country. They point out that atheism is on the rise; they also question the quality of people's faith, emphasizing that Americans are strikingly ignorant when it comes to doctrine.

The Pew research does much to undermine the first claim. America is certainly witnessing a striking rise in the number of people who have no religious affiliation. It's true that only 7.3 percent of Americans say that they were "unaffiliated" as children; today the figure for the unaffiliated is 16.1 percent. But the Pew Survey shows that people who are not affiliated with a particular religious tradition do not necessarily lack religious beliefs. A large portion of the unaffiliated (41 percent) say that religion is at least somewhat important in their lives; seven in ten say that they believe in God; and more than a quarter (27 percent) say that they attend religious services at least a few times a year. One in five people who identify themselves as atheists (21 percent) and a majority of those who identify themselves as agnostic (55 percent) say that they believe in God or a universal spirit![42] This growing group of unaffiliated Americans is not just a product of religious churn, as people drop out of this or that religious tradition. It also provides the basis of more churning in future, as some of these unaffiliated "seekers" will attach themselves to religious groups, just as Obama did in Chicago.

The second point is harder to deal with. How exactly can we measure the quality of people's faith? And should we equate faith with religious literacy? You can certainly be a religious person without knowing much about St. Augustine or Thomas Aquinas. Many advocates of the secularization thesis seem happy to accept highly optimistic estimates of the level of religiosity in medieval Europe. It does not seem unreasonable when judging the level of religiosity in modern America to take people at their word—and accept that if people describe themselves as being religious, then they are religious.

BLAIR'S ALTERNATIVE

Bush's America makes a mockery of the idea that advanced societies inevitably become more secular. But what about Europe? On the face of it, Europe stands at the other end of the spectrum, irretrievably secular. But look a bit deeper and you can see glimmerings of a religious revival: Europe is more likely to move in America's direction than America in Europe's.

Blair's unwillingness to discuss religion was understandable. In his history of Europe, published in 1996, John Roberts argued that "the Europe once coterminous with Christendom is now post-Christian and neo-Pagan."[43] "In Western Europe we are hanging on by our fingernails," observed the Reverend David Cornick, the general secretary of Britain's United Reformed Church, in 2003. "The fact is that Europe is no longer Christian."[44] In a 2004 survey, 44 percent of Britons claimed that they had no religious identification whatsoever, a number that had grown from 31 percent in 1983. Two-thirds of people age eighteen to twenty-four described themselves as nonreligious—and almost half of these young adults didn't even believe that Jesus existed as a historical figure. Over half of British weddings in a typical year are civil rather than religious. The best-known born-again Christian in Britain is Cliff Richard, an endearingly naff pop singer famous for singing about remaining a bachelor boy, who has not translated well into many other countries.

And Britain is a nation of God botherers compared with most European countries. Only one in ten people in France and two in ten in Germany say that religion is "very important" in their lives (compared with one in three in Britain).[45] Only one in twenty people in France attend a religious service once a week.[46] Overall, only 21 percent of Europeans say that God plays an important role in their lives, compared with 60 percent of Americans (and 90 percent in many Muslim countries).[47] Catholic priests are a dying breed. In Dublin, home to a million Catholics, precisely one priest was ordained in 2004.[48]

Still, there are a few glimmers of light on the horizon. Those glimmers are brightest to the east. In Poland, more than 70 percent of the population regularly go to church. In Orthodox countries, religion also plays a strong role: 98 percent of Greeks belong to their church and Orthodoxy is also reviving in Russia, where there are 3,500 Web sites and scores of magazines and newspapers.

But there are some signs that faith is reviving in Western Europe too. Over two million Britons, with an average age of twenty-seven, have taken the Alpha Course, "an opportunity to explore the meaning of life." The course began at Holy Trinity Brompton, a posh church in Kensington, just around the corner from Harrods, and is now taught in over seven thousand churches in Britain and fifteen thousand worldwide, including many in the United States. The number of adult confirmations in the Church of England has risen sharply even as the overall number has fallen. Pilgrimages are booming. Some one hundred thousand hikers a year make the trek across Europe to Santiago de Compostela in Spain and six million people visit Lourdes.

Immigration is playing a dual role in Europe's religious economy. First, the arrival of millions of Muslims is making many lapsed Christians more aware of their religious inheritance. Nominal Christians are much more likely to practice their faith in areas where there are lots of Muslims. Second, mass immigration is bringing in millions of Christians from the developing world as well. On any given Sunday in London, 44 percent of the people going to church are African or Afro-Caribbean, and another 14 percent are nonwhites of other descent.[49] Britain's most successful preacher is arguably a Nigerian missionary, Pastor Matthew Ashimolowo. He founded Kingsway International Christian Center in East London, with a congregation of a few hundred, because he wanted to provide immigrants with the high-octane style of worship that they were used to back home. He now preaches to five thousand worshippers in his Miracle Center auditorium—a larger crowd than you can find in Westminster Abbey or St. Paul's Cathedral—as well as thousands more on cable television and radio.[50] Immigration is even transforming the once-staid Catholic Church in Britain: a church of "nobs and navvies" is now also catering to Africans, Poles, Cameroonians, Latin Americans and Filipinos.

There are also a couple of trends that are familiar from America. First, religious people in Europe reproduce more enthusiastically than secular people, which gives religion an important long-term advantage. Eric Kaufmann calculates that in the most secular parts of Europe, France and the Protestant north, the "nonreligious" majority (currently 53 percent) will peak at around 55 percent in 2040.[51] Thereafter, the proportion of religious people will increase, thanks to their higher fertility.

Second, there are also important changes on the supply side of the religious economy: European religion is finally being privatized. David

Hume used to feud with Adam Smith about the latter's keenness on opening up the religious marketplace. The anticlerical Hume disliked the idea
of "each ghostly petitioner" competing and thus finding "some novelty
to excite the languid devotion of his audience"; he favored an established
clergy that had been "brib[ed] into indolence."[52] Grace Davie, of the University of Exeter, argues that there are two religious economies in Europe.
In the old one, religion is "a public utility": there is one state-backed supplier, and most Christians follow their religion vicariously (in the sense
that somebody else does your churchgoing for you). For instance, around
75 percent of Swedes are baptized as Lutherans, but only 5 percent regularly go to church. The church pockets a staggering $1.6 billion in mem-
bership fees, collected by the state through the tax system. It has been rare
for Swedes to opt out, though that seems to be changing. In Denmark 83
percent of the population is officially linked to the Folkekirke (people's
church); fewer than 2 percent attend church regularly.[53]

Alongside this old religious economy, a new economy, based on personal choice, is growing. Together Evangelicals, charismatics and Pentecostals accounted for 8.2 percent of Europe's population in 2000, nearly
double the proportion in 1970, according to the *World Christian Encyclopedia*.
Pentecostalism is France's fastest-growing religion. London's immigrant-
packed East End is thought to have twice as many Pentecostal congregations as Church of England ones. Evangelicals and charismatics are also
reviving the older religious economy. Richard Chartres, the Bishop of
London, uses Alpha veterans to "rechurch" areas of his diocese.

The optimists point out that Europe's churches are roughly as full as
America's were before the First Amendment separated church from state:
all you need to do is unleash the market and religion will revive. This argument should not be taken too far. Philip Jenkins (who actually believes
that Christianity will stage a mild comeback) points out that many European countries have long had relatively free markets in religion. There
are no rules preventing you from setting up a new church in Britain, for
example: people just haven't felt the call. More than just market forces are
at work in European secularism. One factor is a deep-rooted cultural hostility, irrigated by ridicule and contempt. Another is the fact that the state
provides more social services in Europe, reducing the demand for faith-
based welfare services.

On balance, a revival of religion in Europe is likely to be one of intensity as much as numbers. An important figure in this regard is Benedict XVI. There is evidence that the pope would prefer a smaller but more vibrant Catholic Church in Europe. "The mass church may be something lovely, but it is not necessarily the Church's only way of being," the former Cardinal Joseph Ratzinger once remarked. He has also spoken in favor of what Arnold Toynbee once called a "creative minority."[54] Indeed, Ratzinger's church would appear to bear some resemblance to the "two-speed" European Union: a committed inner core of true believers with a broader group of fellow travelers.

Some worry whether this will reduce the Church's appeal (one leading European politician, who is a Catholic, nicely describes it as being too committed to a "core-vote strategy"). But this shift in emphasis underlines a change in the way that Catholicism views itself. After embracing modernism in the 1960s with Vatican II, the Church has now returned to a more traditional version of the faith, first under John Paul II and now under Benedict. Rather than modernizing Catholicism, the Church wants to Catholicize modernity. "A church that marries the contemporary world soon finds itself a widow," argues one of Benedict's advisers. That often means being more political. Benedict has courted controversy by criticizing Islam. In 2006 the Archbishop of Paris unleashed a storm by denouncing France's annual telethon: raising money was fine, warned the archbishop, but not for the destruction of human embryos (i.e., for stem-cell research). British Catholics, who now outnumber Anglicans, fought bitterly against laws forcing them to let gay couples adopt.

Pope Benedict's relationship with Jürgen Habermas also points to another intriguing development: religion is beginning to return to intellectual life in Europe. Habermas has long been one of the secular left's philosopher kings, a neo-Marxist who once described himself as "tone deaf in the religious sphere." Yet he agreed to a wide-ranging debate with the future pope in 2004 about the Christian underpinnings of Western civilization and the role of reason and religion in a free society. By common consent, the cardinal not only held his own; on the topical issue of whether religion should be part of the European ideal (the debate about the European constitution was in full sway), Benedict won. Or at least Habermas wrote articles later admitting that there had to be some value system.[55]

In fact, Habermas had been moving in that direction. Three weeks after September 11 he shocked the European intellectual establishment by giving a speech arguing that secular society needs to acquire a new understanding of religious convictions. "The liberal state has only expected the believers among its citizens to split their identity as it were into public and private elements," he complained. "It is they who must translate their religious convictions into a secular language before their arguments have any prospect of being accepted by a majority."[56] In 2002 he published a searing critique of biological engineering and human cloning, *In Defense of Humanity*. Habermas appeared to think that traditional religion might perform the same role that socialism had once done in preventing society from being overwhelmed by the demands of capitalist consumerism. Habermas now talks about the emergence of "post-secular societies." He also argues that tolerance is a two-way street—secular people need to tolerate the role of religious people in the public square as well as vice versa.

Indeed, much more certain than the revival of Christianity in Europe is the idea that religion will play a larger role in the European public square. The rise of European Islam makes this unavoidable. "Eurabia" may be a gross exaggeration, but as we shall see in chapter twelve, it is clearly playing an outsized role in the Continent's politics, on everything from Danish cartoons to French headscarves to the fundamental question of whether Turkey should join the European Union. More generally, just as in America, European politicians are being forced to address cultural issues. What is the role of the family? How far should biotechnology go? The next few years will see dramatic advances in our ability to manipulate our genetic code—to clone ourselves, or cure diseases, or enhance our mental and bodily powers. It seems unlikely that these advances will not produce a response from people who take their morality from the Bible.

Blair was also less isolated as a politician of faith than he sometimes seemed. He was succeeded by another prime minister with a religious core: Gordon Brown is a "son of the manse," who claims that he learned his socialism listening to his preacher father's sermons (several every Sunday). Before becoming president of hypersecular France, Nicolas Sarkozy published *La République, Les Religions, L'Esperance,* in which he called for a greater role for religion in public life. Poland's Law and Justice Party was elected on the promise of a "moral revolution"; one of its coalition partners declared that its program was "based on the social teaching of the Catholic church"; the speaker of the Polish Parliament used to cross himself before he sat down. Even Canada, which has traditionally prided itself on its European *froideur* toward religion, as in so much else, is now led by an Evangelical, Stephen Harper.

OBAMA'S WORLD

It would be foolish to claim that Western Europe is becoming as religious as America; or that you will soon be able to identify right-wingers from left-wingers in London by asking how many times they go to church, as you can in Houston. But the American model seems to have more staying power. The same forces that are reviving religion in America—the quest for community in an increasingly atomized world, the desire to counterbalance choice with a sense of moral certainty—are making headway in Europe. And as people increasingly choose what sort of religion they follow, they are going to make more noise about it.

Barack Obama might even end up being an advertisement for the choice-based version of religion. The clever but confused young metropolitan searching for meaning and finding it in a Chicago church is likely to prove a much more compelling story for a European audience than Bush's battle with the bottle in the Texas oil patch.

If Obama becomes a symbol for the world's "seekers," then once again the Hawaiian will be riding a wave rather than creating one. Look around the world and the exception is plainly not today's America but postwar Europe. Despite the most hectic modernization in world history, faith is flourishing—and in many cases that faith has distinctly American characteristics. We will soon turn to the subject of the spread of American-style faith, and the problems that entails. But first we will examine the American model in more detail. Why are so many Americans drawn to God?

PART TWO

GOD'S COUNTRY

❧ ❧

CHAPTER FIVE

PRAY, RABBIT, PRAY:
SOULCRAFT AND THE AMERICAN DREAM

❧❧

THE MAN STANDING in the parking lot looks like a cross between a country-and-western singer and a professional wrestler. He wears mirrored sunglasses, a tasseled shirt, bright blue jeans and a belt with a huge buckle in the shape of a Texas longhorn. He is nearer to seven feet than six feet tall, and built like an ox. But he is neither a singer nor a wrestler; he works for one of the biggest Baptist churches in Houston.

Twenty years ago Houston's Second Baptist Church was a single building with an aging congregation. Today it is a religious boomtown full of boisterous young families. The parking lot has space for a Wal-Mart's worth of vehicles—and even in the middle of a Tuesday afternoon it is far from empty. Thirty-five American flags flutter from giant flagpoles in front of the complex. The "worship center" seats more than five thousand people. And this is only the church's flagship campus: there are four other campuses scattered around this sprawling city (though, admittedly, one of them meets in a multiplex cinema).

Every Sunday more than ten thousand people attend services, which start early in the morning and continue until late at night. (People who cannot attend can catch Ed Young, the senior pastor, on radio and television.) They embrace an uncompromising brand of Christianity. Southern Baptists live by a strict code, foreswearing tobacco, drink and cursing (at least on Sunday morning). They also subscribe to a literal interpretation of the Bible: an eye for an eye means just what it says.

The towering guide proudly displays the church's facilities, each time emphasizing how big and new they are: a school for over twelve thousand students, a day-care center, basketball and racquetball courts, an air-conditioned walking track, a bowling alley, a bookshop, a cafeteria, a twenty-four-hour-a-day phone bank, and the guide's particular favorite, a huge American football field complete with floodlights. Why all these facilities? "They are hooks for the Lord. One moment these kids are out on the streets. The next they're playing soccer over there. Then we've got them praying. We're reeling in thousands every year. And we're not going to stop until we've hooked every man, woman and child in the country." The giant Texan pauses. "And you? Have you been saved?"

There is nothing unusual about Second Baptist Church. It is not even the biggest church in Houston: that honor belongs to Lakewood Church, which has a congregation of forty-five thousand and has taken over the stadium of the Houston Rockets to accommodate its flock. There are megachurches across much of America—and they are getting bigger by the day. Some of the services they provide are just about convenience—crèches where you can drop off your children during services, restaurants where you can grab a bite to eat. Others are about social life—everything from youth clubs to sports facilities to restaurants. One Arizona megapreacher once expressed the hope his church would feel so much like a shopping mall that visitors would say, "Dude, where's the cinema?"[1]

Some critics dismiss megachurches as "country clubs for the sanctified."[2] But the churches clearly fulfill a pressing social need. Peter Drucker, the doyen of management gurus, thought "the large pastoral church" took over from the company as the most significant organizational phenomenon in the second half of the twentieth century.[3] Just as the Methodists helped unite frontier America, megachurches are doing the same for the suburbs, creating social bonds for otherwise atomized suburban man. They also do a lot of social work that in other countries is done by the state: rehab for addicts, counseling for couples who are going through marital problems, shoulders to cry on for people who have lost loved ones, help for battered women, support for people who are going through financial problems. They are certainly full of "hooks for the Lord." But they are also anchors in a mobile society and life rafts for the distressed.

GALTON'S HALF-TRUTH

In 1872 Francis Galton, one of Victorian England's great polymaths, published his *Statistical Inquiries into the Efficacy of Prayer.* Nobody has prayers said on their behalf more than kings and queens, he pointed out. But sovereigns "are the shortest-lived of all who have the advantage of affluence."[4] Nobody prays more than clergymen do. But they are no more long-lived as a consequence. Galton concluded flatly that prayers don't work.

Galton's skepticism has been widely shared by intellectuals. For several centuries they have argued, with growing fervor, that religion is a collection of tall stories that will disappear as human knowledge advances. But lately something surprising has happened in the groves of academe. Having noticed that religion shows no sign of disappearing, scholars from a wide variety of disciplines have decided to investigate the phenomenon. Galton's successors in the hard sciences are demonstrating that religious experiences are "real"—in the sense that they are associated with changes in brain patterns; that there is a correlation between religion and health and happiness; that faith is a powerful generator of social capital; even (irony of ironies) that religion helps in an evolutionary sense. This intellectual revolution suggests that far from being pushed aside by modernity, religion is thriving as a solution to many of modernity's problems. In a world of ever greater competition, displacement and opportunity, faith has become a useful (though obviously not necessary) attribute for prosperous people. But religion also fulfills a role lower down in society, providing support for those who have lost out in global capitalism or feel bewildered by it. Faith acts as a storm shelter.

HOW GOD WORKS

A small but growing band of neurobiologists has taken to studying the links between the brain and spirituality. Andrew Newberg, a professor of radiology at the University of Pennsylvania, has been putting nuns and Buddhist meditators into a scanning machine (separately, of course) to measure how their brains function during spiritual experiences. He discovered that religious experiences have a profound impact on the brain: both nuns and meditators showed heightened activity in the frontal lobes of the brain when they were in spiritual states. Newberg also studied Pentecostals while they were speaking in tongues and discovered exactly the opposite phenomenon—a marked decline in activity in the frontal lobes.

The Buddhists also caught the attention of Richard Davidson, a professor of psychology and psychiatry at the University of Wisconsin, Madison. He scanned the brains of highly trained meditators and discovered that they had the highest synchronization among their neurons that he had ever seen in healthy humans. It seems that meditators are right to claim that the practice can produce "Karma."

A third researcher, Patrick McNamara, the head of the Evolutionary Neurobehavior Laboratory at Boston University's School of Medicine, works with people who suffer from Parkinson's disease, an illness that is caused by low levels of a messenger molecule called dopamine in certain parts of the brain. McNamara discovered that people with Parkinson's had lower levels of religiosity than healthy individuals, and that the difference seemed to correlate with the disease's severity. It seems that there may be a link between dopamine levels and religiosity.[5] And, like all these studies, this makes it harder to dismiss religion as a mere "illusion," as Freud once put it.

At the same time social scientists have produced a mountain of evidence that religion is good for you—that it promotes various measures of well-being and helps to deal with social deviance. Daniel Hall, a doctor at the University of Pittsburgh Medical Center, has discovered that weekly church attendance can add two to three years to your life. Religion is not quite as good for you as regular exercise (which can add three to five years) or cholesterol-lowering drugs (which can add two and a half to three and a half years).[6] But it is certainly better for you than agnosticism. "There is something about being rooted in a religious community," he argues, that is associated with "a substantially longer life expectancy." A study of 7,000 older people by the Duke University Medical Center in 1997 found that religious observance might enhance immune systems and lower blood pressure. In 1992 only three medical schools in the United States had programs examining the relationship between spirituality and health; by 2006, the number had increased to 141.[7] Harvard Medical School's continuing education courses on spirituality and healing draw thousands of people a year, many of them members of the medical profession or clergy. Magazines such as *Science & Spirit* and *Spirituality & Health* attract contributions from respectable writers.

Religion also seems to be correlated with happiness. One of the most striking results of Pew's regular survey of happiness is that Americans who attend religious services once or more a week are happier (43 percent very happy) than those who attend monthly or less (31 percent) or seldom or never (26 percent). White Evangelical Protestants are more likely to report being very happy than white mainline Protestants: 43 percent compared with 33 percent.[8] The correlation between happiness and church attendance has been fairly steady since Pew started the survey in the 1970s; it is also more robust than the link between happiness and wealth. Attending religious services weekly, rather than not at all, has the same effect on people's reported happiness as moving from the bottom quartile to the top quartile of the income distribution—and is a lot easier to do.

Religion can combat bad behavior as well as promote well-being. Twenty years ago Richard Freeman, a Harvard economist, found that black youths who attend church were more likely to attend school and less likely to commit crimes or use drugs. Since then a host of further studies, including the bipartisan 1991 National Commission on Children, have concluded that religious participation is associated with lower rates of crime and drug use. James Q. Wilson, perhaps America's preeminent criminologist, summarizes a mountain of evidence from the social sciences succinctly: "Religion, independent of social class, reduces deviance."[9]

The obvious objection to these studies is that they deal with correlation rather than causation. Jonathan Gruber, a secular-minded economist from the Massachusetts Institute of Technology and an alumnus of the Clinton administration, has tried to find a way around this in a study of church attendance and economic well-being. Gruber started off by noting that people are more likely to go to church if their neighbors share their faith. Poles in Boston (where there are lots of Catholics) are more likely to attend mass than Poles in Minneapolis (where there are more Protestants). He then discovered that a 10 percent increase in the density of coreligionists leads to an 8.5 percent rise in churchgoing, and that a 10 percent increase in the density of coreligionists leads to a 0.9 percent rise in income. Poles in Boston not only go to church more often than Poles in Minnesota, they are also materially better off. This led him to conclude that it must be religious attendance that is driving the difference in income.

Gruber suggests that there are several possibilities why this might be the case. One is that going to church yields "social capital": you establish close relationships with people, which produces trust and makes business easier to transact. A related possibility is that church members enjoy mutual emotional and perhaps financial insurance. That allows them to recover more quickly from a setback, such as the loss of a job; it also saves them from falling between the cracks in the welfare system. A third possibility is that faith and wealth are linked through education. Higher church attendance leads to more years of education. The best churches also promote religious schools that in turn promote higher educational standards. The final possibility is that religious faith is wealth-producing in its own right: the faithful are less worried about life's many travails and thus better able to prosper.[10]

The Gospel of Social Capital

The idea of "social capital" is at the heart of much of the new thinking about religion. Religion seems to provide social bonds in a world in which so much conspires to produce alienation and anomie. There are remarkably few places nowadays where adults can meet and take a trusting relationship for granted. The workplace is competitive. Neighbors are often strangers. The sort of local bars where "everyone knows your name" are rarities in suburbs and bedroom communities. Many fraternal organizations are shadows of their former selves. Churches offer a safe place where people can get to know each other and pool information and expertise.

They put people with problems in contact with people with solutions. They do all this in a very American way: through informal connections rather than bureaucratic fiat.

Robert Putnam, one of America's leading sociologists, has been struck by religion's contribution to America's social capital. In *Bowling Alone: The Collapse and Revival of American Community* (2000) he argues that almost half of America's civic associations were linked to religion in some way. He also suggested that religious-based social capital was probably more durable than secular-based social capital.[11]

Religion's contribution to social capital is particularly striking in the charitable world. Academic research consistently shows that both "frequency of church attendance and membership in church organizations correlate strongly with voluntary service."[12] Arthur Brooks, a former professor at Syracuse University and now the head of the American Enterprise Institute, calculates that, in 2000, religious people gave about 3.5 times more money a year to charity than secular ones, and volunteered more than twice as often. All in all, about a third of America's quarter trillion dollars a year in charitable donations go to religious activities, and about a quarter of volunteer hours go to religious causes. Even a third of secular volunteers—people who do not volunteer for specifically religious activities—argue that their decision to volunteer is related to the influence of religion.

Several evolutionary biologists have also picked up on the theme of religion's ability to reinforce social bonds. The question that puzzles them is what hidden purpose all this worshipping and ritual-following performs. Religion is a ubiquitous phenomenon. It can be found in all human societies. But it also consumes huge amounts of time and resources—and frequently compels people to do things that are pretty irrational from the evolutionary point of view (such as abstaining from sex). What evolutionary function can it serve?

One explanation is that religion is a complicated signaling mechanism. The fact that signs of religious commitment are hard to fake means that they provide a reliable signal to others in the group that people who are engaging in them are committed to the group. Free riders cannot easily trick their way into membership. For instance, Richard Sosis, of the

University of Connecticut, compared nineteenth century American communes, some religious and others secular. He discovered that the secular communes were up to four times more likely than religious ones to dissolve in any given year. He also found that stricter religious communes—as measured by rituals and taboos—had a better chance of surviving than laxer ones. The same principle did not apply to secular communes: what mattered was not just the strictness of the rituals but the fact that the rituals were sanctified. Sosis's theory also held true with contemporary kibbutzim: the religious kibbutzim were better capable of surviving stress than the secular ones.[13]

The notion of social capital may help to explain two of the biggest puzzles of the secularization debate: Why is America so much more religious than Europe? And why is religion on the rise in so many modernizing societies? There appears to be an inverse relationship between the generosity of the welfare state and the success of religion: the more generous the secular welfare state, the more it will "crowd out" religious-based charities and reduce the demand for religion in general. Jonathan Gruber and Daniel Hungerman estimate that church spending on charity fell by as much as 30 percent in the United States in 1933–39, and that almost all of this decline can be accounted for by the expansion of government activity.[14] Nobody has yet produced such a careful study of the impact of Europe's welfare state on religion. But it seems reasonable to conclude that Europe's much more generous welfare state did far more to "crowd out" religion than FDR's New Deal.

It is likely that the rest of the world will follow America's example rather than Europe's. Many developing countries are simply too poor to afford Europe's generous welfare provisions. And even those that are rapidly improving their living standards, such as South Korea and China, have a strong cultural aversion toward providing their people with European-style welfare. Religiosity may well be a rational response to a combination of two things: the turmoil of modernity and the weakness of other social safety mechanisms. In this chapter we will look at the way religion works in two very different versions of America—in the prosperous suburbs and exurbs, and in the deprived inner city.

THE ANGSTROMS AND ANGST

Americans have always been a people in motion. The country was settled by pioneers who were willing to brave a fathomless ocean for principle or profit. Its most visible symbols have been of motion—from wagon trains to the iron horse, from the Model T to the space shuttle. Many of its greatest books have celebrated mobility, from *Westward Ho!* to *On the Road*. Tocqueville described America as a place where "a man builds a house in which to spend his old age, and he sells it before the roof is on; he plants a garden and [rents it out] just as the trees are coming into bearing."[15]

Today America is the only rich country with a dynamic population. In the twentieth century America's population grew by 270 percent, compared with Britain's 60 percent. Over the past decade the number of Americans has risen from 263 million to more than 300 million—the fastest growth in forty years (and faster than developing countries such as China, Brazil and South Korea). Some 35 million Americans were born abroad. One in six move house in any given year (nearly one in three for twenty-year-olds). Twenty-two metropolitan regions have more than doubled in size over the past twenty-five years, with Las Vegas jumping by 250 percent. These sorts of boom cities simply do not exist in Europe.

America's belief in progress and upward mobility explains much of its dynamism. But it also makes social bonds hard to forge and harder to maintain: John Updike's novels about Rabbit Angstrom examine the dark side of Jack Kerouac's "on the road" freedom. Americans work harder than anyone else in the advanced world—as much as three hundred hours more a year than Europeans—but they change their jobs more frequently. And while Continental Europe celebrates social solidarity and Asia values extended family ties, Americans fall back on themselves: they spend some $700 million on self-help books every year.[16]

The United States is the first country in history to classify more than half its population as suburban. That brings every material convenience from two-car garages to spacious rec rooms. But suburbs can also display a soul-destroying homogeneity—from the cookie-cutter McMansions to the anonymous big-box discount stores. Three decades ago Jane Jacobs, an admirer of traditional cities, observed that "every place becomes more like every other place, all adding up to Noplace."[17] Tom Wolfe remarked in *A Man in Full* (1998) that "the only way you could tell you were leaving one community and entering another was when the franchises started repeating and you spotted another 7-Eleven, another Wendy's, another Costco, another Home Depot." This was actually too kind: the recurrence of these corporate franchises is determined by the economics of distance rather than anything as human as "community."

The family once provided a haven in this heartless world—a refuge from the Sturm und Drang of economic competition. But today the family is no more stable than the rest of the culture. About half of American marriages end in divorce or separation. Twenty percent of all first marriages hit the rocks after just five years. Roughly one in three children live with a single parent—and single-parent families are much more likely to suffer from poverty and social problems than two-parent families.

This is where "soulcraft" comes in. By "soulcraft" we mean religion's ability to offer a helping hand where help is lacking. But we also mean something more than this. We mean religion's ability to provide purpose where life might seem purposeless, and community where community is lacking. Religion is more than just faith-based social working. It is a comprehensive solution to both practical and psychological problems. That is why we have dubbed it "soulcraft." We will start off our examination of soulcraft not in a church but in a giant organization in Colorado Springs that specializes in helping families.

SOULCRAFT AS PARENT CRAFT

Focus on the Family looks like a regular corporate office park: a series of redbrick buildings separated by spacious parking lots and neatly manicured lawns. There are no obvious signs that its main business is soulcraft: no giant crosses, no huge statues of Jesus. Indeed, nowadays it is arguably not best known for that: its founder, James Dobson, is one of America's most prominent culture warriors—a staunch supporter of conservative Republicans and uncompromising denouncer of gay marriage.

Yet politics are not really what either Focus or Dobson should be remembered for. Dobson came from a family that helped set up the Church of the Nazarene, a small Christian denomination, in the early twentieth century. His father was an itinerant preacher who spent years on end on the road. Dobson attended a small Nazarene college in Pasadena, California, where he fell in love with psychology. He got his Ph.D. from the University of Southern California and took up his practice at the university and at the Children's Hospital. But the 1960s radicalized him. As a psychologist, he was confronted every day with the victims of the permissive society, in the form of unhappy children; as a "conservative of the heart," he became convinced that moral relativism was destroying the very foundations of Western civilization. The root cause of this crisis of civilization was the breakup of the family. "Marriages were disintegrating rapidly and youth problems were multiplying just as fast," he later reflected. "I became convinced that only a full-fledged return to the Judeo-Christian concepts of morality, fidelity and parental leadership could halt the erosion of the family unit."[18]

In 1970 the budding Jeremiah published *Dare to Discipline,* a countermanifesto about child-rearing techniques. The book could hardly have been better timed. Benjamin Spock, the child-rearing guide to the baby-boom generation, had become a full-time antiwar campaigner and expressed public sympathy for the Soviet Union. Meanwhile, white middle America was convinced that society was spinning out of control, driven mad by drug addiction, rampant sexual experimentation, black-power bullies, single-issue activists, long-haired weirdos, peaceniks and if-it-feels-good-do-it hedonists. Drawing not just on the Bible but on psychology, Dobson spoke out strongly against permissive child-rearing methods, rooting his own advice in traditional moral values and even supporting corporal punishment.

Dobson was soon besieged by people who wanted to know more. He quit his day job as a professional psychologist in order to become a full-time oracle. An hour-long television show called *Where's Dad?* in 1981 increased his fame. As his organization grew, for a while he contemplated

teaming up with a successful young preacher down the road in Orange
County—Rick Warren. But he decided that he had had enough of California: in 1991 he transplanted his family and staff to a green-field site
in Colorado Springs, which was becoming a mecca for Evangelical businesses of every kind.

In media terms, Focus is a giant megaphone. Dobson's long-running
Focus on the Family radio program has twelve million listeners in America
and two hundred million worldwide. Most of his two dozen books have
been best-sellers. Focus's mailing list exceeds four million people. The
organization was a video production company that churns out DVDs;
magazines for every conceivable demographic, from preteens to single
parents, that reach two million readers a month; millions of monthly bul-
letins that appear in churches across the land (often as inserts in Bibles
and prayer books); and conferences on everything from teenage angst to
homosexual temptations. Focus translates Dobson's radio commentaries into twenty-six languages for broadcast around the world. Most of
Dobson's two hundred twenty million foreign listeners live in China, so
local Focus people adapt them for the Chinese context. Dr. Doo, as he is
known in China, is then broadcast on huge state-run outlets, including
China National Radio.

However, the heart of the business remains counseling. The organization receives so much mail—more than thirty-six thousand letters a
week—that the city has provided it with its own zip code, 80995. Altogether, more than seventeen million Americans have contacted Focus
since its foundation in 1977—the equivalent of the combined population
of the cities of New York, Los Angeles, Chicago and Houston. Focus's
campus attracts two hundred thousand visitors a year. A Family Institute
accommodates about eighty college students each semester. Numerous
outreach efforts are made to organizations (such as churches and crisis
pregnancy centers) and groups of people (such as doctors, blacks, baby
boomers). There are Focus affiliates in eighteen countries, including Australia, Costa Rica, Egypt, Ireland and South Africa.

Focus plainly represents a backlash against the permissive society. But
Dobson is a more complicated figure than the crude disciplinarian and
conservative theocrat of public caricatures. He thinks that Spock made

some good points. He advises parents that it is futile to try to prevent their children from masturbating. He accepts that many women need to work to support their families. He has no theological objection to birth-control pills. He has infuriated many social conservatives by refusing to join the campaign against using Ritalin to cure attention-deficit disorders. In his radio broadcasts he comes across more like a kindly uncle than a fire-and-brimstone preacher. If his approach to politics is confrontational, his approach to therapy is emollient.

Dobson likes to think of himself as a man's man. He is fond of shooting and fishing and hero-worships Churchill. But his real genius is for empathizing with women—their frustrations with their monosyllabic partners and their sense that they are being overwhelmed by ever-multiplying commitments. Married women with children age twenty-nine to fifty-nine make up most of Focus's audience, and much of the organization seems specifically designed to deal with the unhappy, stressed-out, overworked soccer mom, phoning in tears from the SUV, having just dropped the kids off at school.

To begin with, every call to Focus's 1-800 number is answered by a real human being in a maximum of three rings. (Focus employs a staff of 120 people to answer the phones.) If the distressed mother arrives in person, she discovers a cornucopia of delights (from a puppet stage to a climb-aboard replica of a B-17 bomber) to distract attendant children. There are around 10,000 requests for advice a day. Most are for books, tapes or pamphlets, which are duly dispatched from a huge computerized warehouse. But around 10 percent of incoming calls require more expert attention—and are routed to a counseling center, where licensed therapists, social workers and a couple of chaplains are waiting. The distress calls might deal with anything from suicide attempts to spousal abuse to addiction to marital breakdown. The advisers give what help they can before referring the callers to one of 1,500 Christian therapists across North America. Each call and letter is logged so that Focus can build a relationship with each writer and caller.

One secret of Focus's success lies in its balance between modern technology and eternal verities. Dobson deals with the oldest questions on the planet—why can't my wife stand me? am I drinking too much? why are my children turning into monsters?—but he deals with them using the latest technology and the most efficient management methods. He changed Christian radio by making it interactive: anybody who took the trouble to write to him got a timely and to-the-point reply. Focus is Christian to its core—every workday begins with morning devotions, with the entire workforce, from the managers to the people who stock the warehouse, breaking into small groups for prayer—but it is equally rooted in the social sciences. Focus employs licensed psychologists and refers its clients to licensed therapists. A typical Focus publication will quote some piece of psychological research on one page and the Bible on the next.

None of this means that Focus is perfect. In Colorado Springs, many locals talk about the organization as if it were a cult. Dobson has been accused by gay-rights groups of misrepresenting data, and criticized by various psychologists and psychiatric outfits. Focus was forced to lay off as much as a fifth of its workforce in late 2008 because it spent so much money campaigning in favor of California's proposition eight, which banned gay marriage in the state. Indeed, Dobson may well have overreached himself politically, with younger soccer moms finding his tirades about gays distasteful. Many of them seem to have moved on to Rick Warren's kinder, gentler "purpose driven life." But the basic model—religion as balm for the suburban soul—endures.

Jesus, CEO

Soulcraft is also entering the American workplace, with some companies adopting overtly Christian principles, still more making room for religion during working hours, and corporate America in general trying to deal with a growing desire that work should offer "meaning" as well as just a paycheck.

America's executive class is probably its second most religious elite in the country after the senior military. Over the past decade plenty of bosses have outed themselves as committed Christians, including the current or former heads of Tyson Foods, Wal-Mart, Raytheon, Alaska Airlines and Blockbuster and, in the Catholic column, the founder of Domino's Pizza.

Lower down the ladder, many towns now have "faith networks" for businesspeople, sometimes run by full-time Evangelical activists. Will Messenger, a former management consultant, runs the Boston chapter of the Business Leadership and Spirituality Network, which brings small groups of CEOs together for monthly dinners and breakfast prayer meetings. The CEO Forum, which was formed in 1996 and is now run by a former Focus on the Family fund-raiser, is designed to help CEOs who run companies with revenues in excess of $100 million to address their spiritual concerns.

Bosses are becoming more open about bringing their faith to work. Lou Giuliano, the former boss of ITT Industries, used to have a plaque in his office that read, "Bidden or not bidden, God is present."[19] The relentlessly entrepreneurial Wayne Huizenga says that he prays for his employees almost every day.[20] The former CEO of Alaska Airlines encouraged his caterers to place cards with Bible verses on every meal tray.[21] Tom Monaghan reserved an entire wing of the Domino's office complex in Ann Arbor, Michigan, for Catholic apostolates, including the Thomas More Society, the Spiritus Sanctus Academies, and Legatus.

Not all the Christian CEOs work out as role models. Both Bernie Ebbers, the former boss of WorldCom, and Ken Lay, the late head of Enron, used to make a huge fuss about their "faith commitments," but ended up on the wrong side of the law. Yet the number who try to run their companies on biblical lines seems to be increasing. Tyson employs an ordained minister as an executive coach.[22] Mark Dillon, the president of Tampa Bay Steel Corporation, tries to solve difficult corporate problems—what should he do about a delinquent customer? should he sack an underperforming employee?—by consulting the Bible.[23] He also provides Bible classes for his employees and Bible camps for their children during the summer. Riverview Community Bank in Otsego, Minnesota, styles itself as a "Christian financial institution," with a Bible buried in the foundations and the words "In God We Trust" engraved in the cornerstone. One of the bank's business tenets, according to its annual report, is to "use the bank's Christian principles to expand Christianity." The bank's founder sometimes "lays hands" on his customers, prays with them when they take out mortgages, helps them to be "saved," and even performs faith healings.[24] ServiceMaster, a moth-proofing company, is so-called because the founder wanted to remind employees that they are "serving the master," Jesus Christ.[25]

Some Evangelical-run companies go even further. Preferred Management, a home-health-care company based in the Midwest, puts Jesus at the center of its organization chart: all department heads report to Him. The company also requires its employees to read the Bible daily, as part of mandatory self-improvement classes, and to share their religious experiences in daily meetings.[26] Interstate Batteries, a Texas-based company, runs company-sponsored mission trips to places like Mexico and Russia. (The employees pay a portion of their own travel expenses and give up some of their holidays.)[27] Chick-fil-A, a fast-food chain that is particularly successful in the South, exists not only to sell chicken sandwiches but also "to glorify God by being faithful stewards of all that is entrusted to us and to have a positive influence on all who come in contact with Chik-fil-A." The company's restaurants are closed on the Sabbath. Employees hold religious services every Monday at corporate headquarters. The company also sponsors church meetings at its annual meetings.[28]

A growing number of big corporations are making it easier to bring religion into the workplace, regardless of their CEO's religious preferences. The trendsetter has been Intel, thanks in part to the fact that its chief technology officer, Patrick Gelsinger, is a Christian who has written a book on faith and work. Other big names have followed suit, including PepsiCo and Coca-Cola, allowing employees to gather for prayer groups (or "higher power lunches," as some people have dubbed them). There is a particular bull market in corporate chaplains. Tyson Foods has more than a hundred of them (most of them part-time).[29] America can even boast a professional association, the National Institute of Business and Industrial Chaplains, and a booming rent-a-chaplain market. Marketplace Ministries and Corporate Chaplains of America can both fulfill your "emergency chaplain needs."

The growing religion-and-business nexus is having all sorts of side effects. A small industry has grown up to fuel the "faith in work" movement, with newsletters, blogs, books with titles such as "God@Work" and "Loving Monday" and a nine-hundred-strong network of "workplace ministries."³⁰ Thomas Nelson, the main religious publisher, created a subdivision devoted to business books in 2003. America has several God-flavored business schools such as Notre Dame's Mendoza College of Business, the Marriott School of Management at Brigham Young University and the Cox School of Business at Southern Methodist University. At Mendoza, faculty meetings start with a prayer; at Marriott, students pray before every class. The schools cater mainly to business-minded Evangelicals and Mormons, but their concerns, especially about business ethics, have won them an audience in the secular world as well.

Why this upsurge in religion in business life? The legal foundations were laid not by George Bush but by Bill Clinton. In 1997 Clinton issued a White House directive that allowed federal employees to engage in "religious expression" at work to the same extent that they were allowed to engage in "non-religious expression." If you could stand around the water cooler talking about last night's game, you could also talk about how Jesus had changed your life. But the bigger question is why there is so much enthusiasm for talking about Jesus at the water cooler. The underlying reason is that America's general quest for meaning is affecting life inside the office as well as outside. Evangelical bosses talk about the importance of focusing on what is important in a world that is dominated by work, money and the pell-mell of daily decisions. The more turbulent business life becomes, Evangelical businessmen argue, the more important it is for them to anchor their life in family and religion. More Mammon-minded businesspeople tie it to the search for talent (Evangelicals are better educated than most Americans) and the chance to offer workers a way to find meaning—whether it is the fulfillment that comes from making a "cool" product, as at Apple, or the satisfaction that comes from fulfilling the old Christian injunction that *laborare est orare*.

American Evangelicals are particularly keen on seeing work as a "calling." They resist attempts to draw a sharp distinction between their public and private lives, and talk about how their careers are extensions of their religious lives. Seventy percent of Evangelicals claim that their religious beliefs have either a "large" (40 percent) or "some" (30 percent) impact on the jobs they choose. As Miroslav Volf, director of Yale's Center for Faith and Culture, points out, the more people choose their religion, rather than just inherit it, the more likely they are to make a noise about it: "It used to be that workers hung their religion on a coat rack alongside their coats. At home, their religion mattered. At work, it was idle. That is no longer the case. For many people religion has something to say about all aspects of life, work included."

The emphasis on "meaning" and "calling" is tied up with the rise of "compassionate capitalism." Evangelicals are generous with their money. Michael Lindsay obtained data on the giving habits of eighty-four Evangelical business leaders. Their collective charitable donations amount to about $143 million in any given year. Evangelical foundations are also becoming more ambitious and professional. The National Christian Foundation, an Atlanta-based charity, has so far distributed more than $1 billion to various Christian causes. Several banks also offer specialized advice to Evangelical savers and investors who want to avoid sinful investments, and various forms of Christian financial planning businesses.

The pressure of modern business is also blurring the line between work and leisure. Americans now work a month a year more than they did a decade ago. They uproot themselves in search of jobs, breaking with their neighborhood churches. They are tethered to their BlackBerrys day and night. They find themselves in lonely airport hotels on behalf of their company. The quid pro quo for this is that they do not feel any guilt about surfing the Net at work, or engaging in a bit of Internet shopping, or taking some time off in the middle of the day to go to the gym. It is only natural that religion should be one of the many "private" activities that has to find expression at work because there is so little time for it at home. Evangelicals are less shamefaced about admitting to their faith in the office. There is a lot of joking about "coming out of the closet" and admitting their true identities to their colleagues.

This has a lot to do with the general upward mobility of the Evangelical community. "Evangelical" is no longer a code word for an uneducated hick. The more that business tycoons and national celebrities are willing to identify themselves as Evangelical, the more rank-and-file workers are happy to attend Bible groups and talk openly about their faith.

THE PHILADELPHIA STORY

If religion seems to work in the McMansions and office suites, it also addresses very different issues at the other end of American society. Philadelphia is about as different as you can get from Houston or Colorado Springs—a proud Northeastern city that is steeped in American history and divided into long-established neighborhoods. If Houston's problem is unrestrained growth, Philadelphia's is relentless decline. The city's earlier preeminence drained away as political power shifted to Washington, DC (thanks to a political deal), and financial power shifted to New York (thanks in part to Andrew Jackson's refusal to recharter the Second Bank of the United States). More recently, Philadelphia lost a quarter of its population in the second half of the twentieth century as whites fled to the suburbs or the Sunbelt. The city has recovered a little: the revitalized downtown is one of the most attractive city centers in the United States. But the city continues to lose population and many of the local statistics are bleak: twenty thousand abandoned properties, ten thousand abandoned lots, a hard core of schools that are characterized by the government as "persistently dangerous." Phoenix, Arizona, recently passed Philadelphia as America's fifth-largest city.[31]

There are all sorts of reasons for thinking that a city that was founded by William Penn as a quasi-utopian religious experiment should have succumbed to the acids of modernity long ago. The likes of Weber and Durkheim argued that cities were some of the great disenchanters of the world. And the Northeast is the most European part of the United States—far less God-obsessed than the religious South and the awakening West. Yet soulcraft is central to life in Philadelphia too.

Ram Cnaan, a secular-minded sociologist at the University of Pennsylvania, has produced one of the most thorough studies of religion anywhere in America in *The Other Philadelphia*. Philadelphia has more than two thousand churches. They are the only voluntary institutions that span the entire urban landscape, rich and poor, and the only ones that provide a wide range of social services free of charge to anybody who needs them.

Forty-five percent of the population are active members of these congregations.[32] But that understates their influence: there are several "multiplier effects" at work in the religious economy. Churches help a large number of people who are not formal members of the congregation. Each church member is linked, in various ways, with a large number of friends and acquaintances. (A member knows a man who knows a man who can help out.) Collective worship and frequent social engagements make for powerful social bonds.[33] Cnaan concludes that the city's churches constitute nothing less than "a massive force, almost a social movement, of doing good locally and beyond." And this "massive force" is arguably growing in strength as the public sector retrenches and other voluntary organizations wither.

Philadelphia's congregations are primarily religious organizations, of course. They bring people together to pray and reflect, to study the Bible and listen to sermons. It is notable that, even in a relatively liberal city, religious people like their spirituality strong. There are more fundamentalist (15.7 percent) and conservative congregations (39.7 percent) than moderate (34.1 percent) and liberal (10.5 percent) ones.[34] The Southern Baptist Convention planted some twenty-three new churches in the city in 2000–2003.

At the same time, the congregations also provide an enormous amount of social assistance. More than 90 percent of the city's congregations provide a social service of one sort or another, with the average church providing three different types of program. Just as the churches come in all sorts of shapes and sizes, from megachurches to tiny storefront chapels, so do the services they provide. Some programs are huge coordinated enterprises, but one small Pentecostal church simply collects money from the congregation and gives it to poor people when they come in. Yet one common feature is flexibility. There is less red tape than government programs (and thus less humiliation for the recipients). Good works are not quite mandatory but they are more than just impulses: they are part of the weft of Christian life in Philadelphia.

The most common form of help is to feed the hungry. Churches run 220 of the city's 350 food pantries. Six of them also provide soup kitchens.[35] The second most common form is child care, ranging from looking after abandoned children to routine after-school care. (Armies of children are left to fend for themselves in the empty hours between the end of the school day and the end of their parents' workday.) Churches provide alternatives to hanging out on the streets—with all the attendant temptations—or vegetating in front of the television. Another focus is the homeless: one church allows one or two homeless families to live in the church building and use the church kitchen. Many run hostels. Churches also look after the homebound. It is common for churches to have a dedicated group of people who spend their time visiting such people or offering them lifts.[36]

Almost half the city's churches provide medical care of one sort or another, a huge boon in a country where the provision of health care for the poor is patchy, to put it mildly. Several churches provide free vaccinations. Many pastors educate their flocks about how to take care of themselves better. Philadelphia's churches are cornucopias of counseling.[37] Many parishioners are happier to see counseling as an extension of spiritual guidance than as an arm of modern psychology. About three-quarters of AA meetings are held in church properties.[38]

Two other focuses are poverty and prisoners. The Northwest Philadelphia Interfaith Hospitality Network links twelve congregations together in an effort to deal with homelessness. This means more than just putting a roof over people's heads. It means getting them back onto their feet and into permanent accommodations.[39] Clients are given all the assistance they need to find a home (including access to telephones and computers). But they are also expected to prepare their own meals and clean up after themselves and have a maximum of three months before they will have to move on. Two other groups, Amachi and REST Philly, try to help the families of prisoners—especially their children. With one in fifty Americans likely to spend some time in prison during their lifetimes, almost 1.5 million children under eighteen have a parent in prison. Half of these are under ten and 20 percent under five.[40] These prison orphans not only suffer from the psychological scars of having a jailbird for a parent, they are also pretty likely to be brought up in poverty. The children of prisoners are six times more likely than people in the general population to end up in prison themselves.

A disproportionate number of these children are black—reflecting the huge role churches play in the life of black Philadelphia, a population that has more problems than the population in general, and is more inclined to turn to the church for help. In *The Philadelphia Negro* (1899), W. E. B Du Bois, a pioneering black scholar who worked at Philadelphia's Wharton School, captured the centrality of the church to black life:

> As a social group the Negro church may be said to have antedated the Negro family on American soil; as such it has preserved, on the one hand, many functions of tribal organization, and on the other hand, many of the family functions. Its tribal functions are shown in its religious activity, its social authority and general guiding and coordinating work; its family functions are shown by the fact that the church is a center of social life and intercourse; acts as newspaper and intelligence bureau, is the center of amusement—indeed, is the world in which the Negro moves and acts. So far-reaching are these functions of the church that its organization is almost political.[41]

Churches were the hub of black America from the very first. They created schools, credit unions, banks, insurance companies, funeral parlors and housing projects, and served as schools for budding politicians and academies for budding musicians. They were, in short, a nation within a nation and a state within a state.

They continue to play an equally vital role today. Sixty percent of America's black adolescents live in one-parent households and 12 percent live with their grandparents. Fifty-six percent of blacks live in cities, most of them in areas where crime is rife and schools are poor.[42] More than 80 percent of blacks believe that the church has improved the condition of black America. Philadelphia's black churches are more likely to provide social services than white churches. They figure particularly largely in the lives of black women, many of those women grandmothers, who bear more than their fair share of the burden of keeping the black community together. Seventy-one percent of the members of black churches are women, compared with 59.3 percent for white churches, thanks largely to the exorbitant incarceration rates of black men.[43]

Latinos are equally hard hit by urban blight: 40 percent of Puerto Rican children, the largest Latino group in the city, are being brought up by single parents. So far Latino churches have not been as successful as black churches in providing social services. Only 31 percent of Latino church members take part in church-based activities other than worship compared with 41 percent of whites and 47 percent of blacks.[44] But this probably reflects the fact that Latinos are relatively new and the social infrastructure is less well established. The place where the churches plainly do make a difference is assimilation. They provide newcomers—legal or illegal; churches are not in the business of discrimination—with friendly faces and familiar landmarks. They provide legal assistance, financial help and what Du Bois called "intelligence"—the necessary tools to rise in America. Church attendance is positively correlated with all sorts of virtues, such as school attendance and parental involvement with children: Latino parents who attend church spend more time reading books to their children and taking them to libraries.[45]

Put all these social services together and Cnaan calculates that it would cost the city a quarter of a billion dollars a year to replace all the work done by the churches.[46] But he also produces a more compelling way to express the same observation: imagine what Philadelphia would be like without religion. Some of the most pristine structures in the city would be replaced by gas stations and run-down apartments. Former addicts would have nowhere to go to hold their 12-step meetings. Scout troops would be homeless. Latchkey children would haunt the street corners. More hungry and homeless people would be roaming the streets and begging for money. The most vulnerable people—inner-city blacks, the poor, grandmothers struggling to raise children—would be left without a vital source of support. The concrete jungle would be more of a jungle than ever.

THE GOD SQUAD

To see what soulcraft means in practice, consider the Faith Assembly of God in northeast Philadelphia. This is about as far as you can get from a "country club for the sanctified." The church is a patched-together building in one of the toughest areas of the city. Many of the local buildings, including the next-door store, are boarded up and dilapidated. Several nearby lampposts are hung with teddy bears and dolls, makeshift memorials to murdered children. "This is not a good area," says a nervous taxi driver. "Drugs and prostitutes and shootings. There's no way I would come here at night."

Pastor Richard Smith is dressed in camouflage trousers, a camouflage belt and a T-shirt emblazoned with the words "Prevention, Treatment, Justice." He and a group of parishioners built the church four years ago. (Before that they had to make do with an even more unprepossessing building.) The basement is full of ancient computers, television sets and video games that they have managed to scrounge. An ex-prisoner is at work turning the attic into a studio where youngsters can make music.

Pastor Smith tells the story of his life. He was brought up in a fatherless home in Detroit. But he was also brought up in the faith—as a member of the Pentecostal Church of God in Christ—and he started preaching on the streets when he was fifteen: "loving the Lord and wanting to reach souls." As a young man he traveled around North Carolina with an older preacher, holding revival meetings in tents ("I've always been drawn to father figures"). He went to Valley Forge Christian College, in Phoenixville, Pennsylvania, before moving to Philadelphia.

As he talks he is constantly interrupted. A heavily tattooed man walks in looking for food for his friends. Pastor Smith hands over a pile of pizzas. A couple of boys are at loose ends. Pastor Smith tells them to hang around and gives them some Doritos. His mobile phone keeps ringing—a crime suspect needs advice on a court appearance; somebody needs a lift home from the hospital; there has been a big shooting over in the projects.

He dates his social activism from his decision, as a new pastor, to try to clean out all the local crack houses. He was met with violent resistance from the resident crackheads—including one man who brandished a sawed-off shotgun. But he kept going. Wasn't he frightened by all the violence? He says that he believes that a miracle-working God will protect him. The man who pulled the shot gun on him joined his congregation and is now a long-distance truck driver.

But Pastor Smith discovered that closing down crack houses was only the beginning of his problems. Where do all the convicted crackheads—and their children—live? How do they keep body and soul together? And how can you encourage them to give up crack for the straight and narrow? The more he became involved with the problem, the more he had to do to treat it. And crackheads were only the beginning. There were latch-key children with nowhere to go (and plenty of drug dealers to provide them with employment). There were ex-prisoners who were dumped in the streets. There were abused and homeless women and young children.

The church has grown into an all-purpose crisis relief agency. The soup kitchen is open seven days a week. A church hostel houses twenty-two homeless men. (Pastor Smith originally housed them in the basement before acquiring a nearby property.) Pastor Smith also has a clothes bank, a toy bank and an emergency kitty to help people buy bus passes and the like. The church is a first port of call for just-released prisoners: the local police frequently bring them to the church doorstep and unlock their handcuffs. The church tries to provide them with everything from accommodation (it has six apartments for ex-cons) to jobs to valid ID (it is a felony in Philadelphia not to carry a valid ID, but it does not seem to have occurred to the prison authorities to provide its ex-charges with even this most rudimentary ticket to returning to normal life).

The church also specializes in outreach to the area's youth, who are beset by the temptations of street crime and the drug culture. It provides a place to go for young people who are at loose ends after school or on weekends. (Making Christian-themed rap music is a particular passion with the church's younger members.) The church holds tent revival meetings with free burgers. And it has two yellow buses that tour the area providing "sidewalk Sunday schools."

Faith Assembly of God is a monument to the power of what Edmund Burke called the "little platoons." Every member of the hundred-strong congregation volunteers for something or other, and many of the most enthusiastic volunteers are people Pastor Smith has saved from the abyss. Several ex-prisoners helped to build the church, for example. Periodically the entire congregation dresses in military fatigues—their T-shirts proclaim that they are "The God Squad: on Duty for Jesus"—and tries to clear the neighborhood of drug activity. They perform rap songs that praise the power of the Lord rather than the attractions of sex, drugs and violence. They hand out food and toys to the street kids who make ends meet as lookouts for drug lords.

The church is also plugged into other volunteer networks. Pastor Smith works with other organizations that deal with young delinquents or chronically homeless people. He sends his toughest drug addicts to free drug rehabilitation programs or to Victory Outreach, a California-based organization that specializes in dealing with hard-core cases. (Several of the pastors and deacons in a nearby Victory Outreach Church are former drug dealers and addicts.) "Some people are just too crazy for us," he says.

For all the power of voluntarism, Pastor Smith is living on the edge. Some 95 percent of his family's income comes from his wife, who is a psychiatrist. "I'm blessed that she works so that I can do what I'm doing," he says. His family is currently trying to save enough money to reopen the women's hostel, which he was forced to close down when the city reclaimed the lease. ("They flipped the scrip on us," he says.) The church makes $1,000 a month from selling disused washing machines and other metal objects that church members find in the streets. Pastor Smith admits that he gets depressed when somebody he has helped breaks in and robs the church, as had happened recently.

The pastor is also aware that it is not enough to deal with the symptoms of social problems. You need to go to the cause. His view of the root cause is surprisingly similar to James Dobson's (and it would seem Barack Obama's): the breakdown of the family. Three-quarters of the children in the area are brought up by one-parent families. Men impregnate women and then refuse to accept responsibility for their children.

Children and parents are so clumsy with their emotions that they cannot create committed relationships. Family quarrels often escalate out of control. (The majority of homicides are committed by people who know each other.) The pastor's sermons hammer away at this theme—accept responsibility for your actions, learn to make commitments to other people, keep your families intact. The church, he argues, is the catalyst of family renewal and community regeneration: crisis management needs to evolve into soulcraft.

AN ANSWER TO GALTON

The evidence from both Houston and Philadelphia, as well as a growing pile of academic studies, is that Galton's disproof of the "efficacy of prayer" is misguided. It seems that religious experiences can be "real" to the people who enjoy or endure them: they are connected with changes in the activity of the brain. It also seems that religion serves lots of social functions, functions that are becoming no less relevant as a result of "modernization." It helps suburbanites to form communities in the atomized world of the Sunbelt. It helps ordinary people all over America to deal with the problems of alcoholism and divorce, wayward children and hopelessness. And it helps the hard-pressed inhabitants of the inner cities to deal with the chaos that surrounds them, inspiring extraordinary acts of dedication from the likes of Pastor Smith and inspiring all sorts of desperate people to turn their lives around.

It is hard to see any flagging in the demand for soulcraft anytime soon: some of the problems it deals with are perennial and some are likely to intensify as the world becomes more turbulent. Part of the genius of America, and one of the things that distinguishes it so sharply from Europe, is that it is outstandingly good at producing a supply of soulcraft to deal with the demand. It is to that supply side that we now turn as we look at one of America's biggest businesses.

CHAPTER SIX

THE GOD BUSINESS:
CAPITALISM AND THE RISE OF RELIGION

❧

THE SIGNS at the Nashville airport welcome visitors to "Music City, USA." It might be worth adding a few signs welcoming them to "Faith City," or "Jesus City," or even, perhaps, "Southern Baptist City." Nashville is not just a global powerhouse in the country music business. It is a global powerhouse in the religion business, as well. The buckle in the Bible Belt is the home of the Southern Baptist Convention, otherwise known as the Vatican of America's largest Evangelical organization, and the home of Thomas Nelson, the world's biggest producer of Christian books, as well as hundreds of churches and religious businesses.

Nashville's founding fathers wanted the city to be the "Athens of the South." The city's columned Capitol and elegant Parthenon certainly make it America's greatest center of Greek revival architecture; and Vanderbilt University, where Al Gore studied theology, has long put it in the first division of southern college towns. But the cultural tenor of the city is more Appalachian than ancient Greek, defined by populist politics (Andrew Jackson based his career in Tennessee) and redneck culture. The Grand Ole Opry House, a country music venue, has forty-four hundred seats; the local metropolitan opera just thirty-eight hundred.

Tennessee was once "a sink of iniquity, a black pit of irreligion," according to Lorenzo Dow. But a succession of Great Awakenings turned it into one of the most religious states in the nation: in the nineteenth century Tennesseans flocked to camp meetings, where they prayed for weeks on end, and once they were fully converted they built a huge infrastructure of churches and chapels. During the Scopes trial, H. L. Mencken mocked Tennessee as a land of bigots and buffoons. But the bigots and buffoons clung to their beliefs regardless.

Today Nashville has more than seven hundred churches—more per capita than any other American city. Sixty-five percent of people in Davidson County, where Nashville sits, describe themselves as religiously affiliated. The religious tenor of the place is Protestant and Evangelical. There are more members of the Church of Christ (8 percent) than Roman Catholics (4.2 percent) and more Southern Baptists (20 percent) than anything else. The city houses the headquarters of the Southern Baptist Convention. Every year ten thousand to twelve thousand delegates converge on the city to attend the SBC's annual convention, the largest in the country. The city also houses the SBC's huge commercial arm, LifeWay Christian Resources, whose building sports a 108-foot-tall cross.

Appropriately enough, the Southern Baptist Convention building is situated on Commerce Street. Nashville is the place where God and Mammon happily coexist. Some of the religious businesses are service businesses catering to the local faithful: 7 percent of the city's business travelers are part of faith-based groups. But, as with country music, Nashville produces most of its religion business for export. Nashville is America's biggest religious publishing center, producing more Bibles than any other city in the world, largely thanks to Thomas Nelson. LifeWay Christian Resources, formerly the Baptist Sunday School Board, claims to publish more religious materials than any other organization: it is also the country's second largest operator of Christian bookstores, with 127 stores around the country; and it runs conferences and summer camps. The United Methodist Publishing House is one of the largest publishing houses in the world. There are also lots of other, smaller businesses that specialize in supplying religious materials to churches.

The city's two great passions are often intertwined. God is a staple theme of country music greats such as Hank Williams ("Jesus Remembered Me," "Jesus Died for Me" and "How Can You Refuse Him Now?")

and Johnny Cash ("I Talk to Jesus Every Day," "Personal Jesus" and "It Was Jesus"). And the post–September 11 period produced a surge of country-flavored religiosity. Carrie Underwood, one of the winners of *American Idol*, sang "Jesus, Take the Wheel." Randy Travis's "Three Wooden Crosses" rose to the top of the *Billboard* country music chart. Tim McGraw's "Live Like You Were Dying" tells the story of a man who, having been told that he has just months to live, takes the opportunity to "finally read the Good Book" as well as to take up skydiving, rock climbing and riding on a mechanical bull.

The Nashville region is littered with vivid examples of the marriage of God and country. One is the Nashville Cowboy Church, which is presided over by Dr. Joanne Cash Yates, a blood relation of the great Johnny, and, like him, a survivor of a broken marriage and a spell with alcohol and drugs. The church's regular broadcasts reach "millions with the Gospel of Jesus Christ and Christian Country Music." Another is Trinity Music City, a Christian entertainment park complete with TV studios, a concert hall, a theater and, of course, a church.[1]

The Competitive Advantage of American Religion

Alfred Marshall, one of the founders of modern economics, once remarked that some skills seem to be "in the air" in certain cities and regions. Marshall was referring to steelmaking in Sheffield. But his analysis also applies to computing in Silicon Valley, design in the Prato region of northern Italy and filmmaking in Hollywood. These are all places where people live and breathe the local specialty, where consumers, producers and suppliers all cluster together, where you cannot get a cup of coffee without hearing about "the business."

The religion business is clearly "in the air" in Nashville—as it is in a remarkable number of other American cities. Go to Fort Lauderdale (home of the Coral Ridge Ministries), Orlando (home of Campus Crusade for Christ and the Wycliffe Bible Translators), Dallas (home to a fine collection of megachurches), Virginia Beach (home to both Pat Robertson and the late

Jerry Falwell's Liberty University) or Colorado Springs, and you feel much the same sort of presence: there are a lot of people in the God business.

Michael Porter, one of America's most prominent management gurus, elaborated on Marshall's insight in *The Competitive Advantage of Nations* (1989). He pointed out that different countries have different competitive strengths (strengths that are reflected in their propensity to produce clusters of world-beating firms in particular industries). The Germans excel in high-quality engineering and chemicals, for example, the Japanese in miniaturization and electronics. Porter argues that competitive advantage is rooted in a country's past. A long history of excellence in one area—pharmaceuticals in Switzerland, for example—produces highly competitive firms and highly sophisticated consumers. The educational system becomes geared to producing workers for successful industries. (The Netherlands has specialized research institutions in flower growing and packaging, for example.) And consumers tend to keep the producers on their toes.

Another vital ingredient is a large number of competing firms. This helps create a flourishing world of suppliers and employees: Los Angeles is chockablock with acting coaches, stuntmen, costume designers, electricians and eye-catching waitresses. Producers are kept on their toes by sophisticated customers. Again and again the quality of the home market has had a disproportionate impact on a firm's capacity to stay ahead of the game. The Japanese have a sophisticated audience for cameras, the Germans for cars, the Italians for clothes, the Americans for entertainment; and these sophisticated customers keep a constant pressure on producers to innovate and excel.

All this is self-sustaining. Companies can hire better people because the educational system is geared to their needs. They can produce innovative products because they have first-class producers and demanding consumers. They can plow money back into education and training, because they reap the rewards of a global market, but they can also use their heft to put pressure on universities to deliver what they need. The more deeply rooted these advantages, the more difficult it is for would-be competitors to catch up with these companies. The competitors would have to build not only a firm but an entire culture.

America amply fulfills all Porter's criteria for competitive advantage when it comes to religion. The country was founded by religious refugees. The constitution mandates a free market in religion. And the combination of relentless innovation and high immigration means that the market is as varied as it is competitive. The *Yearbook of American Churches* for 2005 lists some 217 different church traditions. The American religious marketplace is almost a study in perfect competition: there are no real barriers to entry, the domestic market is big enough to support a mind-boggling variety of religious producers, and new religious entrepreneurs are always rising up to challenge incumbents.

America has the world's largest pool of religious consumers, with more than 225 million church members, according to the *Yearbook*. It also has the world's best religious infrastructure—from religious schools and colleges to religious broadcasters. America has religious specialists of every conceivable variety—an Association for the Development of Religious Information Systems, an Association of Statisticians of American Religious Bodies, a Christian Management Association with its own magazine and audiotape library. The *Yearbook* lists twenty different Baptist governing bodies, twelve different Lutheran bodies, and thirty different Pentecostal bodies. It also lists more than four hundred different religious periodicals.

The American landscape is littered with examples of the country's remarkable religiosity: giant crosses (an illuminated one in Effingham, Illinois, is 198 feet high), billboards warning that "Hell is real," statues of Jesus. *In Roadside Religion: In Search of the Sacred, the Strange and the Substance of Religion* (2005), Timothy Beal, of Case Western University, has provided a fascinating catalogue of some of the weird and wonderful things that you can come across if you rent an RV and go on a pilgrimage across America.

Fields of the Wood, in Murphy, North Carolina, the headquarters of the Church of God of Prophecy, contains the world's largest Ten Commandments (reputedly visible from outer space), the world's largest altar (eighty feet wide) and the world's largest New Testament (thirty feet high and fifty feet wide). Holy Land USA, in Bedford County, Virginia, is a two-hundred-fifty-acre scale replica of the land of the Bible during Jesus' time. The Ave Maria Grotto, in Cullman, Alabama, contains miniature replicas of Jerusalem, St. Peter's in Rome and numerous famous sacred buildings. Cross Garden, in Prattville, Alabama, is an eleven-acre collection of homemade crosses and discarded kitchen appliances. Many of the crosses bear signs reminding people of their fate ("You will die") while the kitchen appliances bear signs pointing out that there are no modern conveniences for sinners in the basement of the afterlife ("No ice water in hell! Fire hot!").

Even miniature golf has caught religion. The Golgotha Fun Park in Cave City, Kentucky, boasts a biblically themed miniature golf course, starting with the Creation at the first hole and ending with the Resurrection at the eighteenth. The Lexington Ice Center & Sports Complex, down the road in Lexington, goes two better with three biblically themed golf courses, the Old Testament, the New Testament and Miracles.

America's religious marketplace has all the features of competitive success. Salesmanship? People like Rick Warren and Joel Osteen are unrivaled when it comes to selling their ideas. Innovation? The Catholic Eternal Word Television Network (EWTN) distributes Catholic programs from a television studio in a monastery in Alabama. Economies of scale? America has huge churches that combine their resources in gigantic parachurch organizations. Product proliferation? There is a different church or religion for every possible market niche. The Scum of the Earth Church in Denver, Colorado, focuses on society's outcasts, or people who like to think of themselves as outcasts, such as homeless people, punks, skaters and ravers. Customer focus? American churches provide their "customers" with everything from cinemalike seats to cafés to crèches. Children can munch on Oreo-and-milk communion wafers or eat birthday cakes for Jesus on Christmas Day. Product variety? You can find everything from Buddhist sects to feuding branches of Judaism in any reasonably-sized city. Branding? The Rock in Evergreen, Washington, sponsors a local rodeo bull chute. Every time a cowboy rides out of the chute the announcer hollers the church's name.[2] Market opportunity? Packaged Facts, a market-research company, estimates that the "religious products" market was worth $6 billion in 2008, compared with $5 billion in 2004.

America leads the world in producing religious entrepreneurs—men and women who build thriving religious empires, often from nothing.

T. D. Jakes was born in a hardscrabble West Virginia mining town. His childhood was overshadowed by his father's lingering death from kidney disease, and he left school early to help support the family. But he had an overpowering sense of God—he was so fond of carrying the Bible around that his friends nicknamed him "Bible Boy"—and he established himself, even when he was still a teenager, as a part-time preacher with his own storefront church.

Jakes is now at the top of his business, a big, burly, jolly man, happy in his life and work, with a mesmerizing preaching style and a proliferating religious empire. His Potter's House Church, in Dallas, Texas, boasts a five-thousand-seat auditorium, a 34-acre campus, a membership of almost thirty thousand and a striking range of auxiliary businesses, including publishing houses, broadcasting networks and schools. His books, starting with his self-published *Women Thou Art Loosed,* the story of a young woman who was raped by her mother's boyfriend, have sold in their millions. A conference based on the book attracted 87,500 women to the Georgia Dome, breaking the attendance record previously held by Billy Graham.

Such popularity has turned him into a power broker. Jakes is a close friend of most of America's black leaders, not least the late Coretta Scott King, Martin Luther King's widow. He was one of the guests at the White House breakfast where Bill Clinton confessed to having sinned in his relationship with Monica Lewinsky. Both George Bush and Al Gore visited Potter's House in 2000, and Bush remained close to "T.J." throughout his presidency. It has also turned Jakes into a secular curiosity: that great national barometer, *Time,* has blessed him with a cover article.

Jakes's message is perfectly tuned to the rising black middle class. He preaches the virtues of self-help and upward mobility—one of his books is entitled *Reposition Yourself: Living Life Without Limits*—and he cheerfully practices what he preaches. He lives in a posh house in a Dallas suburb popular with oil magnates. He wears flashy suits and a diamond ring, and owns a Bentley and a private jet. That said, he also devotes attention to the casualties of the American dream—to drink and drug addicts, women trapped in abusive relationships and men and women who find themselves attracted to members of the same sex.

America's remarkable religious economy is a book in itself. The next two parts of this chapter will concentrate on two segments of it: first, the thriving market for religious products, particularly books and films; then the application of business techniques to the management of American churches.

Onward Christian Shoppers

The religion market is booming in America. The growth is most obvious in the media. The National Religious Broadcasters (NRB) represents sixteen hundred broadcasters with billions of dollars' worth of media holdings. Religious radio stations, most of them Evangelical, outnumber classical, hip-hop, R&B, soul and jazz stations combined. Christian rock is so popular that, in one issue of *South Park,* the foulmouthed heroes contemplate founding a Christian rock group called Sanctified to cash in on the trend. "All we have to do is sing songs about how much we love Jesus, and all the Christians will buy our crap."[3] There is so much Christian media that Sky Angel, one of America's three direct broadcast satellite networks, can carry thirty-six channels of Christian television and radio—and nothing else.

The definition of religious books is vague, but religious publishing is undoubtedly growing at a time when the publishing industry in general is struggling—and religion accounts for a striking number of the "megahits." The *Left Behind* series of novels on the end of the world has brought in $650 million. And, of course, the Bible is the best-selling book of all time—outselling all its rivals year in and year out, decade after decade.

Christian blockbusters of all sorts are dragging a flotilla of other Christian products in their wake—from "Praise the Lord" backpacks, in camouflage colors, to Christian dieting books such as Don Colbert's *What Would Jesus Eat?*; from *Rev!,* a magazine designed for pastors, to Christian horror novels. The boom in religious books is going hand in hand with a more general boom in spiritual books, as Americans, not least aging baby boomers, look for "meaning" in life—and imagine that the likes of Deepak Chopra will supply it.

The religious market is attractive for lots of reasons. Most obviously, there are millions of Christians. But it also comes with a ready-made distribution channel in the form of churches. (America has more than 330,000 of the Protestant variety alone.) Larry Ross, a Dallas-based consultant whose firm specializes in this market, points out that films based on the *Left Behind* series became hits without ever being screened in cinemas; churches showed them. Religious Americans are also willing to do much of the marketing, spreading the message by word of mouth. The *Left Behind* series, initially published by a tiny Chicago house, was passed from Christian to Christian. Mel Gibson promoted *The Passion* by talking to prominent religious figures, who then encouraged their flocks to purchase large blocks of tickets. And church stores filled their shelves with film-related products such as cross-nail pendants. *The Purpose Driven Life* became a surprise best-seller because it became a staple of church sermons and church study groups.

Greg Stielstra, Zondervan Publishing's chief marketing guru (who has to his name eighty-eight best-sellers, twenty-one number-one best-sellers and eight books that have sold more than a million copies), calls this "pyromarketing." Rather than promoting people through mass-market media such as television, pyromarketing relies on "consumer evangelists" who spread the word among like-minded people. (Rick Warren was furious that Stielstra used *The Purpose Driven Life* as an example of pyromarketing; he thinks that its success reflects its spiritual message, and its spiritual message alone.)

The rapid growth of the religion market is attracting a powerful new group of competitors—mainstream media companies. The first big company to spot the potential of the religion market was HarperCollins, which bought Zondervan back in 1988. Now almost all the big publishing houses have religious lines, most of them acquired in the past few years: Random House has WaterBrook and Hachette has FaithWords. Penguin published two new editions of the Bible in 2006, and HarperCollins created a specialized Bible imprint. One of the bright spots of EMI is its Christian music label. Hallmark Cards brought the Arkansas-based DaySpring, America's largest producer of Christian greetings cards, in 1999. NBC hired Amy Grant, a heroine of the Christian music world, to present one of its prime-time programs on Friday evening, *Three Wishes.* NBC also purchased the rights to broadcast *Veggie Tales,* a cartoon that features vegetable-shaped characters that impart a Christian moral message, on Saturday mornings. Not so long ago, people who wanted to buy Christian diet books or Christian detective stories had to go to specialist Christian stores. Now you can find them at your local Wal-Mart—along with a whole library of other Christian books.

Hollywood has been slower to react, thanks to a combination of institutional lethargy and cultural blinkers. Much of the pioneering work has been done by Christians who have enough money or connections to ignore the Hollywood culture. Phil Anschutz, a Denver-based billionaire, has created two production companies, Walden Media and Bristol Bay Productions, that support religious films. Mel Gibson funded *The Passion of the Christ* with his own money, but its success opened the industry's eyes to the moneymaking power of religion, grossing more than $365 million in the United States, despite dialogue in Latin and Aramaic and the lack of a major Hollywood distributor. For *The Chronicles of Narnia,* its version of the C. S. Lewis books, Walden teamed up with Disney, which had been a bogeyman among Evangelicals because of its penchant for organizing "gay days" at Disney World. Disney hired Motive Marketing, the company that promoted *The Passion,* to get the message to the Evangelical audience, particularly in churches and Bible study groups.

The industry's enthusiasm for religious cash also survived Gibson's anti-Semitic outburst in 2006. *The Passion of the Christ* and the two *Narnia* films are among America's biggest moneymaking films. Bristol Bay had a hit with *Amazing Grace,* a film about William Wilberforce and the abolition of the slave trade, which many Evangelicals liken to the crusade against abortion. What Joe Eszterhas, the screen writer of *Basic Instinct* who has since become a born-again Christian (presumably to atone for the appalling *Showgirls*), calls the "faith express" still has a long way to run. C. S. Lewis's children's books provide plenty of material for future films. Several mainstream studios have formed religious subdivisions such as Fox Faith; Sony has bought the rights to the *Left Behind* series.

Even churches have gotten in on the act. In October 2008, *Fireproof,* a film about a Christian firefighter, which cost just $500,000 to make, sneaked into fourth place at the American box office, with $6.5 million in sales.[4] The movie was the third film from Sherwood Pictures, which is tied to Sherwood Church in Albany, Georgia. The pastor was executive producer and the twelve-hundred-strong cast were mostly volunteers from the congregation. In the movie the hero's life is changed by reading a book called *The Love Dare* that uses a piece of scripture every day to teach couples how to love each other. Some six hundred thousand copies of a book called *The Love Dare* were rushed into print—and it became a best-seller. The star of the film, Kirk Cameron, had a role in the *Left Behind* series, though he might be best known to secular audiences as one of the youthful stars in the television show *Growing Pains*. Asked by *The New York Times* about how his Christian values survived in Hollywood, he replied, "As a teen idol who makes it to thirty-seven without being a crack-smoking transvestite stuck in a drug-rehab center over and over, I'd say, wow, those values have served me pretty well."[5]

OF MAMMON AND MURDOCH

The arrival of big corporations inevitably provoked some worry among Evangelicals about getting into bed with Mammon. There has been much talk about "Godsploitation." Zondervan is part of Rupert Murdoch's News Corporation, which has given the world the Page Three girls and *The Littlest Groom,* a television show about a dwarf trying to find love among women of various heights. Its sister publishing companies have included ReganBooks, which published *How to Make Love Like a Porn Star* by the experienced Jenna Jameson, and which flirted with publishing *If I Did It* by O. J. Simpson, and Avon, which publishes *The Satanic Bible.*

Back in 1992 some of the staff of Zondervan tried to buy out their company to preserve its purity. More recently, Evangelicals have been up in arms about the fact that Zondervan prints Bibles in China, because of that country's persecution of Christians. Many Evangelicals worry that traditional faith-based bookshops are being squeezed out of business—by big chains that can demand huge discounts and by mainstream agents who can poach religious writers with huge contracts.

In fact, the arrival of News Corp et al. has led to many fewer disasters than predicted. The behemoths have been sensible enough to give their religious subsidiaries plenty of latitude. Zondervan has lost none of its old character: it is still based in Grand Rapids, Michigan, and its corporate lobby is dominated by a life-sized bronze sculpture, *The Divine Servant,* showing Jesus washing Peter's feet. Random House set up its Water-Brook subsidiary in Colorado Springs, the command center of Evangelical America.

Meanwhile, the traditional faith-based media companies have fought back. They have the advantage of intense brand loyalty. (Across the American South it is common for Evangelicals to mark professional advertisements with a cross in order to attract the custom of fellow Evangelicals.) They are getting much more businesslike in the way they run their affairs, colonizing new markets, particularly for videos and video games, and invading old ones. If America's biggest media companies are pushing into the religion market, many of America's faith-based companies are pushing back, into the mainstream market. The Southern Baptist publisher Broadman & Holman, for example, had a mainstream hit with *Mission Compromised,* a thriller about covert operations by Oliver North, of Iran-Contra fame. "It's covert in its message and in its content and story line," its marketing man observed. "But it's also covert in the sense that it offers a clear message of hope through Jesus Christ."[6]

One of the best of the independents is in Nashville. Thomas Nelson is the country's largest Christian publisher, its second-largest Bible publisher after Zondervan and its ninth-largest publisher overall. The company's annual sales have increased from a mere $4 million in 1960 to $233 million today. The company's oeuvre includes plenty of Christian best-sellers, thirty-four hundred different Bibles, biblical reference products and study guides. Thomas Nelson has now established a secular imprint, WND Books, which publishes conservative authors such as Katherine Harris, a former Republican congresswoman, and Andrew Napolitano, Fox News's in-house legal expert.

Many smaller faith-based companies are rapidly upgrading their management skills. The old mom-and-pop outfits are being replaced by professional businesses that are, as publisher Jane Friedman, puts it, "profit and loss driven as well as mission driven." The Christian Booksellers Association helps its members plan marketing and publicity. Independent Christian publishers are clubbing together to form purchasing groups in order to compete with the big retailers. Larry Ross even provides advice on crisis management (which came in particularly handy for one of his clients, Billy Graham, when a tape was unearthed in early 2002 that had him exchanging anti-Semitic remarks with Richard Nixon in 1972).

This growing professionalism reflects a more general recognition that Christians need to come to terms with today's media-saturated culture if they are to get their message across. Biola University, a Christian university south of Los Angeles that is a stronghold of fundamentalism, once banned its students from watching Hollywood's products; now it has a flourishing mass communications department (and an alumnus who already has one hit film under his belt, *The Exorcism of Emily Rose*). Biola and Regent University both have state-of-the-art film studios. Act One, a Los Angeles–based group founded by a former nun, Barbara Nicolosi, provides two courses, one for aspiring Christian screenwriters and the other for aspiring Christian entertainment executives, oxymoronic though the latter may sound. George Barna, an Evangelical pollster, has launched BarnaFilms Preview Night, which allows Evangelicals to preview "significant" or "outstanding" new films.[7] Christian film festivals highlight the best in religiously inspired films, prayer groups steel would-be Christian producers and actors against the manifold temptations of La-La Land, and the Church on the Way in Van Nuys caters to Evangelical Hollywood figures, such as they are.

Christian entrepreneurs are also proving successful at borrowing ideas from mainstream American culture and adapting them to religious ends. America boasts several religious theme parks and museums. Christian Nymphos, an Evangelical Web site, offers an eye-popping guide to married sex, "spicy, the way God intended it," with information on everything from "anal sex: what does the Bible say?" to "tasting his fruit." Joseph "Reverend Run" Simmons, a former member of the hip-hop group Run-D.M.C., launched a "clean" reality show, *Run's House*, on MTV. "The show is like my pulpit," he says. "I want the world to get into spirituality and lead people to Christ."[8] *The Logan Show* is a Christian version of *Late Night with*

Conan O'Brien. A Christian men's magazine, *New Man,* features stories with titles like "Porn Again" and "A Porn King Finds God." *Christian MotorSports* recently featured an article on "outlaw bikers" discovering the Lord.

Left Behind: Eternal Forces, one of many Christian video games, offers you a choice between killing or converting enemy soldiers. Scripts Footwear gives you a chance to have your feet fitted with the "gospel of peace," or so the advertisements claim. Prayer Circle Friends, a clone of Build-A-Bear, allows children to assemble a stuffed animal and then insert a self-recorded audio chip of a prayer. Life of Faith dolls, a clone of American Girl dolls, portray ordinary girls throughout history who have displayed noteworthy acts of faith. There is even a clothing line called Jesus Is My Homeboy.

TOTAL SERVICE EXCELLENCE

The desire to blend Christianity with the modern world is more than a matter of marketing. It is a vital ingredient in Evangelical worship. Visit Willow Creek Community Church in South Barrington, Illinois, an upscale exurb of Chicago, for example, and you are immediately confronted with a puzzle: where in God's name is the church?

Willow Creek has every amenity you can imagine, from food courts to basketball courts, from cafés to video screens, not to mention enough parking spaces for 3,850 cars. But look for steeples and stained glass, let alone crosses and altars, and you look in vain. Surely this is a slice of corporate America rather than religious America? The corporate theme is not just a matter of appearances. Willow Creek has a mission statement ("to turn irreligious people into fully devoted followers of Jesus Christ") and a management team, a seven-step strategy and a set of ten core values. The church employs two MBAs—one from Harvard and one from Stanford—and boasts a consulting arm. It has even been given the ultimate business accolade: a Harvard Business School case study.

Willow Creek is only one of a growing number of Evangelical churches that are deliberately borrowing techniques from the corporate world. Forget about those local worthies who help out with the vicar's morning coffee and the flowers. American churches have started dubbing their senior functionaries CEOs and COOs. (North Point Church in Alpharetta, Georgia, even has an executive director of service programming.) Forget about parish meetings in which nice old dears throw out random ideas about how to keep the church going. America is spawning an industry of faith-based consultancies. In a nice example of how the lines between religion and business are blurring, John Jackson, the senior pastor of Carson Valley Christian Center, a "high-impact" church in Minden, Nevada, has taken to describing himself as a "pastorpreneur" (and has published a book of that title, to boost his consultancy).

Willow Creek is based on the same principle as all successful businesses: putting the customer first. Back in 1973 the church's founder, Bill Hybels, conducted an informal survey of suburban Chicagoans asking them why they did not go to church. He then crafted his services to address their concerns. He removed overtly religious images such as the cross and stained glass. He jazzed up services with videos, drama and contemporary music. And he tried to address people's practical, everyday concerns in his sermons.

This emphasis on user-friendliness continues to pervade the church. Hybels's staff tries to view their organization through the eyes of newcomers (or "seekers," as they call them). This means dedicating themselves to "total service excellence." The grounds—or what they call "the avenue of first impressions"—are impeccably kept, with the lawns mowed, the trees trimmed and the parking lot perfectly organized. The staff is welcoming without being over the top. ("Evangophobia" is a big worry.) The huge congregation is broken into lots of smaller "affinity" groups. Lots of "hooks" are used to attach seekers to the church.

Willow Creek has dozens of affinity groups for everyone from motorcycle enthusiasts to weight watchers. The church provides all sorts of social services, from counseling for alcohol and sex addicts to providing help with transportation, which is a serious problem in the far-flung exurbs. (The "CARS ministry" fixes up donated cars and then gives them to needy people, particularly single mothers; in case you hadn't guessed, "CARS" stands for Christian Auto Repairmen Serving.) The church also provides entertainment, from sports (hence its basketball courts) to video areas.

Willow Creek is particularly careful to make sure that everything is age-appropriate. The church provides child care for thousands of children every Sunday: this started out as a necessity (parents won't come if their children aren't taken care of) but has become a hook in its own right (parents can relax over the service while children are royally entertained). The church also has a youth auditorium. Willow Creek's adolescent members have taken over an entire hall, tearing up the carpet to expose the concrete floors, painting the whole thing black and littering video screens all over the place.

Across America churches now compete to provide "total service excellence." These pastorpreneurs don't just preach on Sundays. They don't just provide services for the great rituals of birth, death and marriage. They keep their buildings open seven days a week, from dawn to dusk, and provide a mind-boggling array of services: some megachurch complexes even contain banks, pharmacies and schools. Counseling and guidance groups are routine. So are children's ministries.

Part of "total service excellence" is serving every possible market niche. This is not just a matter of providing liberal churches for liberals and conservative churches for conservatives. There are biker churches for bikers, cowboy churches for cowboys, sports-minded churches for the sporty (Prestonwood Baptist Church in Plano, Texas, has eight playing fields and sixteen thousand people on its athletic teams) and gay-friendly churches for gays, such as the Cathedral of Hope in Dallas, which is famous, among other things, for its Great Annual Yard Sale (GAYS). Many seem prepared for every eventuality. Visit the First Assembly Church in Phoenix and they show you proudly a cupboard full of medical equipment they lend out to the needy. The World Changers ministries in Georgia offer help preparing for tests, filling out tax forms and buying houses (and even a network of mortgage brokers and real estate agents). Carson Valley Christian (motto: "Friends helping friends follow Christ") offers a seminar on how to slay the "Goliaths" of procrastination, resentment, anxiety, temptation and loneliness, presumably aimed at people who write books about the global revival of faith. It also offers classes in martial arts "the Christian warrior way."

All this emphasis on customer service is producing a predictable result:

growth. John Vaughan, a consultant who specializes in megachurches, argues that 2005 was a landmark year for church growth. This was the first time an American church passed the thirty-thousand-a-week attendance mark when Lakewood moved into its new home in Houston's Compaq Center—though, as we will see, it is still smaller than some churches in the developing world. It was also the first year that a thousand churches met the megachurch range. (Broadly you qualify if you get three thousand worshippers a week.) Willow Creek has seating for seventy-two hundred. And when they say "seating" they mean "seating": comfortable thrones with room for even the most expansive bottoms, not wooden pews.

Rapid growth brings all sorts of advantages in its wake. The most obvious is that it allows churches to put on megaspectacles. Willow Creek regularly invites celebrities such as Randy Travis, a country singer, or Lisa Beamer, the widow of Todd Beamer, the man who tried to take back United Flight 93 on September 11. Lakewood has a five-hundred-strong choir. Potter's House in Dallas has produced a Grammy Award–winning record. Westlink Christian Church puts on an outdoor display of extreme sports that includes skateboarders jumping over a fire in order to illustrate salvation.

Equally important is the fact that rapid growth allows pastorpreneurs, powered by a combination of large cash flows and economies of scale, to exploit every possible channel to get their message across. Joel Osteen, the chief pastor of Lakewood, a church that raises more than a million dollars a week in offerings,[9] has a television ministry that reaches seven million people around the world, and a best-selling book, *Your Best Life Now,* which was such an obvious money-spinner that his publisher provided him with a private jet for his book tour.[10] Warren's *The Purpose Driven Life* has spawned a huge follow-up industry of PDL books, tapes, courses and a CD of songs featuring a Christian chanteuse. Bishop T. D. Jakes, the chief pastor of the Potter's House, reaches two hundred sixty prisons a week via satellite.

Most successful churches seem to have almost as much high-tech equipment as NASA. Willow Creek has four video-editing suites. World Changers ministries has a music studio and a record label. The Fellowship Church in Grapevine, Texas, employs a chief technology officer (and spends 15 percent of its $30 million annual budget on technology). Worshippers don't have to worry about finding their place in the hymn book or catching cold in a draft. Computers project the words of the hymns onto huge screens, and the temperature is perfectly controlled.

SPOILED BY SUCCESS?

But this rapid growth brings problems in its wake too: problems that almost invariably end up forcing churches to become yet more business-like and management-obsessed. The most obvious problem is the simple one of managing size. You can't just muddle through if you have an annual income approaching $100 million (like Lakewood) or if you employ 450 full and part-time staff (like Willow Creek). You need to establish a proper management structure with finance departments and even human relations departments. You even need to start thinking—like Hybels—about the relationship between the religious leadership and the management team.

The other problem is subtler: how do you continue to speak deeply and directly to individual parishioners when you have a stadium the size of a football field? Some megachurches have begun to see some members drift away in search of more intimate organizations. And many mega-preachers have begun to worry that they are producing a tribe of spectators who regard religion as nothing more than spectacle. So they have begun to adopt techniques that allow churches to be both big and small, spectacular and intimate, at the same time.

One technique is to break the congregation down into small groups. Most big churches ask members of their congregation to join small groups of eight to ten people who have something in common (age or marital status, for example). These groups are not only designed to provide people with company, they are also designed to transform "baby Christians" into "mature Christians" and to produce the next generation of church leaders.

A second technique is to segment the religious market. Willow Creek has two very different services. The Sunday service for new "seekers" is designed to showcase the Christian faith in a "relevant and nonthreaten-ing way." Willow Creek estimates that half of the people who come to its services on a Sunday would otherwise be "unchurched." The Wednes-day service for people who are committed to Christianity is designed to deepen and refine their faith. By the same token, Willow Creek has two different seven-step growth strategies: an external strategy designed to bring the unchurched to church and an "internal" strategy designed to deepen the involvement of the churched.

A third technique is to set up satellite churches—a form of religious franchising. Willow Creek has set up several satellite churches in the Chicago area so that nobody has to travel more than fifty miles to get the Willow Creek message. (The thinking is that you should run into the same people in church that you do in the grocery store.) Life Church has franchised various campuses around the country. NorthWood Church in Keller, Texas, has fathered a hundred daughter churches.

Growth in religious organizations is proving just as addictive as it is in corporate ones. And once again these successful churches are reach-ing deep into business theory in order to feed their habit. They use stra-tegic planning and strategic visions to make sure they know where they are headed. They use branding to expand their market share: Willow Creek finished in the top 5 percent of one survey of 250 major American brands.[11] Rick Warren has used alliances with retailers such as Wal-Mart and Costco to get his book onto their shelves. And they have started using measurement to make sure they are doing their job properly. Willow Creek measures its success in turning "seekers" into Christians through biblical concepts that they have dubbed the five G's (they include grace and good stewardship).

These pastorpreneurs are committed not just to applying good man-agement techniques to their own organizations but also to spreading them around the worldwide Christian community. Willow Creek has a consulting arm, the Willow Creek Association, which has more than twelve thousand member churches, puts on leadership classes for more than a hundred thousand people a year (guest speakers have included Jim Collins, the business guru who wrote *Good to Great,* and Bill Clinton) and earns almost $20 million a year.[12] Rick Warren likens his "purpose-driven

formula" to an Intel operating chip that can be inserted into the moth-
erboard of any church—and points out that there are more than thirty
thousand "purpose driven" churches. Warren has also established a Web
site, pastors.com, that gives a hundred thousand pastors access to e-mail
forums, prayer sites and precooked sermons, including twenty-two years'
worth of Warren's own offerings.

Indeed, in a nice turnaround, some businesses have also started to
learn from the religious sector. The management thinker Peter Drucker
used to point out that these churches are superb at motivating their
employees and volunteers, and superb, also, at transforming volunteers from well-meaning amateurs into disciplined professionals. The
best churches have discovered the secret of low-cost and self-sustaining
growth—transforming seekers into Evangelicals who will then go out and
recruit more seekers. How many businesses could boast such committed
customers?

THE DISNEYFICATION OF GOD

However, even if Evangelicals and corporations have made happy bed-
fellows, there is still the problem that religion is not quite the same as a
business. What matters in religion after all is the Truth, not attendance
figures. One criticism of these megachurches, for instance, is that they
represent the Disneyfication of religion. Forget about the agony and
ecstasy of faith. Some claim that Willow Creek and its ilk serve up nothing more challenging than Christianity Lite—a bland and sanitized faith
that is about as dramatic as the average shopping mall. Another criticism
is that these churches are not really in the religion business but in the self-
help business. Osteen and his compatriots preach sermons full of reassuring words about how you are "victors not victims," about how you can be
"rich, healthy and trouble free," and about how "God wants you to achieve
your personal best."

True to this picture, the center of gravity of religious books is shifting—
not just from nonfiction and didacticism to fiction and entertainment, but
also from guilt-inducing wrath to feel-good self-help. The touchstone for

the Christian dieting movement in the 1950s was Charles Shedd's classic, *Pray Your Weight Away,* which pulled no punches: "When God first dreamed you into creation, there weren't a hundred pounds of excess avoirdupois hanging around your belt."[13] Today's Christian diet books ooze sympathy for the obese, who are naturally exempted from any personal responsibility for their condition.

The critics note that all this is extraordinarily good for the pastorpreneurs themselves, who are growing suspiciously prosperous out of preaching the gospel of prosperity. Jakes is not the only churchman who does not have to fly commercial. The wonderfully named Creflo Dollar, the chief pastor of World Changers Church International in Georgia, drives a Rolls-Royce and flies around in a Gulfstream jet.[14] Joyce Meyer, who promises that God rewards people with His blessings, counts among her own blessings a $2 million home and a $10 million jet.[15] Keith Moore, the founder and head of Moore Life Ministries and Faith Life Church in Branson, Missouri, has even given a series of lectures on the subject of whether Jesus would wear a Rolex. The answer, not surprisingly, is yes: Jesus happily accepted expensive personal gifts, and it was actually Judas who suggested giving them to the poor.

Hardly edifying. But do incidents of hucksterism discredit all attempts to mix religion with business? The simplest defense of Jesus, Inc., is indeed growth: modern management is bringing more people to God, and providing more cash for the churches to spread his word. For instance, the target audience for the megachurches consists of baby boomers who left the church in adolescence, who don't feel comfortable with overt displays of religiosity, who dread turning into their parents, and who apply the same consumerist mentality to spiritual life as they do to every other aspect of their experience. The megachurches are simply using the tools of American society to spread religion where it wouldn't otherwise exist, and persuading corporations to bring advertising and sponsorship dollars to Christian America that would otherwise go elsewhere. Jakes persuaded a group of big-name companies, including Ford, Coca-Cola and Bank of America, to sponsor his MegaFest conference. Meanwhile, corporations have also provided Christian artists with bigger audiences for their ideas, not to mention bigger rewards for their efforts. When Joyce Meyer joined

Warner Faith, for example, she more than doubled her sales. Two decades ago Christian recording artists could not get their work into mainstream music shops. Now you can pick them up along with the latest records by Satan-worshipping heavy metal bands.

The Disneyfiers also have some history on their side. The marriage of religion and business has deep roots in American history. Itinerant Methodist preachers from Francis Asbury onward borrowed the latest marketing techniques from business. Aimee Semple McPherson borrowed the latest techniques from Hollywood moguls. And the gospel of self-help and prosperity is as American as apple pie. In his 1925 best-seller *The Man Nobody Knows,* Bruce Barton, an adman turned evangelist, pictured Jesus as a savvy executive who "picked up twelve men from the bottom ranks of business and forged them into an organization that conquered the world." His parables were "the most powerful advertisements of all time."

Yet the main response is that if you listen closely to Disneyfied American religion, it is actually much less Disneyfied than it first appears. It contains plenty of good old-fashioned fire-and-brimstone stuff. LaHaye's *Left Behind* series pulls no punches when it comes to the end of the world and the fiery fate that awaits all those scoffing unbelievers. The megachurches may be soft on the surface, but they are hard on the inside. The people at Lakewood believe that "the entire Bible is inspired by God, without error." Cuddly old Rick Warren believes that "heaven and hell are real places" and that "Jesus is coming again." You may start out in a Disney theme park but you end up in the heart of Evangelical America.

CHAPTER SEVEN

EMPIRES OF THE MIND:

GOD AND THE INTELLECTUALS

❧❦

KEY WEST is famous for many things. It is the most southerly point in the continental United States, just ninety miles north of Cuba. It provided vacation homes for Ernest Hemingway, who tried hard to drink the place dry, and Harry Truman, who located his southern White House there. It is, above all, one of the raunchiest party towns in the country—an awe-inspiring and money-swallowing collection of bars, strip clubs and T-shirt shops. (The prize for the worst taste: a Harley-Davidson T-shirt on the back of which is written, "If you can read this, the bitch fell off.") Key West boasts a "clothing-optional" bar, the Garden of Eden, and, for those who find that too hygienic, a "clothing-optional" restaurant, the Naked Lunch. Wander down the main street and you can meet drag queens, bikers and their molls, aging stoners, sun-baked dropouts, drunken Midwesterners and cruise passengers, disgorged from the huge cruise ships that dock there regularly, eager to see the freak show.

Key West is also the venue for a regular conference on religion and public life that is sponsored by the Pew Forum on Religion and Public Life. Twice a year a group of journalists travel to Key West to listen to somber presentations from academics, policy makers and religious leaders. The conference was established in the late 1980s by Michael Cromartie, an Evangelical Christian who is based at the Ethics and Public Policy Center in Washington, DC, in order to educate journalists—particularly political reporters—on the subject of religion. Washington hacks had started phoning him because they wanted to understand the Christian right. Cromartie was shocked by their ignorance. They treated religious figures as caricatures. They knew little about the Bible or doctrinal disputes. They might as well have been investigating a tribe of head-hunting pygmies. How better to remedy their ignorance than to take them to Key West?

There are many reasons why countless journalists (including one of us) have leapt at Cromartie's invitations. There are worse assignments than standing on the deck of the Pier House hotel, drinking wine and contemplating a Florida sunset, all in the name of work. The speakers are excellent. They have included Rick Warren, Michael Gerson, Peter Berger and Mark Noll. But there is a bigger reason than this: the resurgence of interest in religion among America's intellectual elite.

In one way this is just following the news. We live in a world where fanatics strap on suicide belts and blow themselves to smithereens in the name of God. There is also less dramatic evidence of the revival of religion—politicians invoking God's name, religious groups taking on new responsibilities. Any serious commentator can hardly ignore questions such as whether the world is on the verge of a "clash of civilizations" between Islam and Christianity. But it is driven by more than intellectual curiosity. A growing number of intellectuals are finding themselves caught up in the religious revival. The speakers at Pew have included a number of religious-minded thinkers—people such as Noll, Gerson, Stephen Carter and Philip Jenkins.

GOD AND THE QUAD

For most of human history religion has been central to the life of the mind: the intellectual elite has also been a religious elite. Most of the great European universities were founded by religious orders. Academics devoted their efforts to the dual tasks of training a clerical elite and providing the gentry with grounding in the rudiments of religion. Theology was the queen of the sciences. The fieriest debates were on religious subjects. The majority of books were on religion.

As we have already seen, colonial America tightened the links between intellect and religion: the Puritan oligarchy was one of the most highly educated in history. But all this changed in the late nineteenth century, when secular academics began to take over American universities. As the avante garde intelligentsia turned against religion, Evangelicals increasingly responded by rejecting the life of the mind in favor of dogma and raw emotion. The supply of religious minds did not dry up completely. Reinhold Niebuhr was one of the most prominent public intellectuals of the twentieth century. Nor did demand disappear. During the 1950s students scandalized their secular professors by turning up to lectures by Paul Tillich, Reinhold Niebuhr, Fulton Sheen and Billy Graham.[1] Nevertheless, both supply and demand for divine education went into long-term decline. The focus of intellectual life moved elsewhere—to technocratic social science in the 1950s, to the counterculture in the 1960s, to the debate about the relationship between the market and the state in the 1980s.

Most academics all but ignored the study of religion. When Harvard University designed its core curriculum for undergraduates in the 1970s, in an attempt to encourage students to broaden their minds rather than succumb to premature specialization, it decided to ignore religion. John Rawls, Harvard's leading political philosopher, argued that people should set aside their religious views before they could participate in the public square.[2] Religion was even out of favor in schools of religion: a report by the Rockefeller Foundation in 1976 found that fewer than half of the graduates of the country's top five divinity schools—Harvard, Yale, Chicago, Vanderbilt and New York's Union Theological Seminary—went on to work for the church or engage in further study of religion, down from four-fifths a couple of decades earlier.[3] In 1988, fresh from his triumph with *The Bonfire of the Vanities*, Tom Wolfe told students at Harvard, not entirely happily, that they lived in an era of "freedom from religion."[4]

Now God is returning to intellectual life. The revival was supercharged by September 11. After the terrorist attacks large numbers of what David Brooks of *The New York Times* has diagnosed as "recovering secularists"[5] went back to church, and religious courses in universities swelled dramatically. Al Qaeda inevitably focused intellectual inquiry on both Islam and religion in general. But even before the twin towers fell there were growing signs that faith was reviving as a force for the mind as well as the soul.

Religious-minded thinkers formed associations such as the Society of Christian Philosophers (in 1978) and founded journals such as *First Things* (1990). The churches found their intellectual sap rising. A few far-seeing public intellectuals began to grasp the importance of religion, most notably Samuel Huntington of Harvard, who published *The Clash of Civilizations and the Remaking of World Order* in 1996. Meanwhile, other intellectuals, not just on the right, began to realize that moral problems, such as family breakdown, might have huge social consequences. Dan Quayle was roundly condemned in 1992 for criticizing the fictional heroine of *Murphy Brown* for choosing to have a child out of wedlock. A year later the *Atlantic Monthly* ran a cover story, based on a mass of social scientific evidence, entitled "Dan Quayle Was Right."

Interest in the study of religion once looked like a hobbyhorse of the cultural right; now it is a normal part of intellectual discourse. Father Richard John Neuhaus points out that when he set up the Center for Religion and Society in 1984 there were "to the best of my knowledge only four centers of religion and public life in America; now there are more than 200 think tanks and faculties devoted to the subject." Even leftish intellectuals are finding God—at least as a subject. Mike Davis, a Marxist sociologist, has decided that "for the moment at least, Marx has yielded the historical stage to Muhammad and the Holy Ghost. If God died in the cities of the industrial revolution, he has risen again in the postindustrial cities of the developing world."[6] Davis argues that Islam and Pentecostalism today occupy a "social space" analogous to early twentieth century socialism. Marx has reemerged in the guise of radical imams and Pentecostal preachers. One of the most widely discussed philosophical tomes of 2007 was Charles Taylor's lengthy meditation on the relationship between faith and secularization, *A secular Age*.

Stanley Fish, one of America's loudest supporters of poststructuralism, and one of its most sensitive weather vanes, also regards religion as the new big thing:

> When Jacques Derrida died, I was called by a reporter who wanted to know what would succeed high theory and the triumvirate of race, gender and class as the center of intellectual energy in the academy. I answered

like a shot: religion. . . . Announce a course with "religion" in the title, and
you will have an overflow population. Announce a lecture or panel on
"religion in our time," and you will have to hire a larger hall.[7]

This created an odd sensation for many conservative intellectuals.
They had gotten used to being marginalized by their interest in religion. They had also gotten used to reacting to an agenda that was largely
set by the secular left. But by 2001 they found themselves at the very center of a general reassessment of the role of religion in public life: prophets with a certain amount of honor. Nowadays three groups of religiously
minded thinkers are prominent: neoconservatives, theoconservatives and
Evangelicals. But the best place to begin analyzing the American intelligentsia's rediscovery of religion is with a young conservative iconoclast at
Yale in the 1950s.

GOD AND MAN AT THE *NATIONAL REVIEW*

The man who did as much as anybody to reintroduce God into America's
political debate was a brash young graduate named William F. Buckley.
The publication of *God and Man in Yale* in 1951 was a seminal moment for the
conservative movement. It made young Buckley's reputation as a liberal
bête noire, and it linked together two themes that were to power intellectual conservatism—opposition to Keynesian economics (the "man" part
of the title) and hostility to secular intellectuals.

God and Man was a firecracker of a book. A Yale man dared to charge
faculty members by name with fostering atheism and socialism. He called
for the firing of particular professors. He urged rich alumni to step in and
save the university from godless communism. No wonder Yale students
lined up around the block to buy the book. No wonder the Yale establishment mobilized to denounce the young rebel. And no wonder the book
became a national best-seller.

This might sound like adolescent bomb throwing. But Buckley had a
more serious point. He rejected the idea that the university was a mere
educational marketplace (especially a bazaar where all the stalls were run

by socialists, atheists and other bearded misfits). He believed that the purpose of education was not to keep students up to date, but to introduce them to eternal truths and provide them with the means for defending them. Buckley was a Catholic, but he wanted to restore the Yale that existed before the industrial and scientific revolutions (and before Catholics were welcomed into the institution): the church-based college that dedicated itself to producing God-fearing all-Americans.

Buckley used his newfound celebrity, together with his considerable family wealth, to found the *National Review* in 1955. The *Review* rapidly established itself as a rallying point and mouthpiece for religiously minded conservatives. Many members of the inner circle were Catholics by birth (Buckley and his sister Priscilla) or by conversion (Brent Bozell, Russell Kirk and Buckley's former tutor, Willmoore Kendall). So were many regular contributors such as Hugh Kenner and, in his youthful conservative incarnation, Garry Wills. The *National Review* crowd were not exactly monks (Buckley's milieu was more St. Moritz than St. Peter's), but they were convinced that religion was a synapse of the conservative mind. And they resisted the temptation to narrowness and nostalgia. In 1961 they recruited as their religion editor Will Herberg, the author of *Protestant Catholic-Jew* (1955), who helped to forge good relations with a rising group of East Coast intellectuals—the soon-to-be neoconservatives.

The neocons were, for the most part, secular Jews who came to God much later than the *National Review* crowd and by a very different route— the sociological rather than the theological. For the Kristols and the Podhoretzs, religion eventually became a sort of superglue that held society together and protected it from the excesses of capitalist economics. But the neocons' enthusiasm for traditional culture began as a reaction against the student radicals of the 1960s: the same disgraceful peaceniks who burned American flags, worshipped Che Guevara and badmouthed Israel also hated the church (and indeed the synagogue). Gradually, this solidarity with their enemy's enemy grew into a deeper enthusiasm for religion.

The Reagan presidency made the neocons look more sympathetically at his Evangelical base. But there was also an intellectual link. The neocons' journey toward God started with a sociological conundrum—the propensity, first spotted by Daniel Bell, of consumer capitalism to eat its own children by undermining the culture of discipline and self-restraint. Those "cultural contradictions," as Bell dubbed them, loomed ever larger for the neocons as the affluent children of the 1960s tuned in, turned on and dropped out. Capitalism, they decided, needed to be supported by old-fashioned bourgeois virtue if it was to succeed—and the obvious place to find such virtue was in the churches. Indeed, there was an opportunity to bond the two groups their enemies on the left most disliked to the conservative cause—the business class and the pious. If capitalism needed to be saved from itself with a healthy dose of traditional morality, capitalists also had to be protected from their critics, through an alliance with the vast army of religious Americans.

Another spur to reconsider religion was the neocons' dismay at the growing black underclass. They broke with their fellow social observers in insisting there was a moral dimension: Daniel Patrick Moynihan, a rare Catholic in the mainly Jewish neocon club (and a friend of Buckley), argued that black poverty was rooted in family breakdown. As the underclass swelled in the 1980s and 1990s, the neocons attacked the welfare state for treating a moral problem as a merely technical one. You could not solve the problem of poverty simply by giving poor people more money and jobs (particularly when the economy was at nearly full employment). You needed to teach them habits of self-respect and discipline.

Gertrude Himmelfarb, Irving Kristol's wife and the iron lady of the neoconservative movement, touched on all these themes in her numerous books on nineteenth and twentieth century Britain—a country that was one of the most religious in the world when it was at the height of its power. She argued that religion had played a vital role in powering Britain's astonishing success. This involved her in trying to rescue Victorian values from what the British Marxist E. P. Thompson, in a different context, had called "the enormous condescension of posterity": making the case in favor of the army of religious workers who campaigned against drink, debauchery and sin. Victorian Britain saw a dramatic decline in drunkenness, one-parent families and crime, evils that have all returned with a vengeance in secular Britain. Himmelfarb lauded the nineteenth century patchwork "welfare state" that the churches ran. In her view, the decline of religion had gone hand in hand with the demoralization of society: the government version of the welfare state had perversely decoupled the provision of basic services from any attempt to reform personal behavior.

The neocons' attitude toward religion certainly had a smell of intellectual opportunism. In 1979, for example, Irving Kristol described himself as a "nonpracticing" Jew who was nevertheless "sympathetic, very sympathetic, to the spirit of orthodoxy."[8] The neocons often come across like those eighteenth century British clergymen who preached their sermons in order to keep the masses (and indeed their wives) under control, then went back to their studies to read Gibbon and Voltaire. The neocons treated religious Americans very much as Marxists treated proletarians—as the people who provide the muscle for the inevitable revolution. Leo Strauss, the neoconservatives' favorite philosopher, praised a Platonic intellectual elite that was willing to use religion to make the Republic work better. He sided with religious conservatives when they blamed liberals for a "crisis of modernity," but the tradition that he valued was the Greco-Roman tradition, with its emphasis on civic virtue, rather than the biblical tradition, with its preoccupation with sin and salvation.

Still it was more than just opportunism. There was nostalgia for the old Jewish faith—a nostalgia that, in recent years, has given way to a more personal enthusiasm in some cases. There was also the belief that religion is on the rise whatever the intellectual elites want to do about it. It is not surprising that Daniel Bell was one of the first intellectuals to spot the return of religion—he delivered a compelling lecture at the London School of Economics in 1977 titled "The Return of the Sacred" that deeply shocked the sociological establishment.

RUNNING ON FAITH

The charge of opportunism is much harder to level against the theocons. These are a group of mainly Roman Catholic intellectuals who have been at the heart of the intellectual revival of religion—Michael Novak, George Weigel, Robert P. George and, most importantly, Richard John Neuhaus. For most of these men religion is at the very center of their life. Neuhaus was a leftish Lutheran minister in the 1960s who converted to Catholicism

in 1990 and became a priest the following year. Novak enrolled in a seminary at the age of fourteen, studied at Stonehill College, the Gregorian
University, the Catholic University of America and Harvard for twelve
years before finally deciding against ordination. Weigel is one of the most
fluent Catholic theologians in America, and the author of a heavyweight
biography of Pope John Paul II.

The term "theocon," which they don't particularly like, has often been
used to imply kinship with the neocons. The theocons came from a different generation from Irving Kristol et al.: they came of age in the 1960s
rather than the 1940s. They were also of a different faith—Christian
rather than Jewish. But there are still parallels. Like the original neocons,
they did their time on the left. Neuhaus began his political career marching alongside Martin Luther King in the civil rights and anti–Vietnam
War movements. He called for a "Christian Marx" who could rescue
America from both capitalism and a pervasive "crisis of meaning"—and
even looked forward to a socialist conflagration. Novak was even more
immersed in the counterculture—first turning against the Vietnam War
and then moving to the radical wing of the antiwar movement. He berated
"corporate liberalism" and proposed a Fonda-esque "theology for radical
politics," to quote the title of one of his books, and called for the destruction of "the idol of inhibition, repression and shame." "The enemy in
America" he argued, "is the tyrannical and indifferent majority: the good
people, the churchgoers, the typical Americans."[9]

But Neuhaus and Novak eventually broke with their radical past, dismissing the 1960s as a "slum of a decade." They feuded with their former
comrades, and moved smartly to the right, in due time finding a comfortable home in the bosom of the conservative establishment. The guests
at Neuhaus's ordination ceremony to the Catholic priesthood included
Buckley and Robert Bork, the right's leading judicial thinker; George W.
Bush referred to him simply as "Father Richard." Novak is now a cardinal
in the Papal College of neoconservatism, the American Enterprise Institute. (When he first arrived at the AEI, some of the economists and social
policy people seemed at a loss as to what to make of a scholar of religion,
wondering if he was there to say grace; now they defer to him.)

The theocons started from a tricky position. As Americans, they were treated with suspicion by the curia in Rome; as Roman Catholics, they were treated with suspicion in America by both the Evangelicals, who dominated the religious right, and the secular Jews, who wielded growing influence on the intellectual right. Yet, again like the neocons, they succeeded in making their influence felt both nationally and internationally by founding magazines and think tanks, by writing books, by forging working alliances with other conservatives and, above all, by producing new ideas.

They created an intellectual infrastructure for theoconservatism that mimicked, even if it did not equal, the intellectual infrastructure of neoconservatism. The Ethics and Public Policy Center is one of the more serious Washington think tanks that largely operates above the fray of day-to-day politics. *First Things,* which was designed to "advance a religiously informed public philosophy for the ordering of society," attracts contributions from prominent intellectuals. It now has thirty-five thousand subscribers, but Neuhaus's essays were distributed much more widely. (One archbishop who loathes their message admits to admiring their style.) The theocons also produced two of the most thought-provoking, and widely discussed, books on religion of the past forty years—Novak's *The Spirit of Democratic Capitalism* (1982) and Neuhaus's *The Naked Public Square* (1984).

The former was a Catholic defense of democratic capitalism: Reaganism in a priest's collar. Novak launched a sustained attack on the idea that capitalism and religion were like oil and water. Quite the contrary, he argued: capitalism is based on theological underpinnings. Much of the book was devoted to examining "the life of the spirit which makes democratic capitalism possible."[10] Novak was not content to argue that democratic capitalism is the only political system that has ever guaranteed both growth and human liberty. He also argued that capitalism is fully compatible with Christian thinking about the fate of man in the world. He insisted that the engine of capitalism is not individualism but communalism—not the isolated entrepreneur of American legend but the corporation that pools risks and binds individuals together in a collective enterprise. Novak was not averse to spiritualizing capitalism—he talked about "the sense of communal religious vocation in economic activism" and argued that corporations "offer metaphors for grace, a kind of insight into God's ways in human history."

The book could not have been better timed. It not only caught the heady mood of the Reagan years, it was taken up by the opposition in Eastern Europe, who were in the process of overthrowing Soviet hegemony, and by Latin American Catholics, who were tiring of the excesses of liberation theology. The book seemed to offer a new and exciting way forward for Catholics: challenging them to abandon their long-standing suspicion of capitalism and instead embrace it as a guarantee of both liberty and prosperity.

Neuhaus's *The Naked Public Square* was a jeremiad against liberal secularists who wanted to drive religion out of political life. He argued that there was an asymmetry at the heart of the separation of church and state as understood by liberals: secularists were allowed to express their moral views in the public square while religious people were excluded. "We insist we are a democratic society, yet we have in recent decades systematically excluded from policy consideration the operative values for the American people, values that are overwhelmingly grounded in religious belief."[11] The secularists had been aided in their project of advancing the "naked public square" by the mainline churches—churches that had once provided America with much of its soul and verve but which had recently shrunk demographically and suffered a collapse of morale. Neuhaus's prescription for Christians—stop censoring yourselves and start participating in the public square—caught the mood of conservatives across America.

The theocrats helped to redirect Catholicism. Neuhaus criticized Catholic nervousness about involvement in the public square, nervousness that was created by the religion's outsider status and reinforced by Kennedy's insistence that his religion was a private affair. Novak played a role in persuading the Vatican to drop some of its more extreme anticapitalism. The theocrats also brokered a successful deal with Evangelicals. Neuhaus was personally uncomfortable with Evangelicals, disliking their "overly confident claims to being born again," recoiling from their happy-clappy ways and suspicious of their lack of intellectual heft. But he and his colleagues were responsible for launching, in July 1993, a highly successful alliance under the (somewhat happy-clappy) title of "Catholics and Evangelicals Working Together." This is more than just a matter of sharing the same enemy; Evangelicals and Catholics increasingly began to share ideas as well as war stories.

Indeed, one of the theocons' achievements was to fashion a nonde-nominational language that allowed conservatives to talk about religion and morality in the public square. This was an area where Evangelicals had struggled. Falwell found it hard to discuss a political issue like gay rights without bringing in scripture and indeed sin almost immediately. Neuhaus discussed it in terms of philosophy and social policy. This made it more difficult for secularists to hide behind John Rawls's idea that religion was too private and personal to influence public debate. And it made it easier for Jews and Christians, Catholics and Protestants, to make their way back into the public square together. The new public language provided social conservatives with both an argument to rally around and a language in which to present that argument.

Like the neocons, the theocons can be easy targets. They sometimes lack common sense. In 1996 *First Things* ran an issue seriously discussing the case for a revolution against the morally corrupt American "regime" because of its support for abortion. (Walter Burns, Gertrude Himmel-farb and Peter Berger resigned from the magazine in disgust, and many other prominent conservatives sent letters of protest.) Neuhaus lik-ened Bill Clinton's Washington to the pre–Civil War capital where all branches of the government were in the hands of "pro-slavery forces."[12] More recently, the theocons have been distressingly quick to pronounce the death of Europe.

Another criticism of the theocons is their selectivity. They are guilty of cafeteria Catholicism—as strict as you can get when it comes to papal doctrine on contraception and euthanasia but willing to second-guess the Vatican when it comes to its opposition to the "war on terror." Far from following the papal condemnation of the Iraq war, Neuhaus suggested that in some conflicts it might be possible to conceive of "military action in terms not of the last resort but of the best resort."[13] Meanwhile, Novak penned a blogospheric hymn of praise to Donald Rumsfeld, describing him as one of the best defense secretaries ever, a few days before his defenestration. The movement takes an equally à la carte approach to the wisdom of the American people too. Damon Linker, the author of an excellent book on the theocons, points out that, when conservatives are in power, "Neuhaus and his colleagues are inclined to sanctify the country, its leaders, and its people, and to counsel extreme deference to political authorities, who are assumed to be doing God's work in the world. But when the people fail to conform to theocon expectations—throughout the 1960s, for instance, or during Bill Clinton's presidency—the theocons lurch to the opposite position, demonizing the country, its leaders, its people, and even going so far as to declare that the nation is on the verge of totalitarianism, civil war, justified revolution, or perhaps all three at once."[14]

Still, not all the criticisms of the theocons are justified. The most damning attack (at least from the left's point of view) has been the charge that they set about trying to create a theocracy at home under George Bush. The theocons certainly exercised some influence. Neuhaus, who served as an adviser to Bush on the 2000 campaign, was treated with great reverence by everybody in the White House—by Evangelicals such as Gerson as well as Catholics. "Compassionate conservatism" owed a great deal to the Catholic notion of "subsidiarity"—the idea that social problems are best solved by voluntary organizations rather than the all-powerful state. But as we have already seen, Bush did not follow up. The theocon agenda on abortion and gay marriage did not get far at the federal level either. The one area where you can spot their influence is stem cells—especially through Leon Kass, a Chicago professor who mixed neoconery with theoconery: Bush made him the head of the President's Council on Bioethics from 2002–5 and he remained close to the administration thereafter.

THE OPENING OF THE EVANGELICAL MIND

A third group of religiously minded intellectuals emerged from an unlikely location—the Evangelical world. If the closing of the Evangelical mind was one of the most dramatic developments in religious America in the first half of the twentieth century, then the opening of the Evangelical mind promises to be one of the most interesting developments of the first half of the twenty-first century.

The Evangelicals are perhaps the most anti-intellectual religious group in America—lacking the rich theological and philosophical tradition of the Catholics or the gentlemanly scholarship of the mainline churches. Mark

Noll has observed bluntly that "the scandal of the Evangelical mind is that there is not much of an Evangelical mind." Evangelicals have succeeded in creating a boisterous popular culture: there are Evangelical television channels, choirs and pop groups. They have nourished millions of believers in the simple verities of the faith. But they have singularly failed when it comes to sustaining serious intellectual life, abandoning the universities and high culture to a secular elite that looks down on them as simpletons.

To many people this is just as it should be. Evangelicalism is a religion of the heart rather than the head—a religion that emphasizes first and foremost the experience of being born again and the practice of conversion. But Evangelicals have not always been as anti-intellectual as they are today. They are heirs to a profoundly intellectual Protestant tradition that emphasized the Word and thus learning. (Martin Luther described parents who neglected the education of their children as "despicable hogs and venomous beasts.") The Puritans who settled America believed that Godliness entailed good learning. But Evangelicals turned sharply against the intellectual establishment.

For most Evangelicals, the split with the mainline Protestant churches a century ago was a split between piety and intellect: it was a matter of emotion and faith. But for some it was also a debate. Evangelical intellectuals, such as they were, parted company with the mainline establishment over how to deal with science: the mainliners believed that you needed to adjust religion in the light of reason, while the Evangelicals clung to a literal interpretation of the Bible. This meant more than just sticking to ancient verities: Evangelicals invented (or substantially refined) anti-scientific theories. Creationism was the most obvious; nobody had been so wound up about when God created the world before. "Dispensationalism" was an even more complex structure, splitting human history into seven parts. Evangelical scholars devoted more time to searching the Bible for signs of the precise timing of Armageddon than they did to studying nature or writing history.

Evangelicals were driven from the world of higher education far more completely than members of other religious traditions. They responded to this ruthless marginalization by creating a counterestablishment of Evangelical colleges and Christian schools (and sometimes resorted to home schooling). But this counterestablishment is in academic terms a pretty poor thing. It is not just that Evangelical colleges lack the prestige and resources of the great research universities. Many of them were founded by charismatic preachers who were not exactly first-rate intellectuals in their own right—the likes of Oral Roberts, Jerry Falwell and Pat Robertson. Some of them were downright eccentric. Bob Jones University, in South Carolina, banned interracial dating until 2000 and still teaches "young-earth" creationism. America has no shortage of Catholic universities and Jewish institutions that promote the Catholic and Jewish understanding of God. But there is no first-rate research institution that advances the Evangelical understanding of God.

The Evangelical rejection of the life of the mind was partly driven by revenge. Ever since the Scopes Monkey Trial, intellectuals have been pouring scorn on Evangelicals as brain-dead dolts (though there has been a marked downturn in the quality of the invective since H. L. Mencken laid down his pen). Evangelicals responded in kind. They not only questioned the value of these intellectuals (effete snobs leeching off hard-working Americans). They questioned their patriotism as well. During the Cold War every liberal intellectual exposed as a Communist fellow traveler cheered the Evangelical heart. Evangelicals delighted in Eisenhower's definition of an intellectual as "a man who takes more words than are necessary to tell more than he knows," and in Buckley's quip that he would rather trust the first hundred names in the Boston telephone directory than the first hundred names in the Harvard faculty.

The Evangelical rejection of the life of the mind also had a lot to do with their obsession with "market share." The very thing that made Evangelicals so successful—their drive to spread the Good News—also led them to eschew highfalutin theologizing in favor of preaching and conversion. The heroes of the Evangelical world were not deep thinkers but great orators. The scenes of the great Evangelical triumphs were not private studies and lecture theaters but camp meetings and crusades. The result was that the Evangelical mind took on many of the features of America's commercial society. Evangelicals emphasized rapid results rather than prolonged concentration. They put their faith in their own judgment (however untutored) rather than in the wisdom of tradition (however long considered).

Nowadays the standard bearer of this anti-intellectual tradition is Mike Huckabee. There is no doubt about the former governor's intelligence: he is arguably the best debater on the right and he can easily hold his own with the lions of the mainstream media. But he hardly wears his learning on his sleeve, and his education, at Ouachita Baptist University and Southwestern Baptist Theological Seminary, was entirely confined to the Evangelical subculture. On foreign policy, he said his two greatest influences were Tom Friedman, of *The New York Times,* and Frank Gaffney, a leading neoconservative, who hardly sing from the same hymn sheet. Told that it was mathematically impossible to win the nomination, Huckabee quipped, "I majored in miracles, not math," and dismissed evolutionary science thus: "If you want to believe that you and your family come from apes, that's fine. . . . I just don't happen to think I did."

But in this at least Huckabee is unrepresentative. Something remarkable is happening: Evangelicals are rediscovering the life of the mind. Many of them now admit the costs of exclusion and ignorance; they are starting to produce intellectuals again, after a respite of a century; and they are getting more self-confident. Academics who never would have mentioned their faith a few years ago for fear of ridicule are now emboldened by their growing numbers.

After the Second World War, thousands of Evangelicals, like many other working-class Americans, discovered university for the first time. Evangelicals also established campus ministries such as the Campus Crusade for Christ (1951). In some cases, this encounter between the most religious and the most secular parts of America proved a bruising experience; but the more Evangelicals stuck their heads out of the shell into which they had retreated in the 1920s, the more they began to exercise their minds. Once again, Billy Graham was important: he initiated conversations with other religious traditions and set up *Christianity Today* and various Evangelical study centers. Another influence was C. S. Lewis, who won a huge following among Evangelicals with *Screwtape Letters* (1942) and *Mere Christianity* (1952). He turned Oxford into something of a paragon in Evangelical circles. (Even today you are much more likely to find starry-eyed admiration for the dreaming spires among Evangelicals than among Harvard professors.) Lewis also loathed anti-intellectualism, warning that "God is no fonder of intellectual slackers than of any other slackers."[15]

The intellectual revival has grown. Over the past thirty years the proportion of Evangelicals earning at least a college degree has increased by 133 percent—more than any other religious tradition.[16] Evangelicals have also become more familiar figures on Ivy League and other elite campuses. Michael Lindsay calculates that about 10 percent of the undergraduate body is regularly involved in Evangelical groups. Brown University has about four hundred students who regularly attend Evangelical meetings—more than the number of active mainline Protestants.[17] Several universities have "Veritas" forums that bring students and professors together to discuss "life's hardest questions and the relevance of Jesus Christ." The rise of these Ivy League Evangelicals is also tied to demographic trends. People from the South and Midwest who never would have dreamed of sending their children to Harvard now do so; and they have gained from the growing diversity of America's elite, especially the presence of Asian Americans. At Yale, for example, 90 percent of the members of the Campus Crusade are Asian Americans.[18]

Evangelicals have formed an impressive array of academic associations ranging from the Affiliation of Christian Geologists to the Christian Society for Kinesiology and Leisure Studies. The Conference on Christianity and Literature has a membership of more than a thousand, and publishes a journal and monographs. The Society of Christian Philosophers is one of the largest subgroups in American philosophy. Indeed, there are so many of these groups that they have even formed an umbrella organization, the Council of Christian Scholarly Societies. *Books & Culture* is an Evangelical version of the *New York Review of Books*. *Christianity Today* has taken to reviewing art and culture.

They are being helped by Evangelical businesspeople and foundations, which are pouring money into creating an intellectual infrastructure. The Pew Charitable Trusts, which were cofounded by an Evangelical oil magnate, J. Howard Pew, support some of the best work on religion being done anywhere; they also back Evangelical scholars at universities, including Yale, Emory and NYU. The Lilly Endowment, which was established by the family behind the Eli Lilly pharmaceutical company, has invested more than $171 million in religious studies at over a hundred campuses since 2001.[19] The John Templeton Foundation, set up by the late investor, gives away around $60 million a year in an attempt to reconcile religion and science: its annual $1.6 million Templeton prize is one of the biggest in the intellectual world.

Several Evangelical philanthropists focus on the Ivy League, because of its outsized influence on American culture. Steve Forbes, who has run for president twice, has helped establish Princeton's James Madison Program in American Ideals and Institutions, which has a soft spot for conservatives and Christians. Harvard now has a chair in Evangelical Theological Studies thanks to Alonzo McDonald, a former McKinsey consultant. The Harvey Fellows Program was set up by Dennis Bakke, an energy magnate, along the same lines as the White House Fellows Program: it helps Evangelical-leaning students who are pursuing graduate studies at "premier institutions."[20] Matt Bennett, the son of the founder of a hotel chain, launched the Christian Union to reclaim "the Ivy League for Christ" and thus shape "the hearts and minds" of the elite.[21] It already has student centers, where Christians can gather for Bible study and discussions, at Brown, Cornell and Princeton; more will follow "as God provides the funding." The Union is also training a cadre of young Evangelicals to work as missionaries to the Ivy League.

This intellectual infrastructure is not restricted to universities. The Trinity Forum, which was founded in 1991 as an Evangelical version of the Aspen Institute, puts on by-invitation-only retreats for intellectual and business leaders in swanky resorts. Its Trinity Forum Academy gives young Evangelicals a chance to spend nine months on Maryland's eastern shore meditating on great works of theology and philosophy. Socrates in the City holds discussions on "the unexamined life" for the Manhattan smart set. The C. S. Lewis Institute, which is based in Washington, DC, sponsors year-long study groups in theology. Charles Colson's Centurions Program tries to forge public intellectuals who are steeped in the biblical worldview. The World Journalism Institute in New York holds seminars for Evangelicals who want to mix holiness with hackery.

The revival goes deeper than the Ivy League and posh symposiums. Enrollment in Evangelical colleges grew by 60 percent in 1990–2002 at a time when the general college population was static.[22] Many conservative-minded Americans are reluctant to send their children to the sort of institution that Tom Wolfe portrays in *I Am Charlotte Simmons*, with their coed dormitories and unrelenting performances of *The Vagina Monologues*. Evangelical colleges are trying to raise their standards—particularly when it comes to original research. Fuller Theological Seminary has recently raised more than $125 million. Baylor University is trying to triple its endowment by 2012 (it has already raised $500 million). They are also forming closer relations with Catholic institutions: Notre Dame is their favorite model not just because of its tradition of combining religious commitment with academic success, but also because it is home to some noted Evangelical scholars.

One of them, Mark Noll, is perhaps the best example of the Evangelical intellectual revival. The very fact that he has written a book lamenting the scandal of the Evangelical mind is significant in itself: you don't lament the lack of something that you do not value. But Noll is also a first-rate historian. He has produced a series of outstanding books on religious history that emphasize the role of faith in shaping America without endorsing Evangelical myths about America being founded as a Christian nation. In some ways Noll is the Thomas Babington Macaulay of the Evangelical resurgence (though without the cockiness): a man who expresses the confidence of a community that has a growing sense of its vital role in history.

Evangelicals are still weak intellectually—it is hard to think of an Evangelical leader who could have debated Jürgen Habermas in the way that the future Benedict XVI did. Yet that will surely change. History is full of examples of the extraordinary intellectual energy that is released when closed religious communities open up and try to come to terms with the modern world: think of the Jewish intellectual renaissance in late nineteenth century Austria. The idea that the next Freud will appear in Texas may be ambitious. But something is plainly going on—and, like everything else in religious America, it will have consequences for the rest of the world as well.

PART THREE

GOD'S EMPIRE

CHAPTER EIGHT

EXPORTING AMERICA'S GOD

⚜

IT IS THE THREE P.M. exorcism at the Universal Church of the Kingdom of God on the Avenida Brigadeiro Luís Antônio in São Paulo. The
other two Tuesday exorcisms take place at eleven a.m. and eight p.m. The
air is sticky and the afternoon has a lazy siesta feel. Across the road, a
café blasts out Guns N' Roses and the news kiosk displays porn alongside soccer magazines. Middle-class Paulistas drift into the cool, calm
church, which, with its comfortable seats, sparkling granite floor and
raised stage, has a very American feel, more like the in-house conference
center of a decent-sized multinational than a place of worship. Most of
the arrivals, who eventually number about two hundred, are women, some
with children. There are plenty of shopping bags. The three p.m. exorcism seems to be squeezed in between the school run, the laundry and the
groceries.

The preacher, Pastor Eginaldo, emerges without fanfare, wearing a
white shirt and slacks. He asks people to bring forward trinkets belonging to loved ones whose souls are in torment. The congregation sings a
hymn—there is no accompanying music, no big production, but they sing
lustily and some hands are already raised. Pastor Eginaldo talks about the
rudimentary problems of life—of marriage and family, of body and soul.
The hands reach higher. These problems, these demons cannot be driven
out by going to the hospital, he says. The power of science is limited, the

power of God unlimited. Ushers hand out shoulder bands bearing the words "Break the curse."

Then all the people in the church link hands in a huge circle. They close their eyes. The emotional level rises a few notches. Pastor Eginaldo proceeds from person to person, talking all the while, louder than before but still calm. He lays his hands on peoples' heads, willing the evil spirits out of them. Around the circle there are ripples of great trauma. A woman in a pink T-shirt collapses, writhing, screaming. Some of the helpers are a bit aggressive: they order people who open their eyes to shut them. But their main job is to catch people who fall over when the pastor cries out, "Leave in the name of Jesus!" The expelling of devils is a rough business—involving lots of head jerking and genuflection.

Eventually, the pastor asks people to return to their seats. His tone is now conversational, whimsical, almost postcoital. He talks about the tithe—the tenth of their incomes church members are supposed to hand over—and he sells a few newspapers, having blessed them first. But if the intensity has gone from his own performance, the screaming and writhing continues in the background, as people are released by the helpers. There is a hymn—and then the congregation streams out. Most seem completely unperturbed by the agonies they have just endured or witnessed. They are in a hurry: the shopping and the school run are calling. The children seem oddly relaxed about what they have just seen their mothers go through.

Pastor Eginaldo explains that this was a fairly typical service. Many of the exorcised were regulars. The Tuesday service is about spiritual liberation, he says; yesterday's service was about solving financial problems. His style is that of a professional surgeon who has just emerged from an operating theater: everything has gone pretty well. He discusses the American preachers whom he admires; this is a global business, just like medicine, where you have to learn from the best practitioners. In the background, in his operating theater, his helpers are extracting one last devil. "I'm stronger than you!" shouts one of the helpers, cradling a young woman's jerking head, while she howls and her small, exhausted body shivers.

YO YOIDO

Pentecostalism is growing like crazy in Latin America, where it has shattered the Roman Catholic Church's monopoly of religion. An eighth of the population of Brazil claim to be Pentecostals and just over a third "charismatic."[1] Indeed, according to the World Christian Database, there are now 24 million Pentecostal Christians in Brazil, compared with 5.7 million in the United States. In Chile, the "cathedral" of the Jotabeche Methodist Pentecostal Church in Santiago can seat 18,000.

But if you want to see the full power of Pentecostalism—the organizational heft to balance the emotion on display in São Paolo—there is only one place to go: David Cho's Yoido Full Gospel Church. For most people the word "megachurch" summons up an image of a Wal-Mart-sized spiritual supermarket in the American suburbs. In fact, five of the world's ten biggest megachurches are in South Korea. Yoido, the largest of them, sits opposite the national assembly in Seoul, an astute piece of political positioning, akin to Westminster Abbey. It looks somewhat unprepossessing—a brownish blob surrounded by office buildings—but Yoido boasts 830,000 members, a number it says is rising by 3,000 a month. One in 20 people in Seoul is a member.[2]

Each of the seven Sunday services at Yoido is a logistical challenge: apart from the twelve thousand people in the main sanctuary, another twenty thousand follow the service on television in overflow chapels scattered around neighboring buildings. Some thirty-eight thousand children attend Sunday school during the day. As one service begins and the next ends, around sixty thousand comers and goers are ushered by white-jacketed traffic directors. If you want to get into one of the two services starring the church's founder, you have to arrive an hour early.[3]

Not that you will lack entertainment while you wait. The massed choir (one of twelve) is already belting out hymns, backed by a large orchestra (one of three). The audience sings along, with huge television screens supplying the words, karaoke-style. The mother church beams pictures of the service to hundreds of satellite churches around the world and to Prayer

Mountain, a grueling religious camp close to the border with the North. It offers translations in English, Japanese, Chinese, Spanish, French, Indonesian, Malay and Arabic.[4]

By the standards of American preachers, Cho is a remarkably restrained figure: with his glasses, tie and tidy red cassock, he looks like one of the more bureaucratic kinds of Asian politician. His tone is logical and unrelenting. His theme today is, "Deliver us from the Evil One." Sin and Satan are omnipresent, he argues, but if you ignore their enticements, "your grave is already empty." As he cites scripture, the passages appear on the big television screens. Cho urges the liberation of North Korea, quotes Edward Gibbon and cites unknowingly Ted Haggard as the man who drove out demons in Colorado Springs by exorcising the telephone book. (Sadly, it seems that the devil who drove Haggard to buy sex and drugs from a male prostitute was not listed.) As he closes, Cho then invites people to touch the part of their body that most needs healing. There are shouts of success but no obvious miracles. After Cho sits down, a young opera singer performs while the money is collected—by the sackful in gold and scarlet bags—and piled up in front of the pulpit.

The Yoido Church's resemblance to American megachurches is more than a matter of size or razzmatazz. Its whole culture is deeply American. The church is organized like a business (too much so, according to some of its critics). It is broken up into small cells that try to preserve the benefits of face-to-face organization. Most of the praying and converting is done at home, in groups of around a dozen people. The idea is that these cells, like their biological equivalents, will multiply. Just as with an American church, they see no geographic limit to that multiplication. Yoido sends out six hundred missionaries a year. One target is North Korea, which used to be the more Christian end of the country. (Locals still talk stirringly of the Pyongyang Revival in 1907, which supposedly hooked Kim Jong-il's grandmother). Plans already exist at Yoido to build a second sanctuary in Pyongyang, as well as forty other churches. China is another target—and also a road into North Korea. The Yanbian Korean Autonomous Prefecture in the Jilin Province near the North Korean border is chockablock with missionaries.

Yoido attracts the upwardly mobile middle class—exactly the sort of people who flock into the megachurches of Dallas and Orange County. Asked in 2004 which faith had most spurred on their country's modernization, 43 percent of South Koreans named Protestantism and 11.3 percent Catholicism. The churches provided many of the democracy movement's leaders. Hahn Meerha, a professor and chaplain at Korea's Hoseo University, points out that 42 percent of the chief executives of listed companies are Protestants.

A VERY AMERICAN RELIGION

In their different ways, Pastors Eginaldo and David Cho reflect three things: the global spread of American-style religion in general, and Pentecostalism in particular; the push by Evangelical Protestants into politics; and the way that global religion is a two-way street, with American-style Christianity spreading to the developing world and then developing-world Christianity returning to America.

Pentecostalism is the great religious success story of the twentieth century. Today there are more than five hundred million "renewalists" in the world (i.e., members of Pentecostal denominations plus "charismatics" in traditional denominations).[5] It is not just spreading in Asia and Latin America: in large swaths of Africa Pentecostalism is expanding faster than Islam, which is provoking no end of Islamic resentment. It is also expanding twice as fast as Roman Catholicism, and three times as fast as other forms of Protestantism in Africa.[6] Renewalists make up 30 percent of the population of Nigeria, and about 50 percent of the populations of Zimbabwe and Kenya.[7] In South Africa there are nine hundred congregations in Soweto alone.[8]

The Pew Forum on Religion and Public Life, which completed a survey of Pentecostalism in late 2006, argues that "renewalism" is the world's fastest-growing religious movement: renewalists now make up about a quarter of the world's Christian population compared with just 6 percent thirty years ago. The evidence of this can be seen everywhere in the developing world: in churches the size of football stadiums across Latin America, in twelve-thousand-acre "redemption camps" in Nigeria, in storefront churches in the slums of Rio and Guatemala City, in brick and mud tabernacles with metal roofs and dirt floors in rural South Africa. Across the world fiery preachers are delivering the same message: live your life according to God's law, read the Bible as the literal word of Truth, be on the lookout for miracles and wonders, and, above all, prepare yourself for the end of history and the beginning of the millennium.

The success of Pentecostalism is a strange mixture of unflinching belief and pragmatism, raw emotion and self-improvement, improvisation and organization: it is as if somebody had distilled American-style religion down to its basic elements and then set about marketing it globally. The Azusa Street Revival in Los Angeles began with a global mission: the faithful dispatched hundreds of missionaries abroad. And subsequent revivals over the years released yet more energy and dispatched yet more missionaries abroad. Pentecostal preachers drew on America's vibrant religious traditions, for instance bringing large open-air Methodist-style "camp meetings" to Africa. They also planted churches wherever they went. Some of the most impressive evangelizers were little known outside their circles. Gordon Lindsay, a Texas-based preacher, planted over three thousand churches in eighty-three countries. His books were translated into forty-six languages, and his Bible schools and tapes educated young Pentecostals the world over.

Others became household names. Jimmy Swaggart's tears were even more familiar (and revered) in Latin America than in the United States. Pat Robertson, a Southern Baptist who has always been close to Pentecostals, has arguably been more influential in Africa and Latin America than back home. In 1990 Robertson flooded Guatemala, a favorite Evangelical stomping ground, with "Proyecto Luz" ("Project Light"), launched from his Christian Broadcasting Network. He reached 60 percent of Guatemalan homes with televisions, and galvanized thousands of Pentecostal churches.[9] He also flew to Guatemala City in 1982 to embrace Ríos Montt, a Pentecostal, after his coup, and raised millions to support his regime in "Operation Love Lift."[10]

Korea was converted by American missionaries. Cho started his career as a translator for Samuel Todd, an American Assemblies of God faith healer who staged a revival tour of South Korea in the 1950s. He founded

Yoido in 1956 in a battered tent that he bought from the Marine Corps for $50. Throughout his career he has kept in close contact with American Evangelicals—particularly with those at the Fuller Theological Seminary in Los Angeles. American preachers visit South Korea to play to enormous crowds; and Cho also visits America. One of his most important satellite churches is in Chicago.

Like all marketing successes, Pentecostalism owes some of its success to its ability to adapt itself to local traditions. For instance, exorcism has always been a big part of religion in Brazil. (One of Pastor Eginaldo's rivals talks about the curse of Africa. Many Brazilians are descended from slaves; when they arrived in slave ships, their old religions cursed the new land. Their descendants feel fated.) The Pentecostals have taken this legacy of folk tradition and incorporated it into their weltanschauung. In Africa, they have performed the same trick, blending the old Azusa Street formulas—speaking in tongues and spiritual healing—with ancient spiritual practices. The names of Pentecostal churches speak to their adaptability. What other Christian movement can produce churches with names like the Mountain of Fire and Miracles (in Nigeria) and the Church of Christ's Spit (in Brazil)? Pentecostal services take place everywhere: you can be woken up in a respectable hotel in Guatemala City by amplified rock music and hallelujahs; but the services are also going on in disused shops in the poor part of town, as well as huge modern stadiums. So Pentecostalism adapts, but it is nevertheless a very American product.

BORN IN THE USA

Indeed, one of the things that attracts people around the world to Pentecostalism is its very Americanness. The Pentecostal world is dominated by pastorpreneurs who model themselves on their American equivalents, building megachurches and establishing entrepreneurial empires. In Guatemala, where 20 percent of the population is Pentecostal and 40 percent charismatic, they have just finished the largest building in Central America. Like Yoido, Mega Frater (Big Brother) is not ashamed of its American roots: it boasts a twelve-thousand-seater church, a parking lot with room for twenty-five hundred cars, a vast baptism pool, and a heliport. Magnificently, the road to the church is called "Burger King Drive." Down the road, Harold Caballeros, the pastor of the El Shaddai Ministries, another huge outfit (and no relation to the Catholic charismatic movement of the same name), makes no bones about his admiration of America. He studied at Lakewood Church in Houston with John Osteen, who was responsible for ordaining him, and still keeps in close contact with the church and its current pastor, John's son, Joel. His heroes, other than familiar American figures, include Korea's Cho.

You can also see this Americanness in the Pentecostals' determination to reach as many people as possible. While the Catholic Church sticks to Spanish in Mexico and Guatemala, Protestants also use indigenous languages. In Brazil the ratio of Protestant pastors to worshippers is eighteen times higher than that of priests to Catholics, according to a study by the Fundação Getulio Vargas, a business school.[11] The Pentecostals also use the talents of all the people—especially women. In Latin America, the Catholic Church is perpetually short of priests, not least because it limits its recruits to well-educated celibate males. In Pentecostal churches women not only fill the pews, they get up and testify. And they are increasingly becoming preachers in their own right—a particularly striking development in patriarchal Latin America. In South Korea, Yoido has broken with cultural tradition to give women a prominent role in spreading the faith. For years Cho's right-hand woman was his mother-in-law, Jashil Choi, a figure known as "Hallelujah Mama." Today Yoido boasts 62,580 female deacons—over twice the number of male ones.

There is also a very American emphasis on worldly success and upward mobility. In Brazil Bishop Edir Macedo advertises his church as a place where the faithful are rewarded for their sacrifices, usually of a financial kind. "The church of results" will reward them for their 10 percent not just in the next world but in this one. Those little envelopes are "investments." The bookshops of the megachurches are full of books not only by pastors like T. D. Jakes and Rick Warren but also by management gurus such as Peter Drucker and Jim Collins. The churches exude a boundless confidence in the power of self-help and smart management. The business model works: 44 percent of church donations in Brazil come from Pentecostals, and only 31 percent from the far more numerous Catholics.[12]

Sometimes the pay-and-pray-to-play philosophy can sound crude. But many of the new generation of Pentecostal preachers, particularly in the biggest churches, are notable for their sophistication, both entrepreneurial and intellectual. Caballeros litters his conversation with references to Max Weber and Michael Porter. (He has recently returned from a semester at Harvard.) He believes that "culture matters"—borrowing the title from one of the many sociological texts he has absorbed—and that the best way to shift the culture in the right direction is through religion. He argues that Pentecostalism can lift his country out of poverty by two strategies: teaching individuals to be sober and thrifty (he himself turned to religion when he was seventeen after a period when he drank too much) and teaching officials to abandon corruption. He points to the role that Protestantism played in creating modern institutions in America, and to the role that Pentecostalism played in supercharging economic growth in South Korea. Caballeros hopes that his own church will play the same catalyzing role in Guatemala—providing the framework for a successful civil society but also inculcating a pro-growth psychology in the population.

But just as important is what might be called the religious ecology. The same force that shaped American religion for centuries is shaping Christianity in both Latin America and Korea—the embrace of the free market and individual choice. In Brazil and Guatemala, there are hundreds of smaller religious entrepreneurs. ("We have to work against the competition as well as the devil," says one young preacher.) And there is also a fight-back by the Catholic Church. Having lost worshippers at a rate of 1 percent a year since 1991,[13] mainly to Pentecostal churches, Rome is finally responding. That has meant getting rid of a lot of liberation theology; and also imitating the Pentecostals. Brazil's most famous priest is now Marcelo Rossi, a former physical-education teacher who has been known to perform aerobics during his services. One American academic, Andrew Chestnut of the University of Houston, calls this "the Pentecostalisation of Latin American Christianity"; he estimates that 75 to 80 percent of Protestants in the region are Pentecostals and that in Brazil at least half of active Catholics have gravitated toward the charismatic movement.

The Getúlio Vargas study found that in Brazil defections from Catholic ranks have stopped. The number of Pentecostals continues to grow but at the expense of the irreligious.[14]

The Yoido Church operates in one of the most competitive religious markets in the world. A typical Evangelist will make thirty-five visits a week and drink an unhealthy amount of coffee in the process. That has produced incredible results. In 1950 only 2.4 percent of the population in South Korea was Protestant. Now the figure is close to 20 percent. Counting Catholics (which many Korean Protestants don't), Christians make up close to 30 percent of the population.[15] "Koreans don't play church," says an American elder at Yoido.

The Protestant surge has slowed down a bit recently, a development that is variously blamed on changes in education laws and the abuses of some clerical families. Cho has been criticized for letting his son run the church's newspaper, the fourth-largest in the country. Again, a little like America, the Protestant push in Korea has coincided with a spurt in secularism. If one part of the middle classes has flocked to the megachurches, another is increasingly cross about religion's role in society: a 2004 poll found that 59 percent of Koreans thought the churches were going in the wrong direction. When a group of clueless young Korean missionaries were captured by the Taliban in Afghanistan in 2007, there were widespread complaints in Seoul that the youngsters had been brainwashed into going there merely to provide a marketing pretext for South Korea's churches.

But Protestantism's problems have given a push to South Korea's Catholic Church (where the priests do not have sons to inherit the churches). And there has even been a competitive response of sorts from Buddhism, the religion whose market share has dipped most over the past century. Buddhism remains more passive than its Christian competitors—believing people should discover faith for themselves rather than be energetically introduced to it—but there are some signs of awakening. In South Korea Buddhist monks, often hidden away in inaccessible rural shrines, have set up meditation areas in cities to fight off the Protestants. The market is still working—and even Buddhists are being drawn into the American-inspired revival and reshaping of global religion.

Finally, there is the political angle. Many rising Korean politicians claim that they owe their success to their religious faith. A third of the country's senators are Protestants, according to Hahn Meerha, and monthly prayer breakfasts at the national parliament are well attended, with the occasional American political visitor. Lee Myung-bak, the country's president, is the elder of a megachurch. (He was seen helping to park cars before his election.) South Korea even has its own religious right. South Korea's megachurches are formally banned from endorsing politicians; but in 2005 one of the leading pastors, Jin-Hong Kim, set up the New Right Movement. It already has about two hundred thousand members, two-thirds of whom are Christians. Set beside its American equivalents, the New Right's views are somewhat vague. Kim complains about the country's leftward drift, America-bashing, the timid policy on North Korea and corruption. His enemies say the New Right was really a device for helping his friend, Lee, win the presidency. But even if that is the case, he has already been helpful. Protestants voted overwhelmingly for Lee in both the primary and the election. In the bidding prayers at Yoido, there is a prayer "to help us choose the right president (and let the spirit overflow us in that choice)."

In Brazil, the founder of the Universal Church of the Kingdom of God, Bishop Macedo, owns the country's second-largest television station, several radio stations and newspapers and, perhaps most important of all for his fellow countrymen, a soccer team. He also runs a political party, the Partido Republicano Brasileiro. Majorities of Pentecostals in nine of the ten countries studied by Pew said that religious groups should express their views on day-to-day politics—and sizable minorities (including in the United States) said that the government should take steps to make their country a Christian one.

FROM GEOGRAPHY TO CHRISTIANOGRAPHY

It is hardly surprising that American-style religion should exercise such a profound influence on the development of global Christianity. America looms large in everybody's mind as the world's military and cultural hegemon (seldom more so than in South Korea). America has been living with the world's new religious ecology—an ecology defined by choice and competition—since the founding of the Republic. And, partly as a result of that ecology and partly as a result of its native missionary zeal, America has always been in the business of exporting religion—first to the wild lands of the American West and eventually to the far corners of the earth.

In America religion was born global. When John Winthrop told the first settlers of the Bay Colony that they were to be "a city upon a hill," he added that "the eyes of *all people* are upon us." "Far from seeking permanent separation from the Old World," Robert Kagan writes, "the Puritans' 'errand to the wilderness' aimed to establish a base from which to launch a counteroffensive across the Atlantic."[16] The American Board of Commissioners for Foreign Missions was founded in 1810. By 1835 it had opened 63 overseas missions with 311 members of staff, started 474 schools for 80,000 pupils, and distributed 90 million pages of religious tracts. By 1869, America already supported about as many overseas missionaries as Continental Europe and half as many as Great Britain. By 1910, American missionaries outnumbered Continentals by two to one and even surpassed the British. Some 2 million American women were involved in missionary-support organizations—with China a particular target.

Missionaries also spread American ideas abroad, planting American-style Christianity in such far-flung places as China, Korea and Guatemala, and American-style universities, such as the American University of Beirut, around the world. Many of China's most prominent universities were founded by missionaries. Missionaries often functioned as encyclopedias of local knowledge and Rolodexes of local contacts, turning them into indispensable guides to both American diplomats, when they moved to a new posting, and American businessmen, when they entered a new market.[17] Horace Allen, a Presbyterian medical missionary, became the most influential foreigner in Korea. Samuel Zwemer, known as the "Apostle to Islam," traveled throughout Arabia in 1890–1905 and was the first American to establish close relations with the al-Saud family. The hospitals that he established treated some three hundred thousand Arabs, including ibn Saud himself.[18]

There was a period in the twentieth century when this missionary zeal appeared to wane. The Scopes trial reduced Evangelicals' enthusiasm for fishing for souls in New York, let alone New Guinea. Decolonization produced a sharp reaction against missionary work both in the United States and the developing world. The mainstream churches were gripped by colonial guilt—and much more likely to celebrate indigenous African spirituality than old-fashioned muscular Christianity. A literary genre, produced mostly by writers who came of age in the 1960s, sprang up that vilified missionaries as agents of imperialism and sexual repression: Caryl Phillips's *Crossing the River,* Linda Hogan's *Mean Spirit,* Nora Okja Keller's *Comfort Woman* and, most famously, Barbara Kingsolver's *The Poisonwood Bible.*

Yet if the missionary drive slowed, it did not stop. For instance, Billy Graham's global crusades turned him into one of the best-known Americans in the world. In 1956, Graham was greeted as a prophet throughout Asia. "No American in the postwar period has made so many friends for America," William Stoneman, a distinguished foreign journalist, concluded, "and gone so far toward offsetting the widespread conviction that material rather than spiritual matters are America's sole significant concern as Billy Graham during his amazing tour of Asia."[19] Graham has preached to more people than any other Protestant in history, reaching more than 2 billion people in person or over the airwaves during his long life, and inspiring 2.8 million people to "accept Jesus as their personal savior" during his crusades.

Nowadays, Evangelical America has shed any reticence it once had about "going global." Everywhere you look in religious America, Christians and churches are taking the Bible's "great commission" to "make disciples of all nations" to heart. This is partly to do with upward mobility. The teachers and bankers who now fill America's megachurches want to spend their political capital on more than just abortion and gay marriage. Cheaper transport and faster communication also make it even easier to travel abroad and, thereafter, preserve the links that you forge there. But the most important reason is the shift in the balance of power in global Christianity, which is pulling American Christianity southward.

In 1900, 80 percent of the world's Christians lived in Europe and the United States; today, 60 percent live in the developing world. On any given Sunday, more Roman Catholics attend church in the Philippines than in Italy, or any other European country for that matter, and more Scottish Presbyterians attend church in Ghana than in Scotland; and, as we saw in the introduction, there is the conversion of China to come. This shift is particularly dramatic in the Evangelical world.[20] If you are in the business of duck hunting, you go where the ducks are.

The combination of the shrinking of the world and the shifting of the Christian population has given rise to a vigorous "Christian solidarity" movement in America. American Christians hear from visiting Christians from Africa or Asia. Or they visit the developing world on holiday or as missionaries. Or their churches collect money for persecuted Christians or take in refugees.

The issue that solidified Evangelical interest in "the suffering church" was religious freedom.[21] Many Americans were astonished to discover how many Christians and other believers are persecuted for their faith. A Freedom House survey in 2000 found that 36 percent of the world's population live in places where religious freedom hardly exists and another 39 percent in places where it is only partially honored. The campaign against religious persecution quickly developed into a wide-ranging campaign against everything from sex trafficking to slavery. Evangelical Christians have done as much as anybody to draw attention to the horrors of Sudan and North Korea, and to persuade the Bush administration to provide over $15 billion to fight AIDS in Africa.[22] During a meeting to discuss the AIDS initiative the president turned to Michael Gerson, his chief speechwriter and a committed Evangelical, and asked him what he thought of the policy. "Mr. President," he answered, "if this is possible—and we don't do it—we will never be forgiven."

Export businesses have a way of becoming import businesses too. People like Cho absorb American Christianity, change it—and then reexport it back. It is also a template that other religions are beginning to grasp. We will come back to those ideas at the end of this chapter. But first we will look at four things that shape this export industry—pastorpreneurs, philanthropy, the Christian media and missionaries.

The Global Megachurch

The desire to go global begins at the top. Many of America's leading pastorpreneurs are focused on export. Take three of the figures we have already looked at in America. T. D. Jakes is probably as well known in Africa as he is in the United States. In the summer of 2006, when he preached to forty thousand in Atlanta's Georgia Dome, inmates in South Africa's Drakenstein Correctional Center, where Nelson Mandela was once incarcerated, got up at two a.m. to watch him perform.[23] Indeed, Jakes says that Africa is where he feels most at home, outside his own country. In October 2005 he took four hundred followers, most of them black, with him to Kenya, including his church choir, political dignitaries, business leaders and fellow pastors. He delivered two sermons at Nairobi's Uhuru Park that attracted an estimated crowd of a million people, and hobnobbed with the president (and election stealer) Mwai Kibaki.[24]

Jakes brought over doctors and medical supplies to help heal the sick and established a well-digging project. But on the grounds that it is better to give people a fishing rod than fish, he is teaching entrepreneurship. Many Africans responded ecstatically to his gospel of God and self-help. Jakes represented not just the message of Jesus but also the promise of American life. Kenyan clergy compared his arrival to the return of the biblical Joseph—a man who was born into slavery and was now returning with enough wealth to help his brothers. "We will give you your past," they said to their American visitors, "if you will help us find our futures." "African Americans may have left in slave ships," Jakes declared, "but we're returning in 747s."[25] And the same goes for a variety of other black preachers who cultivate close relations with Africa—notably Charles Blake, the senior pastor of a Pentecostal megachurch in West Los Angeles, who has visited Africa every year since the 1980s and set up the Pan-African Charismatic Evangelical Congress in 2000.

Both Bill Hybels and Rick Warren have also embraced globalization. The consulting arm of Hybels's Willow Creek Church has more than twelve thousand member churches from ninety denominations and thirty-five countries. Nearly half of the association's members are non-American. Warren is also an increasingly international figure, spreading purposefulness around the world and branching out into international politics. (He is on the advisory council of Tony Blair's foundation.) When he arrived in Busan, South Korea, in July 2006, five thousand rural pastors marched to the town spontaneously in order to get him to train them.[26]

The Evangelical superstars are almost all involved in global philanthropy. Warren claims that the astonishing success of *The Purpose Driven Life* brought a divine rebuke. God told him that he could not spend the rest of his life tending to his megachurch in southern California, training pastors and watching his bank account swell; he was morally bound to serve the world's downtrodden, particularly in Africa. He points out that churches are uniquely placed to help the world's poor. There are "a million villages around the world that don't have a school, a clinic, a hospital, a fire department or a post office . . . but have got a church," he argues. "What if that church could be networked together with millions of other churches to become a distribution center not just for spiritual truth and salvation, but also for job training and health care, for education, for business development? The church is the only possibility." Warren's church, Saddleback, sends hundreds of missionaries a year to Africa, starting with Rwanda. He distributes a clinic-in-a-box, a portable supply of medicine that people in isolated villages are trained to dispense. His kit also includes a school-in-a-box, a business-in-a-box and a church-in-a-box. "We've got more volunteers than anybody else," says Warren. "Government doesn't have a billion volunteers. Business doesn't have a billion volunteers."

Religious superstars like Jakes, Hybels and Warren sit on top of a religious establishment that is increasingly worldly-wise and globally connected. Evangelical businessmen are exploiting their global power and connections to spread the Word. Tyson Foods deploys corporate chaplains in Canada and Mexico as well as the United States. Marketplace Chaplains USA and Corporate Chaplains of America are both going global, providing chaplains to companies in Mexico, Puerto Rico and perhaps even China.[27] Interstate Batteries runs company-sponsored mission trips that allow employees (who bear some of the travel costs themselves and give up some of their vacation time) to work with the needy in places such as Mexico and Russia. This is not just confined to big companies; most of the action happens at a smaller level. For instance, Greg Newman, a San Francisco–based venture capitalist, has helped set up a candle company in Thailand that offers victims of sex abuse jobs, training and, if they are amenable, counseling from Evangelical missionaries.[28] Pura Vida Coffee, another Christian outfit, was set up to "serve and empower at risk children and families" in coffee-growing countries.

CHARITY BEGINS ABROAD

Indeed, global philanthropy, always a strong part of grassroots Christian America, is now thriving. The Hudson Institute estimates that religious organizations provided $8.8 billion worth of foreign aid in 2006, the equivalent of 37 percent of all U.S. government foreign aid.[29] In a survey by Robert Wuthnow, a sociologist at Princeton University, three-quarters of active church members claimed that they had personally given money to international relief or hunger projects. The same number said that their congregations had also given money collectively. The survey also showed that 29 percent belonged to congregations that had helped to support a refugee over the past year.

Both religious denominations and individual churches are deeply involved in charitable work. The Presbyterian Church is in the forefront of antimalaria programs in Africa. The United Methodist Church runs farms in the Congo. The Mormon Church sent $79 million worth of goods and services to the developing world in 2004. Damascus Wesleyan Church, just north of Washington, DC, runs an orphanage for three hundred children in Zambia. And Christian organizations are particularly important when natural disasters strike. For instance when the Asian tsunami struck, the Southern Baptist Convention, which is sometimes derided as the official church of American rednecks, collected $16 billion for the victims. Religious charities have an impressive record of being the first to arrive in disaster zones and the last to leave.

It is not just churches and individuals. There is a broad sweep of religious NGOs, some of which get funding from the government as well as private sources. Nearly half of the seventy largest NGOs that engage in international relief work are religious organizations. The largest religious NGOs (or RNGOs)—the Salvation Army, World Vision and Catholic Relief Services—enjoy combined annual revenues of over $1.6 billion and reach almost a hundred fifty million people. Evangelicals support some forty-eight NGOs through their own umbrella organization, the Association of Evangelical Relief, and their own development organizations. Some religious NGOs keep faith in the background. Others are more up front: World Vision International requires its entire field staff to sign a "statement of faith" as part of their contracts, and establishes evangelism committees wherever it operates.

Evangelicals are also forming much closer relations with global institutions. Some of their contact with the United Nations has been combative (see chapter twelve); but in the field such ideological differences matter less. UN agencies have realized that religious NGOs possess remarkable resources: one of the largest distribution systems in the world, with a presence in almost every community; an army of highly motivated volunteers; and a remarkable degree of trust. (Polls consistently show that faith-based NGOs enjoy more confidence than secular ones.) American missionaries play an important role in distributing aid from the United States Agency for International Development, (USAID) in Africa, for example.

GOD'S MICROPHONE

The Trinity Broadcasting Network's headquarters in Santa Ana, in California's Orange County, is not likely to win any prizes for refined taste. The spacious parking lot leads onto an Appian Way of faux-marble pillars and colonnades. The bright white entrance hall is dominated by a "sculpture" of the angel Michael slaying the serpent. The frieze on the ceiling looks like a paint-by-numbers version of something you might find in an Italian church—though the bambini are a good deal fatter than anything that even the Italians might dare to produce. The Gold, Frankincense and Myrrh gift shop takes up much of the ground floor—a treasure trove of religious schlock of every variety from plastic manger sets to Galilee candles. The sounds of organs and hymns float through the air—along with the regular cries of "Hallelujah" and "Praise be the Lord." Ubiquitous signs warn that disturbing religious meetings is a felony under California's penal code.

This is a depressing place rendered all the more depressing by the sight of impoverished-looking handicapped people lining up to buy the Jesus junk from the gift shop. But it is also the headquarters of a global business. TBN is the largest religious broadcasting organization in America (and the seventh-largest one of any description). It was also born global: Paul Crouch, who founded the network in 1973 with his wife, Jan, along with Jim and Tammy Bakker, even entitled his autobiography *Hello World*. The company now reaches every corner of the planet, except Antarctica, and broadcasts in numerous languages, including Arabic. TBN produces more religious programming than any other body (with titles like *The Omega Code, More Than a Carpenter* and *To Hell and Back*); but it is also helping established American preachers, such as Creflo Dollar, Kenneth Copeland, Joyce Meyer, John Hagee and Joel Osteen, to take their brands global.

Evangelicals like to point out that God had dominated the airwaves from the first. The first words sent by Samuel Morse, in his telegraph from Washington to Baltimore, were "What hath God wrought?" The first radio broadcast, on Christmas Eve, 1906, was a religious service. Charles Fuller's *Old Fashioned Revival Hour* was the most popular radio program in America in the 1940s. Father Charles Coughlin attracted more than forty million listeners in the 1930s. In the 1970s Jimmy Swaggart was one of America's most successful global broadcasters, with supposedly a name recognition of 73 percent in Latin America.

TBN has plenty of competition. The Christian Broadcasting Network, Pat Robertson's broadcasting arm, broadcasts to two hundred million people in more than two hundred countries, boosted by broadcasting facilities in Ukraine, Lebanon, India and the Philippines. CBN produces local programming in Indonesia and Thailand as well as local versions of the 700 Club. (An Indonesian program features female converts from Islam discussing matters of the day.) CBN also employs "broadcasting blitzes" in less-developed markets, trying to get the message across by buying up as much airtime on as many media as possible.

The Christian media is also devoting more energy to keeping Christian America informed about what is going on abroad.[30] This trend started even before the September 11 attacks: several Christian radio networks, such as American Family Radio, established news operations in the late 1990s. But Al Qaeda's assault enormously reinforced the trend. CBN launched *NewsWatch,* the first nightly Christian television news program, shortly after the Al Qaeda attacks. FamilyNet TV, part of the Southern Baptist Convention's media empire, also expanded its news operations as the war on terror progressed. In 2005 Christian television networks from around the world joined forces to form a news co-op, intended to improve the global Christian community's coverage of the news by pooling footage and other resources.

These Christian organizations put a very different spin on the news from their secular competitors. They devote a lot of attention to the persecution of Christians in places like China and Sudan, where they covered the gathering genocide in greater detail. They are also a lot more sympathetic to Israel. Several of the leading Evangelical figures, including Pat Robertson, sometimes broadcast live from Israel. CBN's only international news bureau is in Jerusalem. Some Evangelical news programs go even further than sympathizing with the Jewish state: *Prophecy in the News* interprets world events in the light of biblical prophecy, putting particular emphasis on Israel's role in the Second Coming.

THE MISSIONARY POSITION

One reason why the American Christian media cover overseas events is that so many members of their families are working there as missionaries. According to the *International Bulletin of Missionary Research,* America had 115,700 full-time missionaries serving abroad in 2005, almost a quarter of the world's stock of full-time Christian missionaries (443,000) and a significant increase on the previous decade. In fact, the number of Americans engaged in some kind of missionary activity is probably significantly higher, thanks to the surge of Pentecostalism and the rise of short-term missionaries. Another survey, by Robert Wuthnow, discovered that

74 percent of American church members said their congregation supported a missionary working in another country during the past year. Four in ten said that their congregation had a committee that focuses on overseas missions or other international programs. One in five reported that their congregation had a full-time staff member with special responsibility for global ministries.

Missionary work is dangerous, given the rising tide of anti-Americanism, the fervor of radical Islam and the fact that many of the souls being chased live in some of the most unstable places in the world, particularly the Middle East, Africa and Southeast Asia. Yet the number of people with the stomach for it is growing, thanks to three developments.

The first is the success of hot religion. In 1918, eight out of ten of American Protestant missionaries belonged to the mainline churches. By 1996, the mainline churches mustered fewer than 3,000 missionaries out of a total of 40,000. In 2007, the Southern Baptist Convention's International Mission Board had a budget of $289 million, a full time staff of 500 people in Richmond, Virginia, and some 5,000 foreign missionaries, a fivefold increase since 1955. The board claims that its missionaries baptize some 500,000 people around the world every year and provide help in almost 135,000 churches. The Mormon Church sends so many people abroad as missionaries that the state claims that the 2000 Census undercounted Utah's population by 14,000 (and deprived the state of a rightful congressional seat). Bill Bright's Campus Crusade for Christ International grows ever larger: it now has annual revenues of $650 million and employs more than 25,000 people.

The second development is the boom in short-term missions, lasting from a week to a year, driven by a messy mixture of religious enthusiasm, technological advance (the falling cost of air travel, the rise of the Internet), and the spectacle of suffering on the television. Wuthnow argues that 1.6 million American churchgoers go on short-term missions abroad every year, generating about 30,000 man-years of missionary work, worth about $1.1 billion, or about a quarter the amount provided by professional missionaries. *The Mission Handbook,* published by the Billy Graham Center, puts the figure for short-term missionaries lower, at 364,000, up from 64,000 in 1996, but that is still a significant contribution to missionary activity.

Some missionaries dismiss short-term ventures as mere mission-themed holidays. (The coordinators promise such perks as adventure, fun and, that all-important ingredient, meaning.) Some worry that they do more harm than good when it comes to gathering in new souls. People who are so young and inexperienced inevitably take a lot of effort to manage. Even so, the movement is plainly having a big impact not just on the developing world but also on the next generation of Evangelical America: youngsters who grew up knowing nothing but suburban America now understand something about third-world slum cities; they have friends with enormously different backgrounds just an e-mail or text message away. Anecdotal evidence suggests these are exactly the sort of young conservatives who are turning away from the old religious right toward the likes of Warren.

The third development is the growing sophistication of missionary activity. *The Mission Handbook* contains more than six hundred pages of information on North American missionaries serving overseas. Many Christian universities offer advanced training in missionary work. The Billy Graham Center at Wheaton College has an Institute of Strategic Evangelism and an Institute for Cross-Cultural Training. Biola University has a school of intercultural studies. The Assemblies of God Theological Seminary has established a doctoral program in missiology. Seattle Pacific University has trained more than thirteen hundred short-term missionaries since 1983.[31] The Fuller Theological Seminary offers an online MA in global leadership that missionaries can complete without leaving their posts. Campus Crusade for Christ now boasts an innovation center to allow virtual missionary work. There are companies that specialize in arranging missionary trips, such as InterVarsity, and providing insurance to the bold souls in the field, such as Adams & Associates.

A TWO-WAY STREET

The global trade in religion is more complicated than it was a century ago, when the West—and particularly the Anglo-Saxon West—did most of the exporting. The number of foreign missionaries produced by the developing world has increased from about three thousand in 1973 to more than a hundred thousand today. South Korea is the world's second-largest exporter of missionaries, after the United States, with an estimated fifteen thousand Koreans working abroad as missionaries in 2006, nearly double the number in 2000 and up from barely a hundred in 1979.[32] A great deal of missionary activity bypasses the West completely. South Korea is the biggest exporter of missionaries to North Korea and China. Missionaries are sent from Indonesia to Thailand and from Goa to Brazil.

The United States nowadays is once again an importer of religion—but this time from the developing world rather than Old Christendom. The original immigrant church, the Catholic one, now echoes to the sound of Latin American voices: more than three thousand churches across the country celebrate mass in Spanish. But it is much broader than that. Today, as throughout American history, immigrants tend to become more religious as they put down roots: the church provides them with a way of adapting to American mores as well as preserving some of their culture. Churches in New York's Chinatown, for example, provide housing, food, employment and a safe haven for Chinese immigrants.[33] More generally, churches also plug people into social networks that can make it easier to get mortgages, housing, jobs, business openings and even political influence. (Religiously active immigrants are more likely to vote.)

Immigrants are helping to reshape American religion. Pentecostalism, which divided into black and white branches after the Azusa Street Revival, is returning to its multicultural and multiracial roots. The Catholic Church is being infused with Latino blood and culture. Twenty-eight percent of the seminarians ordained in the United States in 2001 were born elsewhere, including 5 percent in Mexico and 5 percent in Vietnam.[34] In the Boston area about half the active congregations worship in languages other than English. Brazilian Protestants hold an annual prayer festival in Boston Garden.

Developing countries have even started to send missionaries to convert American heathens. Nigerian churches such as the Deeper Life Bible Church are active in the United States, particularly in Houston, with its large Nigerian population. Argentine evangelists regard the United States as a fertile recruiting ground, using Philadelphia as a bridgehead. Both the

Brazilian Assemblies of God and the Universal Church of the Kingdom of God have missions in Los Angeles. The Universal Church broadcasts on Spanish-language channels in New York City. The El Shaddai Catholic charismatic movement, which is a powerful force in the Philippines, is active among Filipino Americans.

One of the nicest examples of "spiritual recycling" is provided by Aimee Semple McPherson's International Church of the FourSquare Gospel (ICFG). The church sent its first missionaries to Brazil after the Second World War, establishing its first church in São Paulo in 1951.[35] Thereafter the church grew relentlessly, first dwarfing its American mother and then returning home to help her out. Sitting in his São Paulo office, Pastor Marco Oliver boasts that the Brazilian arm has around eight thousand churches—roughly ten times the number in America. There are more than thirty thousand ICFG pastors and church workers in Brazil. His own church in a lower-middle-class part of São Paulo started in a tent. Now it is part of a network of thirteen churches, which also produce some three hundred radio programs a week. (They don't own a station.) Pastor Marco ascribes the church's relentless growth to the fact that it adopts a more aggressive business style than the Catholic Church, and to the popularity of exorcism. His new focus is politics: the ICFG sponsors a hundred city councillors across the country. The ICFG opposes both gay marriage and abortion (though some Pentecostal outfits in Brazil, such as the Universal Church, support abortion in part to differentiate themselves from the Catholics). The Catholics, meanwhile, are fighting back: they are using radio and television more effectively, notes Pastor Marco, and they have become far more charismatic.

The Brazilian arm of ICFG has its own corps of missionaries, with seventy at work in places like Cuba, Guyana and rather magnificently Rome. (A Brazilian-Italian pastor fishes for souls within reach of the Vatican.) People warm to Brazilians, points out Pastor Marco; they are less threatening for many people than Americans are. In Senegal, where conversion to Christianity is banned, Brazilian missionaries sneakily set up a school of soccer. But a growing focus of the Brazilian church is America itself.

Some five hundred thousand Brazilians now work in the United States, often illegally. This surge of emigration from Brazil persuaded the church to follow its members abroad (its leader estimates that at least a third of the church's members have emigrated to the United States). The church sends pastors to look after its American flock. It also puts on frequent revivals to give their faith an extra boost. Often a Brazilian pastor will attach himself to an American ICFG church, offering services in Portuguese late at night. Visas are a repetitive problem: it took five years to get one missionary a work permit. "With good laws, we could send many, many more people." Pastor Marco says he would love to help the American mother church more: he thinks it is a little staid.

A UNIVERSAL OPERATING CHIP

For all the southward shift in global Christianity, America continues to have a huge influence on the shape of religion. For one thing, American preachers historically did more than the preachers of any other country, with the possible exception of Great Britain, to turn Christianity into a truly global faith. For another, material wealth matters in the spread of religion, as in so much else. As Wuthnow points out, the average American Christian has an annual income of $26,980 compared with just $3,640 for the average Brazilian Christian. America has twice as many Catholic parishes as Brazil, despite having only half as many Catholics, and six times as many priests per parishioner. Catholic and Protestant churches in America take in nine times as much money annually as churches in Brazil. There are at least twenty-three hundred Christian "service organizations" in the United States compared with two hundred and fifty in Brazil.

Above all, America's influence is guaranteed by its soft power: in much of the world, particularly developing countries, the most ambitious preachers look to America as a model of how to organize their affairs. Such deference has long been true of Christianity. Now American-style religion is also acquiring imitators among leaders of other faiths.

Sometimes you have to dig a bit to uncover the American influence. For instance, sitting on a hilltop in the heart of Bangalore, the Iskcon Sri Radhakrishna Temple still has the feel of the old eternal India. Chants of "Hari Krishna" and "Hari Rama" fill the air. The building is a riot of

Hindu color: everywhere you look there are alcoves filled with brightly colored statues of Gods and portraits of Krishna as a young child. Monks in orange robes offer food and flowers, bang cymbals, bow in prayer and blow conch shells.

In fact, the megatemple, which is backed by several software titans from India and America, was only founded in 1997. It uses every modern method to entice and service believers. A Web site that is as user-friendly as that of any American megachurch lets you download Krishna screen-savers and Krishna ring tones. Touchscreen terminals in the reception area allow visitors to register suggestions and complaints.

Chanchalapathi Das, a former electrical engineer who is now both the chief monk and the vice chairman of the temple, explains with a swish audiovisual presentation how the community has reengineered its chari-table work. Rather than just waiting for the hungry poor to turn up at its doorstep, it has become a food distribution giant, providing free school meals to 200,000 schoolchildren a day in Bangalore and, via sister tem-ples, another 600,000 across the country. This miracle of abundance has been achieved by combining modern technology with modern supply-chain management and marketing pizzazz. The trucks that distribute the food display advertisements from global firms such as Philips, partly to raise revenue and partly to reap the benefits of what Chanchalapathi calls cobranding. His temple's "strong and credible delivery model" is tested by his advisory board (which holds quarterly board meetings) and a "very tough" audit by KPMG, a giant accountancy firm. Harvard Business School has written a case study on the temple.

Buddhism is generally more reluctant to embrace American models, though evidence that American methods can work is provided in, of all places, Myanmar.[36] A seventy-one-year-old monk called Sitagu Sayadaw has no time for the traditional Buddhist principles of self-effacement and asceticism: a camera crew films him wherever he goes, and he is raising money to build a huge convention center on the banks of the Irrawaddy River, to be followed, he hopes, by a nationwide network of self-branded schools and colleges. Sayadaw's inspiration (and some of his funding) comes from the United States: he fled to Nashville, Tennessee, in 1988, after taking part in prodemocracy demonstrations, and studied world religion there; he has also opened a monastery in Austin, Texas. Today he gets on relatively well with the junta (some of whose wives follow his teaching), but he is also capable of kicking at the dictatorship's shins. During the cyclone in 2008 many foreign donors funneled relief money to Sayadaw and his followers.

The most obvious imitators of American-style pastorpreneurship are to be found in the Muslim world. Across the Middle East and Asia a younger generation of religious innovators are looking to America not just for signs of the devil's work but also for models of how to adapt a traditional religious message to modern audiences. The new-wave preachers of the Islamic world are very different from both old-fashioned imams (who preach as if nothing has changed) or religious fundamentalists (who rage against the modern world). They preach a very American mixture of traditional values and upward mobility. Without Islam, you will get drowned by commercial culture; with Islam, you will thrive in a demanding world.

Until 2006 one of the clear leaders of this new wave would have been Abdullah Gymnastiar, Indonesia's favorite preacher. Usually known as Aa Gym (or elder brother Gym), he used all the modern conveniences of the preaching trade—a wireless mike, a backing quartet and a dry-ice machine—together with an informal, sometimes chatty style. He dressed in blazers and embroidered shirts rather than clerical garb. His voice rising to a shout and then falling to a near whisper, he mixed advice on self-help and personal relationships with more traditional religious themes and the occasional bit of politics. His mainly female audience was as different from the Muslim norm as he was. They wept, applauded and tried to touch the preacher. Gym built up a huge empire on the back of this, including fifteen broadcasting and publishing businesses, a school and a speaking business. (He was able to charge up to $100,000 an hour for television broadcasts during Ramadan.[37]) He was also something of a technological innovator, for instance setting up a text-message system to distribute his personal analysis of bits of the Koran.[38]

All this did not endear Gym to traditionalists: the head of one local group condemned him as "the Britney Spears of Islam."[39] The fanatics of Jemaah Islamiyah, Al Qaeda's Southeast Asian offshoot, loathed the ground he walked on. But Gym's message of "Manajemen Qulbu" (or

"Heart Management") seemed to give him a lock on the rising business class of the cities and suburbs.[40] With approval ratings above 90 percent, there was talk of him being a vice presidential candidate. Then, in the best televangelist tradition, he was brought down by a sex scandal—albeit a less saucy one than the likes of Swaggart and Bakker. In December 2006 he announced that, with his wife's permission, he had taken a second wife. Uproar followed, with politicians lining up to denounce polygamy, Gym's female followers shredding pictures of their idol and television contracts drying up.[41] Yet again in the best televangelist tradition, Gym seems to have made something of a comeback, appearing with both his smiling wives and repositioning himself as a more conservative voice.[42]

Amr Khaled is an even more American figure. He turned himself first into Egypt's most popular preacher and then into Islam's answer to Billy Graham by eschewing almost everything associated with traditional imams. He has no official religious credentials or position. He dresses in Western clothes—suits and polo shirts mostly—rather than religious robes. He performs on television and in cavernous conference chambers rather than in mosques—and he puts on a dramatic performance, raising and lowering his voice and sometimes bursting into tears. He addresses many of his remarks to the women in the audience, alternately flattering them (the first convert to Islam was a woman) and cajoling them to observe traditional practices (women are so precious that they need to be covered in a veil). Faithful Muslims are also successful Muslims. He urges his audience to take control of their lives and make sure that they succeed in business.

Like Gym, Khaled is no slouch at practicing what he preaches or on pointing to the Prophet's own career as a businessman. His Web site allows his fans to download his sermons and buy hooded sweatshirts branded with his logo. He has sold more than five million cassettes of his sermons and is a regular columnist in Arabic women's magazines. His natural home is the television studio. Khaled noted that traditional Islamic television consisted of nothing more exciting than old men mumbling bits of the Koran. So he teamed up with a friend to produce an entirely new kind of show. His 1999 television series *Words from the Heart* featured interviews with famous actresses and sports stars, who had turned to God, and clips of ordinary Muslims testifying to the wonder-working power of faith. The audience held their hands open, palms facing upward, much as Evangelical audiences do; some wept. Since then he has created several other shows. One of the most popular, *Life Makers,* encourages Muslims to improve the world around them—teach people to read, fix the potholes in the street, give up smoking, take their fate into their own hands.[43] He likes to boast that he is more popular than Oprah Winfrey.

Khaled has now gone global. This was partly involuntary: the Egyptian authorities made it clear that they would no longer tolerate him speaking to such large crowds, and he and his family decamped to Birmingham, England. But even without the helping hand of the Egyptian authorities he would have become an international figure. He is a hot commodity throughout the Arab world and the Muslim diaspora, and a friend of many Muslim leaders, including Queen Rania of Jordan.

Hopeful Westerners regard Khaled as a possible bridge to the Islamic world. But in fact, much as with Billy Graham, there is a hard core to his soft-edged faith. He tells people that Allah loves them, that Allah is merciful, that it is easy to earn Allah's forgiveness. But he also insists on the literal truth of the Koran. He talks about women's empowerment. But he also supports sharia and is an important force behind the growing fashion for the veil. In one lecture he condemned "Western" Muslim girls who reject the veil: "Who respects the woman more? Islam or the ones who cannot even sell a box of matches without painting a half-naked woman on it? Are they the ones who have respected women or ill-treated them? Has not Islam respected women, covered them and liberated them from such exploitation?"[44]

FROM SOFT POWER TO SOUL WARS

The global reach of American religion is adding a new dimension to the country's "soft power." For a growing number of people abroad, "America" means Rick Warren and T. D. Jakes as well as Tom Cruise and Britney Spears. It is also posing an explosive new question. Will Islam's enthusiasm for embracing American techniques such as marketing soften religion's hard edges? Will the likes of Rick Warren and Amr Khaled meet together on the common ground of self-help and spiritual uplift? Or will competition and modern marketing techniques only make the edges of religions sharper—as has sometimes happened to Christianity in America? Television helped sell fire and brimstone as well as soap and self-help.

It is not clear how the world's religions will fare in a gradually more "American" environment. One reason to be fearful is that many people, especially in traditional societies, do not separate out religion from everything else. They see their faith as an answer to a terrible turmoil in their lives, a crude, cruel Western maelstrom, again stemming from America. Globalization is not just helping America export its God; the insecurity it creates is also stirring up a reaction that is driving many people toward faith.

CHAPTER NINE

ALL THAT IS HOLY IS PROFANED:
EXPORTING AMERICAN MATERIALISM

SOME MUCH-USED PASSAGES are so good that they are worth quoting again. Here is Karl Marx at his best:

> Constant revolutionizing of production, uninterrupted disturbance of all social conditions, everlasting uncertainty and agitation distinguish the bourgeois epoch from all earlier ones. All fixed, fast-frozen relations, with their train of ancient and venerable prejudices and opinions, are swept away, all new formed ones become antiquated before they can ossify. All that is solid melts into air, all that is holy is profaned, and man is at last compelled to face with sober senses the real condition of life, and his relations with his kind.

Like so much that Marx wrote, this passage combines a brilliant insight with a dangerous error. The insight is that capitalism is by its nature revolutionary. It shakes up certainties and unfreezes orthodoxies. The error is that it also undermines religion—or, as Marx also put it in *The Communist Manifesto,* that capitalism drowns "the most heavenly ecstasies of religious fervor . . . in the icy water of egotistical calculation."

America is a giant example to the contrary. Americans have reacted to the uncertainty of capitalism not by abandoning religion but by embracing it. Faith provides certainty in a world where secular certainties are constantly being undermined. Religious institutions provide a support network in a world where people can feel rootless and vulnerable. Besides, as the success of America's megachurches proves, religious leaders are quite capable of using "the icy water of egotistical calculation" to increase the market share of those "heavenly ecstasies of religious fervor."

The American example is being repeated globally. People everywhere, but particularly in the developing world, are reacting to the hurricane of capitalism by taking cover under the canopy of religion. We argued in our last chapter that American Evangelicals are doing an impressive job of exporting their faith. At the same time, American multinationals are doing an impressive job of exporting the demand for faith. America is thus contributing not once but twice to the global revival of religion—as the world's leading exporter of religion and as the world's leading supplier of the capitalism that increases demand for religion. In Marx's terms, they are both exporting opium and stoking the demand for opiates.

Unholy Hollywood

America occupies much the same position in the world that Great Britain did in Marx's time—that of commercial leviathan, military giant and cultural dynamo. Granted, America's economic dominance is not as pronounced as it once was; and granted, America is not as globalized as many people assume. Germany is a bigger exporter. China is challenging American hegemony, particularly in manufacturing. European multinationals are by some measures more plugged into world markets than American multinationals. Developing-world multinationals are becoming global players. Nevertheless, when most people think of globalization they still think of America. America, with just 5 percent of the world's population, produces a quarter of its GDP. America is also the world's judge-cum-policeman, the country that lays down global rules and penalizes people who transgress them. The American war machine rules the seas and the skies, and stations troops in 150 different countries. The concerted opposition of much of the world did nothing to prevent America from invading Iraq in 2003. America wields a huge influence over the Washington-based World Bank and International Monetary Fund. Even after the credit crunch, supporters of globalization tout what used to be called "the Washington consensus." Antiglobalization protesters make little distinction between globalization and Americanization.

If America is thus the symbol of all that is good and ill about today's global capitalism, it is also the headquarters of the most advanced sort of capitalism—a capitalism that is less about tangible things than it is about intangibles such as images and information. A century ago the barons of capitalism were in the railroad, oil or steel businesses. (U.S. Steel's value in 1910 was equivalent to two-thirds of all the money in circulation in the United States.)[1] Today the economy is light as air. America's biggest companies are in the business of producing images and transmitting data (images and data that are captured on ever-thinner screens and in ever-smaller gadgets). Microsoft, Apple, Google, Oracle, Dell: these are the giants of the information world. Silicon Valley and Hollywood may each have their faults, but these are the clusters of excellence and innovation that most other countries want to imitate. And even old-fashioned companies are bent on mastering the intangible. Coca-Cola and Nike are in the business of selling lifestyles as much as carbonated drinks or overpriced shoes. Accenture, a management consultancy, calculates that "intangible" assets, such as brand names, now account for 70 percent of the value of companies in the S&P 500 compared with 20 percent in 1980.[2]

Much is made in the emerging world of America's thirst for commodities, particularly oil. But as Benjamin Barber has argued in his prescient *Jihad Versus McWorld* (1995), it is America's ability to create entertainment and information that poses the biggest problems for traditional societies. Hollywood projects images of the American way of life everywhere. The American film industry now derives more than half its revenues from overseas, and films are America's biggest export after aerospace. The Internet gives wired people around the world a door into America's huge information-entertainment complex. Consumer-goods companies seduce global consumers with images of rugged cowboys (Marlboro), happy children (McDonald's) and the self-confident women of Revlon and other cosmetic ads.

These value-laden images have become global wallpaper—but electronic wallpaper that is both unbearably garish and constantly reconfigured. American pictures and words speed around the world at an ever faster pace, carried by satellites, cables and the Internet, and delivered not just to televisions and computers but also to tiny handheld devices. They also reach into the farthest corners of the world. Lists of the most popular films around the world are essentially lists of Hollywood blockbusters written in slightly different orders with one or two local products thrown in for the sake of variety. (Even the most successful films from Bollywood or Hong Kong seldom travel outside their local markets.)

Yet the worldview that is projected by America's great image machine is highly offensive to traditional societies. Hollywood films are at best hymns to the virtues of individual freedom and at worst celebrations of the unchained id. Their depictions of female sexuality and raw violence are deeply shocking to people who were not brought up in a media-saturated culture. The number of people killed per minute in the popular Rambo series has increased from 0.01 in *First Blood* (1982) to 2.59 in *Rambo IV* (2008). Quentin Tarantino thinks nothing of showing people's heads being blown off. On the small screen, Tony Soprano spent his life garroting, gouging, beating and drowning his enemies, and committing adultery in a thoroughly animalistic manner, at one point with a one-legged Russian woman. *Sex and the City* made a fetish out of crossing sexual Rubicons. Even family fare such as *Friends* and *Will & Grace* feature casual bed-hopping, homosexual as well as heterosexual. Abercrombie & Fitch blurs the line between fashion catalogues and soft porn. It is one thing for Western sophisticates, with a lifetime's immersion in popular culture, to watch Britney Spears French-kissing Madonna; quite another for people from more traditional societies.

Consumer companies are equally keen on celebrating individual autonomy. McDonald's and Burger King "liberate" women from the role of preparing food; supermarkets produce an ever wider range of ready-cooked meals, making it easier to abandon the home for work or play. Levi Strauss and the Gap offer the same clothes to teenagers of both sexes. Add to this the quasi-religious attitude that these companies bring to their products—the best way to solve life's problems is to buy this or consume that—and you can see why many traditional people find this offensive. Apple has the feel of a cult as much as a company.

For many conservative-minded people American-style capitalism poses a threat to the two basic building blocks of society—time and space. The essence of traditional societies is a due respect for time. You honor old people and established practices. But American-style capitalism is putting the world into overdrive. The Next Big Thing trumps ancient wisdom. Hollywood glamorizes the young and fit. The Internet allows people to question everything that their elders tell them, from the age of the earth to God's existence.

The assault on place is almost as relentless as the assault on time. Shopping malls and hotel chains are the same the world over. The developing world is now imitating not just America's skyscrapers but also its office parks and gated communities (which often bear American names: there is a Beverly Hills in Seoul and a Napa Valley in Beijing). The successful Indians and Chinese who divide their time between gated communities and air-conditioned business parks are living on American time and in American space.

The onward march of Americanization has even reshaped the Islamic world's holiest cities, Mecca and Medina. Abdellah Hammoudi, a Moroccan anthropologist, was shocked when he arrived for the Hajj in the late 1990s. Instead of Medina's glorious old architecture, he saw only "shop windows and consumer displays." The city was full of "restaurants, cafeterias, ice-cream vendors, all American-style: self-service, cardboard plates and cups, plastic forks and knives, menus and prices displayed on neon-lit boards." "Modernity ravaged everything," he concluded.[3]

And then there is power: Westernized elites are increasingly displacing indigenous elites across the developing world. The offices of global companies may be run by locals. But they are locals with a difference. They are the modern equivalents of the historian Thomas Babington Macaulay's Musalmans—"Indians in blood and color, but English in taste, in opinions, in morals and in intellect." These global figures are hard-wired into the global world. They are trained in American-style business schools—the boot camps of globalization—and they spend their time dealing with people who speak the same dismal language. This is a world of "global supply chains" and "value propositions" rather than local traditions and obligations.

Go Forth and Multiplex

The assault on tradition is often an assault on religion. Most of the time this is unintentional: Western companies embody a message about consumption and personal autonomy that raises many hackles. But it is sometimes direct and crude. Think of Madonna and her erotic games with a crucifix. Think of all those Hollywood films that present religious leaders as frauds or freaks—and their followers as stump-toothed imbeciles. It is true that the religious figures who are being badmouthed are usually Christians, especially southern Evangelicals, but many Muslims see this as disrespect for religion in general. (The Koran and the Bible after all have common roots and common themes.)

This assault is at its most striking in the case of pornography. America has applied the same commercial genius to porn that it has to mainstream films and computers. "Silicone Valley" in LA's San Fernando Valley is one of California's great industrial clusters—home to fifty of the world's top porn companies and sugar daddy to twenty thousand porn stars—and that cluster is increasingly looking to the world market to boost its profits. Porn companies have global distribution chains, not least the Western hotel chains that make a habit of providing "adult entertainment" along with CNN. They are also using the global Internet to drum up customers (often with free samples that draw customers into their world).

It is easy to dismiss the attractions of American-style consumerism. Arnold Schwarzenegger is no Laurence Olivier. Proust would not have written a masterpiece inspired by the fragrance of the Big Mac. But one of the problems for traditionalists is that all this schlock is so darned attractive—particularly to the young. Hollywood blockbusters are best-sellers the world over. The products of Silicone Valley are part of a vast global underground economy. Bearded patriarchs and French intellectuals may look at the average American supermarket and see only decadence and excess. But most people from the developing world see a miracle—food for every taste, medicines for every ailment and gadgets for every occasion. The biggest problem for traditionalists is that American capitalism is so seductive.

RELIGION VERSUS CAPITALISM

The history of modern thought over the past two hundred years is, to a remarkable extent, the history of critiques of capitalism. These critiques sing the same tunes. There is the communitarian theme: capitalism destroys ancient ties and reduces everything to a cash nexus. There is the egalitarian theme: capitalism widens inequality and turns comrades into competitors. And there is the vulgarity theme: capitalism sidelines the warrior virtues of heroism or the scholarly virtues of wisdom while promoting the vulgar vice of material success.

Religion has always been part of this. Ever since Jesus in the Temple dealt harshly with the hedge-fund managers of his time, many Christians have been suspicious of finance. For a time the Catholic Church banned usury (and many versions of Islam still do). The religious opposition to capitalism has hardened as capitalism has advanced over the past few centuries. Catholics have worried that the logic of contracts is dissolving the ethic of mutual obligations. Liberal Protestants have urged the church (and increasingly the state) to step in to correct the injustices of the market—and some have even hailed Jesus as the first socialist. Slavophiles have insisted that the Russian soul—particularly as embodied in the Russian Orthodox Church—is superior to Western cash-and-carry materialism. In Latin America devotees of liberation theology have long regarded neoliberalism as the spawn of the devil. Now Evangelicals often back left-wingers in some of the poorer parts of Brazil.

Christianity still produces searing critiques of capitalist modernity, from both the left and the right. John Paul II was a fierce critic of capitalist modernity (though he was never as outspoken as Marcel Lefebvre, the voice of French Catholic conservatism, who likened modernity to AIDS). By the end of his papacy, the old Cold Warrior had come to see American-style globalization as a new evil, condemning a system that "considers profit and the laws of the market as its only parameters, to the detriment of the dignity of and the respect due to individuals and people." The pope was not only worried about global injustice (he compared the world situation to the parable of the rich man and Lazarus writ large), he also argued that consumerism produced "radical dissatisfaction": the consumer's appetite grows in the eating but his "deeper aspirations remain unsatisfied and perhaps even stifled." He condemned "luxurious egoism" and "imperialistic monopoly," and even asserted "the priority of labor over capital."[4]

Such feelings are widely shared. Leaders of the Russian Orthodox Church such as Metropolitan Kirill of Smolensk and Kalingrad openly worry that liberal culture, with its emphasis on individual rights and unbridled consumerism, is undermining Russian civilization. Liberal British clerics regularly inform their congregations that Jesus was a critic of avarice and greed. The Church of England produced some of the most stinging criticisms of Thatcherism in its 1985 report on "Faith in the Cities," prompting Norman Tebbit to label the church's leaders a bunch of Marxists. (True to that caricature, in 2008 Archbishop Rowan Williams duly announced that the credit crunch proved that Marx was right.) Prince Charles, with his eccentric combination of nostalgia for the organic social order and enthusiasm for organic foods, has sided with Islamic criticisms of capitalism: "This crucial sense of oneness and trusteeship of the vital sacramental and spiritual character of the world is surely something important we can learn from Islam."[5]

Still, root-and-branch opposition to capitalism is becoming rarer. Three developments are reshaping attitudes to capitalism in the Christian world. First, in much of the Christian world—particularly Europe—anticapitalism is becoming secularized. The leading critics of capitalism are no longer priests and prophets but professors and pundits. The old religious arguments are now in a hundred university textbooks, restated in the dismal language of sociology and political science. In Pew's survey of global attitudes nearly two-thirds of people in France and Italy and slightly more than half of people in Britain and Germany said that they thought that consumerism and commercialism were endangering their way of life. More than half of Western Europeans said that "burgers and fries to go" had ushered in a change for the worse. Hence the popularity of the "slow food" movement and the cult status of José Bové, who led a peasants' revolt against agribusiness and junk food, bulldozing a half-built McDonald's in his hometown of Millau. The French (and to a lesser extent the Canadians) have imposed quotas on the import of American films while subsidizing their own productions. The schadenfreude during the Wall Street meltdown of 2008 was palpable. Even Nicolas Sarkozy, that most American of Frenchmen, took obvious pleasure in announcing that "self-regulation is finished, laissez-faire is finished, the idea of a market that is always right is finished."[6]

The second force shaping global attitudes to capitalism and religion might be described as accommodationalism. It starts from the same premise that we examined in our chapter on soulcraft. Many religious people regard religion not so much as the enemy of capitalism but as a necessary counterbalance to it. Capitalism is the most successful wealth-generating machine known to man. But it can also be self-destructive—encouraging promiscuous consumerism, undermining traditional values and destroying self-restraint. Religion provides a way of enjoying the fruits of capitalism while protecting yourself from the thorns.

This attitude has always been common in America, with its free market in religion and weak welfare state, but it is now spreading elsewhere. The British Conservative Party has embraced its own version of "compassionate conservatism," arguing that "faith-based organizations" should be encouraged to do more to provide welfare services. This rests on the idea that faith-based organizations are much better at altering the behavior of troubled people than impersonal bureaucracies are.

The third development is that many religious people have abandoned their wholesale opposition to capitalism in favor of a more nuanced approach. People who might once have rallied behind the banner of Christian Socialism are now rallying behind three more modest banners: environmentalism, fair trade and debt forgiveness. The fashion for "creation care" that we have already encountered in Evangelical America is convulsing all religions: as Harvey Cox, of Harvard University, points out, religious people everywhere are questioning "an economic system based on the infinite expansion of finite resources." Fair trade and debt forgiveness have attracted Christians of all varieties. One of the first places that the fair-trade movement took off was in the vestries of Catholic churches. The movement was also blessed by John Paul II. Across the developing world armies of young Christians are working for secular charities with a skeptical approach toward capitalism, like Oxfam. Religious sorts, such as Bono, the lead singer of U2 who was raised by a Catholic father and Protestant mother, played an outsized role in the Jubilee 2000 campaign to cancel third world debt. (When Bono first made the case to Tony Blair at a G8 Summit in Cologne in 1999, the prime minister replied that debt relief was like Mount Everest; the Irishman replied, "When you see Everest, Tony, you don't look at it, you fucking climb it."[7]) Indeed, as Mike Elliott, of *Time* magazine points out, the Cologne summit was a turning point in terms of the relationship between religion and globalization: the first time that faith-based groups and social activists, which had traditionally distrusted each other, came together to tackle global issues of poverty and health.[8]

ASIAN GODS, ASIAN VALUES

However, the greatest religious reaction against American consumerism has taken place outside the Christian world. For non-Christians, the onrush of globalization is doubly threatening. It is not just Mammon that is invading their homes, offices and streets; it is Christian Mammon.

In Asia, leaders who have tried to tame American capitalism, making it more culturally sympathetic, have frequently looked to religion. Lee Kuan Yew, the architect of modern Singapore, argued that embracing Confucian values has enabled Asian countries to build harmonious societies and rapidly grow their economies. Much the same argument is now being advanced by the Chinese government, albeit through clenched teeth. Religion is a way of soothing the savage beast of American materialism.

In India, the same forces have been at work for longer. If Nehru represented the secular side to Indian socialism, then Mohandas Gandhi represented the religious, moralistic side. Gandhi loathed the concept of the survival of the fittest almost as much as the idea that might is right. He was a great believer in self-sufficiency, and one of his favorite means of protest was boycotting foreign-made goods. He preferred eating vegetables rather than meat in part because they required less of a surrender to capitalist civilization. In his great manifesto *Hind Swaraj* (1909), he attacked Adam Smith and denounced machinery as "the chief symbol of modern civilization; it represents a great sin." Shedding Western imperialism meant shedding Western consumerism too.

Today the Hindutva movement wants to create what might be called capitalism with Hindu characteristics. On the one hand, the Hindu nationalists are proud of their appeal to India's rising middle class. On the other, they also make much of the idea that India is different from the West—a spiritual place where capitalism can be adapted and enhanced. Hindutva politicians argue that Western capitalism is a crude two-dimensional thing. The new Indian version, which will include respect for your elders, an accent on the spiritual and a sense of balance, is a more stable three-dimensional affair. This sense of an alternative, higher capitalism manifests itself in several strange ways. There are the early morning exercises that Hindus go through in parks across the country—a form of purification and balancing. And there is also the passion for economic protectionism.

FROM MUSLIM RESENTMENT TO MUSLIM RAGE

The most uncompromising opposition to American-style capitalism, however, is to be found in the Middle East. Many people in the Arab world feel much more threatened by the force of advanced capitalism than do their former colonizers in Europe (who have had much longer to get used to it). And they are increasingly reacting to the threat by taking refuge in the old certainties of religion. The beauty of Islam for traditionalists is that it provides both a shelter from the storm of global capitalism and a fierce critique of everything that the capitalist Goliath stands for.

Unlike Abdullah Gymnastiar and Amr Khaled, the televangelists who stress Muhammad's role as a businessman, and indeed some Islamic historians who point out their culture's leading role in commerce, the traditionalists look at capitalism and see a Western tool. This criticism began in earnest in the early part of the twentieth century. One of the first Muslim intellectuals to pop his head above the parapet was Muhammad Rashid Rida, an Egyptian thinker who argued for a return to the caliphate: only an Islam restored to its former glory and purged of impurities and Western influences could save Muslims from subordination to the colonial powers. Rida was one inspiration for Hasan al-Banna, who founded the Muslim Brotherhood in 1928. Al-Banna was disgusted by the rampant secularism and depravity that he encountered in Cairo. He felt that Egypt's religious and secular elites were merrily colluding with British colonialists in return for wealth and status, and warned that Westernization threatened to engulf Egypt under a "wave of atheism and lewdness," a wave that would bring, in its wake, "devastation of religion and morality on the pretext of individual and intellectual freedom." The only solution to the problem was something he referred to as "the Islamicization of society." The Muslim Brotherhood's credo summed up his philosophy succinctly: "God is our objective; the Koran is our constitution; the prophet is our leader; struggle is our way; and death for the sake of God is the highest of our aspirations." Al-Banna was assassinated in 1949, but his ideas spread throughout the Islamic world, often underground. *Occidentosis: A Plague from the West* by Jalal Al-e-Ahmad, one of Iran's leading intellectuals, had to be secretly published in Tehran in 1962. The book's argument against what he called "west-mania" or "westoxification" had a marked influence on Ayatollah Khomeini.

The Karl Marx of radical Islam was Sayyid Qutb, a member of the Muslim Brotherhood and, many argue, the spiritual godfather of Al Qaeda. Qutb received both a traditional Muslim education (he had memorized the entire Koran by the age of ten) and a secular Western one. He published poems, novels and literary criticism, and earned his living as a teacher and education bureaucrat. The Egyptian government sent him to the United States to study its educational system in 1948–50, in part to get him out of the way. But, to judge from Qutb's accounts of the visit, the government might as well have sent him to hell itself. On the ship across the Atlantic he was revolted by an advance from a sozzled woman.

He found New York's "seductive atmosphere" shocking. He disliked jazz, which he thought was created for Negroes to satisfy their "love of noise and to whet their sexual desires." He was shocked by American women and their sexual knowingness: "The American girl is well acquainted with her body's seductive capacity," he wrote. "She knows it lies in the face and in expressive eyes, and thirsty lips. She knows seductiveness lies in the round breasts, the full buttocks and in the shapely thighs, sleek legs. . . ."

The young prig longed for a conversation that was not about "money, movie stars or car models." He was even appalled by people's behavior in the apparently wholesome town of Greeley, Colorado, particularly at a local church dance. "Songs from the record player whipped the dancing into a fury. The room became a confusion of feet and legs; arms twisted around hips; lips met lips; chests pressed together. The air was thick with passion. . . ." Here is another example of his overwrought prose: "Humanity today is living in a large brothel! One only has to glance at its press, films, fashion shows, beauty contests, ballrooms, wine bars and broadcasting stations! Or observe its mad lust for naked flesh, provocative pictures and sick, suggestive statements in literature, the arts and mass media!"

Qutb can come across as somewhat dated, but he helped define three of the most important innovations in radical Islam. The first was to draw a sharp distinction between "faithful" and "unfaithful" Muslim rulers. Hitherto people had assumed that anyone who called himself a Muslim and prayed like a Muslim was a Muslim. But Qutb argued that many Arab leaders like Nasser were in fact nonbelievers (he was particularly incensed by Nasser's refusal to ban alcohol) and could thus be removed from office. The second was the idea that the best way for Islam to come to terms with modernity was not to embrace the separation of church and state but to reassert the power of Islam in the secular realm. The third was to pronounce a death sentence on decadent Western civilization. "What should be our verdict on this synthetic civilization?" he asked. "Should we not issue a sentence of death? Is this not the verdict most appropriate to the nature of the crime?" Qutb's version of Islam was thus a reaction against the West as much as anything else.

These Islamists fed on idealized images of their own past. For them Islam was the ideal antithesis of the modern West—hierarchical rather than egalitarian, communal rather than individualistic, pious rather than decadent, caring rather than soulless, disciplined rather than licentious. All you had to do was to follow the true path—accept the unlimited power of God not just over your own soul but also over communal life—and the evils of lust and degradation would disappear. Islamists lived in a hybrid world—the world of their imagination, in which Islam was pure and Arab culture great, and the sordid world around them, where Arab countries had fallen to ruin and where most Muslims lived in rural poverty or in sordid slums.

There was a degree of delusion in this. Far from rejecting the West lock, stock and barrel, many Islamists drew heavily on Western critiques of modernity. Arab intellectuals have periodically fallen in love with both Marxism (which justified their economic objections to capitalism) and German pan-nationalism (which justified their admiration for strong leaders and their sentimentalization of the Arab people). Many pan-Arabists dreamed of the victory of Arabs over all other ethnic groups, particularly the Jews: a thousand-year caliphate, as it were. The secular Baath Party modeled itself on the Nazi Party. Qutb borrowed the idea of a "vanguard" of committed activists from Lenin. Many Iranian revolutionaries mixed Marxism with their Islam. All the same, the underlying worry about the West—that it is simultaneously intoxicating and soul-destroying—has resounded ever since in the Islamic world.

When Gallup asked Muslims what they most resented about the West, the most frequent response, across all Muslim countries and among moderates as well as radicals, was "sexual and cultural promiscuity." Benazir Bhutto noted that "within the Muslim world, there is a reaction against the sexual overtones that come across in American mass culture. America is viewed through this prism as an immoral society." Majorities of Muslims in Egypt, Jordan and Pakistan do not believe that women are treated with respect in the West. There is even a marked tendency for movie stars to abandon their Western clothes for the becoming modesty of the Hajib. Yet many of the people who dislike the West are also seduced by aspects of Western culture—hence the phenomenon of alienated Arab youths across Europe dressing in jeans and baseball caps while also dreaming of the time when a purified Islam ruled the civilized world. As Olivier

Roy has pointed out, radical Islam does not just represent "hatred of the other." It also represents "hatred of oneself and one's desires." Many of the Iraqis who chanted, "Women, whiskey, sexy," when the American troops marched into Baghdad later tried to kill them in the name of Allah.

THE BIN LADEN AMBIVALENCE

There is no better example of this ambivalence about the West— intoxification tied with revulsion—than the bin Laden family. As Steve Coll's excellent study of the family makes clear, the second generation of bin Ladens—the children of the founder of the dynasty, an illiterate Yemeni, Muhammad—was full of people who were infatuated with modernity in general and America in particular. As teenagers, the bin Ladens liked Western American films and Western pop music. (The Beatles, Chicago, Jimi Hendrix, and the Rolling Stones were particular favorites.[9]) More than a quarter of Muhammad bin Laden's fifty-four children studied in the United States at some point.[10]

Salem, one of Muhammad bin Laden's eldest sons and his anointed successor, was particularly infatuated with America. He spent a lot of time in his house in Orlando, Florida. He embraced all the technologies of modernity, from mobile phones to airplanes, which he piloted with daredevil enthusiasm. (He eventually died when he lost control of a plane that he was piloting in Florida.) His brother, Hassan bin Laden, was one of the biggest shareholders in Iridium, a pioneering satellite telephone company. He was also a major shareholder in the Hard Rock Café Middle East, which brought the tacky music-themed restaurants to the region.[11] The bin Ladens were also central to the modernization of Mecca, building roads to take the faithful to and from their destination, installing air-conditioning in the holy sites in conjunction with an American company based in Pennsylvania, and constructing several five-star hotels and restaurants.[12]

Not all members of the family were so enamored with America, however. Muhammad bin Laden's most famous son, the much younger Osama, saw the Americanization of his family as a sign of cultural decay, and reacted by embracing the strictest form of Islam. As a student at Jeddah's King Abdulaziz University in the 1970s, he joined the Muslim Brotherhood; he read Qutb's anti-American *Milestones* and *In the Shade of the Koran* and he even attended lectures by Qutb's younger brother, Muhammad. Osama complained increasingly vigorously about "the American alienation project" to alienate his fellow Saudis from their religion.[13] He also became increasingly obsessed with the connections between Americanization and Islamic decay:

> If every Muslim asks himself why has our nation reached this state of humiliation and defeat, then his obvious answer is because it rushed madly for the comforts of life and discarded the Book of Allah behind its back, though it is the only one that has its cure . . . the Jews and Christians have tempted us with the comforts of life and its cheap pleasures and invaded us with their materialistic values before invading us with their armies, while we stood like women doing nothing because the love of death in the cause of Allah has deserted the hearts.[14]

Claiming that Osama bin Laden is typical of anything is an easy way to annoy plenty of Muslims. But in this case he was hardly breaking the mold. Islamic fervor is often closely linked with strong anti-Westernism. Two-thirds of radical Muslims regard holding fast to their spiritual and moral values as something that is critical to their lives, compared with 45 percent of more moderate people. Significantly more radicals than moderates (64 to 51 percent) think that having an enriched spiritual life is essential.

Hatred of the West and zeal for a religion that is regarded as both a source of meaning and as a victim of an existential threat are common feelings in radical Islam circles. Wherever they have gained power Islamists have directed their fury at the local agents of "Westoxification." One of the first things that Mullah Omar and his supporters did when they captured Kabul in 1996 was make an example of the former president (and champion of secularization), Mohammad Najibullah. They cut off his testicles, hitched his battered body to the back of a jeep, and drove him around town. Then they shot him and hung his blood-soaked corpse from a streetlamp. The ex-president's pockets were stuffed with money, while cigarettes were pressed between his broken fingers. The Taliban then set about ridding their country of Western and secular influences. They banned "British and American hairstyles." (Qutb also had a thing about how bad haircuts were in the United States.) They expelled women not just from the workplace but also from public view. They banned music, chess, soccer and kite-flying. They reintroduced sharia law, punishing adultery with stoning, drinking alcohol with whipping and homosexuality with death by various gruesome means.

The Islamists' greatest fury has been reserved for the engine of secular modernity—America. Bin Laden repeatedly denounces America not just as a Crusader state but also as an apostle of secular modernity. America is exporting a uniquely decadent culture around the world: a culture that glorifies immorality in the form of fornication, homosexuality, sex, drink, drugs and trading with interest; a culture that is so decadent that it has produced diseases, such as AIDS, that have hitherto been unknown to man; a culture that corrupts and degrades everything it touches. Ayman al-Zawahiri, bin Laden's deputy, argues that "the freedom we want is not the freedom to use women as a commodity to gain clients, win deals or attract tourists; it is not the freedom of AIDS and an industry of obscenities and homosexual marriages." Al Qaeda supporters regularly refer to America as the "house of unbelief" and the "enemy of God."

For them America is both a mortal threat and a paper tiger. Americans subjugate the Islamic world with their weapons and toxify it with their pop culture. But they are also too decadent to win a prolonged war. (One of the radicals' favorite sayings is that "They love Pepsi-Cola but we love death.")

It is hard to think of a more spectacular rejection of American capitalism than the felling of the Twin Towers of the World Trade Center. The Twin Towers were not only symbols of America's global financial dominance, they were also symbols of New York City—the secular Babylon that had so revolted Qutb a generation earlier and that has so much of the world in its thrall. But September 11—and Islamic radicalism in general—is more than just a rejection of the modern world fueled by crazy dreams of a seventh century caliphate. It is a commentary on the modern world written by people who are familiar with its ways and conversant with modern technology. Al Qaeda used Boeing jets to fell the twin towers. Al Qaeda communicates with the world and its followers through videocassettes and Web sites. (A generation earlier the Iranian revolution was ignited by cassette recordings of Khomeini's sermons that were smuggled into Iran and distributed around the country.) Bin Laden and the leading hijackers were well educated in the ways of the modern world. Bin Laden studied economics and business at university, and was a keen student of both engineering and management techniques when he worked for the family company. Mohammed Atta received a degree in architecture in Cairo. The architects of the slaughter spent a considerable amount of time studying and living in the West. Atta wrote a thesis on modernism and city planning at the Technical University of Hamburg. The 9/11 terrorists also drank alcohol and frequented strip clubs and porn shops. Al Qaeda uses some of the most modern management methods. Bin Laden is in many ways a terrorist entrepreneur running a finely tuned "virtual organization." Peter Bergen, a terrorism expert, points out that Al Qaeda is a franchise operation that does not so much plan atrocities as inspire and fund start-ups that bear the same brand name.

THE FATAL DIALECTIC

It would be naïve to assume that this deadly cycle of Western advance and Islamic reaction has played itself out. There are good reasons for thinking that globalization will gather pace in future years. Technological innovation seems to be getting faster by the day. Big American companies are increasingly dependent on growing demand in the developing world. General Electric calculates that 60 percent of its growth over the coming decade will come from the developing world compared with 20 percent over the past decade.[15] And companies from the developing world such as Infosys and Tata are equally keen on advancing globalization. McKinsey, a management consultancy, reckons that only a fifth of world output—or $6 trillion out of $28 trillion—is open to global competition in products, services or ownership. But in thirty years, as various markets (e.g., China) and industries (e.g., professional services) open up to global competition, that number could rise to four-fifths. This continuing globalization will not only encourage many unhappy people to embrace religion in reaction, it will provide them with the tools that they need to globalize their faith while throwing wrenches into the capitalist machine.

America's position as the world's leading producer of both Evangelical Christianity and popular culture is inevitably creating confusion. Peter Berger, the sociologist of religion, points out that foreigners regard America as a land of both "Puritans and pornographers."[16] Its success in both religion and popular culture spring from exactly the same source: its commitment to free markets. America's churches and film studios have both become global exporters because they are liberated from the state and thus have to compete for customers. But whatever their common roots, pornography and Puritanism produce very different sorts of anti-Americanism.

For many European liberals, American religiosity is its least attractive characteristic. They cannot believe that any modern person can be religious unless that person is either stupid or insane. Britain's *Private Eye* depicted George Bush as the head of an Evangelical group called the "Latter Day Morons." The former German chancellor, Gerhard Schröder, was known to accuse Bush of "hearing voices." The Pew Research Center's survey of global attitudes discovered that Europeans worry that America is dangerously religious.

Yet many cultural conservatives dislike America for exactly the opposite reason—because it is a battering ram for popular culture and an enemy of established beliefs. This is particularly true in the Arab world, where it is America as Mammon rather than America as a Crusader state that most people worry about, but it is also true of many Europeans.

All this makes anti-Americanism extraordinarily hard to combat. How do you address two completely different worries? Do you try to sell America as the land of the free or the home of traditional virtue? But at the same time it also makes America extraordinarily fascinating to the rest of the world. Fascinating because it is so odd: how can you not be gripped by the fact that Los Angeles contains both Silicone Valley and some of the biggest churches in the world? But fascinating also because it points the way to the future. The dialectic that has dominated American culture for so long—between the siren voices of capitalism and the reassuring force of religion—is going global.

PART FOUR

GOD'S WARS

CHAPTER TEN

THE BIBLE VERSUS THE KORAN:
THE BATTLE OF THE BOOKS AND THE
FUTURE OF TWO FAITHS

FOR ALL THEIR manifold disagreements, Christians and Muslims have one striking thing in common: they are both "people of the Book." They both base their beliefs on Holy Books. And they both have an obligation to spread the Word—to get those Holy Books into the hands and hearts of as many people as they can. (The Jews, the third "people of the Book," do not feel quite the same obligation to evangelize nonbelievers.)

Spreading the Word is hard. The Bible is eight hundred thousand words long and littered with tedious passages about "begatting." Many have claimed that the Koran, though only around a tenth of the length of the Bible, is an even more difficult read. Edward Gibbon complained about its "endless incoherent rhapsody of fable and precept." Thomas Carlyle said that it was "as toilsome reading as I ever undertook; a wearisome, confused jumble, crude, incondite." Both books are written in the idioms—and shot through with the assumptions—of antique societies. Scholars who spend their lives studying the holy texts still argue over their ambiguities, literary allusions and obscure references.

Yet both books pour from the world's printing presses in their millions. There are more Bibles and Korans available in more languages than

at any time in history. Over a hundred million copies of the Bible are sold
or given away every year. Annual Bible sales are worth between $425 mil-
lion and $650 million; Gideon's International gives away a Bible every
second. The Bible is available, in all or in part, in 2,426 languages, accessible to more than 90 percent of the world's population.

The Koran is ubiquitous in the Muslim world. Some of the most cher-
ished objects in the Muslim world are handwritten texts, produced by
the great masters of calligraphy, or astonishing feats of human ingenuity,
such as the complete Koran written in such microscopic writing that it
can be housed in a ring. Whole chapters of the book are used to decorate
the walls and ceilings of mosques. The faithful transcribe phrases and put
them around their necks in amulets, or turn them into bumper stickers, or
use them as letterheads.[1]

The Koran is not only the most widely read book in the Islamic world,
it is the most widely recited, too. The word "Koran" means "recitation."[2]
Indeed, many Muslims would politely reject a comparison with the Bible
on the basis that the Koran is more than just a text: it is a living thing
whose power comes from being consumed or recited. Much of the language about the Koran being on people's lips is similar to Catholic veneration of the holy sacrament. Muhammad, the Prophet who bequeathed
the book to the world, was an illiterate who recited the book for others to
write down. There is no more common sound in the Muslim world, from
Morocco to Indonesia, than the sound of the Koran being recited; there is
no higher goal in Muslim life than to turn yourself into a human reposi-
tory of the Holy Book. One of the most prized honorifics in Islamic society is *hafiz,* or "one who has the entire scripture off by heart": the Iranian
government awards an automatic university degree to anyone who can do
it. The great reciters compete in tournaments that can attract audiences in
the hundreds of thousands—the World Cups of the Islamic world—and,
if they are victorious, they produce CDs that become instant best-sellers.

The Koran is the backbone of Muslim education, taught in schools,
often by rote, studied in universities, and pored over by everybody with
a claim to education. Islamic scholars believe that studying the Koran
involves the search for literal truths—facts and laws about the world—that
were made available by God in the seventh century through the Prophet's

revelations. Learning at least a part of the Koran by heart is the single most common experience of all Muslims.[3]

In many Muslim countries the Koran is the foundation of the constitution and the basis of the law. In Saudi Arabia the Koran *is* the constitution. Majorities of people in most Muslim countries want to see sharia law—i.e., the law laid down in the Koran—put into force.[4] Even in countries where they are not the clear majority, such as Nigeria, Muslims have pushed to get sharia introduced in their regions; in Europe, a growing number of Muslims want to be able to "live by the Book," in their legal affairs as much as their private lives.

Two Books, Three Questions

This mountain of Holy Books is a giant refutation of the secularization thesis. "The Book lives on among its people," Constance Padwick, a scholar of the Koran, has written. "For them, these are not mere letters or mere words. They are the twigs of the burning bush, aflame with God."[5] The same can be said of the Bible.

The two books are also an invitation to ask three intriguing questions. Why are today's Christians and Muslims proving so successful at getting the Word out? Second, who is winning the Battle of the Books and getting them into people's hands and hearts? And lastly, does this say anything about the relative conditions of Christianity and Islam?

The straightforward answer to the first question is that Christians and Muslims are both proving remarkably adept at using the tools of modernity—globalization, the media and growing wealth—to supercharge the distribution of their Holy Books. "Give me Scotland or I die," John Knox once demanded of his flock. The modern Knoxes in both religions are content with nothing less than the world. We have already described Christianity's southward march. Islam has also fanned out from its two Arab and Southeast Asian cores—eastward toward China, northward into Europe and southward through Africa. In the course of that struggle they share some of the same problems and the same successes, though there is an interesting split in the way the two religions approach the task.

The similarities begin with the way that devotees of both Holy Books have learned how to use technology. The Islamic world boasts several television channels and radio stations that do nothing but broadcast the Koran, while, at the other end of the technological spectrum, the American Bible Society produces an audio device, powered by a battery or hand crank and no bigger than a couple of cigar boxes, that can broadcast the Bible to a crowd of a hundred. You can consult both books on the Internet. You can read them on your "Psalm Pilot" or mobile phone. You can listen to them on MP3 players or iPods. ("Podcasting" has inevitably given rise to "Godcasting.") Want to "plug into God without unplugging from life"? Then simply buy a GoBible MP3 player. Want to memorize the Koran? Then buy an MP3 player that displays the words as you listen. Want to network with like-minded people? Then the eBible allows you to discuss biblical passages with virtual friends.

Another similarity is more painful. Just because you put a Holy Book in people's hands (or on their iPods), it does not mean they will understand it. For instance, the United States, as the world's most religious rich country, is saturated with Bibles—Americans buy more than twenty million new ones every year to add to the four that sit in the average American house. Yet the state of American biblical knowledge is abysmal. One Gallup survey found that fewer than half of Americans can name the first book of the Bible (Genesis), only a third know who delivered the Sermon on the Mount (Billy Graham is a popular answer), and a quarter do not know what is celebrated at Easter (the Resurrection, the foundational event of Christianity). Sixty percent cannot name half the Ten Commandments; 12 percent think Noah was married to Joan of Arc. George Gallup, a leading Evangelical as well as a premier pollster, describes America as "a nation of biblical illiterates."

The situation is worse with Islam. Muslims believe there can be no really accurate translation of the Koran. Yet the archaic language and high-flown verse, while inspiring to some, can also be difficult to understand for even highly educated Arabic speakers. (Imagine the inhabitants of Greenwich Village trying to understand Chaucer.) Only 20 percent of Muslims speak Arabic as their first language. And illiteracy rates are high across the Muslim world—some 40 percent of Arabs cannot read Arabic, for example. Many students of the Holy Book do not grasp much of what that they are reciting and memorizing.

So the two people of the Book face similar challenges and opportunities. The interesting difference lies in how they are overcoming those hurdles. On the Christian side, the Bible business is very much a bottom-up affair—a collection of businesses with centers of excellence all over the world and new entrepreneurs constantly introducing innovations. An interlinked global network of 140 national or regional Bible societies pools resources to reach its collective goal of putting a Bible in the hands of every man, woman and child on the planet. Most Bibles are no longer printed in the West, but in cheaper places like Brazil, South Korea and China; and the missionaries distributing them are no longer white Westerners either.

The Koran is also going global. But for that it is unduly indebted to a single political power. Saudi oil wealth is supercharging the distribution of the Koran. Saudis only make up about 2 percent of the world's Muslim population, but the combination of geology and history—the country's vast oil wealth and position as the guardian of Mecca and Medina—has turned it into a vast engine for spreading the Word. The Saudi princes also regard the propagation of Islam as one of the central pillars of their foreign policy. Saudi embassies maintain religious affairs departments that are explicitly charged with spreading the state's version of Islam.[6] Some Saudi-watchers claim that the world's largest printing presses are located in Mecca.

A confidential report composed back in June 1973 by the British ambassador to the Kingdom for the British Foreign Office pointed out that the Saudis regarded their oil wealth as part of a God-given plan to spread Islam around the world:

> That God should have endowed His Holy Land with the means to finance it by the accident of oil is seen as a natural part of His plan for a world Islamic revival. Islamic maps in local classrooms show Saudi Arabia at the center of the world, with two concentric circles drawn around Mecca. The Arab and other Islamic countries are colored bright green, and countries with Muslim minorities . . . in gradually paler shades of green. Most other parts of the world are not even named.[7]

Since then the emphasis on exporting Islam and its holy text has grown ever stronger. In 1993 the government established the Ministry of Islamic Affairs, Endowments, Call and Guidance to mastermind the export of Islam.[8] Adel al-Jubeir, a Saudi foreign policy adviser, argues that "the role of Saudi Arabia in the Muslim world is similar to the role of the Vatican."[9] Alex Alexiev, of the Center for Security Policy, estimates that the kingdom is spending three to four times as much exporting its faith globally as the Soviet Union spent on external propaganda at the height of the Cold War. The late King Fahd's Web site simply states that the cost of his "efforts in this field has been astronomical."[10]

The kingdom gives away some thirty million Korans a year, sometimes in the name of the royal family, sometimes thanks to the generosity of individual billionaires, sometimes under the aegis of charitable organizations. These Korans are distributed through a vast network of mosques, Islamic societies, NGOs, embassies and Muslim charities, such as the Muslim World League, the International Islamic Relief Organization, the World Assembly of Muslim Youth or the Al-Haramain Foundation. In the early 1990s King Fahd was reported to have sent one million copies of the Koran to just one former Soviet Republic in Central Asia.[11]

At the same time, the Muslim diaspora is also spreading the Word to areas of the world where it has never reached—and Muslim missionaries are doing their best to ensure that it sticks. The Riyadh-based and Saudi-funded World Association of Muslim Youth (WAMY) advertises itself as the world's largest Muslim youth group dedicated to the spread of Islamic ideals and sacred texts; it supports offices in some fifty-five countries. Abdullah bin Laden, another of Osama's relations, who established an American branch in 1992, was particularly proud of the "kits" of proselytizing material that he created—a silver kit, a golden kit and a diamond kit, all containing translations of the Koran and commentaries by radical Muslims. The organization seems to have survived its association with a radical bin Laden: in 2002 it built twenty-eight mosques in Sudan alone.[12] The Tablighi Jamaat ("Group That Propagates the Faith") is an eighty-country network of part-time preachers who dress like the Prophet, in a white robe and leather sandals, travel in small groups and devote themselves to propagating the Koran. They can be seen anywhere from Boston to Bangalore, and their annual gatherings in India and Pakistan attract hundreds of thousands. They are also the group behind plans to construct a megamosque in East London, next to the site of the 2012 Olympics.

BATTLING FOR GOD'S WORD

Ask who is winning the battle of the books, and many pious Christians and Muslims bristle. The us-versus-them assumption that is at the heart of this question is a distraction. Can't both sides win by converting the heathen? And aren't Christianity and Islam fellow Abrahamic faiths different versions of the Truth? The Koran speaks respectfully of Christians and Jews as "people of the Book." Muslims recognize the biblical prophets and God's revelation to both Moses (the Torah) and Jesus (the Gospels). Musa (Moses) and Isa (Jesus) are common Muslim names. Besides, they ask, isn't there plenty of competition within faiths—between Pentecostals and Catholics, for example, or Sunnis and Shias—as well as competition between different faiths?

None of these objections is convincing. The faithful certainly behave as if they are engaged in a severe competition. The Koran says that God became upset with the "people of the Book" who thought that they did not need Muhammad in order to enter paradise, telling the faithful to "fight against those who have been given the scripture and believe not in Allah." One interpretation—and there are many—is that this means Christianity and Judaism are false religions. The Muslim World League Web site denigrates the Bible as being "corrupted."

The Saudi regime does not just disseminate the Koran, it also produces a lot of literature promoting the regime's stern understanding of Islam, Wahhabism. Although traditional Muslim teaching stresses those passages in the Koran that affirm the Christian Gospel and the Hebrew Torah as valid revelations of God and paths to salvation, the Wahhabis, who take their inspiration from Muhammad ibn Abd-al-Wahhab, an eighteenth century conservative theologian, embrace the harsher view that, since Muhammad delivered the final revelation, Christianity and Judaism have lost their power of salvation. The Saudis will not allow the

Bible to be distributed on their soil—which makes a mockery of many of their claims to be sponsors of interfaith dialogue. Women who convert to Christianity—and flirting with it is reputedly one of the ultimate "dares" for rich, bored women in the kingdom—are treated shockingly.

Christians, though models of tolerance by Saudi standards, fight no less fiercely for souls. Many Evangelical Christians are fixated on what they call the 10/40 window—the vast swath of the Islamic world in Africa and Asia that lies between latitudes 10 and 40. The Southwest Baptist Theological Seminary in Texas has even created a master's degree to train missionaries in the art of converting Muslims. The Bibles and videos that get into Saudi Arabia do not appear there by accident. And there is a long history of Christians mistranslating the Koran with the express purpose of discrediting Islam. Alexander Ross's version of the "Alcoran," published in 1649, set out to expose the "contradictions, blasphemies, obscene speeches and ridiculous fables" in the book. The "Koran" found in Thomas Jefferson's library, produced by George Sale, was intended to give Protestants the material that they needed to "attack the Koran with success."[13] Even today Evangelicals produce counterfeit Korans that are designed to plant doubt into Muslim minds.

And the "Battle of the Books" is certainly at the heart of the battle between the two religions. There may be no guarantee that people who get their hands on Bibles or Korans will read them, still less understand them. But there is every guarantee that people will remain heathens unless they are introduced to the Book. Once again, precise numbers are a problem—there are no systematic figures on the sales and distribution of the Koran, and the front line of the Battle of the Books cuts through some of the most dangerous places on the planet. But even an imperfect report on the Battle of the Books tells us a lot about the state of the world's two great missionary religions.

ONWARD CHRISTIAN SOLDIERS

In general, the main advantages are with the Bible, not the Koran. An immediate problem for Islam, much complained about in the Muslim world, is America's "war on terror," which is certainly making it much more difficult to spread the Koran. Contributions to Muslim charities have fallen since September 11, sometimes dramatically. Several charities have been discontinued completely. The Tablighi Jamaat has come under investigation by Western intelligence services: many active jihadis were members of the organization, including some of the prisoners in Guantánamo Bay. On the other hand, even with the new security restrictions, it is much easier to distribute Korans in the Christian world than it is to distribute Bibles in the Muslim world.

So what are the Bible's longer-term advantages? The first is that Christians are much more enthusiastic than Muslims about translating their Holy Book. Muslims believe that the Koran is the literal word of God—dictated to Muhammad by the angel Gabriel and then written down by Muhammad's followers. The Koran is not just a perfect document but also an eternal one: it has always existed in exactly the form in which it appeared to Muhammad. "The Koran does not document what is other than itself," one scholar notes. "It is not about the truth. It is the truth."

This makes Muslims uncomfortable with translations, or indeed any other "renditions," of the Koran. The Holy Book says sternly that "we have sent no messenger save with the tongue of his people." For much of the history of Islam the authorities regarded translations as impious or even blasphemous (perhaps not surprising, given the ones the Christians were peddling). Today most Muslims tolerate translations—there are now more than twenty translations into English—but it is a begrudging sort of tolerance. And most translations are as literal as possible. Pious Muslims are expected to learn God's language.

By contrast, Christians are much keener to get the Word out—and much less choosy about what form it should take. You do not have to learn Greek or Hebrew to get the Lord's word. There are more than five hundred English translations of the Bible, ranging from the grandiloquent to the colloquial; and it has been translated into more languages than any other book in history. A couple of eccentric geeks have even produced a Klingon version, though the language is spoken only by imaginary space aliens on *Star Trek*.

The headquarters of the American Bible Society, just north of Columbus Circle in New York City, for example, is a monument to Christianity's enthusiasm for translation. The words "In the beginning" are inscribed on the front of the building in more than fifty languages. In 2006 the society celebrated its 190th birthday with a marathon reading of the Bible, outside the front of the building, in twenty-five languages, attracting the interest of tourists from all over the world. It houses a collection of forty-five hundred Bibles in twenty-four hundred languages. (The collection used to be bigger but the society sent eleven hundred duplicates to a sister society in Brazil.) Some date back to the Reformation. But the number of translations increased exponentially in 1800 when the Christian world was seized by what Leonora Lupus, the curator of the collection, calls "translation fever." The British and Foreign Bible Society was founded in 1804. The American Bible Society was founded a few years later. The first Mandarin translation was produced in 1814.

The row upon row of translations—arranged by region and covering the whole world—is a striking reminder of Christianity's global reach. There are Arabic translations dating back to the sixteenth century, as well as translations in obscure African languages. A crowded corner of the collection is devoted to just one country—Papua New Guinea—where the natives speak hundreds of languages. One of the society's most prized possessions is a copy of John Eliot's Indian Bible. The first Bible printed in the New World, this was written not in English but in Algonquin. The fact that the Algonquin people themselves could not read their own language did not deter Eliot from engaging in the incredible labor of translating the Bible into their language and then getting it printed: he wanted the Bible to be the basic building block of the natives' education.

The Bible Society continues to add new translations to this extraordinary store. The society has devoted huge resources, over the past few years, to translating the Bible into Barrow, a language spoken by a handful of people in Alaska, and Gullah, an African language spoken by a small number of African Americans in South Carolina and Georgia. It justifies directing all this effort at such small groups of people on the grounds that the opportunity to read the Bible in your own language confers a sense of dignity on people who might otherwise feel marginalized. Bob Hudson, of the American Bible Society, wants everybody on the planet to be able to claim that "God speaks my language."

The second advantage is Christians' superior talent for turning their Holy Book into a commercial enterprise. Islam is not quite as uncommercial as many Westerners imagine: witness the proliferation of Korans and Koran players. But Koran production is dominated by the state and disseminated by officially approved charities. Commercial Islamic publishing houses tend to be small and rudimentary.

Consider product proliferation. Thomas Nelson, the Nashville-based Bible firm, publishes sixty different editions of the Bible every year. The Good Book now comes in every color of the rainbow, including the colors of your college. There are Bibles for every category of humanity, from "seekers" to cowboys, from brides to barmen. The African American Jubilee Bible contains over three hundred pages on the black religious experience. There is an outdoor Bible with laminated paper and a camouflage Bible for use in war zones. There are Bibles for family prayers, Bibles for personal devotion, Bibles for the theologically minded, with detailed commentaries, Bibles for the historically minded, with historical details, Bibles with commentaries by celebrated Evangelicals. The "hundred-minute Bible" summarizes the Good Book for the time-starved.

Or consider user-friendliness. There are Bibles in everyday vernacular or even street slang ("Even though I walk through / The hood of death / I don't back down / for you have my back"). Bardin & Marsee Publishing has produced the world's first "outdoor Bible," the "perfect all weather companion for campers, boaters, hunters, sports teams, the military, missionaries and any other outdoor enthusiasts." Westminster John Knox has revived an old idea—begun in 1965 with its best-selling *Gospel According to Peanuts*—to give us the *Gospel According to* everyone from Bart Simpson to Madonna.

Or consider innovation. In 2003 Thomas Nelson dreamt up the idea of BibleZines—crosses between Bibles and teenage magazines. The pioneer was *Revolve,* which intercuts the New Testament with makeup tips and dating advice ("Are you dating a Godly guy?"). This was quickly followed by *Refuel* for boys and *Blossom* for tweens. And BibleZines are only a tiny part of the universe of repackaged Bibles for the young. There are toddler-friendly versions of the most famous Bible stories. The Boy's Bible promises "gross and gory Bible stuff." The Picture Bible looks like a super-hero comic. God's Little Princess Devotional Bible is pink and sparkly.

The Bible Society, though not a commercial organization, has also embraced all sorts of innovations in pursuit of its goal of putting a copy of the Bible in the hands of every man, woman and child on the planet. It gives a free copy of the military edition of the Bible, complete with a cam-ouflage cover, quotations from inspirational figures such as Billy Graham, a military code of conduct and a guide to the principles of just war, to all members of the U.S. armed services. (The tradition of giving Bibles to American soldiers began in 1817; during the Civil War the society handed out Bibles to both sides.) It provides booklets of biblical excerpts to people who are trying to cope with tragedies or disasters: the society gave away 5 million specially prepared booklets after September 11 and 1.5 million after Hurricane Katrina. It has also teamed up with Time Warner (whose headquarters are a couple of blocks away) to produce user-friendly guides to the "mysteries of the Bible" and the Life of Christ. It also uses prominent sports stars to spread enthusiasm for the Good Book. The New Orleans Hornets have been known to distribute copies of the Bible. LeBron James, of the Cleveland Cavaliers, is such an enthusiastic Bible promoter that he has been nicknamed "King James."

Publishing and translating the Book is only the beginning. There are now sophisticated dramatizations of the Bible, with well-known actors and state-of-the-art sound effects. Zondervan's *The Bible Experi-ence* features every black actor in Hollywood, from Denzel Washington to Samuel L. Jackson as God. Zondervan has also produced a collection of "five-minute" Bible study videos that combine state-of-the-art graph-ics with interactive techniques. Other businesses are producing films that dramatize bits of the Bible as faithfully as possible. In 2008 the Missouri town of Branson unveiled *Noah—The Musical,* a massive affair that includes seventy-five live animals and seventy-five animatronic ones, as well as forty humans.[14] It was staged in the New Millennium Theatre, the coun-try's largest Christian theater, which resembles an ancient temple. More Bible-themed shows are planned.

And then there are the spin-offs. There are Bible quiz books, stuffed with crosswords and other word puzzles, and Bible bingo games. There are Bible coloring books, sticker books and floor puzzles. There is even a Bible-based jukebox that plays your favorite biblical passages at the push of a button. A "fully posable" Jesus doll recites famous passages of the Good Book.

The third advantage for the Bible over the Koran is the wealth of its believers. It helps the Bible's cause that the world's richest and most powerful country has more Evangelicals, missionaries and media organizations than any other country. By contrast, the fact that the Koran's heartland is relatively poor, with low levels of economic development, technological prowess and popular education, hurts the Book's cause—though Muslims do not see it that way. (What matters is that people are reciting the Koran, not who is doing it.)

The fourth advantage is the West's belief in religious freedom— guaranteed in America by the Constitution, and in Europe by an aversion to religious persecution caused by centuries of it. The heartland of Islam, on the other hand, is theocratic. The Saudi royal family and the official Wahhabi clerisy are intertwined: the clerics confer Islamic legitimacy on the royals and the royals give the clerics a monopoly of religious power. The Saudi Ministry of Islamic Affairs, Endowments, Call and Guidance employs a hundred and twenty thousand people, including seventy-two thousand imams. Clerics vet school textbooks. The Commission for the Promotion of Virtue and Prevention of Vice, the kingdom's religious police, frequently arrests Christians for trying to worship together or for merely possessing copies of the Bible. Filipino Christians, who are usually poor and invariably lack diplomatic clout, are a particularly popular target. Other Islamic countries are almost as tough. Pakistan has witnessed the kidnapping of Christian missionaries. Sudan punishes "religious deviation" with imprisonment.

Christian Evangelists complain that this creates an uneven playing field: Muslims can build giant mosques in "Christian lands" while Christians are barred from distributing Bibles in Saudi Arabia and Iran. But, in the long-run, uneven playing fields weaken the home players. The West's open marketplace in religion promotes innovation, even in something so basic as Bible publishing, while the Muslim world's closed marketplace promotes dull conservatism. *The Book and the Koran* (1990) by Muhammad Shahrur, which tried to reinterpret the Koran for modern readers, was widely banned in the Islamic world, despite its pious tone and huge popularity.

ISLAM, CHRISTIANITY AND MODERNITY

The Battle of the Books is clearly important in itself: the first obligation of both Christianity and Islam is to preach the Word to the faithful. But the battle also tells us something about a bigger issue—the relative ability of each faith to thrive in the face of modernity. Here again Christianity seems to be doing better than Islam.

Many people would regard that judgment as odd. Islam had a much better twentieth century than Christianity did. The world's Muslim population grew from 200 million in 1900 to 1.5 billion today—still about 500 million behind the Christian church, but an enormous catch-up. Christianity shriveled in Christendom's European heart, while Islam was resurgent across the Arab world. Some Christian scholars predict that Islam will overtake Christianity as the world's biggest religion by 2050.

Islam is also thriving in the Islamic world. As Bernard Lewis puts it, Muslim countries are "profoundly Muslim in a way and in a sense that most Christian countries are no longer Christian."[15] Ninety-nine percent of Indonesians, 98 percent of Egyptians and 86 percent of Turks say that religion plays an important role in their daily lives[16]—even higher than the figure for America and enormously higher than the 28 percent figure for Great Britain. The most common response to the question of what people in the Muslim world most admire about themselves is faithfulness to their religious beliefs. The definition of a lackadaisical Muslim is somebody who prays only once a day.

Religion saturates the culture of most Muslim countries. Shops close for prayer several times a day. Office workers adjourn to prayer rooms. Hotel rooms routinely include a small Qibla locator on the desk or nightstand pointing the way to Mecca. Local prayer times are printed in almost every Muslim newspaper. Every year more than two million pilgrims travel from all over the world to Mecca.

Islam is also doing a better job spreading to Christendom than Christianity is into the Islamic world. The talk in neoconservative circles about "Eurabia" may be overstated: Muslims make up only 4 percent of the population of the European Union. But Muslims are highly concentrated—they make up 24 percent of the population in Amsterdam; 20 percent in Malmo and Marseille; 15 percent in Paris, Brussels, Bradford and Birmingham; and 10 percent or more in London and Copenhagen.[17] You can see signs of Islam's spread across Europe, in the mosques that are springing up in cities and small towns (there are twenty-four hundred in Germany, two thousand in France and one thousand in England); in the fashion for headscarves among women; in the proliferation of Islamic bookshops and schools; in the way that Muslim-owned shops increasingly close for prayer times and religious holidays; and, alas, in the number of men who sport beards. In Britain the number of people who attend mosques every week is closing in on the number who attend Anglican churches—despite the fact that Muslims only make up 3 percent of the population and Britain has two thousand years of history as a Christian nation.

The Muslim population is bound to grow. The continent that gave the world Thomas Malthus, the first great worrier about overpopulation, is suffering from a birth dearth. Over the next twenty-five years the number of Europeans of working age will decline by 7 percent while the number of retired people will increase by 50 percent. Europe has little choice but to import workers from the Muslim societies on its southern periphery, where birth rates are high and job opportunities limited. If the number of Muslims triples over the next three decades (just as it did over that past three), France, which is now 10 percent Muslim, could be 25 percent Muslim in 2040. Several European cities will become majority Muslim.

Islam has also gained political clout around the world. In 1975 it seemed like a spent force politically in the Middle East: secular Arab nationalism was the vogue. But Iran has been a militant Islamic regime since the mullahs seized power in 1979. Islamic parties have won free elections wherever they have been allowed to participate in the Arab world. Hamas won a stunning victory in the Palestinian elections of 2006. Turkey is ruled by an Islamic party that is encouraging the spread of piety. In Iraq, Afghanistan, Pakistan and many of the former Soviet republics Islam is a potent political force. In other places, such as Egypt and Morocco, Islamists may well be the government in waiting. Morocco's king styles himself "Defender of the Faith." In 2001 Malaysia's ruler, Mahathir bin Mohamad, controversially suggested that, whatever the constitution might say, Malaysia was "an Islamic state." Indonesia has seen an increase in piety since the 1960s, with notably more women wearing headscarves. Saudi money has been at work building mosques and spreading Wahhabi ideas throughout Southeast Asia—even having some success with the tiny Muslim community in Cambodia.[18]

In Europe too, Muslims are developing political muscle. Muslim groups have begun to rate British politicians on how they vote on "Muslim" issues. In particular, they have taken to reminding Labor politicians that their margin of victory is often smaller than the Muslim populations in their constituencies. George Galloway, a left-wing blowhard, unseated a Labor Party candidate by playing on Muslim anxieties. The largest protest in British history—a two-million-strong march against the invasion of Iraq in February 2003—was co-organized by the Muslim Association of Britain. Prince Charles once suggested that when he becomes king he will change his title from "Defender of the Faith" to "Defender of the Faiths," partly in recognition of Islam's arrival on Britain's shores.

In 2008, Boris Johnson, London's new mayor, helped organize a festival in Trafalgar Square to celebrate the end of Ramadan. Johnson is no fan of political correctness; he was simply being practical. Across Europe mayors have to worry about things like setting up temporary abattoirs to cope with the slaughter of sheep for the annual Eid al-Adha feast in December, or organizing the parking around mosques on Fridays. And an increasing number of those mayors, including the heads of Rotterdam and Leicester, are Muslims.

As for coping with modernity, the Arab world is experiencing not one but two economic booms, in the Gulf and around the Mediterranean. In many ways Dubai is a model of cosmopolitan modernity. The Jumeirah Beach Hotel displays signs noting that there are sixty-five different nationalities of guests and eighty-six of staff. The sail-shaped Burj Al Arab, "the world's only seven-star hotel," allows guests to choose from thirteen different types of pillows on which to lay their heads. Dubai boasts a bizarre ski slope inside a shopping center, an airport that makes either Heathrow or JFK look archaic and now the world's tallest building (symbolically reclaiming for the Arab world a title it lost to the West when Lincoln Cathedral climbed higher than the pyramids at Giza). Dubai's extravagance is the most visible sign of a region awash with oil money. The six Gulf nations—Saudi Arabia, Kuwait, Oman, Qatar, Bahrain and the UAE—pocketed $400 billion from their exports of oil and gas in 2007. One estimate by the McKinsey Global Institute, admittedly based on $100 a barrel oil, reckoned they could reap a cumulative windfall of almost $9 trillion by 2020.

Dubai is interesting because it has no oil of its own. Instead, Dubai has successfully turned itself into a middleman, concentrating on finance, trade and tourism, quintessentially cosmopolitan activities. Over lunch, Dubai's ruler, Sheikh Mohammed, insists that his kingdom is simultaneously both Islamic and modern. Religion is the bedrock of his life and prayer a central part of his daily ritual: he sees himself as an Arab in touch with his roots, disappearing off into the desert frequently. Islam is the state religion in Dubai and the government pays for nearly all the mosques and imams; but other faiths are free to set up shop. Dubai is following the same approach of tolerance and entrepreneurship as Islam's founding Prophet. On the other side of the table, his son nods his head vigorously.

The Saudis are a much less tolerant bunch than the Maktoums, Dubai's ruling family, but they have also learned how to use some of the tools of modernity to reinforce the faith. Consider the example of the annual Hajj—the pilgrimage to the holy cities of Mecca and Medina that faithful Muslims are expected to make at least once in their lifetimes. The Hajj used to be difficult and dangerous—people were robbed or even killed by bandits on the road, and conditions in the holy cities were unhygienic, with pilgrims slaughtering sheep in the street, and dangerous, with crowds getting out of control and people dying in the crush, particularly during the ritual stoning of the devil. But in the 1990s the Saudis poured more than $18 billion into modernizing the Hajj, adding modern roads, hotels and, crucially, air-conditioning.[19] Overhead water sprinklers now cool pilgrims during the Day of Standing. A state-of-the-art slaughterhouse can accommodate 500,000 goats and sheep; another can accommodate

10,000 camels and cattle.[20] About 100,000 pilgrims a year made the Hajj in the early twentieth century. Today there are more than 2 million and they come from 125 different countries.

Saudi Arabia is protected by its oil wealth. But what about the teaming masses of the Maghreb? The southern Mediterranean is also enjoying a boom. The container port in Tangiers, Morocco, is still under construction—a jumble of wire fences, concrete lumps and chaotically driven trucks—but fairly soon it should be the size of Long Beach. On the outskirts of Cairo, work is under way at the Smart Village, a Silicon Valley–style technology park that has attracted the likes of Microsoft, Oracle and Vodafone. Foreign direct investment in the countries along the Mediterranean shore, from Morocco to Turkey, has grown by a factor of six since the turn of the century, to $59 billion in 2006—a figure in the emerging world second only to China.[21] Much of this wealth has been swallowed by three countries—Egypt, Turkey and the decidedly un-Islamic Israel—but there is hope that North Africa and what was once called the Near East will become Western Europe's new backyard. In July 2008 Nicolas Sarkozy welcomed forty heads of state and government from the EU and the southern and eastern Mediterranean to create a new club, called the Union for the Mediterranean.

THE TROUBLE WITH ISLAM

The idea that Islam is incompatible with the modern world is clearly untrue. But the plain fact is that the Islamic world is a long way behind the Christian one in its engagement with modernity. Islam is coming to a succession of epochal religious debates—particularly about the relationship between faith and authority—much later than Christianity. Christianity, particularly in its American version, has resolved those debates in a way that has rendered it well equipped to thrive along with modernity. Muslim scholars' hackles rise when people talk about Islam needing a Reformation: they see that as a Christian solution to a Christian set of problems (such as indulgences and papal corruption). But nothing similar to it or the Enlightenment has happened in the Islamic world.

Look at the relative performance of Christianity and Islam in the light of several centuries of history and the latter's recent growth looks less impressive. Christianity has expanded massively since the sixteenth century, thanks to the dynamism of first Europe, then the United States. During the same period Islam, which once controlled three of the world's economic superpowers—the Ottoman Empire, Persia and India—has suffered from repeated setbacks. The territory ruled by Islam has been shrinking since the Ottomans were turned back at the gates of Vienna in 1683. European powers galloped ahead thanks to the scientific and industrial revolutions.

Despite the blessings of oil, the Arab world—the very heart of Islam, even if it does not contain most Muslims—lags behind the West in most indices of economic success and political maturity, from investment in science to free and fair elections. The total GDP of the Arab League, which contains twenty-two countries and three hundred million people, is about the same size as that of Spain. Islam was once the center of the civilized world: Muslim scholars collected and translated all the great books from the East as well as the West, dominating every sphere of learning, from philosophy to mathematics. ("Algebra" comes from the Arabic word *al-jabr*.) Nowadays, in terms of the knowledge economy, Islam is an also-ran, partly because of its treatment of women. One in every two Arab women cannot read or write. Some ten million children do not go to school at all. Investment in research and development is less than a seventh of the world average. The annual ranking of the world's top universities, compiled by Shanghai's Jiao Tong University, includes not a single Arab institition, compared with six in tiny Israel. There is depressingly little evidence of internal cultural creativity, and even less of curiosity about the outside world. More books are translated into Spanish every year than have been translated into Arabic in the past millennium.

There are problems with both Arab economic booms. Most Gulf countries have an unhealthy reliance on a single windfall, oil, that owes everything to the twin accidents of geology and geography and nothing to the ingenuity and entrepreneurialism of the people. The rest of the world, worried about global warming and political instability in oil-producing countries, is desperately trying to find alternative sources of power.

Earlier this decade, when oil was below $30 a barrel, many Arab governments looked indebted and insecure and the Saudis were facing Islamic insurgents. But even if the oil price climbs again, there will be problems. Roughly two in three private-sector jobs in the Gulf are performed by foreigners. (In the UAE, it is 90 percent.) According to McKinsey, the Gulf economies need to create 280,000 jobs a year to employ their young people. But despite some of the lowest student-teacher ratios in the world, the religious schools give their students few marketable skills: indeed, foreign firms are forced to take quotas of the locals through affirmative action programs. McKinsey reckons a quarter of native employees in Bahrain, Saudi Arabia and the UAE fail to show up for work.[22]

As for the southern Mediterranean, it has a lot of catching up to do. The MEDA ten (a group of southern and eastern economies) have an average income per head of only $6,200, putting them roughly where Western Europe was in 1950 and Romania was in 1975. By one count it would take almost a hundred sixty years for the MEDA ten to catch up with the European Union average. Many of the countries along the coast feel more desperate than prosperous. The Egyptian economy may have been booming, with a prosperous upper class and a spanking-new highway linking Cairo to Alexandria, but most of its seventy-five million citizens are still desperately poor, and Cairo is abuzz with gossip about the eventual departure of Hosni Mubarak. The subtitle of one recent book about the country was *The Land of the Pharaohs on the Brink of Revolution*.[23] The Muslim Brotherhood claims that it would win any fair election. One of the brotherhood's leaders, a doctor who has recently been let out of jail (and has the bruises to prove it), smiles: "We shall overcome . . . eventually."

For every gleaming tower in Dubai, you can find a hundred examples of Muslim economies falling behind. Why is Algeria, once the breadbasket of the Roman Empire, one of the biggest wheat importers in Africa? Why are the air conditioners that cool the pilgrims when they visit the holy cities made by an American company? And why does some of the more complicated equipment have to be installed miles away from the Prophet's Mosque, so that non-Muslims, who are barred from Muslim holy sites, can fix it when it goes wrong?[24] Perhaps most telling of all, why is the oil money still being pocketed by governments or ruling families?

Many European Muslims are also doing badly. Millions of them live in inner cities and impoverished suburbs. Most of the original immigrants were poorly educated people who were imported to do low-skilled jobs that Europeans no longer wanted to do. And the combination of Europe's overgenerous welfare state and its tradition of protecting insiders has hampered integration. Two-thirds of British Muslims live in low-income households. In Holland, the country with the largest proportion of Muslims, as many as 60 percent of Moroccans and Turks above the age of forty are unemployed. In France, the country with the largest Muslim population in absolute terms, there is not a single mainland politician in the Assemblée from Muslim background. In Germany, only 3 percent of young Muslims make it to university. Predictably, many young Muslims have reacted to marginalization by embracing radicalism. The British security services estimate that up to three thousand Britons have passed through Al Qaeda training camps.[25] Many Europeans associate Islam not with the great achievements of its civilization or with the resurgent economies of the oil states but with a succession of religion-fueled atrocities: the death sentence pronounced on Salman Rushdie, the murders of Pim Fortuyn and Theo van Gogh, the train bombings in London and Madrid, a surge in anti-Semitic abominations, riots about cartoons and plays.

Many Muslims protest that such radicalism has little to do with the peaceful religion that they follow. That may be true. But it is hard to ignore two facts. First, a lot of the radicalism is rooted in Islam. Hezbollah is the self-proclaimed "army of God." Suicide bombers in Palestine and elsewhere claim to be engaged in a religious act. Osama bin Laden launched his war in Islam's name, arguing that "to kill Americans and their allies, both civil and military, is the individual duty of every Muslim who is able." And, second, a substantial minority of Muslims agree with all or some of his broad aims. Millions celebrated the fall of the Twin Towers. Solid majorities of Palestinians and Indonesians told Pew's pollsters that they had at least some confidence in bin Laden to "do the right thing regarding world affairs," as did nearly half of those polled in Morocco and Pakistan.[26]

Martyrs or Traitors

Merely posing the question of whether Islam is different raises Muslim hackles. They sense a post-September 11 witch hunt, and with some cause. Every Western schoolboy now "knows" that the Koran promises suicide bombers will be provided with seventy-two virgins (not true) and that in Muslim countries you can get stoned to death for being homosexual (true, sadly, in some places). Yet few Western schoolboys know much about the equally bloodcurdling texts of the Old Testament: if you want illiberal family law, Leviticus is hard to beat (though few Christians or Jews implement it). Islamic politics, Muslims argue, are not uniform: Kano in northern Nigeria is very different from Karachi or Kuwait or Kuala Lumpur. In South Asia, for instance, much is made of the rise of the Taliban and the spread of Saudi Wahhabism; but Sufism, which blends Islam with folk religion and Hinduism, is far more prevalent. Sufism is a much more relaxed, even hedonistic, affair, which focuses on the worship of saints, supposedly descended from the Prophet Muhammad. The number of strict Sufis who devote their life to mysticism is relatively small, but most of the 450 million Muslims in Pakistan, India and Bangladesh (a third of the worldwide total) borrow at least some of its traditions.[27] Sufism explains many of the shrines you see on the roads as well as some of South Asia's largest religious festivals, such as a three-day, somewhat Bacchanalian event in the Pakistani town of Sehwan Sharif, the burial place of a Sufi saint, Lal Shabaz Qalandar.

Muslims might be a little embarrassed by this, but they point out that this lighter, more tolerant side of Islam rarely gets mentioned. Instead, the focus is always on the troubles of Arabia. Here Muslims present a separate explanation. The problems of the Arab world, they maintain, have nothing to do with faith; they were caused by the fact that the Ottoman Empire was amateurishly subdivided by the British and then exploited by a variety of foreign powers.

There is a lot of truth in this political critique. For many Muslims the modern world has brought nothing but disaster: from European imperialism to the arrival of global oil firms to the creation and expansion of Israel to foreign-inspired coups. The current cartography of the Muslim world was largely a poisoned gift from the West. The British drew the borders of Iraq and Kuwait; the United Nations divided Palestine. The French created Lebanon. This often did the inhabitants no favors—artificial borders produced ethnic tensions and political instability, and these in turn generated a demand for strong rulers. The Western powers continued to interfere even when they had formally withdrawn—as when the British and American secret services deposed the prime minister of Iran because he had the temerity to nationalize the oil industry. Arab rulers reinforced their misery by borrowing bad ideas from the West such as Fabian socialism and hypernationalism. The Arab-Israeli War in 1967, when tiny Israel inflicted a humiliating defeat on the massed armies of the Arab world, confirmed their sense that theirs was a civilization in crisis.

The Western elites who eventually took over much of the Islamic world played a particularly traumatic role as messengers of modernity. They not only imported Western technology and economics (often in the misguided form of socialist planning), they also imported the European assumption that modernization entails secularization. Many of them were no doubt sincere in their desire to bring progress to their countries. But they frequently adopted brutal methods. And they were usually bad messengers—closely tied to Western interests and ruthlessly bent on lining their own pockets. The Shah of Iran was the quintessential example of Western-imposed modernity: here was a man who clamped down on Islam, but spent more than $300 million on a party to celebrate the thirtieth anniversary of his accession to the throne, flying in leaders from all over the world and stuffing them with food and wine imported directly from Maxim's in Paris (all at a time when the average annual income in Iran was barely $500 a head).

So there are powerful secular reasons why so many Muslims should be hostile to modernity. But there are still reasonable questions a dispassionate observer of any faith or none should be asking. Why does Islam make so little room for freedom of conscience? Why is Islam involved in quite so many modern wars of religion? Why have so many Muslims coped so badly with modernization? Bad luck cannot explain all of this.

Islam arguably has a bigger problem with the notion at the heart of Western modernity—individual conscience—than has Christianity. Larry Siedentop, of Oxford University, points out that Islam and Christianity draw radically different conclusions from the premise of the moral equality of all believers.[28] Islam emphasizes the "equal submission" of believers to Allah's will, while Christianity, at least in its modern form, emphasizes the "equal liberty" of believers under the Christian God. "Equal submission" puts a heavy emphasis on conforming to certain rules, whereas "equal liberty" stresses the importance of following your own conscience. These differences may have been a result of the different early histories of the two religions: Islam primarily spread by the sword while, much of the time, Christianity spread by persuasion. But it has had a dramatic long-term influence on the political cultures of the two religions: the idea that moral equality entails personal autonomy and respect for the individual conscience eventually led to the Western distinction between the public and the private and the sacred and the profane.

Islam's difficulty with modernity is further complicated by three things. The first is the doctrinal splits within Islam, particularly the splits between Sunnis and Shias, which today yawn much wider than the gap between Catholics and Protestants. An ancient disagreement to do with the primacy of various successors of the Prophet has become a greater schism—exaggerated not just by the sectarian killings in Iraq but also by a power struggle between different Arab states. This is a division that in different countries in different ways divides moderates from extremists, ins from outs: the Shia radicals of Iran and the Sunni radicals of Al Qaeda detest each other. Emmanuel Sivan, an Israeli expert on Islam, points out that in Gaza, Fatah loyalists have accused Hamas of being Shia. The same "insult" is used in Nigeria. (And it gets worse. The Sunni-Shia split also makes relations more difficult with other religions: the sort of Sunnis who contend that apostate Shias should have no rights tend to take a harsh view of other faiths, such as Christainity and Judaism.)

Not that all Sunnis and Shias are united within their denominations either. The Sunni Palestinians have received more help, many would argue, from Shias in Lebanon and Iran than they have from Saudi Arabia. Al Qaeda and the Muslim Brotherhood are both radical Sunni movements that grew out of bitterness over colonialism, but the two groups are locked in a fierce ideological battle over the use of violence: the brotherhood says that it should only be used against occupiers, while for Al Qaeda violence seems to be a tool of first resort. Al Qaeda also has no truck with the way that Hamas and the Muslim Brotherhood embrace democracy, which Al Qaeda believes is a dangerous Western invention.

Christianity is, of course, not entirely innocent in this respect. The bickering between the Orthodox patriarchs of Constantinople and Moscow can be just as petty as anything that the Muslim world has to offer. But recent years have seen a dramatic rapprochement between Protestants and Catholics: so much so that some religious scholars are speculating about "the end of the Reformation." And Christian countries have done a better job of keeping religion and politics separate. Muslims are much more likely than Christians to be riven by wars of religion, with their ugly mixture of schismatic passions and political maneuverings.

The second complication Islam has in coming to terms with modernity is that, at least in theological matters, many Islamic reformers would like to go backward rather than forward. Westerners, as you might expect, like to split Muslims between old-timers and modernizers. In fact, the modernizers (people, say, who would like to let women lead prayers) are a tiny group. Often the main argument within Islam is not between modernizers and traditionalists but between two sets of conservatives.

In one category are Salafists (those who rely only on the teachings of the Prophet and his immediate companions or successors) and neofundamentalists, who argue that nothing of great value has happened in Islam since the first couple of generations of the faith. Like fundamentalist Christians, they feel that believers should disregard most of the writings, customs and ideas which their faith has produced in the last millennium and refocus on holy writ. For Muhammad ibn Abd-al-Wahhab, whose thinking informs modern Saudi Islam, there was a battle to be waged against "new" customs like the veneration of tombs and relics. For his spiritual descendants and other fundamentalists, a similar battle needs waging against television and Western clothes. Among Muslims in the Western world, this neofundamentalist way of thinking can lead people to an intense engagement with democratic politics; but it can also lead some into the nihilist violence of Al Qaeda.

The opposing category of Muslim teachers is traditionalist in a more literal sense. They see themselves as guardians and representatives of a vast corpus of Muslim thought, as it has evolved over the centuries and reacted creatively, in each successive generation, to changing circumstances. Because it acknowledges that circumstances vary, even if the Word of God does not, this school of traditionalism provides a basis at least for Islam's engagement with the contemporary world. Its cautious, scholarly reading of the Koran is often hailed as the best antidote to jihadist violence. But with respect to the role of the sexes, say, or homosexuality, the traditionalists are in a different eon from most Westerners. In any case, this milder form of traditionalism has lost out to the neofundamentalist strain in countless mosques and madrassas around the world.

So much for theology. More depressing, to most modern eyes, is the central political battle within the Muslim world, which has little to do with religion. Rather, as a colleague of ours, Peter David, once described it, it comes down to a separate contest between "martyrs," who are ready to die for change, and the authoritarian "traitors," who now wield power and are too friendly by half with the West. The former have a simple, coherent message that goes well with the Wahhabi and other Islamist causes: failure in Muslim countries has been due to moral dissoluteness and secularism. Society should be rebased on the Koran. The martyrs' strength is that organizations like Hamas or the Muslim Brotherhood are relatively incorrupt and democratic and continue to "resist" Israel and the West. On the other side of the argument are the "traitors"—the Arab world's authoritarian regimes, most of them propped up by some mixture of Western might and oil money. Some, such as Egypt, suppress the Islamists in the name of maintaining secularism; others, such as Saudi Arabia (which is theocratic but from the radicals' point of view not theocratic enough), suck up to the radicals. All the traitors in their different ways feed on the assumption that Islam is incompatible with democracy.

There are some alternatives to this dismal choice. As we have seen, tiny Dubai is relatively open. Some Asian brands of Islam seem better suited to coping with the modern world. Indonesia and Malaysia have their injustices; but their politics do not fit the martyr-traitor split. Neither does Turkey's, perhaps the greatest hope. (We will look at it in greater detail in chapter twelve.) Revealingly, large majorities in Indonesia, Malaysia, Bangladesh and Turkey have rejected the imposition of extreme versions of sharia law. In Indonesia, when a religious scholar named Ulil Abshar Abdalla was issued with a death sentence by conservative scholars for rejecting elements of Islamic law, clerics protested and the conservatives had to deny that any such death sentence had ever been issued.

And there are even a few tentative signs of challenges to the old order. For instance, with the active backing of the Justice and Development Party, scholars at the University on Ankara in Turkey are working on a new version of the Hadith, Muhammad's sayings, putting them in some kind of context. Mehmet Görmez, a theology professor at the University of Ankara, pointed out to *Newsweek* that a Hadith forbidding women from traveling alone (which has been used to ban women from driving in Saudi Arabia) was "clearly not a religious injunction, but was related to security in a specific time and place."[29] In Iran, a popular mullah, Mohsen Kadivar, has attacked the regime for claiming theocratic powers the Koran never gave it.

Still, Islam is clearly a long way behind Christianity when it comes to intellectual freedom: removing religious compulsion from the public square and making room for the free exchange of doubts and ideas. The most important indicator of Islam's failure in coming to terms with modernity is its ingrained hostility to pluralism.

THE PLURALIST IMPERATIVE

Pluralism is the hallmark of all the world's most advanced societies. The rise of Protestantism, with its emphasis on the individual conscience, helped to power economic growth in Northern Europe. The introduction of religious choice antedated the introduction of democracy in most of the modern world. And most westerners regard freedom of conscience as just as important as the freedom to vote, if not more so. Pluralism also seems to toughen religion—or at least it has done so outside Europe, bearing out Adam Smith's insight that in a free market vibrant religious "firms" will grow and lethargic ones contract.[30] Resistance to pluralism is thus a double disaster for Islam: it is holding back economic progress in general and undermining its ability to compete for souls in the long run.

The acid test of pluralism is conversion—the freedom to join a religious community or leave it. Yet across the Islamic world Muslims are either nervous about conversion or adamantly opposed to it. Large numbers of Muslims believe that leaving the faith—apostasy—is at best a grave sin and at worst a crime that should result in punishment. Mainstream scholars in both the Shia and the Sunni traditions defend the death penalty for apostates by pointing out that the Prophet reportedly said on his deathbed that there should not be two religions in Arabia (though some scholars dispute the validity of this particular hadith).

The fiercest opposition to pluralism comes from Saudi Arabia. Apostasy or attempting to convert Muslims carries the death sentence. The Saudis refuse to allow non-Muslims to build religious buildings, despite the fact that there are seven million "guest workers," including up to a million Catholics, in the country, and they only allow them to worship together if they are neither seen nor heard. The Saudi religious police still harass worshippers from other religious traditions and persecute the country's Shia population. The children of expatriate Saudi fathers are presumed to be Muslim simply on the grounds that their fathers are Saudi citizens—and there have been several tragic cases of Saudi fathers kidnapping their children from their estranged Western wives, bringing them back to Saudi Arabia and forcing them to become Muslims.

Saudi Arabia is not alone in its bloodiness. Afghanistan still has the death penalty for apostasy. In 2002 Sima Samar, a women's affairs minister, was charged with the crime of blasphemy when she said that she did not believe in sharia. (She eventually resigned amid death threats.[31]) Abdul Rahman, an Afghan who had spent years living in Germany, was sentenced to death after the police found him with a Bible. Rahman was eventually allowed to emigrate to Italy after international protests, but Afghanistan's democratically elected parliament tried to stop him from emigrating.[32]

"Soft" Muslim countries still have some pretty hard laws. For instance, tolerant Dubai has its limits in this respect: non-Muslims are free to pray as they wish, to build churches and temples, but trying to convert Muslims is a criminal offense; and there are special visa restrictions for Jews. Despite its vote against strict sharia (and the fact that religious choice is enshrined in its constitution), Malaysia has generally moved in the opposite direction. Changing religion used to be a formality, just requiring registration; now sharia courts intervene to stop anybody from leaving Islam. A celebrated recent case involved Lina Joy, who asked a federal court to register her change from Islam to Christianity on her ID card. The judges rejected her bid, telling her that one "cannot, at one's whims or fancies, renounce or embrace a religion."[33]

As this implies, theology and politics are all too entangled. In theocracies such as Saudi Arabia and Iran there is no distinction between questioning religion and questioning the regime. In Lebanon, where political power is allocated on the basis of membership in a confessional group, leaving that group directly affects its power: converting from Islam to Christianity is necessarily a political act. This is obviously not just a Muslim problem: it is true for Catholics and Protestants in Northern Ireland, and for Orthodox and Catholics in the former Yugoslavia. But the theological bias against conversion in Muslim countries is reinforced by the widespread sense that Islam is being threatened by an alien Christian-secular-Western civilization. Indeed, in most of the prominent apostasy cases, public opinion has been behind the hardest possible line. Usama Hasan, a young British imam, ran into a hail of protest on Islamic Web sites when he made the case for the right to change religion.

This aversion to pluralism poisons everything that it touches in the Islamic world. It encourages unthinking deference to authority and tradition. From kindergarten onward Arabs are instructed to seek the truth not in experience but in the Koran. It reinforces autocratic governments, which are intertwined with the clerical establishment. It also limits intellectual life. How can you cultivate the intellectual talents of your own population, let alone attract the world's best and brightest, if you do not allow the free discussion of "first things"? For all the money the Saudis are now pouring into higher education, they have no chance of producing world-class universities as long as they embrace theocracy: talent will inevitably go elsewhere.

There are some reasons for hope. After all, most middle-of-the-road

Muslims across the Arab world live in a world of choice as consumers (and even sometimes as voters). The Shias in particular are less fundamentalist, in the strict sense of the word, than the Sunnis. They put more emphasis on Islam's capacity to react creatively to new circumstances. And some clerics are making much more strident noises. In 2007 Egypt's grand mufti, Ali Gomaa, hardly a squishy liberal, caused a storm in the Islamic world when he published an article embracing the principle of freedom of religion, pointing to three verses in the Koran: "Unto you your religion, and unto me my religion"; "Whosoever will, let him believe, and whosoever will, let him disbelieve"; and (most simply) "There is no compulsion in religion."

There are also grounds for hope regarding the birth of a reformed version of Islam outside the Arab world in three places in particular: Turkey, Europe and the United States. Turkey's Islamic Justice and Development Party (AKP), which took over the government in 2002, is making a valiant attempt to reconcile Islam with modernity. This has not gone completely smoothly. The army, which regards itself as the guardian of Atatürk's secularism, has flirted with coups to depose the Islamic government. The constitutional court came close to outlawing the party completely in 2008. For its part, the AKP has flirted with drives to ban alcohol and downgrade the teaching of evolution. But for all that, the AKP has accepted the basic principles of democracy and pluralism. The party rests on the support of a growing middle class that is both religious and economically vibrant, and it is succeeding in pulling many would-be radical Islamists toward the center. The party has banned the death penalty, given women more rights than ever before, opened up universities to people from poorer backgrounds and refrained from banning abortion.

Despite its radical fringe, Europe provides as many reasons for hope as it does for pessimism. The influx of Muslims into Europe is the largest encounter between Islam and modernity in human history. Europe is producing a growing Muslim middle class—and an emerging Muslim intelligentsia that is trying to reconcile Islam with modernity. Across the Continent Muslim women are getting married at a later date, having fewer children and entering the workforce. A poll for Policy Exchange, a right-leaning think tank, discovered that 68 percent of Muslims said that

Islam and the Western notion of democracy were compatible and 78 percent said that it was possible to be both British and Muslim equally.[34]

The United States also provides a potential source of reform-minded Muslims: linked to a powerful economy and imbued with the principles of pluralism and individual rights. A survey of American Muslims for the Pew Research Center, the first ever nationwide survey of the group, described them as "middle class and mostly mainstream."[35] It might also have said they were quintessentially American: they liked their communities, believed that hard work paid off and backed the idea that Muslims who came to the United States should try to adopt American customs rather than remaining distinct from the rest of the country. By a margin of nearly two to one (63 to 32 percent) they saw no conflict between being a devout Muslim and living in a modern society.

The similarities between American Muslims and American Christians are particularly striking. American Muslims are a little more likely than Christians to say religion is "very important" in their lives (72 versus 60 percent). But they are a little less likely to say that they pray every day (61 versus 70 percent). The two communities are about equally likely to attend religious services at least once a week (40 percent of Muslims versus 45 percent of Christians). Muslims are thus mainstream members of a pluralist religious society.

One optimistic parallel could be Catholicism, which used to take a dim view of what Gregory XVI called, in the 1830s, "this madness that everyone should have and practice freedom of conscience." It was an American Catholic, John Courtney Murray, who played the leading role in persuading the Second Vatican Council to renounce the ancient doctrine that governments should recognize the monopoly of "the one true religion" and instead come to terms with religious pluralism. This embrace of pluralism had a big effect: of the thirty countries that abandoned authoritarianism for democracy between 1974 and 1989, three-quarters were Catholic.[36] Murray was a fervent Catholic who never abandoned the idea that his church was the universal one. What he rejected was the idea that the best way to advance the Catholic cause was to form an alliance with the civil power rather than trying to change people's minds.

From this perspective the current pope's attitude toward Islam is interesting. In his Regensburg speech in 2006 and especially in a later address to the Vatican curia, Benedict XVI made it clear that the Islamic world had to come to terms with the Enlightenment. That did not mean weakening its faith but embracing two ideas, which he also sees as preconditions for any serious interfaith dialogue: first, accepting religious freedom as an inalienable right, and second, drawing some separation between church and state.[37] It is a mark of how far Islam still has to go that this was immediately rejected by many Muslims. But the pope is not giving up. On Easter Sunday 2008, he publicly (and provocatively) baptized Magdi Allam, an Egyptian-born journalist who now lives in Italy and who duly described his liberation from Islam at length. The pope has also publicly defended the right of Christians to proselytize among Muslims.

The Battle of the Books is still on. Two thousand years into the history of the Abrahamic religions, the twigs of the burning bush are still aflame with the fire of God.

CHAPTER ELEVEN

THE NEW WARS OF RELIGION

❧❧

THE FOUR-HOUR JOURNEY through the bush from Kano to Jos in northern Nigeria features many of the staples of African life: checkpoints with greedy soldiers, huge potholes, scrawny children drying rice on the road. But it is also a journey along a front line.

Nigeria, evenly split between Christians and Muslims, is a country where people identify themselves by their religion before they call themselves Nigerians or members of particular tribes. Around twenty thousand people have been killed in God's name in Africa's most populous country since 1990, estimates Shehu Sani, a local chronicler of religious violence.[1] Kano, the center of the Islamic north, introduced sharia law in 2000 (as did eleven other of Nigeria's thirty-six states). Many of the Christians who fled ended up in Jos, the capital of Plateau State, where the Christian south begins. The road between the two towns is dotted with competing churches and mosques.

This is one of many religious battlefields in this part of Africa. Evangelical Christians, backed by American collection-plate money, are surging northward, clashing with Islamic fundamentalists, backed by Saudi petrodollars, surging southward. And the Christian-Muslim split is only one form of religious competition in northern Nigeria. Events in Iraq have helped set Sunnis, who make up most of Nigeria's Muslims, against the better-organized Shias: about fifty people have died in intra-Muslim violence, reckons Sani. On the Christian side, Catholics are in a more peaceful battle with Protestant Evangelists, whose signs promising immediate redemption dominate the roadside. By the time you reach Jos and see a poster proclaiming "the ABC of nourishment," you are surprised to discover it refers to chocolate.[2]

Recently Christians have been returning to Kano, partly because sharia law (which in any case applies only to Muslims) has been introduced sympathetically. None of the bloodier sentences has been carried out, and some Christians are envious of the speed of the courts. Local Muslim officials are proud of the tolerant way in which the law has been introduced. The election in April 2007 was settled in a reassuringly secular way—with the local political barons swapping cash and ballot papers in the bungalow of the Prince Hotel.[3] The young men loafing around in soccer shirts on the road from Kano to Jos know far more about soccer than politics.

Yet they are aware of who is on whose side. Indeed, it would not take much for things to boil over again. The Muslim north resents the Christian south's hogging of Nigeria's oil money. The Christian south still resents the fact that the British administrators, who were worried about religion even in colonial times, favored Muslims and stopped Christian missionaries from making a nuisance of themselves: they complain that Christians are treated as *dhimmi*—second-class citizens. It does not take much to set off violence between Christians and Muslims in Nigeria: in 2002 it was an article by a female journalist for a reputable Nigerian newspaper about the Miss World competition, which made a joke about the Prophet Muhammad choosing a contestant for a wife; in 2006 it was the Danish cartoons of the Prophet. More people died in the "cartoon wars" in Nigeria than anywhere else.

The violence continues. When the shadowy "Black Taliban" struck a police station in Kano in 2007, 20 militants or so were killed. Later that year, Muslim youths set shops on fire based on rumors that a Christian teacher in the area had drawn a cartoon of the Prophet Muhammad. Much of the sectarian violence is shockingly routine. In November 2008 some 300 people died after the "Christian" party won the disputed local elections in Jos. Some 7,000 people were displaced and many mosques and churches burned (one monk had a lucky escape when a Molotov cocktail happened to land in his toilet).[4] Although the death toll was 130, higher than the total in the Mumbai attacks that took place at exactly the same time, it was barely recorded in the Western press and Nigeria's president, Umaru Yar'Ardua, did not consider it worth making the three-hour trip from Abuja to inspect the damage. Meanwhile, the missionaries are still pushing provocatively north. Salihu Garba, a prominent Muslim convert to Christianity (who has survived several assassination attempts), claims that the Evangelical Church of West Africa now has 157 churches in Kano State—double the number five years ago.[5]

Garba prays that America will eventually attack Iran; otherwise, he maintains, there will be no peace in Nigeria. It is the only way, he feels, to halt radical Islam, which surged in Africa after the Iranian revolution. It is not clear that Washington takes quite the same approach. But the West is becoming increasingly worried by what is happening in this part of Africa. America maintains a naval presence off Nigeria's coast, partly to defend its oil supplies and partly to keep an eye on a looming source of terrorism. And the intelligence services are nervous. Asked about potential trouble spots, one intelligence chief names West Africa and the Sahel. "All the symptoms are there," he says gloomily.

The greatest change in foreign policy in the recent past has been the revival of religion. It is impossible to understand international affairs today without taking faith into account. The most important single political act of the twenty-first century so far—the terrorist attacks of September 11—was an act of religious war. The hijackers prepared for battle by performing intricate religious rituals; they went to their deaths shouting, "Allahu Akbar!"; they regarded their monstrous deeds as an act of faith. Muslim fanatics have been involved in many of the worst acts of religious violence since, including the Madrid and London bombings. Iran talks about acquiring a Muslim nuclear bomb. Many commentators worry that the Sunnis and Shias could be on the verge of fighting a Muslim version of the European wars of religion.[6] Many European statesmen are fixated on the possibility of a religious war between radical Islam and Christian America—probably with Israel as the proximate cause. We are living in "the age of sacred terror," to borrow the title of an excellent book by Daniel Benjamin and Steven Simon.

How frightened should we be? In one way, the answer is simple: extremely. There are plenty of nightmare scenarios: some form of nuclear conflagration involving Pakistan and India or an American-Iranian standoff over Israel; a lunatic with a suitcase bomb in Manhattan; and so on. People are right to be terrified of these things. But for the most part, modern wars of religion come in different forms from their predecessors. Rather than being violent and state-driven, they are usually bottom-up affairs—and the main weapon in many squabbles is the ballot box. Dealing with them will require much more subtlety than the West—and the United States in particular—has displayed thus far.

OLIVER'S ARMY IS HERE TO STAY

Begin with the bad news. Consider a recent speech by Iran's president to his country's parliament. Mahmoud Ahmadinejad posed two questions: "Who are our enemies?" and "Why do they hate us?" He described an axis of evil, with Iran's enemies being "all the wicked men of the world, whether abroad or at home." The root cause of their hatred was religious—a loathing of "whomsoever should serve the glory of God." Having described George Bush's atrocities, he told the cheering MPs, "Truly, your great enemy is the American—through that enmity that is in him against all that is of God in you." Fortunately, Iran would not fight alone: it had the support of Muslims around the world. Be bold, he advised, and "you will find that you act for a very great many people that are God's own."

In fact, the speaker was not Ahmadinejad, but Oliver Cromwell; the cheering MPs were English; and the great Satan was not America, but Catholic Spain. The quotations above come from a speech made by Cromwell to the English Parliament in 1656. A year later Parliament passed an oath of loyalty in which English Catholics were asked to disown the pope and most of the canons of Catholic belief, or face losing two-thirds of their worldly goods.

Bloody though Cromwell's religious wars had been, especially in Ireland, the worst in Europe in terms of religion was largely over. For that, people had to thank the Peace of Westphalia in 1648. The Thirty Years'

War that preceded the treaty had brought astonishing destruction, more destruction than the Black Death as Protestants and Catholics slaughtered each other by the millions. The treaty laid down the foundations of the modern state system by giving each ruler the right to determine how God was worshipped within their own territory. This not only brought an end to the era of religious wars between Christians, with their bloody fanaticism, by, in effect, forbidding one country to make war on another country for religious reasons; it led to the secularization of foreign policy.

In his monumental study *History of the Rise and Influence of the Spirit of Rationalism in Europe* (1866), W. E. H. Lecky, one of the great Irish public intellectuals of the Victorian age, celebrated the Peace of Westphalia as one of the turning points in European history:

> It was in this way that, in the course of a few centuries, the foreign policy of all civilized nations was completely and finally secularized. Wars that were once regarded as simple duties became absolutely impossible. Alliances that were once deemed atrocious sins became habitual and unchallenged. That which had long been the center around which all other interests revolved, receded and disappeared, and a profound change in the actions of mankind indicated a profound change in their belief.[7]

The ending of the wars of religion was indeed a huge achievement. As well as being peculiarly bloody, wars of religion built instability into the heart of the diplomatic system. Realpolitik was designed to end all this. People might continue to fight for advantage. But there was a difference between fighting for national interest (which could result in compromise) and fighting for the glory of God (which could bring the Apocalypse). By Lecky's time, the magnificent age of improvement and equipoise in the mid–nineteenth century, statesmen no longer quarreled about religious dogmas or formed alliances on the basis of religious affiliations. Yet almost 150 years after Lecky's masterpiece, new wars of religion are raging.

Religion is seldom the casus belli: indeed, in many struggles, notably the Middle East in modern times, it is amazing how long it took for religion to become a big part of the argument. But once there, it makes conflicts harder to resolve. A squabble over land (which can be divided) or power (which can be shared) or rules (which can be fudged) becomes a dispute over nonnegotiable absolutes. If you believe that God granted you the West Bank, or that any form of abortion is murder, compromise is not really possible. In Nigeria, the tough talking does not just come from radical Islamists and Pentecostals: asked by Eliza Griswold of the *Atlantic Monthly* about an alleged atrocity by the often thuggish Christian Association of Nigeria, Peter Akinola, the Anglican archbishop, replied thus: "No Christian would pray for violence, but it would be utterly naïve to sweep this issue of Islam under the carpet. . . . I'm not out to combat anybody. I'm only doing what the Holy Spirit tells me to do. I'm living my faith, practicing and preaching that Jesus Christ is the one and only way to God, and they respect me for it. They know where we stand. I've said it before: let no Muslim think they have a monopoly on violence."[8]

Once again, politicians are stirring up religious passion. Ahmadinejad may not have told Muslims that the Israelis have "an interest in your bowels" (as Cromwell did of Spaniards), but he has called for Israel's removal from the face of the earth and questioned the Holocaust. Osama bin Laden rages that Islam is under sustained attack: any Muslim who "collaborates" with the West is an apostate. American leaders have been more careful, but many use religious imagery, as we saw with General Boykin. During the Cold War, denouncing the godless communism of the Soviet Union involved some pretty strident language: in his book *God and Gold,* Walter Russell Mead compares Ronald Reagan's "Evil Empire" speech to Cromwell's. Franklin Graham may have been slapped down by Bush for calling Islam a "very evil and wicked religion," but criticism of Islam continues. American conservatives seem undecided on whether the battle against "Islamofascism" is the Third World War (as Newt Gingrich thinks) or the Fourth (Norman Podhoretz).

Once again, outsiders are rushing in to defend their religions: religious fights attract money and soldiers. Some of the most fervent supporters of India's Hindutva movement come from the diaspora. Many migrants define themselves by their faith, not their new home. Just as Guy Fawkes, Britain's most notorious religious terrorist (of Gunpowder Plot fame), hardened his radical beliefs when fighting for Catholicism in the Netherlands, European Muslims have journeyed to defend their faith in Kashmir, Chechnya, Palestine and Iraq. Like Guy Fawkes, many have returned convinced of the need to act against the state. In 2005 a young Muslim Briton, Mohammed Sidique Khan, speaking in a broad Yorkshire accent, justified his participation in the London bombings in a posthumously released videotape:

> Our words are dead until we give them life with our blood. . . . Your democratically elected governments perpetuate atrocities against my people and your support of them makes you responsible, just as I am directly responsible for protecting and avenging my Muslim brothers and sisters. Until we feel security, you'll be our target. Until you stop the bombing, gassing, imprisonment and torture of my people, we'll not stop this fight. We are at war and I am a soldier. Now you too will taste the reality of this situation.

Terrorist outrages are once again presumed to have religious connections, as they would have been in Cromwell's time. In the 1970s terrorism seemed to be the preserve of Maoist guerrillas, middle-class Germans and Italians or the then-very-secular (and partly Christian-led) Palestine Liberation Organization. The only exception was Cromwell's old stomping ground, Ireland. Now three out of the four most likely flashpoints for nuclear conflict—Pakistan-India, Iran and Israel-Palestine—have a strong religious element. The only exception is North Korea.

THE GREAT CLASH

For many observers, the most worrying parallels between the twenty-first century and the seventeenth century are not the surface ones of mayhem and conflict. Rather, they lie in the underlying state of the religions themselves—especially Islam. The old wars of religion were rooted in two things: competition for souls and an internal, schismatic crisis of confidence within one of the world's great religions caused by the splitting of Christianity into Catholic and Protestant. The background for the new wars of religion includes a fierce competition for souls—this time largely between Christianity and Islam; and once again one of the world's great religions—this time Islam—is sharply split between rival sects. To make matters worse, the battlefield this time is global.

Christianity and Islam are both global faiths. Judaism is happy with the chosen people, Hinduism focuses on the Indian subcontinent (or Hindustan, as it sees it), Shintoism is limited to a single country, but Christianity and Islam both regard the world as their parish. Today they are competing for converts in areas of the world, like the road from Kano to Jos, that are already explosive. Across the global south, their main theater of conflict, populations are growing faster than the resources to support them and the average age is getting younger. People are abandoning their traditional villages for ramshackle megacities (the home of half the people of the Middle East, for instance). Large numbers of young men have few traditional structures to keep them under control. Governments in many places are incapable of providing security and welfare services, leaving their unstable and rootless populations ripe for recruitment by religious entrepreneurs. A ring of instability lines Islam's southern frontier, which runs roughly along the tenth parallel from West Africa to the Philippines.

Radical Islam has a huge influence over several countries—notably Iran, Saudi Arabia and Pakistan. Iran is the most bellicose: Ayatollah Khomeini, who seized power from the shah in 1979, preached a messianic form of Shia Islam that involved a continuous war against the forces of evil, by which he meant the infidel West, led by the United States. His successors have preached the same doctrine with varying degrees of fervor. The current Iranian president is on the extreme end of that: he believes that the Second Coming is imminent and seems to think that he has a chosen role in bringing it about. Although it denies it, Iran is suspected of trying to acquire an "Islamic bomb." It is also actively involved in sponsoring Muslim terrorist organizations around the world, particularly Hezbollah, Islamic jihad and Hamas. And, perhaps most important for the Arab world's Sunni regimes, it has also stirred up the region's Shias.

Saudi Arabia is friendlier, but stuck in a devilish pact with radical Islam. Dick Cheney once observed that "the good Lord didn't see fit to put oil and gas only where there are democratically elected regimes friendly to the United States." He might have added that the Good Lord did see fit to put oil and gas supplies in areas where religious passions burn brightest. The largest reserves of oil in the world lie beneath the land of Mecca and Medina. The recapture of the kingdom from its corrupt princes remains the main goal of most Muslim radicals, including Osama bin Laden. The ruling Saudis have ended up playing a double game of appeasement and repression, channeling money to extreme Muslim outfits on the one hand but taking a stern approach to dissent at home. Few people seem to think it can go on forever.

If Saudi Arabia offers radical Islam the chance of gaining control over the world's oil superpower, disorganized Pakistan offers the chance of acquiring a nuclear bomb. Pakistan has also long played a double role with regard to radical Islam—condemning it in public while sponsoring it in private. The Pakistani intelligence service has nurtured Islamic extremists, including terrorists who mount attacks on India, for decades; before September 11, the Pakistani government also had close ties with the Taliban in Afghanistan. Pakistan is about as pro-Western as it will ever be, thanks to intense pressure from Washington (and a lot of money). But its government remains chronically weak: witness the transition of power in 2008 from an autocratic general, Pervez Musharraf, to a corrupt dynast, Asif Zardari, Benazir Bhutto's widower, who is known as "Mr. Ten Percent." The government's inability to control its tribal areas, which the Taliban uses as a base for attacks on Afghanistan, infuriates America, which has responded with air strikes and even armed forays. The combination of America's bloody inefficiency—civilians get killed as well as militants—with the overt breach of Pakistan's sovereignty has in turn inflamed anti-Americanism. Meanwhile, the terrorist attacks in Mumbai by militants with strong Pakistani connections in November 2008 provoked more accusations from India. The Islamists, who have generally done poorly in elections, could yet break through.

Given the number of people who seem to believe that a clash of civilizations is under way, it is hard to rule it out. But look a little deeper and there is nothing inevitable about a clash between Islam and Christianity. For much of the Middle Ages Muslim states were more tolerant than Christian ones: Jews and Christians thrived in Islamic countries, while Muslims and Jews were harassed and massacred in Christendom. Nowadays, for all the introduction of "anti-Christian" sharia in Muslim countries and "anti-Muslim" terrorist legislation in the Christian world, in most parts of the world Christians and Muslims rub along most of the time, sometimes in places of great hardship. (Muslim Palestinians and Christian Palestinians still get along fairly well.)

If Muslims and Christians have proved they can live together, it is also worth stressing, sadly, that they have also proved that they don't need each other to start killing people in the name of the Almighty. Some of the most ghastly religious violence in Africa has come from Christian armies who have preached the Apocalypse and hacked away at their Christian enemies with the zeal of fanatics. In Uganda, for instance, the rebel Lord's Resistance Army has been responsible, over the past couple of decades, for slaughtering an estimated 120,000 people, kidnapping more than 25,000 children, attacking religious leaders and property and forcing 1.5 million people to abandon their homes and take refuge in makeshift camps.[9] The army not only believes that it is doing God's work, but also that magic oils can protect people from bullets.[10]

As for the idea that Islam is stuck in a clash of civilizations with the West, this too seems unconvincing. Put simply, most of the fighting is not taking place in that arena. One great irony of the war on terror is that many of the people on George Bush's "enemies list" have devoted themselves to fighting people other than Americans. The jihadis' most important war is not against the West but against apostate Muslim regimes, notably Saudi Arabia; where they do battle with outsiders, it is mainly against what they regard as occupying powers—Russia in Chechnya, America in Iraq, India in Kashmir and Israel in Palestine. Muslims also slaughter each other in large numbers. In Iraq, the insurgency has killed far more Muslims than Christians. Those numbers will only increase if Al Qaeda gets its way. "We believe that the Shiite heretics are a sect of idolatory and apostasy," claims one bit of Al Qaeda propaganda, "and that they are the most evil creatures under the heavens."[11]

Indeed, the most dangerous power struggle in the Middle East is arguably the one between followers of the two biggest versions of Islam—the Sunnis and the Shias. For most of Islam's history the divide has been relatively peaceful, partly for reasons of geography. Sunnis, who make up about 85 percent of Muslims, dominate both the eastern and western flanks of Islam: Moroccans or Indonesians hardly know what a Shia is.[12] The Shias cluster in the center of the Muslim world—in the Levant, the Indian sub-continent, the Gulf and Persia—and even in their heartlands they have tended to live in isolated communities.[13] The two groups perform similar rituals; indeed, one of India's most respected Muslim scholars claims that the two religions agree on 97 percent of religious doctrine.[14]

The new enmity owes something to globalization, which has hurled Sunnis and Shias together. But there are also more political forces at play: the rise of revolutionary Iran, whose assertiveness has emboldened Shias everywhere; Sunni chauvinism, led by Saudi Arabia's heresy-hating Wah-habists; and, above all, the invasion of Iraq.

As late as the 1950s, Baghdad was a famously cosmopolitan city where mixed marriages were common. But Saddam Hussein, a Sunni, repressed the Shia majority with unusual brutality. The American "liberation" was a chance for payback. With Shias seizing power, ultra-puritan Sunnis, known as *salafis,* claimed that it was legal to kill Shias, as apostates from Islam. Atrocities mounted on both sides. In February 2006, Sunnis blew up the Al-Askari shrine at Samarra, north of Baghdad, an important site of Shia pilgrimage, setting off a sectarian bloodbath that was contained only by the "surge." Sectarian violence has been responsible for most of the two-hundred-thousand-odd deaths in Iraq. This also means that every-thing that happens in Iraq is now seen through sectarian lenses: even the execution of the much-loathed Saddam, on a Sunni feast day, was deemed to be a Shia triumph.

America's invasion of Iraq also disturbed the balance of religious power in the region, removing the biggest barrier to Iran exporting its version of Islam. Rather than being blocked by a Sunni-controlled Baath Party regime on its western flank, Iran now deals with a Shia-dominated gov-ernment over which it has considerable influence (though not the control that many Sunnis fear). Iran has been using religious proxies to expand its influence in Palestine, Lebanon and Iraq itself. It has also spread panic in the Sunni powers about what King Abdullah of Jordan dubs the "Shiite crescent." Sunni governments maintain their support for Sunni extremists across the region as a way of countering Iranian influence. (Various Saudi Web sites claim, mischievously, that Iran's president had declared that he wanted not a Shia crescent, but a full moon.)[15] One of the many nightmarish scenarios that could follow Iran getting a bomb is that Sunni states would also feel compelled to develop an "Islamic" nuclear bomb of their own (or at least cloak their regional rivalries in religious garb).

As with most sectarian splits, it is the quarrels within countries that could end up doing the most damage. Talk of a *fitna,* or sectarian schism, is commonplace across the Islamic world. Many Sunnis see the Shias as a fifth column. In Pakistan, some two thousand lives have been lost in Sunni-Shia violence over the past fifteen years. Even small incidents can produce sectarian conflicts. A skirmish in a cafeteria in Lebanon in 2007 ended up with a street fight that left four people dead.[16] The star preacher on the Al Jazeera satellite channel caused a storm by denouncing Shia Islam as heretical, and warning of a Shia attempt to "invade" Sunni societies by stealth. Sectarian suspicion justifies repression as well as violence.[17] In Bahrain, for instance, the regime justifies limiting the rights of the majority Shias on the ground that they will flock to foreign (i.e., Iranian) ayatollahs. In Saudi Arabia, the government justifies its harsh treatment of Sunnis in part on the grounds that they want to expropriate the country's oil; the Shias, who make up 15 percent of the population, point out that most of that oil is under the parts of the country where they live.

You Don't Need God for a War . . .

Put these things together, and it is certainly possible that the new wars of religion could escalate into something horrifying. What terrified Lecky and European statesmen about wars of faith was that they knew no limits. The revival of religion is multiplying the number of people who are willing to kill and die for their faith. A confrontation between nuclear Iran on one side and Israel and America on the other would reverberate around the globe: billions of people would see it as a faith-based conflict and millions would interpret it in eschatological terms. The dispute between

India and Pakistan over Kashmir could also have global consequences: many jihadists would dearly love to set off a war, which would have the added frisson of going nuclear. In Asia, the (predominantly) Christian Philippines has long-standing tensions with (predominantly) Muslim Indonesia. Each country could stir up the other's religious minorities for political gain—the Philippines firing up Christians in Indonesia and the Indonesians stirring up Muslims in the Philippines.

These are terrifying possibilities, to be sure, but they are not probabilities. Most obviously, humanity can find plenty of reasons for genocide and brutality without troubling God. "The 20th century was the most secular and the most bloody in our existence," argues George Weigel. What he calls "the Godless religions of Nazism and communism" killed tens of millions of people. Each had its utopias, its rites, its prophets and its sacred places; but they did not use God to stir up passions. Some of the worst mass slaughters of the past quarter century—in Cambodia, Congo, Rwanda—were mostly secular.

Many of today's so-called wars of religion would have been wars even if man had never troubled God. For instance, if you dislodge 750,000 people to create a new state, as the Israelis did, those people are likely to object, even if they are atheists. Similarly, if you invade a country, topple a regime and deprive the ruling class of its jobs, as the Americans did in Iraq, then the dispossessed are likely to be miffed, regardless of whether they are Sunnis or Rastafarians. Saddam Hussein hardly cared about God, but he started several wars. The founder of the first pan-Arab Baath Party was a Syrian Christian, Michel Aflaq, who was educated at the decidedly secular Sorbonne.

And you certainly do not need religion for acts of terrorism. According to Europol, 498 terrorist attacks took place in the European Union in 2006: 424 were perpetrated by separatists, 55 by left-wing groups and 18 by various other terrorists. Only one—bloody though it was—was carried out by Islamic terrorists.[18] Or take the act many people identify with religious terrorism: suicide bombings. Until 2000, the practice was most associated with the largely secular Tamil Tigers (who invented the suicide vest); since then jihadist groups in Lebanon, Israel-Palestine, Iraq and, of course, Europe have taken up the practice, egged on by religious fervor. Yet academics who study suicide bombing play down the role of religion. Robert Pape, of the University of Chicago, has identified three things that encourage the phenomenon: a community that feels it is under occupation; an "occupier" that is a democratic society where opinion can be swayed; and a sectarian difference between the perpetrators' community and the target community. Religious differences, for him, are not the main driver. Nichole Argo, at the Massachusetts Institute of Technology, agrees: she stresses the background of support for the idea of insurgency and the sense among self-annihilators that their peers will see them as heroes. Nor is religious indoctrination a big factor, Argo insists; only a fraction of the alumni of hard-line madrassas in Pakistan and Indonesia engage in violence.[19]

There is another important difference from Cromwell's England. Where it does exist, religious conflict is now far less of a top-down affair. No government officially approves of killing people solely because of their religion, and no significant religious leader sanctifies that killing by blessing armadas or preaching crusades. Even the Cromwellian Iranians insist that they do not want to destroy other religions. They claim that the quarrel that they are best known for is not with Jews but with Israel. (That may be hard to believe with the regime, but with regular Iranians it has the ring of truth: one of the country's most popular recent television dramas dealt with trying to save Jews during the Holocaust.) Most Islamic authorities preach nonviolence. Ayatollah Sistani, the most revered Shia on the planet, has often urged restraint in Iraq. From the other side, Pope Benedict XVI has certainly not been shy about taking issue with Islam, but he also opposed the Iraq war and supports ecumenical dialogues with Muslim leaders.

Meanwhile, the ability of governments to control religious politics has declined. The wars of religion took place in a world where confessional states were the rule, not the exception, and where the monarch could shape religion. England rejected Catholicism because Henry VIII found the Catholic Church's rules on matrimony irksome. Even in the direst moments of the Bush administration nobody tried to improve America's relations with the Middle East by marrying off the Bush twins to Arab princes and having them converted to Islam (tempting though that may often have been to their father).

. . . BUT IT HELPS

With national armies no longer marching across borders under religious banners, religious grievances have reappeared in several more subtle guises, none of which is easy for the West to deal with. One is the emergence of culture wars, the subject of the next chapter. There are four other basic types: terrorism; intercommunal violence; state-based repression; and the ballot box.

The one that gets most attention is inevitably terrorism—especially Islamic terrorism. States are certainly actors in this, but much less so than the Bush administration initially imagined. The evidence linking Saddam to Al Qaeda was derisory. Iran certainly has a lot of blood on its hands from backing Hezbollah in Lebanon and Hamas in Palestine, but the relationship between states and religious fanaticism is complicated. Neither Hamas nor Hezbollah are easy to characterize as instruments in a religious war: like the Irish Republican Army, they have political and territorial as well as religious goals.

At the other end of the spectrum, the leading jihadist terrorist organizations are bottom-up affairs. It is noticeable, one of our colleagues argued in a special report on terrorism, how "the most immediate global threat comes from the ungoverned, undergoverned and ungovernable areas of the Muslim world. These include the Afghan-Pakistani border, the parts of Iraq still in turmoil, the Palestinian refugee camps in Lebanon, and swathes of Yemen, Somalia, the western Sahara desert and the chain of islands between Indonesia and the Philippines."[20] Osama bin Laden has always found it convenient to control states (as he once did with Afghanistan). But his organization has been able to mount attacks and recruit volunteers without help from governments. Indeed, Al Qaeda's statelessness makes it more frightening. As a network, it can operate without any clear leadership: in parts of the world it is essentially a franchise operation, with terrorists even setting up shop from the Internet. That makes it much harder to control through decapitation. (British spies worry about the speed with which jihadists regroup after any repulse—much quicker than the IRA.) Similarly, Al Qaeda's taste for unlimited violence stems from its statelessness: unlike the Basque ETA, or even Hamas, it has no domestic constituency or political masters to restrain it. The object is to produce ever more spectacular acts of destruction.

The second way in which religion thrusts itself into politics is intercommunal violence. Once again, other forces are often at work, such as tribalism in Nigeria or nationalism in India. But religion adds enormously to the underlying viciousness. In Ulster, for instance, there were all sorts of socioeconomic and territorial reasons for Catholics to resent the descendants of Cromwell's army, but several thousand Protestants marching through your town singing, "Our fathers knew thee, Rome of old, and evil is thy name," added to the tensions.

The astounding thing about intercommunal violence is how such conflicts grind on beneath the surface. Iraq may have captured the headlines but sixty-eight thousand Sri Lankans have died since 1983. Outside parties can play a role in stoking up such struggles (and supplying arms), as Iran has done in Iraq and Syria has done in Lebanon. But most of these fights are local, tit-for-tat affairs. The violence is often set off by events such as marches, feast days or elections.

Intercommunal violence will always be a potential problem because so many countries are deeply divided over religion. Some, mainly Muslim, countries have significant Christian minorities (Indonesia, Egypt and Sudan). Some mainly Christian countries have significant Muslim minorities (the Philippines, Congo and Uganda). And, most worrying of all, some countries are almost evenly divided between Muslims and Christians (Nigeria, Ethiopia and Tanzania).[21] In general, the closer populations move toward parity, the more tensions increase. For instance, Indonesia's tiny Papua region used to be seen as mainly Christian or animist. Now Muslims account for up to half the two-million-strong population. (The official figure of 23 percent is widely disbelieved.[22]) American and Canadian Evangelical preachers have arrived, alongside the Indonesian chapter of Hizb ut-Tahrir, which wants to unite Muslims worldwide under one "caliphate." A lot of goading goes on: the Christians, for instance, erected an iron tower shaped like a Christmas tree, topped with a Star of David. They have also boasted about converting Muslims, priming worries in Indonesia that there is a plot between America, Australia and the Philippines to pry Papua away.[23]

Religious wars often flare up from nowhere, suggesting that even the most happy-go-lucky society may suddenly be consumed by religious passions. The former Yugoslavia was once famous for its relaxed attitude toward faith. Marriages across religious lines were commonplace. But civil war divided the country into religious groups, with foreign fighters joining the fray and combatants targeting religious buildings, and the combination of ethnic and religious passions rendering the violence particularly bloody. The Serbian massacre of Bosnian Muslims at Srebrenica in 1995 was the most gruesome single crime in post-1945 Europe. The Ivory Coast has traditionally been a fairly tolerant place (about 40 percent of the population are Muslim and 33 percent Christian), but the country has recently witnessed bloody religious strife and calls for a partition along religious lines.[24]

Third, there is state-based repression where religion is either the target or the motivation. In the Muslim world the repression is sometimes by theocracies (like Iran or Saudi Arabia) against irreligious sorts, such as adulterers, heretics and homosexuals. Part of Sudan's many problems stem from the fact that its government, which seized power in a coup in 1989, has been bent, ever since, on Islamizing the country, reshaping the country's laws, institutions and policies in accordance with the Koran. But repression also goes the other way, with secular states (Syria, Egypt, much of North Africa) cracking down on religious organizations. In the most bizarre example, in 2007 China banned Buddhist monks in Tibet from reincarnating without government permission. The religious-affairs agency explained that this was "an important move to institutionalize management of reincarnation." The real purpose was to prevent the Dalai Lama, Tibet's exiled spiritual leader, from being succeeded by someone from outside China.[25]

Yet the foremost way in which religion has found expression around the world has been more peaceful: the ballot box. Religious people have either formed religious parties—such as India's Bharatiya Janata Party (BJP)—or converted secular ones into more faith-driven outfits (such as America's Republican Party). In places where religion was frowned upon by the state, such as Mexico or Turkey, greater freedom has allowed the pious to form parties, such as the Catholic-oriented PAN Party or the Islamic Justice and Development Party. Indeed, some commentators spot a link between the spread of democracy and the rise of religion. Timothy Shah, of the Council on Foreign Relations, argues that more than thirty of the eighty or so countries that became freer in 1972–2000 owed some of the improvement of their condition to religion. Sometimes established churches helped to push for democracy—the Catholic Church in Poland is a dramatic example—but more often it was pressure from the grassroots: religious people, he points out, usually look for a degree of freedom, if only to pursue their faith.[26]

In fact, many conflicts include at least two or three of these elements—a bit of terrorism, a bit of democracy, a bit of intercommunal rivalry. Consider two examples: first the world's most intractable intercommunal conflict—the Middle East—and then the religious conflict within the world's most religious country—India.

THE OVERPROMISED LAND

Sheikh Yazid Khader and Rabbi Yaacov Medan both live in the occupied West Bank. Both are devoutly religious men who feel that they have been betrayed by secularists. The sheikh, a local Hamas leader, has been in and out of Fatah custody (depressing when the rival Palestinians, he says, should both be fighting "the Zionist enemy"). The rabbi, a leader of the settler movement, is still seething about the Israeli government's forcible ejection of its own settlers from Gaza.

Both men are towering obstacles to any chance of peace in the Middle East. Not that they see it that way. Both insist that their religions are peaceful, and each has solutions to the current impasse. Of course Israel should keep its settlements in the West Bank (illegal under international law), argues the rabbi: it is part of the land God gave us. But a system of tunnels could be constructed for the Palestinians to find their way around them. For his part, the sheikh refuses to accept Israel's right to exist: Palestine is a *waqf,* a land placed by God in Muslim hands for eternity. But if Israel retreats to its 1967 borders, Hamas would generously grant the infidels a *hudna,* or "truce," initially for ten years.[27]

If you are concerned about religion's effect on politics, there is no more discouraging place to visit than the tiny slither of land that is Israel-Palestine. Forty years ago the trouble there amounted to a territorial dispute between two fairly secular tribes. In the aftermath of Israel's creation in 1948 both Israel and its leading adversaries regarded themselves as secular states. The Zionists who founded the country were secular nationalists who wanted to make the Jews more "normal." Some of the Palestinians were also secular sorts. George Habash, founder of the Popular Front for the Liberation of Palestine, was a Greek-Orthodox Marxist, educated at the American University in Beirut. Israel's main enemies, Egypt and Syria, were ruled by secular regimes who dreamed of a pan-Arab region rather than a pan-Islamic one.

But the 1967 war unleashed a new religious fervor on both sides of the divide—a fervor that has only grown and curdled with the years. In Israel, the miraculous victory gave greater voice to religious groups who regarded Zionism as the fulfillment of the biblical promise rather than a practical alternative to wandering. The settlement movement, which previously would have been mocked as a blatant land-grab, acquired a fiery theological backing—to the despair of many of Israel's founders. In the Arab world, the shattering defeat further delegitimized the secular regimes and added credibility to their Islamic challengers.

The emergence of Hamas has only dramatized the religious divide between the Jewish state and an overtly Islamic Palestinian Authority.[28] Polls show that most people on both sides still want a two-state solution, but many of the growing number of people determined to stop such an outcome now claim that God is on their side. And many of the most ardent fanatics live far from the Holy Land.

For Muslims the indignities heaped on the Palestinians are part of a systematic attack on Islam that must be resisted to the bitter end: the level of routine anti-Semitism in Arab societies is startling. On the other side, many American Jewish groups will not tolerate the sort of criticism of Israel that is routine in the Jewish state itself. In Jerusalem, disagreeing with the views of the Likud Party is hardly controversial (Likud, after all, is just one of many parties); but Likud has a lockhold on the Israeli lobby in Washington. And, as we have already seen, now there are America's Christian Zionists to deal with.

Ignorance rules on all sides. Most Muslims are unaware that Arabs can vote in Israel. A surprising number of them cling to the idea that Israel's 5.2 million Jews are somehow responsible for the poor economic performance of the region's 221 million Arabs. Many Jews, even in Israel, are separated from the routine miseries of Palestinian life by the wall that divides them. Evangelicals are shocked to discover that some Palestinians are Christians. Describing the ignorance of American Protestants about the plight of the Palestinians as "willful," one Catholic priest, working at the Church of the Holy Sepulchre, points to the way that Evangelical tours of the Holy Land avoid biblical sites that might affect their prejudices. A few hundred yards away in the Armenian quarter, an elderly Christian relays with horror his attempts to explain to American Evangelicals why he, a Palestinian Christian born in Jerusalem, has to give up space for a newly arrived Russian Jewish immigrant: "Their pastor said I was making it up."

The picture is not all bleak. Most of the Palestinians who vote for Hamas do so out of despair over Fatah's corruption rather than out of religious fervor. Israel is such an engagingly disputatious place that religious people pop up on different sides, depending on the argument. The Ultra-Orthodox, who make up approximately 9 percent of the population, traditionally attach less importance to land than some more secular Israelis. Many see the same dilemma that has convinced a succession of prime ministers, including Ehud Olmert, of the need for a two-state solution. Thanks to the fast-growing Palestinian population, the dream of a greater Israel increasingly conflicts with the still more precious idea of a Jewish state.

One sad irony of this dispute in the Holy Land is how few holy people are trying to make peace. Rabbi David Rosen, chairman of the International Jewish Committee for Interreligious Consultations, argues that the Oslo peace process collapsed in part because no religious people were involved. It was not until 2002 that a small group of leading rabbis, Muslim clerics and bishops signed the Alexandria Declaration, which condemned violence and insisted that the holy places should be kept open. There have been subsequent meetings, including some with Tony Blair and Condoleezza Rice, but progress is beset by practical problems, such as the inability of Palestinian clerics to get through Israel's West Bank barrier. Whatever the reason, when suicide bombers strike Israeli towns, too few imams condemn the violence; and when Israeli bombs or shells fall on Palestinian civilians, too few rabbis speak out. Until that changes, the various children of Abraham will find peace elusive.

A Passage to India

If the Middle East is famous for its fractiousness, India is more commonly seen as a peaceful, spiritual place. On the face of it, Praveen Togadia is just the sort of Indian the modernizing Jawaharlal Nehru might have been proud of. Urbane and sophisticated, he is a cancer surgeon, with more than ten thousand operations to his credit. He hails from Gujarat, one of India's more go-ahead states, currently run by his friend Narendra Modi, perhaps the most free-market-oriented of the state leaders.

Yet Togadia is also the international general secretary of something Nehru would have abhorred—the Vishwa Hindu Parishad (VHP), one of the main organs of the Hindutva ("Hinduness") movement. Togadia drifted away from medicine toward politics because he became convinced that Hinduism, like Judaism, was a persecuted faith, especially by Muslims. He has played a leading role in the campaign to rebuild a temple at Ayodhya, the birthplace of Lord Rama, one of Hinduism's great trinity of gods. In 1992 Hindu activists tore down a mosque built there by a Muslim ruler.

For Togadia, the crucial difference is that "we [Hindus] believe in peaceful coexistence; Islam does not." But his definition of peaceful coexistence would be queried by India's 150 million Muslims, especially those in Gujarat. The state is still haunted by the riots of 2002, which began after a train carrying Hindu activists on their way back from Ayodhya caught fire in a Muslim neighborhood, and Muslims were blamed for the dozens of deaths. In the ensuing pogrom, 2,000 people died.[29]

In one of Gujarat's commercial centers, Ahmedabad, many Muslims are now stuck in an eastern ghetto known as "little Pakistan." Abeda, a widow housed in a gloomy resettlement complex, Sibbaka Bab, recalls how her family took sanctuary in a local MP's house, only for her Hindu neighbors to force their way in, "stabbing, hacking and burning." There was so little left of Abeda's husband and one of her daughters that she had trouble getting death certificates for them. Many of the mob were wearing Hindutva gear—saffron headbands, or the khaki shorts favored by those who take part in the movement's early-morning physical exercises.

The place is more peaceful now. Sophia, a middle-class lawyer who was also forced to retreat to "little Pakistan," calls Togadia "a fanatic," but she thinks most Muslims have given in: "They are too scared and poor to get anything." Although Modi's reputation has suffered—he was refused a visa to visit America in 2005—he was reelected comfortably in 2007.

Ghettoization has radicalized the women of Sibbaka Bab. They go to the mosque more often and talk approvingly of Osama bin Laden. The otherwise mild Abeda is proud that her son is called Saddam (like the Iraqi leader "who died for Islam") and she wishes a horrible death on Modi and his friends. Togadia has survived several assassination attempts. One of his preoccupations is trying to stop the (mainly secular) Congress Party from blowing a hole in a holy bridge, supposedly built by Lord Rama, that links India to Sri Lanka. Many people in Congress say that the bridge, which is mainly underwater but visible from the air, is really just a ridge blocking shipping.[30] He has also objected to Christian conversions of Hindus, insisting on the right to retaliate against Christian violence in Orissa.

Today's India is a test tube for religious politics. The birthplace of four big religions (Buddhism, Jainism, Sikhism and Hinduism), it has remained religious even as it has modernized. It was founded in the throes of a religious conflict—the partition between Hindu India and Muslim Pakistan. And religion informs three different political conflicts: the external one with Pakistan; an internal one between the Hindu majority and the sizable Muslim minority; and a rip-roaring debate about religion in the public square.

India has had three big wars with Pakistan, in 1947, 1965 and 1971, and one minor one in 1999. The wars were not explicitly about religion but about the disputed territory of Kashmir and, in 1971, the independence of what was then East Pakistan, now Bangladesh. But religion is crucial to Kashmir, because Pakistan claims that the mainly Muslim state was ceded to India unlawfully by its Hindu maharajah. And some in the Hindutva movement think the real territorial crime is the existence of Pakistan itself. Hinduism, they claim, is the religion of "Hindustan," the whole subcontinent. Maps in Hindutva offices have a habit of leaving out the Pakistani border.

The terrorist attacks on Mumbai in November 2008, which left more that 170 people dead, were designed to inflame the situation. The sea-borne militants who attacked India's commercial capital came from Pakistan. Hindutva politicians promptly demanded revenge and lacerated the Congress Party for being soft on Pakistan. This was a step backward because India's relationship with Pakistan has in general been relatively peaceful, partly because Pakistan is not in a state to challenge India overtly. But both sides now have nuclear weapons. And Hindus persistently worry that Indian Muslims are a fifth column. One Hindu nationalist suggests that, if Indian Muslims will not do the decent thing and move to Arabia, they should at least be forced to take an oath of loyalty.

An uneasy relationship with Pakistan was perhaps inevitable; but what would have distressed Nehru particularly is the prominent role played by religion in domestic politics. India's constitution writers tried to get around this in two ways. The first was to embrace pluralism: "The keystone of Indian culture and religious tolerance is the bedrock of Indian secularism." The second was to go out of their way to provide protection for the (generally poor) Muslim minority. Many Hindus would add that India was also born with a third force for tolerance: Hinduism. As a religion with countless gods and many sacred texts, it does not lend itself to extremism: there are no rules for governments to enforce.

How did things go wrong? The short answer is that many Hindus, like Togadia, came to see India's secularism as a code for favoritism toward Muslims—especially by Nehru's Congress Party (which until recently most Muslims voted for). Muslims are allowed to live by their own family law and enjoy plenty of positive discrimination, including subsidies to fly to Mecca. There was also a change in Hinduism: the more mystical strain,

Vedanta, which preaches the unity of all religions, was challenged by the stauncher Hindutva message. Vedanta Hindus stayed with the Congress Party; Hindutva ones moved to the BJP, which became the main party of the aspiring middle class.

Hindutva wants three things, all of which create tension: a federal ban on the slaughter of cattle; the introduction of a "uniform personal code" (which is itself code for getting rid of a separate family law for Muslims); and rebuilding Hindu temples, especially Ayodhya. The movement has cleverly broadened its arguments, couching them in nonreligious terms. Cows, for instance, need to be kept alive for their milk (a "white revolution," they argue), not just because they are sacred. Lord Rama's bridge to Sri Lanka is essential as a bulwark against tsunamis.

None of Hindutva's main goals has been met. Although most of India's states ban the slaughter of cows, there is no central government ban; the Ayodhya temple remains unbuilt; the uniform code unpassed. For this, many Hindu nationalists blame the BJP; but the truth is that, having never won more than 26 percent of the vote, it has had to rely on coalition partners, who, like most of the country, are less militant. When they think about it, many Hindus would like a temple built at Ayodhya. But they tend not to think about it, and are appalled at the violence the dispute has spawned.[31]

For all its social organizations, in the end the Hindutva movement is based on a culture war, similar to that waged by the religious right in America. The sprawling offices of its main arm Rashtriya Swayamsevak Sangh (RSS) in Delhi are strangely similar in spirit to the Focus on the Family campus in Colorado Springs we described in chapter five. Neither organization is overtly political: the RSS's motto is "United Hindus, capable India" and most of its energy is plainly taken up with social welfare (just as Focus does indeed focus on families). But just like the Christians in Colorado, the Hindus at the RSS are obsessed by politics—and feel just as let down by the BJP as Focus does by the Republicans.

Meanwhile, the Hindutva movement has set off a counterreaction. Secular members of the Congress Party, who privately admit that they may have indulged Muslims too much, adamantly defend secularism in public. Muslims too are on their guard. One Muslim politician says he would get into trouble if he visited a Hindu temple. The minority, he argues, will always be insecure—especially if that minority used to rule India. Asked whether religion will ever leave Indian politics, he shrugs. "That was the dream—but it did not work out that way."

TAMING THE BEAST

Atypical though they may be, both the Middle East and India illustrate several things about modern wars of religion. First, they are mercifully less violent and all-consuming now than in the past; second, tackling the politics of religion is more awkward than it used to be. For instance, when the West considers radical Islam, should it focus on the tiny number of angry Muslims with guns, or the millions who have voted for Islamic parties in Egypt, Pakistan, Turkey, Algeria and Palestine? If most religious fanatics were bent on conquest and terror rather than democracy, their causes would be easier to discredit. This is a subject we will return to in our conclusion.

CHAPTER TWELVE

THE CULTURE WARS
GO GLOBAL

❧❧

APART FROM a firm belief in God, a transparent decency and a penchant for tea, Hidayet Tuksal and Rowan Williams might seem to have little in common. But both are stuck in one of the loneliest places in modern public life—trying to fight culture wars from the middle.

Williams is much the better known. As Archbishop of Canterbury, he is head of the 80 million-strong Anglican Communion. That gives him a splendid home at Lambeth Palace and a global pulpit, but it has surely been a hellish job for the former divinity professor. Nobody would want to be chief executive of a business with the Church of England's profit trajectory. Its regular Sunday attendance is down to 871,000; at more than half its 16,200 churches it is below 50.[1] On current trends, it will be down to 350,000 people by 2030, forcing it to close another 6,000 churches.[2] As it happens, Williams is adamant that religion is about more than numbers in pews. It is possible that he would have been well suited to overseeing gentle decline. Instead, he has gotten embroiled in a series of distinctly ungentle controversies.

In 2003, the year that Williams became Primate of All England, the Episcopal Church, America's branch of Anglicanism, allowed the ordination of Gene Robinson, a divorced father of two who lives with his male partner, as Bishop of New Hampshire. This set off a firestorm among conservative Anglicans, not just in America (more than twenty-five hundred gathered in Texas and called on the church to "repent") but also in Africa. In the same year Williams narrowly persuaded another gay priest, Jeffrey John, to withdraw from becoming Bishop of Reading. (He made him Dean of St. Albans instead.) But the issue kept coming back. In 2008 Robinson married his partner, Mark Andrew, first in a civil ceremony and then in a service of thanksgiving at a New Hampshire church. Robinson said he went ahead in part because of threats to his life—he was worried about providing life insurance for his partner—but the timing was nightmarish for Williams. It happened just before the Lambeth Conference, the once-a-decade gathering of Anglican bishops, which Robinson had already been tactfully excluded from and which many African prelates were already boycotting. (The conservatives held their own event in Jerusalem.) Meanwhile, two male English vicars married each other with full pomp in a medieval London church that was used in the film *Four Weddings and a Funeral.*

If gay bishops were one bane in Williams's life, women bishops were another. The ordination of women was approved back in 1992, but he inherited a row over women prelates. Conservative Anglican vicars want to keep an opt-out, allowing them to report to male-led dioceses; liberals, many of them newly ordained women, regard this as the last vestige of discrimination. Both sides quote the Gospel at each other, one pointing out that Jesus appointed men, the other that he was unusually female-friendly for his age. As with the gay bishops, Williams has oscillated between the two extremes, sometimes favoring the liberals, but trying desperately to keep conservatives in the fold.

As if that were not controversy enough, Williams also created a stir in 2008 when he appeared to argue that Britain, with its large and growing Muslim population, needed to introduce some form of "supplementary" sharia law if social cohesion was to be preserved. He talked about something similar to Jewish family-law courts, pointing out that plenty of legal matters are already decided outside the established court system. Rather less cleverly, he called the principle of one law for everybody "a bit of a danger." The press had a field day, with commentators lining up to talk about the prospect of hands being cut off in Leicester Square; the tabloids ridiculed mad old "Beardie" for sounding off again. In later interviews, Williams softened his tone, saying that he did not want to introduce a parallel legal system and denouncing the application of sharia in Saudi Arabia as "grim." Some months later he received support from the Lord Chief Justice, Lord Phillips, who pointed out that English law had always made allowances for religious practices.

The mosque-state argument about Islam that Williams blundered into has been the defining part of Hidayet Tuksal's life. Headscarfed and imposing, Tuksal looks like a sterner figure than the cuddly archbishop does. Born in 1963, she grew up in a strict Muslim household in Ankara. At university in the 1980s, she focused on the Koran's teaching about women. She has since made a name for herself arguing that much of the discrimination against women in the Islamic world has scant basis in the sacred text. (Though Eve was described as weak and flawed, it does not follow that all women are.) For this she got into trouble with traditionalists. On the other hand, she is no fan of Turkey's secularist laws, especially when it comes to that headscarf. Because she wears it, she has been periodically banned from teaching at university. (Had she been younger, she could not have studied there either: the army tightened up the laws on what students could wear in 1997.) From her perspective, Turkey's secularists are preventing her from educating Muslim women about their freedoms.

Turkey is buzzing with such arguments. This is a country whose history is profoundly Muslim—indeed, Turkey arguably *was* Islam from 1517, when the Ottoman sultan adopted the title of caliph, or spiritual leader, to 1924, when Atatürk abolished the caliphate. Yet thanks to Atatürk, it also has the most organized secular regime in the Muslim world and the biggest party of committed secularists. When the mildly Islamist Justice and Development (AK) Party came to power in 2002, the nervous joke in cosmopolitan Istanbul was that it was like electing the Taliban. In fact, under Recep Tayyip Erdoğan, the AK Party's main emphasis has been on freeing markets and stamping out corruption. Like many other true believers, the Islamists mellowed in government. ("AKP members of parliament wear Zegna suits and happily shake women's hands," wrote one of our colleagues at *The Economist* in 2008. "Their wives get nose jobs and watch football matches; their children are more likely to study English than the Koran."[3]) In 2007 Erdoğan survived some rumblings from the army, the traditional guardian of Turkish secularism, and won a second term. In 2008 he had a narrower escape from the (pretty secular) supreme court, which came close to banning the AK Party on the grounds that its religiosity was against the constitution.

That might seem a crazy reason to outlaw a popular elected party, but secular autocrats have banned other Muslim parties on the same grounds. The army is also guilty of hypocrisy: it initially encouraged Islamism as a counterweight to communism, making religious teaching mandatory in schools. But there are plenty of examples of creeping Islamization for less virulent secularists to be worried about. Opinion polls suggest that most people now identify themselves primarily as Muslims, not as Turks.[4] Restaurants in the Anatolian hinterland have become nervous about serving lunch during Ramadan. In 2007 a young woman wearing a knee-length tunic and leggings was arrested in Istanbul for "indecent exposure," and things are much tougher in the more pious countryside: in Tarsus two teenage girls were sprayed with an acidic substance because their skirts were "too short." AKP mayors began by banning drinking alcohol at state-owned restaurants, but have since been sporadically trying to exile drinkers to "red zones" outside their cities. Fierce rows about creationism are also roiling the country's classrooms.

Yet it is the headscarf that is the biggest issue. Erdoğan tried to overturn the ban at universities, but the Supreme Court stopped him. His friend Abdullah Gul, who became president in 2007, is chiefly controversial because his wife wears the headscarf. Secularists dislike the new Islamic sororities at schools, known as the *tarikat,* partly because they require girls to wear headscarves (in exchange for free accommodation). And more generally, more Turkish women are covering their heads: the number wearing turbans, the least revealing headscarf of all, has quadrupled.[5]

Optimists say this is much ado about nothing. Polls show that most Turks do not object to headscarves.[6] Erdoğan might have been able to overturn the headscarf ban if he had been less arrogant and consulted his opponents more. Moreover, the practice may have more to do with class than religious fervor. Most of the new young scarf-wearing women in towns (who so worry the secularists) are rural Anatolians, who have come to the big cities for jobs. As the families get richer and more urbanized, their fathers, in theory, will no longer be so strict. Yet it does not stop the debate about headscarves splitting Turkey. For secularists they are a sign of religion invading politics; for Tuksal, they are an issue of personal religious freedom.

The interesting thing about both Tuksal and Williams is that, until recently, the lives of these two eminently tolerant academics might have been less awkward. Both give the impression that they would rather concentrate on other things: Tuksal shuns publicity; having tea with Williams, you can almost sense his pain when you mention Gene Robinson. But both of them live in an age in which questions of identity and faith have become the bloodiest battleground in politics and in which the combat has been driven not by the Williamses and Tuksals of this world but by fundamentalists on both sides.

An American Export

Culture has always played a part in politics, of course, and, indeed, in wars. The Indian Mutiny started because of rumors that the British were forcing sepoys to use grease cartridges made with beef and pig fat (thus insulting both Hindus and Muslims). This time, there are three big things at work. The first and most obvious is that "God is back"—religious people are no longer content to leave their beliefs (or their headscarves) at home. The second is the rise of Islam in the West, particularly Europe. But the best place to begin is the export of America's culture wars.

The term "culture wars" first captured the public imagination at the 1992 Republican Convention in Houston, when Pat Buchanan, a right-winger who had run a spoiler campaign against the incumbent president George Bush, Sr., singled out the Clintons as the symbol of everything that was wrong with America. "There is a religious war going on in our country for the soul of America," he argued. "It is a cultural war, as critical to the kind of nation we will one day be as the Cold War itself. And in that struggle for the soul of America, Clinton and Clinton are on the other side, and George Bush is on our side."

In fact, the phrase "culture wars" was coined by a man who was as different from Buchanan as you can get—a mild-mannered sociologist at the University of Virginia, James Davison Hunter. In his 1991 book *Culture Wars: The Struggle to Define America,* Hunter argued that America was increasingly divided along cultural rather than political lines, casting social conservatives against secular liberals. Traditionalists, he pointed out, felt their world was under siege from the forces of liberalism—and they were increasingly responding to this siege by creating their own cultural and political organizations.

Hunter was on to something. What bound American conservatives together as much as anything was a feeling of "that ain't right." Some of the grievances were economic—for instance, fury with "big government" that took too much money in taxes. But culture, as we saw earlier in this book, was a huge part of the anger. In election after election from the late 1960s until 2008, blue-collar workers, who were once loyal Democrats, flocked to the Republican camp because they distrusted left-leaning, God-ignoring elitist liberals, who had pushed religion too far out of the public square.

In a growing number of countries politics is moving toward the American model, driven by problems of identity and values as well as economic concerns. Communities are dividing, much like Hunter's America, into liberal and conservative camps. Abortion and gay marriage, stem cells and cloning, headscarves and sharia law: these are every bit as central to modern politics as welfare reform. And religion is at the heart of these values debates. Secularists hoped that science would marginalize religion. In fact, the advance of science—particularly biotechnology—is raising all sorts of religious questions. Secularists hoped that social progress would make religion a private affair. In fact, many modern social movements—particularly the campaign for gay marriage—have pushed religious questions into the heart of the public square. William Buckley, the grand old man of the American right, once argued that a conservative's duty was to stand athwart history shouting, "Stop!" It would be an oversimplification to say that all pious people are standing up to yell, "Stop!" They disagree about what to do; but they all agree that you cannot simply treat cloning or gay adoption as nothing more than technical issues or private preferences. Confronted with growing evidence of a global battle of ideas, they are damned if they are going to let others boss them around—and they are forging alliances with all manner of people to make their case.

FIRST THINGS AND LAST RITES

Four culture wars stand out. The two most obvious are over "life" and "family"—or abortion and gay marriage. The other two wars, over science and the proper dividing line between church and state, have stirred up great debates of yore: biotechnology is rekindling the great nineteenth century debate about evolution, while Islam's progress in Europe is renewing Enlightenment arguments about religious authority. In this chapter we will look at each of these four debates and then conclude by looking at the way many of these culture wars now appear at the once-secular parliament of man, the United Nations.

Abortion inevitably remains central. It is the most important political issue for the Catholic Church. (Even senior bishops now admit that the battle over contraception has been lost, and many priests would say that the battle was an ill-chosen one in the first place, given the suffering it caused in the developing world.) In some Catholic countries, such as Ireland, the pressure for change comes from liberals trying to make regimes more permissive. (Irish women have to travel to Britain to get abortions.) But there is also a countervailing trend in permissive countries where science is helping conservatives. Ultrasound pictures have probably done more for the pro-life cause than any number of papal encyclicals. And the fact that babies can survive if they are born only twenty-five weeks after conception has created pressure for legislatures to reduce the time limit for abortion.

In Britain the effective limit was twenty-eight weeks from 1967, when abortion was legalized, until 1990, when it was brought down to twenty-four weeks. A huge campaign was waged in 2008 to reduce the time limit from twenty-four weeks' gestation to, at most, twenty-two weeks. It failed largely because the evidence for babies surviving below twenty-four weeks did not seem compelling. Yet several Catholic ministers in Gordon Brown's Labor government forced him to give them a free vote (where they did not have to follow the party line) on the issue. In Italy, which legalized abortion in 1978, Catholics managed to get a line inserted into the country's IVF law in 2004 that conferred rights on embryos from the moment of conception. There was a fracas in Italy in February 2008 about a murky case in which a woman in Naples was questioned by police after a nurse claimed that a fetus had been murdered.[7] After doctors explained that the fetus suffered from the sterility-inducing Klinefelter's syndrome, the woman was let off, but pro-choice campaigners saw it as an ominous development.

Occasional flashes of American-style abortion politics reach the Old World. One came with the Kaczynski twins, whose conservative Catholic coalition ruled Poland until October 2007. Shortly before they were voted out, the Polish government blocked a routine European Union motion in Brussels ordaining a "European day against the death penalty," saying it preferred to celebrate the broader "right to life." But Poland's junior justice minister, Andrzej Duda, was not finished there. At lunch he turned to the Danish justice minister, Lene Espersen, and read out the number of abortions carried out in her country. That might have been a bold statement of principle, but in Europolitical terms it came across as dotty: it barely got reported in Poland and its only effect within the EU was to annoy the Danes, who had been staunch supporters of Poland's membership in 2004 and were also a potential ally in a spat with Russia about a pipeline.[8]

This sort of grandstanding, though, is rare in Europe. This is not really to do with different values. Although slightly more people oppose abortion absolutely in America, most Americans take the same messy stance as Europeans. They want abortion to be "safe, legal and rare" (to use Bill Clinton's phrase). The difference has to do with the courts. Ever since *Roe v. Wade,* abortion law in America has been determined by the Supreme Court, not politicians. It has become a problem with a binary solution: either the right to terminate your pregnancy is a basic private freedom or it is murder. It has also made judicial appointments a litmus test for extremists on both sides of the debate: it is hard to be a pro-choice Republican or a pro-life Democrat.

Outside America, abortion is less a matter of left and right. In Britain there are probably slightly more pro-life Conservative MPs and pro-choice Labor MPs, but abortion has always been a "free" nonpartisan vote. Rowan Williams, for instance, is generally seen as being on the left (he has opposed the Iraq war, capitalism and American imperialism), but nobody thinks it is particularly odd that he is against abortion. In Latin America, some of the most intolerant Evangelical churches are pro-choice, perhaps to distinguish themselves from the Roman Catholic Church.

One person who symbolizes the transatlantic divide on abortion is Italy's best-known pro-lifer—an atheist who admits that in his twenties three of his partners had terminations. Giuliano Ferrara is the provocative editor of the pro-Berlusconi *Il Foglio* (and, we should add, a disputatious friend of ours).[9] He has campaigned for the UN to pass a global moratorium on abortion, similar to the nonbinding one it has on the death penalty. But most of his work has been at home. Ferrara stood for parliament in 2008 on a nuanced pro-life stance: he would not try to overturn the 1978 abortion law, but he would stop the introduction of a new drug that induces abortion and would also allow the resuscitation of aborted fetuses without the parents' consent. Some people suspected this was a gambit to lure Catholics to the Berlusconi camp and Ferrara failed to win his seat. But his opposition to abortion was based on a genuine view that it coarsened society. Famously well proportioned, he challenged the Klinefelter's syndrome case on the basis that he himself possessed its abnormalities (small testicles and large breasts) and invited others to take a look.[10] This is all rather a long way from the sort of stuff on Pat Robertson's 700 Club.

OUT OF THE CLOSET, INTO THE CHURCH

The prospect of homosexual unions is unpopular with most religious people pretty much everywhere. Homosexuality, even between consenting adults, is illegal in most Muslim countries, including those that are generally tolerant of gays. Parts of Morocco, for instance, have long viewed physical male friendships kindly, and some very senior figures in the country are believed to be gay. But a storm erupted in 2007 when rumors spread of a gay wedding in Ksar-el-Kebir. In fact, it seemed to be nothing of the sort—more like a party that got out of control. (The main evidence was a YouTube video of a man dancing in women's clothes.) Still, six people were sent to prison, accused of homosexual acts. Roughly the same thing happened in the same year in Bauchi, capital of one of the twelve states in Nigeria that practice sharia law: eighteen young men were put on trial for cross-dressing while celebrating an alleged gay marriage. When the charges were reduced from sodomy, which carries a death sentence, to idleness and vagabondage, punishable by a year in jail plus a few lashings, the locals rioted in protest and the charges were stepped up again—to ones that could send them to prison for ten years.

The situation with Jews and Christians is more complicated. Orthodox Jews still take a dim view of gays: in the past, gay-pride marches through the Orthodox areas of Jerusalem have caused riots. Legalized gay marriage in Israel looks unlikely, because the only sort of domestic union recognized for Jewish citizens is a religious ceremony, as laid down by the rabbinate. Yet the Israeli courts have said that the state must recognize gay marriages (just like other secular marriages) if performed abroad. The court has also allowed lesbian spouses to adopt children born to their partners.

Developed Christian countries have been more tolerant. As usual, *The Simpsons* provides the best barometer: when a Gay Pride march paraded through Springfield chanting, "We're here! We're queer! Get used to it!" Lisa Simpson replied: "You do this every year. We *are* used to it." Some half dozen countries and several American states have followed the Netherlands' lead in 2001 and fully endorsed gay marriage, with many more agreeing to civil partnerships. But that is misleading. In most of these cases (as in Israel) the pressure has come from the courts, trying to apply antidiscrimination legislation, or liberal elites, rather than popular opinion. Tolerance toward gays does not necessarily extend to thinking that gay marriages are normal. For instance, the biggest rally in Spain before the 2008 election was a "Christian Family Day" that drew 150,000 people to Madrid and featured Spain's Catholic bishops tearing into the permissive policies of the Socialist prime minister, José Luis Rodríguez Zapatero.[11] The bishops failed to oust Zapatero, but it was an impressive display of power.

The opposition to gay marriage from Christians in the developing world is much more uncompromising. Much of the fury against Gene Robinson's ordination came from Africa, where Anglicanism is a much more combative creed. The Archbishop of Kenya spoke of "a devil" entering the church; his counterpart in Nigeria described gays as lower than dogs.[12] Some African churches broke their ties with the Episcopal Church as a whole; others have just ruled out the American parishes that accepted gay marriage. Some two hundred African and Asian bishops refused to attend the 2008 synod, if only because some American bishops (though not Robinson) would be there. They have also gone on the offensive, offering shelter to disgruntled American parishes.

Consider, for instance, the case of Falls Church near Washington, DC, a church that once numbered George Washington among its vestrymen and is now the church of choice for the capital's conservative power elite. Michael Gerson, George Bush's former speechwriter, Porter Goss, a former head of the CIA, and Fred Barnes, the executive editor of the *Weekly Standard,* all worship there.[13] In 2006 eight parishes in Virginia, including Falls Church, voted overwhelmingly to break with the American Episcopal Church and put themselves under the authority of a foreign bishop. Liberals, accusing traditionalists of putting their personal prejudices above their duty to the church authorities, unleashed a quiver of lawsuits to reclaim church property. (Falls Church is one of the richest in the country.) The Reverend Susan Russell, president of Integrity, a group that champions gay and lesbian rights in the Episcopal Church, denounced offshore bishops as "intercontinental ballistic weapons of schism and division."[14] Nevertheless, more than two hundred American churches have put themselves up for adoption, with thirty-five joining Nigeria's Anglican Church.

Submitting to places like Kenya, Bolivia and Rwanda is the religious equivalent of corporate offshoring. American conservatives acquire the protection of foreign masters, a more sympathetic religious atmosphere and a new sense of purpose: the newly minted American bishops frequently return to the United States from their African ordinations with a renewed enthusiasm for a traditional interpretation of the Bible. All the same, there is something a little odd about well-heeled clergymen from suburban Virginia, where sports utility vehicles are standard issue, bowing the knee to bishops in Uganda, where people get by on a dollar a day. And many people in developing countries go far beyond just opposing the ordination of homosexuals. In Uganda, for example, homosexual acts are illegal, and priests denounce them as satanic. Nigeria's Peter Akinola, who runs the largest province in the Anglican Communion, supports legislation that would make it illegal for gays to form associations, read gay literature or even eat together.[15] Indeed, conservatives and liberals have switched. Time was when liberal Episcopalians were all for listening to the voices of the developing world, while their conservative brethren were not so sure. Now the reverse is true.

Still, the splits are likely to continue. Although opinion polls suggest that America is moving inexorably toward sanctioning gay marriage, about nine hundred churches have joined the Anglican Communion Network in order to fight a guerrilla war inside the Episcopal Church against the liberal establishment. Conservatives are convinced that they have both God and history on their side. The balance of numbers in the global Christian community is shifting toward the conservative developing world. American Episcopalians only account for 2.4 million of the world's 77 million Anglicans. The erstwhile multiculturalists of the Episcopal establishment could find themselves preaching to a dwindling band of ageing white liberals. And the lily-white conservative power brokers of George Washington's old church could find themselves bowing the knee to the Episcopal authorities of far-off Kigali or Abuja.

THE TESTAMENT VERSUS THE TEST TUBE

The science wars are almost as noisy as the gay and the abortion wars. The most dramatic intervention in science policy has been in America: George Bush's decision to curtail stem-cell research. But America is not alone. Until recently, religious people everywhere had been shamed into silence on such issues by the accusation that any questioning of biotechnology would mean that they were an enemy of scientific progress. Nobody wanted to be likened to the Grand Inquisitor who tried to silence Galileo. But recent breakthroughs in biotechnology—particularly the cloning of Dolly the sheep in Scotland in 1996—have given religious people the chance to refight the battle with science on a much flatter playing field.

For instance, the attempt to bring Britain's abortion law below twenty-four weeks in 2008 was technically a series of amendments to an assisted reproduction law. That law sparked three other controversies. First, it removed a previous requirement that fertility doctors consider a child's need for a father, on the grounds that this discriminated against single women and lesbians. (Conservatives called it antifamily.) Second, the opposition tried to get the law to ban "chimera" embryos—ones where you place human DNA in the eggs of other species. Finally, there was a fight over "savior siblings"—where an embryo is created only to harvest cells for a sick brother or sister. In Britain secular liberals won all these arguments in 2008. But it is noticeable how much more confident social conservatives have become in addressing scientific subjects.

Most religious traditions have come out strongly against cloning. The most absolute response is that of the Roman Catholic Church, which is opposed to cloning in all its forms—therapeutic as well as reproductive—because of its basic theological position on the moral status of the embryo. Embryos must be treated with the same respect with which we treat other human beings and therefore cannot be used as a means to an end. Some Protestants are equally opposed. Gilbert Meilaender, a leading Evangelical theologian, worries that cloning would result in children who were "made," not "begotten": children who are instruments of our will—projects, as it were—rather than equal partners.

Like many Protestants, Muslim scholars make a distinction between therapeutic cloning, which they accept, and human cloning, which they abhor. There have been a succession of fatwas condemning it. The basic objection is the same as it is for Christians: man is playing God. But there is also a more specifically Muslim objection to do with kinship and Islamic values. Who would count as the father, mother, sister of the clone?[16]

Another set of religious people are also reviving one of the great culture wars of the Victorian era—over evolution. In some cases, their methods are as unsophisticated as the fundamentalists in the Scopes Monkey Trial. In 2007 Evangelicals in Kenya denounced the exhibition of the Turkana Boy—the most complete prehistoric human skeleton—because he inconveniently lived thousands of years before Adam is supposed to have met Eve. A lavish new $27 million Creation Museum in Petersburg, Kentucky, aims to set the record straight, showing how huge dinosaurs could have mingled with humans shortly after time began in 4004 BC, and how Noah managed to squeeze all the world's animals into a boat only 135 meters long.

The doctrine of "intelligent design"—the notion that evolution does not explain everything, so there must be an intelligent Creator—is clearly one level up from this. Much of this is refashioned creationism: believers still trying to prove that man might be descended from angels, not apes. But it is plainly gaining ground. In Britain, a group called Truth in Science has sent videos to every school in Britain making the case for intelligent design, and some of the country's hundred state-supported Muslim schools teach creationism. Intelligent design is now taught in some Turkish schools, thanks in large part to Adnan Oktar, a preacher who set up the Bilim Araştirma Vakfı ("Scientific Research Foundation"). He claims to have 4.5 million followers, and his lavishly produced *Atlas of Creation* has been distributed around the Muslim world and Europe. His organization also sees links between Darwin and various evils, including terrorism, fascism and communism.

The crusade to get intelligent design taught in schools has suffered a number of legal setbacks—in Russia, where evolution was opposed by the Orthodox Church, in Britain, where it brought down the wrath of the scientific establishment, and most notably in America, where a judge ruled against a Pennsylvania school board in 2005. But scientists would be wrong to think the issue is dead. In a *Newsweek* poll in 2007, 48 percent of Americans surveyed reckoned that God had created humans in their present form in the past ten thousand years. More surprisingly, a poll for the BBC in 2006 discovered that more than 40 percent of Britons thought that creationism or intelligent design should be taught in school science lessons.[17]

What is really driving this resistance to science is not reasoned argument but much the same emotion that American conservatism drew on: the worry that it "ain't right." There is a widespread fear that man is getting arrogant, playing with things he barely understands. Many people who would never question stem-cell research draw the line at cloning, chimera cells or merging men with animals. Religious people are fond of quoting C. S. Lewis's warnings about the "abolition of man." Lewis worried that man's triumph over his own nature might in fact represent nature's triumph over man. The bid to take control of our lives, including our genetic makeup, is also a bid to turn ourselves into an object to be manipulated.

Islam and the Public Square

Once again, Islam is sufficiently sui generis to produce its own set of culture wars. Many of the battles over where to draw the line between mosque and state mimic those that have been fought in the Christian world. But Islam stands out as the religion that brooks the least distinction between the secular and the religious.

In the Christian world, with the tiny exception of the Vatican, clerics have lost their urge to rule over the secular realm. The Church of England seems embarrassed by having a few bishops in the House of Lords. Christian Democrat parties everywhere treat the first part of their name as silent. The idea of a bright line between God and Caesar is embedded not just in the Gospels but also in Christian history: hence the Holy Roman Emperors' multiple disagreements with the pope.

Islam has always left less room for the secular. Unlike Jesus, Muhammad was a ruler, warrior and lawmaker. Islam, which means "submission," teaches that the primary unit of society is the *umma,* the brotherhood of believers, and it provides a system of laws—sharia—for people to live by. As Mark Lilla of Columbia University puts it, there has been no "great separation": pious Muslims still turn to holy texts for guidance on all aspects of their lives.

Countries can roughly be divided into three groups when it comes to the debate about Islam and the public square. In the first group there is no real debate, because sharia, a system rooted in medieval traditions, is so strictly interpreted that it is hard to see how people can lead modern lives. In Saudi Arabia, for instance, women cannot drive or go to the gym (something Condoleezza Rice learned to her cost). There is no debate about where you can drink, as in Turkey, because alcohol is forbidden. Indeed, in practice the only culture war in Saudi Arabia is over how much the royal family and the elite can get away with in private. (If you write a book about religion, you encounter a lot of humbug, but there is little to compare with an elite Saudi singing the praises of strict Islam during an interview and then inviting you to come around to his mansion for a "proper"—i.e., alcohol-laden—party.)

In the second group are countries like Nigeria and Bosnia, where sharia has been introduced but where there is still recourse to the secular system. In northern Nigeria, as already noted, the sharia system has not been as disastrous as many Christians had feared. Most Muslims prefer the sharia courts to the federal courts for the simple reason that it is cheaper and quicker, and the harsher punishments have generally been avoided. But that does not mean that everything is hunky-dory. There have been a few amputations and some of the lesser punishments have been pretty nasty, as the cross-dressing revelers in Bauchi discovered.

Sharia law has had indirect effects as well. Companies take a stricter line on workplace attire, for both Muslims and Christians. In Kano schools only Muslim children are legally required to wear the *hijab,* but Christians inevitably try to fit in too. And Islamic dress codes have begun to extend beyond sharia states. For a brief period women were arrested in the streets of (generally cosmopolitan) Lagos for "indecent dress," though the cases were thrown out.[18]

The last group of countries trying to deal with Islam and the public square are also the most interesting: secular countries that do not permit sharia. That essentially means two places: Turkey and Western Europe.

TURKISH PROMISE

Turkey is a long way from Saudi Arabia. Its courts are secular and so is much of its culture: several of the erotic exhibits at a recent modern art fair in Istanbul would have had Saudi Arabia's religious police reaching for their scimitars. Yet it is a long way from Europe too. Atatürk's secular revolution was not based on the idea of separating religion from the state in the same way as the American Revolution or even the French Revolution. Rather, he subordinated religion to the state. Religion in Turkey is run by a government department, the *diyanet,* which interferes with many details of religious life. It distributes money to mosques, regulates prayer times, appoints imams to Turkey's seventy-seven thousand mosques and tells them what to preach, even sometimes writing their sermons. The current *diyanet* president, Ali Bardakoğlu, who serves in the AK government, has followed a liberal course. (Hidayet Tuksal approves of his fierce opposition to honor killings.) He has also sent out the firm message that Christian Evangelicals, who have sometimes been beaten up in the past, should be left to go about their business. In Europe, by contrast, Islam is in the minority, and there are no government departments to run mosques.

The Old World's attitude toward culture wars has changed remarkably in the past decade. Europeans used to watch America's culture wars with a mixture of bemusement and contempt, like an even wackier version of *The Jerry Springer Show.* Now Europeans are also arguing about the expression of faith in the public square and the right of journalists to offend religious minorities. They are once more debating—and sometimes dying over—questions that they had long ago consigned to the attic. The reason for this is Islam.

Islam is clearly on the march in Europe. Muslim immigrants are strengthening their commitment to their faith—or rediscovering a commitment that had begun to fade—and reasserting their unique cultural identity. Many Islamic communities are trying to build their own parallel universe of institutions, much as conservative Christians did in the United States. Ghettoization is part of this: from Bradford to Barcelona, Muslims are segregated. There is also an element of collective self-help, understandable when the jobless rate is 24 percent among Turks in Germany and 39 percent among North Africans in France.[19] But such self-help also has the effect of creating an all-embracing religious cocoon that separates its inmates from wider society and reinforces a sense of cultural exclusiveness.

As a result, Islam is introducing an old European problem in a new form—the ultramontane problem. Just as kings used to worry about Catholics' loyalty to the pope, the parallel societies that are emerging in many European cities are closely linked to the global Islamic community. Religious enthusiasts can use the Internet to watch services in Mecca and chat with fellow Muslims all over the world. Many preachers are trained in the Arab world. Arab countries—particularly Saudi Arabia—are pouring huge amounts of money into building mosques, supporting social services and training religious activists. The Union of Islamic Organizations of France (UIOF), a large umbrella group, admits that it gets about a quarter of its annual budget of 2.75 million euros from abroad, especially Saudi Arabia, the United Arab Emirates and Kuwait.[20] The Muslim Brotherhood and its offshoots operate throughout Europe. This is producing an army of Europeans whose first loyalty is not to their nation-state or their Continent but to their global religion.

European Muslims are partly caught up in the global revival of their faith. But another reason for their enthusiasm is peculiar to the immigrant experience: they regard Islam as a source of pride and identity in a continent that sometimes threatens to rob them of both. Enthusiasm for religion is particularly marked among the children and grandchildren of immigrants who arrived during the 1960s. The first generation of immigrants often concealed their religious roots—either because they wanted to fit in with their host societies or because they were happy to escape from their claustrophobic communities. Their children and grandchildren, on the other hand, are reembracing public symbols of their faith (such as headscarves and beards). They are turning to religion as a way of inoculating themselves from the temptations of secular society. Europe's ghettos are full of young religious activists who flirted with alcohol and drugs but were rescued by religious activists who preached self-help and austerity.

Some of these young activists are attracted to Islam in its most perverted form. Olivier Roy points out that when Islam is torn from its traditional moorings of custom and family, as it sometimes is in immigrant societies, it can easily succumb to the twin temptations of fundamentalism and fanaticism. Alienated youths are particularly attracted to a back-to-basics version of Islam that refuses to acknowledge reasonable limits on its authority.

At its worst, this strays from culture wars into real wars. A more common problem is vehement rejection of the values of mainstream Europe.
A poll of British Muslims, conducted by YouGov and the *Daily Telegraph* a
week after the terrorist attacks on the London transport system on July 7,
2005, discovered that 24 percent of those surveyed sympathized with the
bombers (even though only 1 percent said they would do the same thing
themselves).[21] This reflects both contempt for Europe's permissive ways
and worry that permissive mores will infect the Muslim population. In
Islamic ghettos, women who don't wear headscarves are harassed, and
people who consume food or drink during Ramadan are ostracized or
publicly criticized.

Once again, it is worth stressing that Muslim alienation can be
exaggerated. There are still far fewer Muslims in Europe than there
are Latinos in the United States (and they have far less electoral clout).
Moreover, many European Muslims are doing pretty well. A Muslim, for
instance, now runs Cazenove, the queen's stockbroker. And, as Roy has
pointed out, there are double standards aplenty: why only criticize Islam
as discriminatory? Should we not stigmatize the Catholic Church for not
allowing women to be priests? Why not ask Jews to give up the notion of
the "chosen people"?

Still, it is interesting how many Muslims, especially young Muslims,
want to reorder European society to accommodate their preferences. A
1997 survey of twelve hundred young Turkish Germans discovered that
about a third of them said that they believed that Islam should come to
power in every country in the world, Europe included, and that using violence against nonbelievers was perfectly justified if it served the greater
Islamic good. In 2007 a poll for Policy Exchange found that 37 percent
of Muslims age sixteen to twenty-four wanted to introduce sharia law. In
2008 another survey, this time of Muslim students at British universities for the Center for Social Cohesion, produced some fairly spectacular numbers.[22] Two in five Muslim students wanted to incorporate sharia
codes into British law—the same proportion as thought that it was unacceptable for Muslim men and women to associate freely. One in three
supported the introduction of a worldwide caliphate based on sharia, a
proportion that rose to 58 percent among active members of campus

Islamic societies. A third thought that killing in the name of religion was justifiable. A quarter said they had no respect for homosexuals. Once again, the poll was not universally depressing: 68 percent said Islam and the Western notion of democracy were compatible and 78 percent said that it was possible to be both British and Muslim equally.

THE EUROPEAN REACTION

Culture wars require two sides. In retrospect, Islam could not have found a more problematic sparring partner than European secularism. Many Europeans emerged from the Second World War with a fresh determination to rid the Continent of a "history written in blood." This meant evolving beyond reactionary forces such as nationalism and religious strife. It meant reasserting the primacy of Enlightenment values such as reason and tolerance. And it meant making the maximum possible room for individual freedom and self-expression. All this has made it peculiarly difficult for Europeans to come to terms with the influx of a large religious minority.

To begin with, the European elites who masterminded mass immigration simply expected Muslims to undergo the same process of secularization that they themselves had. Back in 1966, Roy Jenkins, then Britain's Labor home secretary, argued for a multicultural model of immigration: "Not a flattening process of assimilation but equal opportunity accompanied by cultural diversity in an atmosphere of mutual tolerance." The elites introduced Muslims to Europe's secular institutions without much heed to religious sensibilities. But when second-generation Muslims began to reembrace the faith of their fathers, muddle and then fury set in.

The muddle has come in government policy, which has veered between assimilation and multiculturalism—and made a hash of both. Take two extreme examples: France and the Netherlands. In 1905 the French introduced laws making the separation of church and state even stricter, in a bid to discipline the Catholic Church, which then controlled primary schools, habitually interfered in political life, and played a disgraceful role in the Dreyfus affair. For years they tried to apply this principle to Muslims. In 1989 the government banned girls from wearing headscarves in schools. (The law also banned the wearing of Christian crosses and Jewish yarmulkes but there was no doubt who was really the object of the law.) The UIOF organized protests against the ruling and encouraged girls to wear bandannas rather than headscarves to evade the new rules. In 2003, Jacques Chirac commissioned a blue-ribbon report from Bernard Stasi that duly reasserted the importance of banning the display of "conspicuous" religious symbols in public places such as schools.

This was largely counterproductive. It made Muslims more Muslim: many were furious about the headscarf ban. It also made religion much more of a political label, separating Muslims from the state. As Roy has put it, "*laïcité* creates religion by making it a category apart that has to be isolated and circumscribed. It reinforces religious identities rather than allowing them to dissolve in more diversified practices and identities." Yet it also, perversely, entangled the state still further with religion. The report urged the establishment of a national school of Islamic studies and laid down detailed rules of religious conduct in the public square (hardly most people's idea of the separation of church and state). Isolated, poor, angry and (in their view) discriminated against, the Muslim *banlieues* erupted in violence in 2005.

On the other hand, Dutch multiculturalism has hardly been a roaring success. Three-quarters Protestant and a quarter Catholic, the Netherlands has traditionally relied on "pillarization," developing a system of church-affiliated secular institutions. Catholics and Protestants lived in their own institutional worlds, with their own schools, newspapers, trade unions, social clubs. The 1960s saw a revolt against church-based organizations and the creation of Holland's famously libertine public square. Convinced that Muslims would repeat the same pattern, the Dutch tried to build a Muslim pillar of the Dutch state, creating Muslim schools and pouring public money into the construction of mosques. The more that Muslims felt at home, the argument went, the more they would embrace secular values. The result has been the opposite: Dutch Muslims are just as isolated and angry as their French coreligionists.

Nowadays, most people would argue that posing a choice between multicultaralism and assimilation is the wrong way to frame the debate.

There are good and bad bits to each. But the convolutions governments have gone through has angered many voters: why was society trying so hard to tolerate Islam's intolerance?

This has helped spawn a new form of European politician—the secular culture warrior. In some cases the beneficiaries at the polls have been far-right politicians who loathed immigration anyway—Jean-Marie le Pen in France, the late Jörg Haider in Austria and various BNP thugs in Britain have all singled out Islam for criticism—and profited politically. But Europe has also produced some much more unusual figures who hardly fit the far-right stereotype. Pim Fortuyn was a flamboyant gay sociology professor turned politician who reluctantly concluded that Islam posed a fundamental threat to the Dutch tradition of toleration. ("I have nothing against Moroccans," Fortuyn quipped. "I have them in my bed all the time.") In March 2002, just before his assassination, the party he headed, Livable Rotterdam, won the local Rotterdam election.

It is also notable how many liberal intellectuals have rallied to the idea that Islam is a repressive and reactionary force. Holland's other best-known culture warrior was a leftish documentary filmmaker, Theo van Gogh. His death warrant was a short movie about the abuse of Muslim women called *Submission* (the English for "Islam"): semi-naked women kneel to tell their stories, as if they are talking to the Prophet, while verses of the Koran are projected onto their bodies. Liberal English writers, such as Martin Amis and Ian McEwan, have also torn into Islam. Flemming Rose, an absolutist on free speech who published the controversial cartoons of Muhammad, compares the Muslim world with the Communist world: for him, people who renounce Islam are heroes on the level of the ex-Communists who contributed to *The God That Failed*. No Muslim Gorbachev has yet emerged, but there have been a few Voltaires. Afshin Ellian, an Iranian-born scholar, argues that Islam needs its own versions of Nietzsche, Voltaire and Marquis de Sade. Ayaan Hirsi Ali, who wrote the script for *Submission,* has described Muhammad as a "perverted tyrant" and cowrote an article with Geert Wilders calling for a "liberal jihad."

THREE BATTLEGROUNDS

These, then, are the warriors in Europe's new culture wars. At their core, these battles pit an increasingly aggressive Muslim minority against lib-eral secularists. Both sides have their villains, hangers-on and rent-a-mobs. And the battleground ranges far and wide—from religious freedom to food, from clothing to arranged marriages. The three most potent bat-tlegrounds are over freedom of speech, sharia and Turkey.

Two centuries after the princes of the Enlightenment excoriated "*l'infame*" for trying to repress open debate, Europe has witnessed a suc-cession of attempts by Muslims to censor offensive speech. The opening shot was the fatwa against Salman Rushdie for insulting the Prophet in *The Satanic Verses* (1988). Rushdie survived his death sentence. Theo van Gogh was less fortunate: he was slaughtered for insulting the Prophet in 2004. Hirsi Ali was eventually hounded out of the Netherlands. Geert Wilders still receives death threats: "It is our wish to kill you by decapi-tation. Your infidel blood will flow freely on cursed Dutch streets." The publication of cartoons of Muhammad in Flemming Rose's newspaper ignited another mass assault on free speech. Muslims across the world called for a "holy war" against Europe. Thousands of people openly called for Rose's head. "Bomb, bomb Denmark," shouted Muslim demonstrators outside the Danish Embassy in London. "Europe, you'll come crawling when Mujahideen come roaring." One demonstrator dressed up as a sui-cide bomber.

The "suicide bomber," who turned out to be a convicted drug dealer, duly apologized. More worrying for many liberals is the fact that the European authorities have frequently caved in on free speech. In Berlin a performance of Mozart's opera *Idomeneo* was canceled in 2006 because it depicts the beheading of Muhammad.[23] In Spain villages have been forced to change centuries-old festivals.

Meanwhile, other religions have also jumped on the censorship band-wagon. British theaters dropped plans to produce *Jerry Springer—The Opera* because of complaints from Christian activists. (The show features a diaper-wearing Jesus Christ who admits to being a "bit gay.") A Sikh playwright was forced to go into hiding when she received death threats because of her supposedly unflattering portrait of her religion. Suddenly, old-fashioned blasphemy laws or newfangled antiracism laws are being considered to protect Muslims from religious insults. The Dutch government has even created a sinister-sounding organization called the Inter-departmental Working Group on Cartoons.[24]

The second culture war has to do with sharia. As Rowan Williams pointed out, the idea of religious-based add-ons is actually part of Western law. The religious courts, or *beth din,* used by Orthodox Jews have been recognized by statute in Britain; Anglican canon law is also used for church property. Nor is it that odd for religions to get opt-outs from rules others follow: for instance, in British Columbia Sikhs can ride motorcycles without helmets. But "sharia" is a much more potent word, both because it is broader (it implies a divine ideal about how society should be organized) and because in some forms it is more violent—all that corporal and capital punishment. The idea of a Muslim state within a secular state scares the daylights out of most Europeans.

The earliest example of Western angst about sharia appeared in Canada (an honorary part of Europe) in 2003, when Syed Mumtaz Ali, a retired Ontario lawyer, said he was setting up a sharia court to settle family law disputes for Muslims. This was allowed under the province's 1991 Arbitration Act. Panic ensued—and eventually the province's premier stopped all settlement of family matters based on religious principles under the Arbitration Act. Religious arbitrators could still offer services in the settlement of disputes, but their rulings would have no legal status.

In the real Europe, there have been few attempts to treat sharia so generously. But there are recurring debates about the deeper issue—how far can societies go in making special rules for particular communities—and there has been a pronounced tendency to accommodate the activists. In both France and Britain, some local swimming pools have been segregated by sex because of Muslim protests. Leicester even provides a swimming session for women who want to swim fully clothed in chadors.[25] One housing estate in Bristol provides apartments for Muslims with the lavatories facing away from Mecca.[26] British local authorities have banned calendars and toys that depict pigs from local government offices. Doctors are asked to issue Muslim girls with "virginity certificates." In March 2008 a French judge allowed a man to nullify his marriage on the grounds that he discovered that his wife was not a virgin, though the judgment was reversed on appeal.

This sounds as if the secularists are capitulating. But in other ways, legal systems are toughening up. Many countries are tightening their requirements for citizenship, imposing citizenship tests and banning arranged marriage. The main thing that Europe is doing to get tougher, however, is one that it may come to regret: raising the bar for Turkey to join the European Union. The hypocrisy is sometimes breathtaking. The European Union famously failed to mention God or Christianity in its lengthy (and now aborted) constitution. But confront a European leader with the prospect of admitting seventy million Muslims to the Union, and they suddenly discover Europe's "Christian heritage": Silvio Berlusconi has flatly stated that Christian civilization is superior to Islamic civilization.

To be fair, the "European project" does indeed have Christian roots. The European Union was founded by Christian Democrats like Konrad Adenauer and Jean Monnet. The Vatican provided long-term support for European unification and Catholic intellectuals created a network of Europe-spanning institutions and alliances. (Catholic countries are almost always more enthusiastic about "federalism" than Protestant ones.) "A Christian club" is a favorite jibe of Turkish politicians trying to shame the EU into opening membership to its southern neighbor.

The irony of this, of course, is that Europe's preference for remaining a "Christian club" is reducing Islam's chances of modernizing. And that will only make future culture wars all the more ferocious. But that, as America long ago discovered, is the way that culture wars work: overreach encourages overreach.

GOD AND MAN AT THE UNITED NATIONS

Perhaps the most surprising new battlefield for the world's culture warriors is the United Nations. The UN was established to end real wars rather than accommodate cultural ones. Its permanent bureaucracy is dominated by secular technocrats who regard religion as a dangerous atavism.

In recent years, however, the United Nations has been the scene of impassioned battles about women's rights, sexual freedom—particularly access to contraception and abortion—homosexual rights and family values. Conservatives accuse liberals of trying to undermine the basic building blocks of society. Liberals accuse conservatives of consigning women to back-street abortions. Conservatives accuse liberals of engaging in the ultimate imperialism against the world's poor—preventing them from having children. Liberals accuse conservatives of getting into bed with theocracies such as Sudan.

The most experienced conservative culture warrior is the Catholic Church. The Vatican has had permanent observer status at the UN from its foundation, but its appetite for a fight increased dramatically under John Paul II. The Vatican increased the number of countries where it has diplomatic representation from 85 to 174. John Paul delivered a series of homilies denouncing the UN Conference on Population and Development in Cairo, calling on faithful Catholics to adopt a conservative stance on birth control, abortion and the family. In 1996 the Vatican suspended its financial support for UNICEF in protest of the organization's growing support for feminism and reproductive rights.

In the 1990s America's religious right also joined the fray. The prompt was a familiar one: overreach by the progressive establishment. During the 1990s the UN sponsored a succession of global conferences that infuriated social conservatives. Two proved particularly irksome: the International Conference on Population and Development in Cairo in 1994 and the Fourth World Conference on Women in Beijing the year later. Both conferences were dominated by liberal NGOs—Beijing saw as many as forty thousand activists flocking to the Chinese capital—and they were saturated by language promoting "rights" and "reproductive choice."

This was big enough for conservatives in America to sit up and take notice. They worried that secular liberals were using global institutions to redefine the basic building block of civilization, the family. They sensed an attempt to "mainstream" homosexuality. (The Beijing Conference on

Women featured "workshops" on "lesbianism for the curious," "lesbian activism from the interfaith perspective," "lesbian flirtation techniques.") They also saw parallels between the UN and American law courts: in both cases unaccountable liberal elites had sneaked up on conservatives. Heavens, the two were even intertwined. The American Supreme Court cited UN findings in the 2003 *Lawrence v. Texas* decision that created a constitutional right to sodomy.

Deciding to engage with the UN was not an easy decision for social conservatives. Most Evangelicals were deeply suspicious of the organization. In Tim LaHaye's wildly popular *Left Behind* series the Antichrist returns to earth in the form of the secretary general of the United Nations. And most conservatives regarded it as little more than a gravy train. John Bolton, George Bush's short-lived ambassador to the UN, spoke for most of his fellow travelers when he quipped that the UN building might benefit from having the top ten stories knocked off.

Yet over the past ten years social conservatives have flooded into the halls of global power. Three titans of America's Christian right—Focus on the Family, the Family Research Council and Concerned Women of America—have now all become accredited lobbyists at the UN with rented offices in the UN village. The Mormon Church also joined the fray, establishing the World Family Policy Center in 1997. The arrival of Concerned Women of America was particularly dramatic given that the organization was founded by Tim LaHaye's wife, Beverly. The Heritage Foundation, a conservative think tank, now also has consultative status at the UN. "Our presence will break the 'liberals only' roster of present NGOs," a Heritage spokesman noted, "and as the skunk at the UN party, we will be in a much stronger position to influence media coverage and public perception."

The arrival of these Christian right activists produced a culture clash as well as a culture war. Jennifer Butler, a long-standing left-leaning representative of the American Presbyterian Church at the UN, has written with striking honesty about how her fellow progressives reacted to the arrival of the Christian yahoos. In March 2000 she was sitting in the balcony of the UN's conference hall listening to the opening speeches of the Beijing Plus Five Conference (which was designed to reflect on the UN's progress in meeting the goals it had set itself at Beijing five years earlier). The female activists in the audience and on the platform were all of a kind. They wore free-flowing dresses and carried book bags covered with feminist stickers. They were middle-aged and graying. Friends and colleagues for years, they spoke a private language that was part UN-speak and part women's-studies patois.

Then suddenly an army of smartly dressed young people filed into the hall. "They wore professional business suits like the ones bankers and lawyers prefer. Their hair was short and clean-cut. The few women among them wore power suits and perfectly coifed hair. All of them wore bright campaign buttons emblazoned with a single word: "motherhood."[27] The reaction was one of shocked disbelief—as if a bunch of rednecks had invaded Wellesley with cries of, "Iron my shirt." When Butler told friends that she intended to write a book cataloguing this strange new phenomenon, many of them asked her if she feared for her life.[28]

George Bush's election in 2000 had given this emerging counterestablishment a big boost. On January 22, 2001, his first working day in office and also, by coincidence, the twentieth anniversary of the signing of *Roe v. Wade*, he issued an executive order reinstating the "Mexico City Policy," a policy that had been imposed by Ronald Reagan and then withdrawn by Bill Clinton, which prevents organizations that help with abortions in any way from receiving money for family planning from the American government. Bush appointed a succession of solid social conservatives to represent America at the UN.

Bush's troops scored the odd victory. In March 2005 the General Assembly voted to ban all forms of human cloning, to the fury of European countries. But it hardly turned the tide. The UN's permanent bureaucracy is instinctively liberal and secular as are most global NGOs. Yet the conservative culture warriors have three important things on their side.

One is the Catholic Church, which has a permanent seat at the UN table, a professional and dedicated papal diplomatic corps and a global network of missionaries and organizations. Another is the gradual emergence of social conservatism as a global movement. Focus on the Family has divisions in twenty countries. Mexico's home-grown Red Familia, or "Family Network," is devoted to defending traditional values and enjoys

strong support from both conservative businessmen and politicians such
as Vicente Fox. The third is a great deal of youth and energy. "Give me
a flyer announcing the themes for a progressive event," Jennifer Butler
observes, "and I can tell you who the speaker is—for they have spoken
for the past few decades to the same topic." The conservative NGOs, by
contrast, have proved much better at recruiting the younger generation.
The World Youth Alliance, which claims a million members, has set itself
the task of fighting "the dehumanizing, anti-life, anti-family trends of an
increasingly decadent western culture."

One of the most conspicuous culture warriors at the UN is a man with
a foot in both the Catholic camp and the American one. Austin Ruse is a
member in good standing of the religious right. (His wife works for Heritage.) He is also a committed Catholic. He has devoted the past fifteen
years of his life to combating the progressive agenda at the UN. Ruse is
the head of CFAM, a six-person outfit with offices in Washington, DC,
and New York that keeps a permanent watch on the UN. He knows the
corridors of the global leviathan like the back of his hand. He is fluent
in UN-speak ("Beijing Plus Five" and the rest of it). Ruse is convinced
that the liberal elites have embedded themselves in the corridors of global
power and are intent on "mainstreaming" abortion, feminism, adolescent
autonomy and homosexuality "in every country around the world."

Ruse is trying to stop this by creating a broad coalition of pro-family
groups—including pro-family Muslims. He says that he wants all the
"children of Abraham" to join together to do battle with the forces of
secularism and "sexual colonialism." ("I have a joke with my Mormon
friends," he likes to say, "that after we defeat the radicals then we can fight
each other.") He devotes much of his time to throwing wrenches in the
works. (One of the good things about the UN bureaucracy is that it is
slow-moving and consensus-oriented.) But he also wants to change the
culture of the institution so that it is more sensitive to what he regards as
the heart of the Christian message.

The point about Ruse and his kind is they challenge assumptions.
For instance, most outsiders admire the UN's battle against overpopulation. For Ruse, it is wrongly conceived and horribly executed. The biggest problem facing the world, in his view, is underpopulation rather than

overpopulation. Europe's aversion to childbearing will render its welfare state unsustainable. China's one-child policy will hobble its economy and unbalance its society. Now the UN is helping to justify immoral practices such as forced abortion and an immoral philosophy that tries to deprive poor people of their right to have children.

There are, of course, many arguments on the other side of this debate. Many Catholics, for instance, would disagree with Ruse about contraception; a few would say that their church's opposition has caused far more pain than the UN has. But the battle has plainly been joined. The UN will no longer be able to treat issues of overpopulation and bioengineering as mere technical issues to be decided by committees of experts. Religious people are standing athwart history, shouting, "Stop!"—and setting off a debate that will surely last for most of this century.

CONCLUSION:

LEARNING TO LIVE
WITH RELIGION

❧

THE EMPIRE STATE BUILDING is the world's most famous sky-scraper—the symbol of modernity par excellence. It was the world's tallest building from 1932 to 1971; and, with the felling of the Twin Towers in 2001, it is once again the tallest building in New York. With 6,500 windows, 73 elevators, 1,860 steps to the top floor and wonderful Art Deco decorations, it is an embodiment of technological prowess and an icon of modern pop culture, the building where King Kong met his tragic end.

Yet this icon of modernity is also home to one of America's leading Evangelical seats of learning. King's College, which moved into the building in 1999, now occupies two floors of the skyscraper. "For all of the sophistication and prestige of the secular colleges," Stan Oakes, the college's chancellor, writes in the college handbook, "almost all of their professors traffic in spent ideas that do not work—bad ideas that have had a myriad of disastrous consequences in our generation. They are wrong about God, human nature, wealth, power, marriage, poverty, family, sex, America, liberty, peace and many other decisive issues. You deserve better."

The stated mission of King's College is to create "ambassadors of Jesus Christ to lead and serve the world": it wants its students to leave with a biblical worldview but also prepared to beat the best and brightest from the secular world. It offers two majors, business and what Oxfordians call PPE (politics, philosophy and economics). It focuses on "three freedoms," spiritual freedom, political freedom and economic freedom. Indeed Oakes is almost as enthusiastic about Adam Smith as he is about the Almighty. The curriculum concentrates on Great Books, particularly the Bible. The students live a few blocks away in one-bedroom apartments in a high-rise. Some look down on a local porn shop. They are grouped into nine "houses," each of which boasts a coat of arms, to give life a more human scale. The houses are named after conservative heroes (Winston Churchill, Ronald Reagan, Margaret Thatcher), Christian eminences (C. S. Lewis, Sojourner Truth) and one, for no clear reason, after Elizabeth I (probably not because she pledged never to "make windows into men's souls").

Oakes, a stalwart of the Campus Crusade for Christ, likes to convey what it is like to be a conservative Evangelical in the heart of Manhattan with a joke about Sammy Davis, Jr., boarding a bus. "Go to the back of the bus," the driver orders. "But I'm Jewish," Davis replies. "Then get off!" retorts the driver. So far some 250 students from thirty states have decided to board Oakes's bus. Many Christians deliberately retreat from the temptations of the big city, attending Bible schools and Christian universities in small towns. Oakes has no time for "hiding in the holy huddle" or retreating to the "Christian ghetto." King's College deliberately brings young Christians to the heart of the beast. "Every sin in the world is within five blocks of The Empire State Building," he says. Where better to strengthen your faith than a city that is rife with temptations? And where better to train people to exercise influence on the world than the capital of the media and financial world, not to mention the home to the United Nations? Oakes dreams of a day when his school will have a student body of 2,500 rather than 250.

And why not? The New York elite may be one of the least religious groups in the country, but look beneath the surface of the secular city and you find a religious heart beating—a place of crammed churches, storefront temples, raucous revival meetings and charismatic preachers. The Times Square Church, in the heart of neon-lit consumer capitalism, has eight thousand congregants a week. Billy Graham attracted tens of thousands when he preached his final sermon in New York; Creflo Dollar attracts thousands to his weekly sermons in Madison Square Garden (where, incidentally, the young Graham led his first revival meeting in New York back in 1957, worrying that "no other city in America—perhaps in the world—presents as great a challenge to evangelism").

Many of the people flocking to worship are immigrants who, like so many new Americans before them, "cling to" religion (to borrow Barack Obama's phrase) far more enthusiastically in the strange new city than they did in their home country. The Catholic Church celebrates mass in thirty-two languages. The Faith Bible Ministry in Flushing provides services in three dialects of Chinese. The Fountain of Salvation in Washington Heights is headquartered in Latin America. The congregation at the Redeemed Christian Church of God in Flatbush wear kente cloth and dance to an African beat.[1]

Nor is religion just something for immigrants, a staging post for newcomers on the way to the cosmopolitan Manhattan of Woody Allen and *Sex and the City*. New York has long been home to large Roman Catholic and Orthodox Jewish populations; it also boasts more than seven thousand Evangelical churches with a collective congregation of about 1.5 million people. New York even has its own megachurches. The Christian Cultural Center in Brooklyn boasts twenty-nine thousand members and a commercial complex that includes a restaurant and a café. The Brooklyn Tabernacle has ten thousand members and a three-hundred-strong choir that produces some of the best gospel music in the country. The suburban churches around New York are full of doctors, lawyers and Wall Streeters—sophisticated people who do not see religion as an alternative to modern life, but as an answer to it.

URBI ET ORBI

This book has pointed out that the secularization theorists are wrong to claim that modernity and religion are incompatible. Religion has always thrived in the world's most modern country (and in its most cosmopolitan city). Now it is also thriving in much of the modernizing world too, from Asia to the Middle East. The great forces of modernity—technology and democracy, choice and freedom—are all strengthening religion rather than undermining it.

Give people the freedom to control their lives and, for better or worse, they frequently choose to give religion more power. Give religious people modern technology and they frequently use it to communicate God's Word to an ever-growing band of the faithful. George Bush (either revealing his inner secular liberal or completely ignoring the story of America) saw democracy as a way of defanging Islam. But, in fact, the more democratic the Middle East has become the more "parties of God" thrive. The democratization of China, if it ever occurs, could produce one of the greatest upticks in Christianity in world history. "Democracy is giving the world's peoples their voice," Timothy Shah and Monica Toft have written, "and they want to talk about God."[2]

Religion is proving perfectly compatible with modernity in all its forms, high and low. It is moving back toward the center of intellectual life. But it is also a vital part of popular culture, with Christian barbershops and tattoo artists, skateboarders and stand-up comedians. Christian rock music is so ubiquitous that, in an episode of *King of the Hill* entitled "Reborn to be Wild," Hank Hill decided that he had had enough: "You're not making Christianity better. You're making rock 'n roll worse."

We have argued throughout this book that the world is generally moving in the American direction, where religion and modernity happily coexist, rather than in the European direction, where secularization marginalizes religion. But it is worth adding three caveats in escalating order of importance.

First, the relationship between religion and modernity is far from smooth for many believers. If religious people are surprisingly keen on harvesting the fruits of capitalism, they are equally keen on rejecting what they regard as its thorns. Evangelicals like Oakes abjure stem-cell research even as they admire the free market. Technophile Muslims set up snazzy Web sites to condemn liberalism.

Pentecostalism is particularly striking in this respect. It is a great force for social progress and upward mobility across the developing world. Indeed, it acts rather like Max Weber's Puritanism in the seventeenth century—providing people with the right psychological disposition to thrive in a capitalist economy. Women are notable gainers: Pentecostals have already done more for feminism in Africa and Latin America than Betty Friedan. Meanwhile, Pentecostal megachurches use every technical and commercial trick in the book: David Cho's Yoido Full Gospel Church is the religious equivalent of a Korean *chaebol*. Yet most Pentecostals believe things that might make Benedict XVI, let alone Voltaire, wince. David Martin, a British sociologist, calls Pentecostalism "a potent mixture of the pre-modern and the postmodern, of the pre-literate and the post-literate, of the fiesta and the encounter group."[3]

The second caveat is that the triumph of the American model does not mean that the alternatives disappear. Its status is closer to "first among equals," or, to borrow Peter Berger's phrase, first among "alternative modernities." The American version of modernity is certainly spreading faster than the European one, but that does not mean that it will conquer every corner of the world. We think that religion is likely to become more vibrant in Western Europe, but Europe will nevertheless remain a predominantly secular continent.

The third caveat—and the most important—is that the natural accompaniment of modernity is not religiosity but pluralism. A country can be modern and religious at the same time (or modern and irreligious). But it is exceedingly difficult to be modern without being pluralistic. Religious identities are becoming something that people craft rather than take for granted. It is notable that many of America's Founding Fathers were great religious tinkerers. Franklin experimented with all sorts of religious beliefs, from Puritanism to Deism to polytheism, and even rewrote the Lord's Prayer to make it punchier. Jefferson went through the Bible cutting out the bits that he liked. This spirit of self-discovery changes the relationship between authority and worshippers. It could have revolutionary consequences, especially in the Islamic world.

The triumph of pluralism means that all religious beliefs (and indeed all secular beliefs) become competitors in the marketplace. Much though some countries struggle against it, globalization is throwing different religions together. Thus more than half of the 13.7 million members of that most American of churches, the Church of Jesus Christ of Latter-Day

Saints, live outside the United States: its twice-yearly conferences in Salt Lake City are translated into 86 languages.[4] Islam too is surging outside its heartlands. Olivier Roy calculates that between 10 and 25 percent of radical Islamic activists are converts.[5]

Many churches—even the "universal" Catholic Church—seem happy with this marketplace. But choice does not always promote tolerance and brotherly love. The more that people weave their own religious narratives, the more some fundamentalists insist on the unique virtue of their own narratives: they want to restore the taken-for-grantedness of traditional religion. That can mean, at its worst, resorting to coercion or violence to promote your vision of the holy.

WAR WITHOUT END?

Europe's secularists were clearly wrong to predict the death of religion. But they were right about one big thing: religion can be a dangerous force in politics. This book has repeatedly hinted at two big challenges, both of which have historical echoes: first, in foreign affairs, how to deal with the new wars of religion; and, second, at home, how to construct a liberal political regime that recognizes man's religious instinct but also preserves individual rights.

The most striking danger is on the international level. In the seventeenth century religion produced a Thirty Years' War. Many people are acting as if we are eight years into another such war between Islam and the West—ten years, if you go back to bin Laden's fatwa against Jews and Crusaders. Look at the world's potential flashpoints and in most of them you can see the fires of religion burning. Look at the world's most intractable problems, particularly in the Middle East, and they have acquired a religious edge. For that matter, look closely at an outwardly stable regime such as China's, and you can see a religious revival gathering under the surface. As Scott Thomas, a British academic, has remarked, "We live in a world that is not supposed to exist."

Before September 11, 2001, liberal thought was at its laziest on the subject of religion. Discussions of modernization were dominated by secular

questions. Does modernization entail democratization? Or are enlightened autocracies better at ensuring stability and growth? And what is the
proper relationship between governments and the market? Few had time
to think about God when there were so many earthly things to worry
about.

The roots of this ignorance reach right back to the Peace of Westphalia
in 1648. Europe's wars of religion proved so bloody that the Continent's
rulers devised an elaborate set of rules to keep religion out of warfare.
There have been plenty of bloody evils to deal with since, including fascism and communism, but they have been secular evils. During that long
religious cease-fire, diplomats became thoroughly secularized. Those diplomats who preserved an interest in religion regarded it as a purely private
affair—rather like a taste for bondage—and certainly not something that
ought to feature in their policy calculations.

As we have seen, religion returned to politics long before September
11; by the 1970s it was a powerful force in plenty of countries, not least
America. Yet Washington's diplomats and think-tankers remained locked
in their Westphalian box—obsessed with the balance of power or the pursuit of economic interests or the clash of secular creeds. Looking back,
Madeleine Albright cannot remember during her adult years "any leading
American diplomat (even the born-again Christian Jimmy Carter) speaking in depth about the role of religion in shaping the world."[6] She points
out that, for diplomats of her generation, the subject of religion was "above
and beyond reason; it evoked the deepest passions; and historically, it was
the cause of much bloodshed."[7] Thomas Farr, an American diplomat who
spent several frustrating years working for the State Department's Office
of International Religious Freedom, describes the department as "one of
America's most avowedly secular institutions."[8]

The mistakes that flowed from this were costly. American analysts
underestimated the opposition to the Shah of Iran: indeed, senior figures
in the CIA dismissed the only intelligence analysis of Iran in the 1970s
that noted a stirring of religious passion against the shah as "sociology,"
the ultimate term of contempt.[9] The alliance with the Mujahideen in
Afghanistan in the 1980s can certainly be justified in terms of the damage it did to the Soviet empire, but it also sowed the seeds of September 11.

America ignored the religious basis of politics in Lebanon for years, treating it as a left-right split, even though "Hezbollah" means "Party of God."

Washington was hardly alone. Nobody in the Western foreign policy establishment predicted that John Paul II, a fiercely antiCommunist Pole, would play a central role in bringing down communism, attracting huge crowds across Eastern Europe and stiffening the spines of activists. The secular Israeli security establishment initially underestimated the rise of Islamic radicalism, encouraging it as a way to destabilize Yasser Arafat. Even the theocratic Saudis followed the secular line, nurturing radical Islam as a creature to bite global communism.

You might have imagined that September 11 would change this dramatically. In fact, Western policy makers have alternated between two contradictory responses: either continuing to underplay the role of religion in foreign affairs or overplaying it.

A good example of the first, as we have already seen, was the Bush administration, which was particularly backward in grasping the religious dimension in statecraft. The administration managed to ignore religion even as Iraq was erupting in a religious war. When Canon Andrew P. B. White, an Anglican clergyman known as the "Vicar of Baghdad," urged the Coalition Provisional Authority to pay close attention, he was told that "Iraq is a secular nation so religion should only be thought about after water and electricity arc dealt with."

At times the level of ignorance about religion—and Islam in particular—in Washington has been mind-boggling. In 2005, Gary Bald, then the FBI's counterterrorism chief, drew a blank when asked, during a legal deposition, whether he understood the difference between Sunnis and Shias. In his defense, he added that such expertise was not as important as being a good manager.[10] This bathetic episode inspired Jeff Stein, of the *Congressional Quarterly,* to conduct an exhaustive study of what exactly official Washington knew about Islam. He discovered that most of the officials and politicians he interviewed were clueless. The head of the FBI's new national security branch acknowledged that it was important to recognize the difference between Sunnis and Shias. He then misidentified Iran as a Sunni country. The Center for Strategic and International Studies has found that some diplomats refuse to engage with religious issues because

they fear "being personally attacked—via litigation or public oppro-
brium—for possibly violating the Establishment Clause."[11]

CARTOONS ABOUT THE PROPHET

If one response has been to pretend that religion does not exist, the
opposite response has been to exaggerate the role of religion in foreign
policy—especially in fomenting a clash of civilizations with Islam. After
September 11, faith, so long ignored, began to assume cartoonish dimen-
sions in much of the commentary about foreign policy.

As with all caricatures, the idea contains elements of truth. Samuel
Huntington was correct to point to the divergence between the West and
Islam. In the name of Islam, jihadists *do* wage a holy war that sanctions
suicide bombings and the mass slaughter of innocents. This book has
hardly stinted in pointing out Islam's problems with modernity. But commentators from the American right have taken Huntington's insight and
blown it up out of all proportion. In *World War IV* (2007) Norman Podhoretz argued that America has been thrust into a long, drawn-out war
with radical Islam. In *America Alone* (2006), Mark Steyn cautioned that
America would be exactly that as European elites surrendered to their
growing Muslim populations. The term "Islamofascism" is standard on
the right. In 2003 a Christian college near Los Angeles took the "clash of
civilizations" thesis to its logical conclusion when it announced a special
program entitled "God v. Allah: Who Will Win?"

The clash of civilizations also appeals to the atheist left. "It is time
we admitted that we are not at war with terrorism," Sam Harris has said.
"We are at war with Islam." A *Washington Post*/ABC News poll in 2006
found that 46 percent of Americans harbor a negative view of Islam.[12]
The proportion of Americans who believe that Islam promotes violence
against non-Muslims has more than doubled over the past six years. A Pew
Research Center survey found that 45 percent of Americans say Islam,
more than other religions, encourages violence among its adherents.[13] Olivier Roy points out that, across the Western world, "The terms 'Islamism,'
'Islamic radicalism,' 'terrorism' and 'fundamentalism' (and, in France, the

word '*intégrisme*') are used more or less interchangeably, and always with the implication that there is something particular about Islam, something in the religion that makes it more prone to fomenting violence."[14]

But the clashing civilizations are highly diverse. Are Malaysia and Indonesia really Islamofascist states? The world's 1.2 billion Muslims spread out across five continents: only one in five Muslims live in the Arab world. Oil-rich Gulf states such as Qatar and the United Arab Emirates have little in common with impoverished countries such as Mali and Yemen. Islamic republics such as Iran do not share a worldview with secular regimes such as Egypt's. Most of the conflicts in the Middle East involve Muslims fighting Muslims. Iran shares a long history of rivalry not just with Iraq, but also Saudi Arabia. The Ayatollah Khomeini saw the Saudi royal family, who were both Sunni and pro-American, as the biggest obstacle to the spread of the Islamic revolution, and even pronounced himself to be the "custodian of the two sanctuaries" (Mecca and Medina); the Saudis treat the Shias as if they are a fifth column.[15] Iran's Mahmoud Ahmadinejad, the leader of Islam in many neocon tracts, has closer relationships with secular-minded populists in Latin America, particularly Hugo Chavez, than he does with his coreligionists next door.[16]

The irony is that American conservatives make exactly the same mistake looking at Islam as European caricaturists do with America—lumping divergent peoples together and then tagging them all with the opinions of a zealous fringe. But this has consequences. It can lead to extremism of its own sort: Guantánamo and Abu Ghraib, deeply un-American places, were created at a time when the war on terror was cast in terms of good and evil. It is not accurate even when it is dealing with real terrorists. The war on terror sounds fine in a Washington lecture theater. But on the ground there is a substantial difference between the way you deal with nihilist groups like Al Qaeda, with whom there is little room for compromise, and more territorially minded ones like Hamas. (Indeed, perhaps the only tragedy of the passing away of the Irish Republican Army, a Catholic group with territorial aims, is that its survival would have made the "war on terror" seem a vacuous term much earlier.)

Speechifying about a "clash of civilizations" makes it difficult for Western policy makers to register the divisions between Sunnis and Shias. It makes it nearly impossible to win the hearts and minds among the Muslim majority. And it bolsters bin Laden's claim that he speaks for those under siege from the West. Sensible policy should be based on recognizing divisions within the Islamic world rather than turning all Muslims into enemies. Divide and defuse is a more sensible policy than unite and inflame.

If this habit of drawing cartoonish pictures of Islam risks treating Muslims as an undifferentiated (and threatening) mass, it also risks dividing the Atlantic alliance. European liberals and American conservatives spent much of the Bush era hurling insults at each other over religion. Dominique Moisi, a special adviser at the French Institute for International Relations, called the combination of religion and nationalism in America frightening: "We feel betrayed by God and by nationalism, which is why we are building the European Union as a barrier to religious warfare."[17] François Heisbourg, the director for the Foundation for Strategic Research in Paris, opined that "the biblical references in politics, the division of the world between good and evil, these are things that [Europeans] simply don't get. In a number of areas, it seems to me that we are no longer part of the same civilization."[18]

On the other side of the Atlantic, American theocrats argue that Europe's secularism is responsible for everything that has gone wrong with the Continent, undermining its will to fight for what is right, weakening its ability to resist Islamic expansionism and turning its citizens into pampered eunuchs. In 2004 the White House's favorite Arabist, Bernard Lewis, warned that Europe would turn Muslim by the end of this century, becoming "part of the Arab West, the Maghreb." A plethora of books with titles like *While Europe Slept* followed. In *The Cube and the Cathedral: Europe, America, and Politics Without God* (2005) George Wiegel described the European elites as not just secular but positively "Christophobic."[19] The "Eurabia" myth defies basic mathematics and lumps together plenty of Muslims who feel little affinity for each other; but like the "American theocracy" caricature, it is enormously powerful—and affects policy. It is not easy for the Western alliance to deal with, say, Iran if Europe thinks America is bent on holy war, and America thinks Europe is really part of the Islamic *umma*.

THE MISSING DIMENSION

If the rhetoric about religion in foreign policy has been all over the place, what about the practice? There is no clear institutional solution to the new wars of religion. We cannot use international law to separate faith and power. Broadly speaking, the West, and especially America, has made two big mistakes: failing to draw on its own domestic success in dealing with religion, and not appreciating the ability of religion to solve problems as well as create them.

One of America's oddest failures in recent years is its inability to draw any global lessons from its unique success in dealing with religion at home. It is a mystery why a country so rooted in pluralism has made so little of religious freedom. During the Cold War, America gained the high ground on human rights by getting friends and foes (including the Soviet Union) to sign the Helsinki Accords. That made it hard to be accused of favoritism. By contrast, the U.S. Commission on International Religious Freedom produces useful annual reports for Congress on persecution, but it has two irretrievable limitations. First, unlike the multilateral Helsinki approach, it looks to foreigners as if it is an arm of American policy, one steered not just by diplomacy but by domestic politics. It took some time for the commission to consider religious freedom in Iraq; and it still has not examined Israel. Even when the commission is making good points, it lacks credibility with non-Americans. Yet, second, as one of its former leading lights has catalogued, its brief is also too narrow.[20] The commission analyzes and condemns religious persecution; it does not make a robust intellectual case for religious freedom as a fundamental building block of a civilized and successful liberal society.

Similarly, in its battle for hearts and minds, America has made scant use of its own Muslim population. "The people of Iran and Pakistan have no idea that American Muslims are free," laments one former Bush adviser. Notwithstanding his isolated use of the word "crusade," Bush had a good record of visiting mosques and a genuine respect for other religions, founded in his belief that all human rights come from the Creator. This got hopelessly lost in Rumsfeldian shock and awe. So often did the West's focus on democracy. Presented with a choice between martyrs and traitors in the Arab world, America has backed the latter. It has often been hard to do otherwise: who would choose Hamas over Fatah? But when secular Arab governments, like Egypt, lock religious opposition parties like the Muslim Brotherhood out of power, they push pious people toward the extremes. The cost of excluding Islamist groups from discussion is often higher than that of letting them in.

If one part of America's problem has been its failure to exploit its natural advantage, the other, oddly, has been its refusal to admit how much religion is part of public life. For once religion is part of a conflict, it must also be part of the solution.

If you gather together a group of credentialed foreign-policy experts—whether they be neoconservatives, realpolitickers or urbane European diplomats—you can count on a smirk if you mention "interfaith dialogue." At best, the professionals say, it is liberal waffle; at worst, it is naïve appeasement. But who is being naïve?

"Faith is a source of conflict," reads a sign at St. Ethelburga's Center for Reconciliation and Peace in the city of London. But it goes on to say that faith may be "a resource to transform conflict." The Good Friday peace settlement in Northern Ireland, for example, was cemented only when preachers from opposite sides of the religious divide joined together in condemning the bloodshed. (Appropriately enough, St. Ethelburga's Center was built in a church destroyed in 1993 by Irish terrorists.) The two religious leaders, the Reverend Roy Magee, a Protestant, and Father Alex Reid, a Catholic, were acquainted with hard-line terrorists through their congregations, and they applied their moral sway to induce each side to the negotiating table. Reid, in particular, brokered a momentous summit that brought together John Hume, leader of the nationalist Social Democratic Party, with Gerry Adams, leader of Sinn Féin.

The pattern plays out across the globe. In northern Nigeria the Catholic Archbishop of Jos has been widely criticized by his fellow Christians for setting up meetings with the local imam and visiting mosques. "You are sleeping with a snake," one Protestant preacher told him. But nowadays whenever there is a flare-up between Christians and Muslims, the imam and the bishop go together to try to sort it out—and that seems to help. Another alliance is between Muhammad Ashafa, a leading imam, and James Wuye, a Christian pastor. Both men began their lives as religious warriors. Wuye lost a hand in battle. Ashafa lost two brothers. Transformed into peacemakers, they cofounded the Interfaith Mediation Center, an organization that tries to, and does, quell religious strife. When other regions of Nigeria were torn asunder by the cartoon controversy, Ashafa and Wuye kept their own area completely still.

A few people in the citadels of power are also beginning to realize that religion can promote peace as well as war. In 1994, Douglas Johnston, a national security expert, produced a prescient book called *Religion: The Missing Dimension of Statecraft*. Since then he has labored to bring together religious leaders. His efforts are easy to mock. Johnston talks proudly about getting groups of southern Sudanese Christian and Muslim leaders together in 2000; the result has hardly been perfect peace. But the religious dimension in the conflict has decreased—and that has increased the (slim) chances of a solution.

Another little-known Washington-based group called the Fellowship has also been active in the Sudanese talks. Douglas Coe, the publicity-averse leader of the Fellowship, has been dubbed a "stealth Billy Graham," his organization hailed as an "underground State Department." Coe says that the Fellowship intends to create a worldwide "family of friends" by extolling the Word of Jesus to those in power. Arguably the world's most successful spiritual networker, Coe has been a close friend to a succession of American presidents, as well as foreign leaders. When James Baker, an active member of the Fellowship, became one of the first Western diplomats to visit post-Communist Albania, the country's foreign minister, Muhamet Kapllani, shook him by the hand and said, "I greet you in the name of Doug Coe." In 2001 the Fellowship arranged a secret meeting in Virginia between the warring leaders of Congo and Rwanda.

There has always been a degree of "interfaith dialogue" between religions, but since September 11 there has been a dramatic growth in the number of such conversations. The World Economic Forum has launched the "Council of 100 Leaders," an eclectic group of bishops, rabbis, imams and academics; the United Nations launched an "Alliance of Civilizations";

there is the Cordoba Initiative (named after the Andalusian town where religions used to coexist).[21] Muslim leaders who feel caught between Islam and the West are often prominent, notably the Malaysian government, the Jordanian royal family and various moderate Gulf states. Even the Saudis have gotten in on the act, with, for instance, King Abdullah summoning five hundred Shias and Sunnis to Mecca in 2008. It is hard to decry any of this: any attempt at talking is useful. Yet from a political perspective such gatherings are dogged by unmentionables (Muslims and Jews discuss Abraham but not Palestine) and by absentees (usually the hard-liners on all sides). There is something rather unreal about the Saudis babbling about interfaith dialogue, when they take such a dim view of other religions at home. Meanwhile, the Western side of the equation has lacked hard-edged political savoir faire.

It is thus arguably good news that the latest omnipresent figure at such gatherings is a man many Muslims associate with holy war and many Britons link to the cynical politics of spin. Nevertheless, the Tony Blair Faith Foundation, launched in 2008, deserves to be taken seriously. Blair has assembled a powerful team of advisers from the world's biggest religions, including Rick Warren, David Rosen and the Grand Mufti of Bosnia-Herzegovina; and he says he wants to devote most of the rest of his life to it.

Blair argues that in a global world, where people and ideas are being thrown together, faith will either be a source of strength (a way of making sense of the world) or of tribalism and division. Education and dialogue are a large part of his solution: the more religious people realize how much they have in common, the less likely they are to retreat into divisive ghettos. But Blair also plainly wants to get involved in the sharp end of religious conflict, notably in the Middle East, where he is working as the envoy for the Quartet of outside powers. He points out that for many Muslims, Islam has replaced political ideology, so religion is inevitably politicized. His own experience in Northern Ireland taught him that bringing religious people into the peace process was a necessary, though far from sufficient, precondition for peace. He believes that the same is true of the Holy Land.

Blair's erstwhile colleagues are not always kind about his motives—

some see a quest for personal redemption by a cynical manipulator, others point out that he has always been "funny" about religion. Either way, he has spotted a genuine opportunity. Faith-based diplomacy is no panacea. At the ground level things are too messy for that. In Nigeria, for instance, the archbishop and his new Muslim friend failed to prevent the bloody riots in Jos in 2008; Ashafa and Wuye cannot always control their troops. In Israel-Palestine, attempts to bring rabbis and imams into the process would no doubt have the same disappointments. But it is extremely difficult to imagine a lasting peace without their involvement.

THE PROBLEM AT HOME

Even more profound than the argument about the new wars of religion (and indeed the cause of some of these wars) is the issue of religion in the public square. Is there anything that we can learn about how to construct a constitutional regime that makes room for religion without sacrificing the fundamental principles of liberal pluralism? The answer is to be found in the foundation texts of modern liberalism and in the practical solution they inspired from America's Founding Fathers.

John Locke's great contribution to the religion debate that raged throughout seventeenth century Europe was to argue that the problem lay not with religion itself but with the fusion of religion and power. In his *Letter Concerning Toleration* (1689) he argued that the "whole jurisdiction of the magistrate" is limited to secular affairs—securing fundamental human rights (life, liberty, property) through the impartial implementation of the law. It definitely does not extend to the "salvation of souls." Governments should leave theological issues to private debate rather than weighing in on one side or another:

> If a Roman Catholic believes that to be really the body of Christ, which another man calls bread, he does no injury thereby to his neighbor. If a Jew does not believe the New Testament to be the Word of God, he does not thereby alter anything in men's civil rights. If a heathen doubts of both Testaments, he is not therefore to be punished as a pernicious citizen.

The power of the magistrate and the estates of the people may be equally
secure whether any man believe these things or no.

If governments should leave religion alone, then religion should return
the compliment: "The care of each man's salvation is a purely private
affair." False religious beliefs do not violate another man's rights. And
true faith cannot be imposed by force.

Some of Locke's successors added important details to this argument.
Adam Smith and Voltaire both pointed out that a variety of religious sects
tend to promote toleration. "If there were only one religion in England,"
Voltaire wrote in his *Letters Concerning the English Nation,* "there would be
danger of tyranny; if there were two, they would cut each other's throats;
but there are thirty, and they live happily together in peace." But the great
breakthrough came with America's Founding Fathers.

Whereas Locke had advocated mere "toleration"—an established religion with other faiths legally tolerated—the Founders eventually argued
for the universal freedom of religion with no established church and
therefore no religious dissent. Tom Paine put the case for going beyond
mere tolerance best: "Toleration is not the *opposite* of intolerance but the
counterfeit of it. Both are despotisms: the one assumes to itself the right of
withholding liberty of conscience, the other of granting it."[22]

The Founders understood the appeal of religion: they did not want to
abolish or marginalize it. But they also understood how dangerous it is
when mixed with political power. They talked about the horrors of the
wars of religion in much the same way that people today talk about the
horrors of the First and Second World Wars. With memories of religious
persecution still alive in the collective consciousness, they were determined that the New World would not repeat the mistakes of the Old.
John Adams argued that "aristocratical tyrants are the worst species of all;
and sacerdotal tyrants have been the worst of aristocratical tyrants in all
ages and nations." One of his principles was to "mix religion with politics
as little as possible." Thomas Jefferson referred to the "loathsome combination of church and state."[23] "History," he said, "furnishes no example
of a priest-ridden people maintaining a free civil government." William
Livingston, the first governor of New Jersey, pointed out that "whenever

Men have sufferenced their Consciences to be enslaved by their Superiors, and taken their Religion upon Trust, the World has been over-run with Superstition, and held in Fetters by a tyrannizing Juncto of civil and ecclesiastical Plunderers." This inspired the Founders to produce one of the great paradigm shifts in the history of religious thought—by breaking up that "Juncto" on the basis that the separation of church and state could be good for both religion and the state.

THE GENIUS OF THE FOUNDING FATHERS

The idea that America has "solved" the problem of religion might strike many people, particularly in Europe, as far-fetched. Hasn't America had plenty of problems with religion over the centuries? Anti-Catholic riots have resulted in church burnings and murder. And hasn't America had too much religion in politics? Kevin Phillips, who has written the book *American Theocracy*, describes today's Republicans as "the first American religious party."[24] And doesn't America, of all countries, still preserve an informal religious test for its highest office? Americans would no more elect an atheist to the presidency than they would a self-confessed child molester; indeed, all of the candidates for the presidency go out of their way to demonstrate their religious bona fides: 2008 was no exception, to put it mildly.

None of these objections really tips the argument. America's problems with religion have been small compared with Europe's. The death toll from religious riots numbers in the hundreds rather than the tens of thousands—and this is in spite of the fact that America's religious settlement, which was largely carved out by English-speaking Protestants, has been subjected to huge strains, such as a vast influx of Catholics and a diverse and polyglot population.

America does a better job than any other country of combining religious vitality with both religious diversity and religious toleration. Religious groups that were once persecuted for heresy—Quakers, Catholics, Unitarians, Jehovah's Witnesses and Southern Baptists—have all groomed men who have ended up in the White House. The Supreme Court has five Catholic members, and the Senate contains five Mormon senators. George Bush hosted a Ramadan dinner at the White House. A Hindu priest has opened a session of the House of Representatives.[25] A Muslim congressman has taken his oath of office on the Koran. Large majorities of religious Americans tell Pew's pollsters that there is more than one religion that can lead to eternal life and more than one way to interpret the teachings of their faith.[26] Whatever Kevin Phillips thinks, Bush and his fellow "theocrats" ended up doing almost nothing to undermine American secularism. Women can still get abortions very late in pregnancies, something that shocks Europeans. Pornography is ubiquitous. Religious Americans participate in politics, but not under banners of faith; they appear as social conservatives rather than as theocrats.

The religious settlement embodied in the Constitution has never been easy. There is a permanent tension between a godless Constitution and an overwhelmingly godly people. There are unavoidable arguments about how to draw the line between church and state. How high should the wall be? (Secularists want it as "high and eternal as the Andes," as one nineteenth-century figure put it.[27]) And what exactly constitutes a hole in the wall? The Supreme Court spends a lot of time on issues such as whether a Christmas crib in a public place can be rendered secular by the presence of a plastic reindeer (yes, though preferably with a Santa as well), or where a state court can display the Ten Commandments (the garden is fine; the building not).

All very messy. But the First Amendment still achieves its two goals. First, it keeps churches firmly apart from the state. There are no bishops in the upper chamber, as in Britain, no church taxes, as in Germany. But the amendment has done this without denying religious people their right to enter the public square. The two greatest social movements of the past two centuries—the antislavery movement of the nineteenth century and the civil rights movement of the twentieth century—were both religious at heart, led by religious people, nurtured in churches, justified in religious language.

The Constitution, in turn, has also protected churches from the state. Unlike France's avowedly secularist laïcité, which is written into the legal code, America has been content to let religious people get on with their business. There has been no fuss about headscarves. As a result, the country's religious life is marvelously varied. Mark Silk of Trinity College in Connect-icut argues that there are in fact eight regions of American religion, vary-ing from California's New Age spirituality to Southern Protestantism. The pagan Pacific Northwest's unofficial religion, says Silk, is environmentalism.

Nobody would claim the American system is perfect. It did not prevent Protestants in the nineteenth century from using the state to give both Mormons and Catholics a hard time. And it has pushed moral debates, notably the one about abortion, toward the courts, rather than toward the lawmakers, who are more likely to come up with a messy but work-able compromise. But on the whole it has struck the right balance between secularism and religion, allowing religious people to thrive but prevent-ing them from imposing their views on other people. America's religious settlement has the same advantage that Winston Churchill claimed for democracy: it is the worst way for a modern society to deal with religion, "except for all those other forms that have been tried from time to time."

There is thus a compelling argument for universalizing the American commitment to the separation between church and state. This is slowly beginning to happen in Europe as the Continent tries to adapt to an ever more religiously diverse population. Britain abolished its last blasphemy laws in 2006. Sweden has finally disestablished the church. Islam is more difficult, but not entirely hopeless. Places like Indonesia and Turkey have separation between mosque and state. Many Islamic theologians are grap-pling with the problem of pluralism.

However, there is plainly a lot further to go. Most obviously, Islamic politicians have been considerably less adventurous than those theo-logians in considering pluralism. The westernized leader of one Islamic state, asked privately about anticonversion laws on a visit to London, con-cedes that the status quo is unfair but pleads: "Frankly, changing them now is politically impossible." Is that really true? The individual in question has done very little even to test the temperature on the subject of pluralism.

European politicians and churchmen could also surely learn from America's example. For instance, the continuing existence of an estab-lished church in England is bad for both church and state. Even if its canons and vicars are no longer engaged in a Trollopian quest for cushy livings (there is nothing cushy about the lifestyle of an inner-city cleric), the Anglican Church's desire to represent the whole nation at prayer has left it desperately seeking consensus where none really exists. Shorn of its privileged status, the church would surely become a much more competitive outfit, able to focus more single-mindedly on defining and spreading the Anglican faith. As for British politics, there is no earthly reason why twenty-six lords spiritual from what is now a minority religion should be granted an automatic seat in Britain's Upper House, no matter how symbolic their presence. Symbols matter, not least to those they exclude: witness also the law banning the monarch from marrying a Catholic. Jefferson and Madison would regard the existence of the lords spiritual as a perfect example of how a religious establishment enfeebles the church and corrupts politics.

God Is Back, for Better

This book has been on a long journey—from Wang's house church, through some of the poorest and most violent places in the world, and ending up in New York. No doubt its overall message will depress many secularists; at times it has depressed us too. Some terrible things have already happened in this century in God's name. More are undoubtedly on the way. But in the end the basic message of this book is a profoundly liberal one.

Unevenly and gradually, religion is becoming a matter of choice—something that individuals decide to believe in (or not). There are plenty of reasons why intellectuals of all stripes might want to turn up their noses at the choices other mortals make. Secularists can scoff at the laboratory scientist in Wang's house church who thought that stem cells were proof of intelligent design; atheists can worry about the contorting woman in the São Paulo exorcism; believers can pity disbelievers and their godless ways; and everybody, save a few fanatics, can worry about people who strap bombs to their bodies and blow themselves up in the name of eternal life.

So the choices can be tragic, or indeed wonderful. But neither side of the religious divide can sneer at the fact that more people nowadays are making those choices for themselves, rather than having those choices imposed upon them. Secularists need to recognize that the enemy that "poisons everything" is not religion but the union of religion and power— and believers need to recognize that religion flourishes best where it operates in a world of free choice, that, as that doughty free thinker Benjamin Franklin once put it, "When a religion is good, I conceive it will support itself; and when it does not support itself, and God does not take care to support it so that its professors are obliged to call for help of the civil power, 'tis a sign, I apprehend, of its being a bad one." Amen.

ACKNOWLEDGMENTS

A GREAT MANY PEOPLE helped us with this book. We would like to thank Anne Foley and Mark Doyle for helping us to check our facts and for expunging some of the more basic errors, such as our injudicious use of the spellchecker that changed "Wahhabi" to "washbasin." Needless to say, any errors that have crept past these high priests are ours alone.

Several saints were also kind enough to read parts or all of the drafts, including Ann Wroe, Laura Beatty, Bruce Clark, Peter David, David Landau and Grace Davie. Out in the field, we were taken under the wing of various protectors who have guided us through the local religious landscapes: Gideon Lichfield, Xan Smiley and Nuha Musleh (Israel-Palestine); Max Rodenbeck (Saudi Arabia, Dubai and Egypt); Richard Cockett and Beth Dickinson (northern Nigeria); John Parker, James Miles and Zhou Yu (China); John Prideaux (Brazil); James Astill and Mian Ridge (India); Catherine Lee (South Korea); Amberin Zaman (Turkey); and Rosemarie Ward (New York).

We would like to thank Bill Emmott for originally giving us permission to write the book and *The Economist* for letting us reuse some passages. We would also like to apologize to those colleagues who have been condemned to the Hades of putting up with us at close quarters, including Camilla Longin, Emma Duncan, Daniel Franklin, Robert Guest, Zanny Minton-Beddoes, Greg Ip, Brendan Greeley, Jon Fasman, Erica Grieder, Stephen Stromberg and especially Rachel Horwood and Sheila Allen.

The fallen angel that is Gideon Rachman hovered over our efforts, spurring us on whenever we were tempted to rest.

We have accumulated numerous debts outside *The Economist*. Michael Cromartie regularly invited one of us to the Faith Angle Conference in Key West, Florida, one of the most pleasant as well as one of the most instructive experiences in journalism. Walter Russell Mead was extremely gracious in including one of us in a wide-ranging seminar on religion at the Council for Foreign Relations. Eugene Rivers was a wonderful guide to Pentecostalism (and a standing rebuke to those who think that faith and intellectualism are incompatible). Ram Cnaan, of the University of Pennsylvania, shared his Rolodex of faith leaders in Philadelphia. Like everybody who writes about religion, we are particularly grateful to the Pew Foundation, whose work is the gold standard in this area and whose staff is unfailingly helpful.

We have been fortunate to work with one of the most harmonious teams in publishing. We remain extremely grateful to our agent, Andrew Wylie, and to Sarah Chalfant in London. We would especially like to thank Scott Moyers, who bought our book for Penguin in New York, repented for that sin and defected to the Wylie agency. We were very lucky that Penguin recruited Eamon Dolan in Scott's stead, who has been a joy to work with, often under quite testing deadlines. We would also like to thank Laura Stickney. This is our second book with our British editor, Stuart Proffitt; we defy anyone to find a more precise editor.

However, the main burden of book writing has fallen on our families. If our wives fail to reach heaven, then that will be because we have turned them against God in much the same way as we previously poisoned their minds against American conservatives, management gurus and joint-stock companies. Having studied the tricks of the pulpit, we have repeatedly promised Fev and Amelia that salvation is just around the corner, that the book will eventually be finished, that we will eventually be helpful in some unspecified way. They, strangely, have taken the distinctly worldly attitude that instant gratification would be somewhat preferable. And our children—Tom, Guy, Edward, Ella and Dora—have treacherously, though understandably, sided with their mothers. The only family members we have managed to convince that this book would actually be finished are our dogs, Tumble and Louis. It is now over.

NOTES

INTRODUCTION

1. To avoid identification, the names in this section have been changed. Wang is not his real name; and he works for a company that is similar to Intel.

2. David Frum diary, http://frum.nationalreview.com/post/?q=ZTg1Y2RiYTM0Y2M5ZjdlZG VhOTFlOTMzMTdhNzBkMWU.

3. "When Opium Can Be Benign," *The Economist,* February 1, 2007.

4. China treats Catholicism as a different religion from Protestantism. This is not just clumsy state bureaucracy. Ask Protestants in Asia how many Christians there are in their country—and they leave out the Catholics.

5. In China we heard reports of above 100 million. There are claims in America that the director of the body that supervises religions in China admitted to 130 million Christians in 2008—see "Sons of Heaven," *The Economist,* October 4, 2008.

6. See Pew Forum on Religion and Public Life, "Religion in China on the Eve of the 2008 Beijing Olympics," May 2, 2008.

7. Ibid.

8. "When Opium Can Be Benign," *The Economist,* February 1, 2007.

9. We visited the shrine but agreed not to reveal its location; the confessor gurus are based on firsthand accounts from Tibet.

10. "When Opium Can Be Benign," *The Economist,* February 1, 2007.

11. http://www.newsweek.com/id/96795.

12. He plays a prominent role in David Aikman's excellent *Jesus in Beijing: How Christianity Is Changing the Global Balance of Power* (New York: Regnery 2003).

13. "When Opium Can Be Benign," *The Economist,* February 1, 2007.

14. Jason Dean and Loretta Chao, "In search of . . . Something," *Wall Street Journal,* April 12, 2008.

15. Josef Joffe, *Überpower: The Imperial Temptation of America* (New York: W. W. Norton, 2006).

16. Friedrich Nietzsche, *Ecce Homo,* in Kaufmann, trans., *Basic Writings of Nietzsche* (NewYork: Modern Library Classics), 783.

17. T. S. Eliot, *Idea of a Christian Society* (New York: Harcourt, Brace, 1940), 64.

18. Quoted in Noel Annan, *Our Age* (London: Fontana, 1990), 18.

19. Thomas Altizer, *The Gospel of Christian Atheism* (Philadelphia: Westminster Press, 1966). In the same year he also published, along with William Hamilton, *Radical Theology and the Death of God* (Indianapolis: Bobbs-Merrill, 1966).

20. Three honorable exceptions were Gilles Kepel's *The Revenge of God* (University Park, PA: Pennsylvania State University Press, 1994), Samuel Huntington's *The Clash of Civilizations* (New York: Simon & Schuster, 1996) and Benjamin Barber's *Jihad vs. McWorld* (New York: Ballantine, 1996).

21. "The lesson from America," in the special report on religion and public life, *The Economist,* November 1, 2007.

22. Andrew Jack, *Inside Putin's Russia: Can There Be Reform Without Democracy?* (Oxford: Oxford University Press, 2006), 75.

23. http://www.russiablog.org/2006/12/are_russians_becoming_more_rel.php.

24. Pew Global Attitudes Project Report, September 2008, 5.

25. This estimate comes from the World Christian Database run by the Center for the Study of Global Christianity at the Gordon-Conwell Theological Seminary.

26. Pew Forum on Religion and Public Life, "Spirit and Power: A 10-Country Survey of Pentecostals," October 2006.

27. Philip Jenkins, *Climates of Faith,* discussion paper shown to authors.

28. Rick Warren, *The Purpose Driven Life: What on Earth Am I Here For?* (Grand Rapids, MI: Zondervan, 2002).

29. Lawrence Freedman, *A Choice of Enemies: America Confronts the Middle East* (New York: Public Affairs, 2008), 29.

30. *The Doctrines and Disciplines of the Methodist Episcopal Church, 1860* (Cincinnati, OH: Swormstedt & Poe, 1854), 62.

31. World Christian Database.

32. "Marching as to War," *The Economist,* September 27, 2008.

33. "The Crescent and the Very Cross," *The Economist,* Sept 13, 2007.

34. Pew Forum on Religion and Public Life, "US Religious Landscape Survey," February 2008, 10.

35. Ibid., 12.

36. Timothy Shah and Monica Tuft, "Religion's Flame Burns Brighter than Ever," *Baltimore Sun,* August 20, 2006.

37. Philip Jenkins, "The Next Christianity," *Atlantic Monthly,* October, 2002.

CHAPTER ONE: THE EUROPEAN WAY

1. http://www.vexen.co.uk/UK/religion.html#ChurchAttendance.

2. Rodney Stark, "Secularization, R.I.P—Rest in Peace," *Sociology of Religion,* Fall 1999.

3. Friedrich Nietzsche, *The Gay Science, 1882,* Republished by Cambridge University Press, 2001.

4. Tom Stoppard, *Jumpers* (New York: Grove, 1974), quote from George, Act 1.

5. Peter Gay, *The Enlightenment: The Rise of Modern Paganism* (New York: Norton, 1966), 400–401.

6. Ibid., 3.

7. The phrase was from John Morley, one of Gladstone's most dedicated lieutenants. Quoted in Owen Chadwick, *The Secularization of the European Mind in the 19th Century* (Cambridge: Cambridge University Press, 1975), 152.

8. David Hume, *Enquiry Concerning the Principles of Morals* (1751).

9. Peter Gay, *The Enlightenment,* 26.

10. *Philosophical Dictionary* (London: Penguin Classics, 1972) 63.

11. Michael Burleigh, *Earthly Powers: The Clash of Religion and Politics in Europe, From the French Revolution to the Great War* (New York: HarperCollins, 2006), 23. An especially useful source.

12. Ibid., 95.

13. Alexis de Tocqueville, *The Old Regime and the Revolution* (Chicago, 1998), 1:101.

14. Pierre Jean George Cabanis. Quoted in Ronald Schechter, *The French Revolution: The Essential Readings* (Oxford: Blackwell, 2001), 317.

15. Michael Burleigh, *Earthly Powers,* 227.

16. Ibid., 230.

17. Ibid., 240.

18. Quoted in Owen Chadwick, *The Secularization of the European Mind in the 19th Century* (Cambridge: Cambridge University Press, 1975), 108.

19. Michael Burleigh, *Earthly Powers,* 265.

20. Ibid., 27.

21. Jeffrey Cox, *The English Churches in a Secular Society* (New York: Oxford University Press, 1982), 109–110.

22. Daniel Bell, *The End of Ideology: On the Exhaustion of Political Ideas in the Fifties* (Glencoe, IL: Free Press), 370.

23. Quoted in Alister McGrath, *The Twilight of Atheism: The Rise and Fall of Disbelief in the Modern World* (New York: Doubleday, 2004), 57. This book has been a useful source throughout.

24. Quoted in Daniel Bell, "The Return of the Sacred?" in *The Winding Passage: Sociological Essays: Essays 1960–1980* (London: Transaction Publishers, 1991), 326.

25. Karl Marx, *Critique of Hegel's Philosophy of Right,* 1843.

26. Tennyson, *In Memoriam A.H.H,* canto 56.

27. T. H. Huxley, "Origin of Species," *Westminster Review,* April 1860.

28. Owen Chadwick, *The Secularization of the European Mind in the Nineteenth Century* (Cambridge: Cambridge University Press, 1975), 164.

29. Ibid., 224.

30. As Philip Rieff puts it: "It is on the subject of religion that the judicious clinician grows vehement and disputatious." *Freud: The Mind of the Moralist* (New York: Anchor Edition, 1961), 281.

31. Ibid., 291.

32. Peter Gay, *The Enlightenment: The Rise of Modern Paganism* (New York: Norton, 1966), 59.

33. Ibid., 527.

34. Edward Gibbon, *The Decline and Fall of the Roman Empire,* 1:30–1.

35. Quoted in A. N. Wilson, *God's Funeral* (New York: Norton, 1999), 69.

36. Mikhail Bakunin.

37. Stephan Collini, *Public Moralists: Political Thought and Intellectual Life in Britain, 1850–1914* (Oxford: Clarendon Press, 1991), 192.

38. Paul Hollander, *Political Pilgrims: Travels of Western Intellectuals to the Soviet Union, China and Cuba* (Oxford: Oxford University Press, 1981), 137.

39. George Bernard Shaw, *Man and Superman.* Quoted in A. E. Dyson and Julian Lovelock, *Education and Democracy* (London: Routledge & Kegan Paul, 1975), 270.

40. Matthew Arnold, *Culture and Anarchy* (New York: AMS Press, 1970), XLI.

41. Michael Burleigh, *Earthly Powers:* 272–3.

42. Ibid., 341.

43. Ibid., 153.

44. Robert Nisbet, *The History of the Idea of Progress* (New York: Basic, 1988), 281.

45. Karl Popper, *Hegel and Marx* (London: Routledge, 1966), 62.

46. Michael Burleigh, *Earthly Powers,* 147.

47. Hugh McLeod, *Religion and Irreligion in Victorian England: How Secular Was the Working Class?* (Bangor, Wales: Headstart History, 1993), 32.

48. Michael Burleigh, *Sacred Causes: The Clash of Religion and Politics, from the Great War to the War on Terror* (New York: HarperCollins, 2007), 40.

49. Niall Ferguson, *The War of the World* (London: Penguin/Allen Lane, 2006), 243–5.

50. "The Abolition of the Caliphate," *The Economist,* March 8, 1924.

51. Michael Burleigh, *Sacred Causes,* 124–5.

52. Tony Judt, *Postwar: A History of Europe Since 1945* (London: Pimlico, 2007), 228.

53. Christie Davies, "The Death of Religion and the Fall of Respectable Britain," *New Criterion* 23, no. 23, Summer 2004.

54. "A Bleak Outlook Is Seen for Religion," *New York Times,* February 25, 1968.

55. Bill Clinton, *My Life* (New York: Knopf, 2004), 30.

56. Ibid., 249.

57. Ibid., 250.

58. Amy Sullivan, *The Party Faithful: How and Why Democrats Are Closing the God Gap* (New York: Scribner, 2008), 81.

59. Ibid., 104–5.

60. D. Michael Lindsay, *Faith in the Halls of Power: How Evangelicals Joined the American Elite* (New York: Oxford University Press, 2007), 21.

61. Quoted in Randall Balmer, *God in the White House: A History: How Faith Shaped the Presidency from John F. Kennedy to George W. Bush* (New York, HarperOne, 2008), 139.

62. D. Linsday, *Faith in the Halls of Power,* p. 163.

63. Amy Sullivan, *The Party Faithful,* 83.

CHAPTER TWO: THE AMERICAN WAY I

1. Finke and Stark, *The Churching of America*, 31.
2. Justo L. Gonazalez, *The Story of Christianity, Volume 2: The Reformation to the Present Day* (New York: HarperSanFrancisco, 1985), 221.
3. Mark Noll, Nathan Hatch and George Marsden, *The Search for Christian America* (Colorado Springs: Helmers & Howard, 1989), 33–6.
4. Jon Butler, *Awash in a Sea of Faith: Christianizing the American People* (Cambridge: Harvard University Press, 1990), 62.
5. Finke and Stark, *The Churching of America*, 39.
6. Roger Green, *Virginia's Cure* (1661), quoted in Butler, *Awash in a Sea of Faith*, 45.
7. Justo L. Gonazalez, *The Story of Christianity*, 221.
8. Perry Miller and Thomas H. Johnson, *The Puritans: A Sourcebook of Their Writings* (New York: Courier Dover Publications, 2001), 183.
9. Steven Waldman, *Founding Faith: Providence, Politics, and the Birth of Religious Freedom in America* (New York: Random House, 2008), 8.
10. Ibid., 9.
11. Garry Wills, *Head and Heart: American Christianities* (New York: Penguin, 2007), 18, 22.
12. Butler, *Awash in a Sea of Faith*, 53.
13. Sydney Ahlstrom, *A Religious History of the American People* (New Haven: Yale University Press, 1972), 2.
14. See Philip Gura, *Jonathan Edwards: America's Evangelical* (New York: Hill & Wang, 2005), 36.
15. Waldman, *Founding Faith*, 31.
16. Noll, Hatch and Marsden, *The Search for Christian America*, 51.
17. Gordon Wood, *The American Revolution: A History* (New York: Modern Library, 2004), 16.
18. Finke and Stark, *The Churching of America*, 62.
19. Gura, *Jonathan Edwards*, xi.
20. Mark Noll, *America's God: From Jonathan Edwards to Abraham Lincoln* (Oxford University Press, 2002), 163.
21. Butler, *Awash in a Sea of Faith*, 177.
22. Ibid., 203.
23. Noll, Hatch and Marsden, *The Search for Christian America*, 73; Wills, *Head and Heart*, 167.
24. Noll, Hatch and Marsden, *The Search for Christian America*, 204.
25. Waldman, *Founding Faith*, 34.
26. Wood, *The American Revolution*, 129–30.
27. George Marsden, *Religion and American Culture* (New York: Thomson, 2001), 55.
28. Noah Feldman, *Divided by God: America's Church-State Problem and What We Should Do About It* (New York, Farrar, Strauss and Giroux, 2005), 35.
29. Quoted in Wills, *Head and Heart*, 187.
30. Wills, *Head and Heart*, 189–202.
31. Ibid., 216.
32. Finke and Stark, *The Churching of America*, 4.
33. Quoted in Lipset, *The First New Nation*, 143.
34. Finke and Stark, *The Churching of America*, 151.
35. Noll, *America's God*, p, 180.
36. Ibid., 330.
37. *The Democratization of American Christianity*, 86.
38. Hatch, *The Democratization of American Christianity*, 136.
39. Finke and Stark, *The Churching of America*, 114.
40. Ibid., 112.
41. Ibid., 156.
42. Ibid., 186–8.
43. Ibid., 23.

44. Nathan Hatch, *The Democratization of American Christianity* (New Haven: Yale University Press, 1989), 4.

45. Noll, *America's God*, 371. Hatch, *The Democratization of American Christianity*, 141.

46. Noll, *America's God*, 8–9.

47. Ibid., 3.

48. Quoted in Lipset, *The First New Nation*, 142.

49. Philip Schaff, *America: A Sketch of the Political, Religious and Social Character of the United States of North America* (New York: Scribner, 1855), 94.

50. Noll, *America's God*, 196.

51. Ibid., 199.

52. Ibid., 201.

53. Ibid., 199.

54. As quoted in Mark A. Noll, *A History of Christianity in the United States and Canada* (Grand Rapids: Wm. B. Eerdmans, 1992), 163.

55. Mark A. Noll, *The Scandal of the Evangelical Mind* (Grand Rapids: Wm. B. Eerdmans, 1995) 97. The quote, which may have been a complaint, is attributed to John W. Nevin, an American theologian.

56. Hatch, *The Democratization of American Christianity*, 20.

57. Ibid., 49.

58. Marsden, *Religion and American Culture*, 68.

59. Karen Armstrong, *The Battle for God* (New York: Ballantine, 2001), 91.

60. Wills, *Head and Heart*, 303.

61. Finke and Stark, *The Churching of America*, 130.

62. Ibid., 149

63. Marsden, *Religion and American Culture*, 142.

64. Walter McDougall, *Promised Land, Crusader State* (New York: Marine, 1998), 55–6.

65. Wills, *Head and Heart*, 76.

66. McDougall, *Promised Land, Crusader State*, 77.

67. Ibid., 174.

68. Walter Russell Mead, *Special Providence: American Foreign Policy and How It Changed the World* (New York: Knopf, 2001), 147.

69. Wills, *Head and Heart*, 391.

70. Martin E. Marty, *Modern American Religion Vol 1: The Irony of It All, 1983–1919* (Chicago: University of Chicago Press, 1986), 307–8.

71. McDougall, *Promised Land, Crusader State*, 119.

72. Ibid., 112.

73. Quoted in George Marsden, *Fundamentalism and American Culture* (New York: Oxford University Press, 2006 edition), 32.

CHAPTER THREE: THE AMERICAN WAY II

1. George Marsden, *Understanding Fundamentalism and Evangelicalism* (Grand Rapids: Wm. B. Eerdmans, 1991) 12.

2. George Marsden, *Religion and American Culture* (Belmont, CA: Thomson, 2001), 107.

3. Jeremy Rabkin, "The Culture War That Isn't," *Policy Review*, August–September 1999.

4. Garry Wills, *Head and Heart*, 342.

5. Stephen Prothero, *American Jesus: How the Son of God Became a National Icon* (New York: Farrar, Straws & Giroux, 2004), 94.

6. Wills, *Head and Heart*, 406.

7. Laurence Moore, *Selling God: American Religion in the Marketplace of Culture* (New York: Oxford University Press, 1994), 245.

8. Harvey Cox, *Fire from Heaven: The Rise of Pentecostal Spirituality and the Reshaping of Religion in the Twenty-first Century* (Cambridge, MA: Da Capo Press, 1995), 54.

9. Ibid., 67.

10. Philip Jenkins, *Mystics and Messiahs: Cults and New Religions in American History* (Oxford: Oxford University Press, 2000), 65.

11. Cox, *Fire from Heaven*, 75.

12. Matthew Avery Sutton, *Aimee Semple McPherson and the Resurrection of Christian America* (Cambridge: Harvard University Press), 142.

13. Edith L. Blumhofer, *Aimee Semple McPherson: Everybody's Sister* (Grand Rapids: Wm. B. Eerdmans, 1993) 343.

14. There is a good summary of the evidence in Sutton, *Aimee Semple McPherson*, 142.

15. Matthew Avery Sutton, *Aimee Semple McPherson and the Resurrection of Christain America* (Cambridge: Harvard University Press), 151.

16. Martin Marty, *Pilgrims in their Own Land: Five Hundred Years of Religion in America* (Boston: Little, Brown, 1984), 338.

17. Ibid., 352.

18. James Moore, *One Nation Under God*, 206.

19. Martin Marty, *Pilgrims in Their Own Land*, 377.

20. Garry Wills, *Under God*, 108.

21. Moore, *One Nation Under God*, 304.

22. Marsden, *Religion and American Culture*, 223.

23. James Patterson, *Grand Expectations* (New York: Oxford University Press, 1996), 17.

24. Ibid., 328.

25. Moore, *Selling God,* 240.

26. Will Herberg, *Protestant, Catholic, Jew,* 53.

27. Quoted in Herberg, *Protestant, Catholic, Jew,* 54.

28. Herberg, *Protestant, Catholic, Jew,* 259–60.

29. Ibid., 47.

30. Ibid., 60.

31. Quoted in Wills, *Head and Heart*, 461.

32. Herberg, *Protestant, Catholic, Jew,* 258.

33. Moore, *One Nation Under God,* 335.

34. North American Jewish Databank. Mandell L. Berman Institute, University of Connecticut.

35. Richard Fox, *Jesus in America: Personal Saviour, Cultural Hero, National Obsession* (San Francisco: HarperSanFrancisco, 2004), 329.

36. Herberg, *Protestant, Catholic, Jew,* 38.

37. Martin E. Marty, *Modern American Religion: The Noise of Conflict, 1919–1941* (Chicago: University of Chicago Press, 1997), 392.

38. Brink Lindsey, "The Aquarians and the Evangelicals," *Reason,* July 2007.

39. James Patterson, *Restless Giant,* 567.

40. Maurice Isserman and Michael Kazin, *America Divided: The Civil War of the 1960s* (New York: Oxford University Press, 2000), 209.

41. Rick Perlstein, *Nixonland: The Rise of a President and the Fracturing of America* (New York: Scribner, 2008), 115.

42. James Patterson, *Restless Giant,* 80.

43. Quoted in Rick Perlstein, *Nixonland,* 113.

44. Kenneth Heineman, *God Is a Conservative* (New York: New York University Press, 1998), 4.

45. Laurence Moore, *Selling God,* 249.

46. Richard Quebedeaux, *The Worldly Evangelicals* (San Francisco: Harper & Row, 1973), xi.

47. Heinemann, *God Is a Conservative,* 66.

48. Ibid., 73

49. Steven Hayward, *The Age of Reagan,* 487.

50. James Reichley, *Religion in American Life,* 321.

51. Patterson, *Restless Giant,* 139.

52. Robert C. Liebman and Robert Wuthnow, *The New Christian Right: Mobilization and Legitimization* (New York: Aldine, 1983), 55.

53. Balmer, *God in the White House*, 117.

54. David Kuo, *Tempting Faith: An Inside Story of Political Seduction* (New York: Free Press, 2006), 27.

55. Robert Sullivan, "An Army of the Faithful," *New York Times*, April 25, 1993.

56. Heinemann, *God Is a Conservative*, 7.

57. Ibid., 9.

58. Ibid., 147.

59. Mark Pinsky, *A Jew Among the Evangelicals: A Guide for the Perplexed* (Louisville, KY: Westminster John Knox, 2006), 61.

CHAPTER FOUR: BUSH, BLAIR, OBAMA AND THE GOD GAP (2000–2008)

1. Quoted in Michael Elliott, "Tony Blair's Leap of Faith," *Time*, May 28, 2008.

2. Kamal Ahmed, "And on the Seventh Day Tony Blair Created . . . ," *Observer*, August 3, 2003.

3. Adam Boulton, *Tony's Ten Years: Memories of the Blair Administration* (London: Simon & Schuster, 2008), 244.

4. Philip Jenkins, *God's Continent: Christianity, Islam and Europe's Religious Crisis* (Oxford: Oxford University Press), 38.

5. The question was asked by Jeremy Paxman on BBC's *Newsnight*, February 6, 2003.

6. David Kuo, *Tempting Faith: An Insider's Story of Political Seduction* (New York: Free Press, 2006), 168.

7. Quoted in Marsden, *Religion and American Culture*, 196–7 (see chap. 3, note 2).

8. Dana Milbank, "Religious Right Finds Its Center in Oval Office," *Washington Post*, December 24, 2001.

9. Pew Forum on Religion & Public Life, John C. Green et al., "The American Religious Landscape and the 2004 Presidential Vote."

10. Kevin Phillips, *American Theocracy: The Peril and Politics of Radical Religion, Oil and Borrowed Money in the 21ˢᵗ Century* (New York: Viking, 2006), 103.

11. Jonathan Raban, "September 11: The View from the West," *New York Review of Books*, September 22, 2005.

12. Ron Suskind, "Faith, Certainty and the Presidency of George W. Bush," *New York Times Magazine*, October 17, 2004.

13. Peter Ford, "What Place for God in Europe?" *Christian Science Monitor*, February 22, 2005.

14. Quoted in Timothy Garton Ash, *Free World: Why a Crisis of the West Reveals the Opportunity of Our Time* (London: Allen Lane, 2004), 55.

15. Dale Bus, *Family Man: The Biography of Dr. James Dobson* (Wheaton, Illinois: Tyndale House, 2005), 341.

16. Ibid., 217.

17. Garry Wills, "A Country Ruled by Faith," *New York Review of Books*, November 16, 2006.

18. Walter McDougall, *Promised Land, Crusader State: The American Encounter with the World Since 1776* (New York: Houghton Mifflin, 1997), 15.

19. John Judis, "The Chosen Nation: The Influence of Religion on U.S. Foreign Policy," Carnegie Endowment for International Peace, Policy Brief no. 37, March 2005.

20. McDougall, *Promised Land, Crusader State*, 169.

21. Michael Oren, *Power, Faith and Fantasy: America in the Middle East: 1776 to the Present* (New York: Norton, 2007), 476.

22. Eugene Rostow, *A Breakfast for Bonaparte: US National Security Interests from the Heights of Abraham to the Nuclear Age* (Washington, DC: National Defense University Press, 1993), 22.

23. http://religions.pewforum.org/comparisons#.

24. Pew Forum on Religion and Public Life, "Young White Evangelicals: Less Republican, Still Conservative," September 28, 2007.

25. Michael Oren, *Power, Faith and Fantasy: America in the Middle East: 1776 to the Present* (New York: Norton, 2007), 83.

26. Walter Russell Mead, "The New Israel and the Old: Why Gentile Americans Back the Jewish State," *Foreign Affairs*, July/August 2008.

27. Michael Oren, *Power, Faith and Fantasy*, 135.

28. Ibid., 142–3.

29. Mead, "The New Israel and the Old."

30. Dan Raviv and Rossi Melman, *Friends in Deed: Inside the US-Israel Alliance* (New York: Hyperion, 1994), 351–3.

31. :http://pewforum.org/docs/?DocID=80].

32. Mariah Blake, "Air Jesus," *Columbia Journalism Review*, October 3, 2008.

33. "Human Rights and Advocacy in the Mainline Protestant Churches (2000–03)," Institute on Religion and Democracy, 2004, Washington, DC.

34. Bob Woodward describes the frantic scene inside the White House on election night 2004, when the outcome seemed to hinge on the result in Ohio. The man in charge of certifying the tally was Kenneth Blackwell, a leading social conservative. "I'm the president of the United States," Bush fumed, "waiting for a secretary of state who is a nut."

35. Jim Wallis, *God's Politics: Why the Right Gets It Wrong and the Left Doesn't Get It* (San Francisco: HarperSanFrancisco, 2005).

36. Amy Sullivan, *The Party Faithful*, 126.

37. The Pew Forum on Religion and Public Life, "U.S. Religious Landscape Survey: Religious Beliefs and Practices: Diverse and Politically Relevant," June 2008, 5.

38. Ibid., 34.

39. Ibid., 95.

40. Ibid., 39.

41. Ibid., 50.

42. Ibid., 8.

43. J. M. Roberts, *A History of Europe* (London: Penguin 1996), 583.

44. Frank Bruni, "Faith Fades Where It Once Burned Strong," *New York Times*, Oxtober 13, 2003.

45. Andrew Kohut and Bruce Stokes, *America Against the World: How We are Different and Why We are Disliked* (New York: Times Books, 2006), 102.

46. "Faith Fades Where It Once Burned Strong," *New York Times*, October 13, 2003.

47. Philip Jenkins, *God's Continent*, 27.

48. Ibid., 33.

49. Ibid., 92.

50. Philip Jenkins, *The Next Christendom: The Coming of Global Christianity* (Oxford: Oxford University Press, 2002), 98–9.

51. Eric Kaufmann, "Breeding for God," *Prospect*, November 2006.

52. The Hume quote comes from a letter to *The Economist* from Professor Andrew Sabl of UCLA, published on August 23, 2008.

53. Philip Jenkins, *God's Continent*, 49.

54. Ibid., 70.

55. Jurgen Habermas and Joseph Ratzinger, *The Dialectics of Secularization: On Reason and Religion* (San Francisco: Ignatius, 2006). Habermas generously admitted this in newspaper articles.

56. Habermas's speech on "Faith and Knowledge" was given in Frankfurt after he received the peace prize from the German Book Trade on October 15, 2001.

CHAPTER FIVE: PRAY, RABBIT, PRAY

1. Christine Wicker, *The Fall of the Evangelical Nation: The Surprising Crisis Inside the Church* (New York: HarperOne, 2008), 40.

2. Ibid., 101.

3. As quoted by Rick Warren at a conference held by the Pew Forum on Religion and Public Life on "Myths of the Modern Megachurch," May 23, 2005.

4. Francis Galton, "Statistical Inquiries into the Efficacy of Prayer," *Fortnightly Review* 12, 125–35, 1872.

5. "Where Angels No Longer Fear to Tread," *The Economist*, March 21, 2008.

6. Daniel Hall, "Religious Attendance: More Cost-Effective than Lipitor?," *Journal of the American Board of Family Medicine* 19, 130–109, 2006.

7. John Dilulio, *Godly Republic: A Centrist Blueprint for America's Faith-Based Future* (Berkeley: University of California Press, 2007), 183.

8. Pew Research Center, "Are We Happy Yet?," February 2006.

9. John Dilulio, "Supporting Black Churches: Faith, Outreach and the Inner-City Poor," in E. J. Dionne and John Diiulio, eds., *What's God Got to Do with the American Experiment?* (Washington, DC: Brookings Institution Press, 2000), 122.

10. "Wealth from Worship," *The Economist,* December 24, 2005.

11. Robert Putnam, *Bowling Alone: The Collapse and Revival of American Community* (New York: Simon & Schuster, 2000), 65–79.

12. Andrew Greeley, "The Other America: Religion and Social Capital," *American Prospect* 32, May–June, 1997.

13. "Where Angels No Longer Fear to Tread," *The Economist,* March 21, 2008.

14. Jonathan Gruber and Daniel Hungerman, "Faith-Based Charity and Crowd Out During the Great Depression," NBER Working Paper No 11332.

15. De Tocqueville, *Democracy in America,* Book II, Chapter XIII.

16. "Centrifugal Forces," a survey of America, *The Economist,* July 16, 2005.

17. Peter Wollen and Joe Kerr, eds., *Autopia: Cars and Culture* (Chicago: Reaktion, 2002), 259.

18. Dale Bus, *Family Man.*

19. D. Michael Lindsay, *Faith in the Halls of Power* (New York: Oxford University Press, 2007), 187.

20. Ibid., 171.

21. Ibid., 177.

22. Ibid., 183.

23. Phred Dvorak, "Some Bosses Mix Managing with Their Faith," *Wall Street Journal,* October 9, 2006.

24. Russell Sholto, "Faith at Work," *New York Times Magazine,* October 31, 2004.

25. Rick Williams, "Serving the Master," *Christian Business Daily,* April 29, 2005.

26. Patti Waldmeir, "US Companies Fall Prey to Religious Lawsuits," *Financial Times,* December 6, 2005.

27. Lindsay, *Faith in the Halls of Power,* 176.

28. Ibid., 180.

29. Neela Bannerjee, "At Bosses' Invitation, Chaplains Come into Workplace and onto Payroll," *New York Times,* December 4, 2006.

30. Russell Shorto, "Faith at Work," *New York Times Magazine,* October 31, 2004.

31. Ram Cnaan, *The Other Philadelphia Story: How Local Congregations Support Quality of Life in Urban America* (Philadelphia: University of Pennsylvania Press, 2006), xvi.

32. Ibid., 25.

33. Ibid., 68.

34. Ibid., 39.

35. Ibid., 82.

36. Ibid., 72.

37. Ibid., 71.

38. Ibid., 116.

39. Ibid., 232.

40. Ibid., 236.

41. W. E. B. Du Bois, *The Philadelphia Negro: A Social Study* (Philadelphia: University of Pennsylvania Press, 1995 edition), 201.

42. Ram Cnaan, *The Other Philadelphia Story,* 133.

43. Ibid., 139, 116.
44. Ibid., 157.
45. Ibid., 160.
46. Ibid., 102.

CHAPTER SIX: THE GOD BUSINESS

1. William Lobdell, "Pastor's Empire Built on Acts of Faith and Cash," *Los Angeles Times*, September 19, 2004.
2. Christine Wicker, *The Fall of the Evangelical Nation* (New York: HarperOne), 103.
3. Pinsky, *A Jew Among the Evangelicals*, 123.
4. Julie Bloom, "Sustained by Faith, Film Reaches Top 5 at Box Office," *Herald Tribune*, October 6, 2008.
5. Ibid.
6. Pinsky, *A Jew Among the Evangelicals*, 114.
7. Lindsay, *Faith in the Halls of Power*, 132 (see chap. 1, n. 60).
8. Kathy Bruner, "Thinking Outside the Trivial TV Box," in Quentin Schultze and Robert Woods, eds., *Understanding Evangelical Media: The Changing Face of Christian Communication* (Downers Grove, IN: IVP Academic), 55.
9. Ralph Blumenthal, "Joel Osteen's Credo: Eliminate the Negative, Accentuate Prosperity," *New York Times*, March 30, 2006.
10. John Leland, "A Church That Packs Them In, 16,000 at a Time," *New York Times*, July 18, 2005.
11. William Symonds, "Earthly Empires," *BusinessWeek*, May 23, 2005.
12. Inés Peschiera, "Keeping an Eye on the Holy Rollers," *Consulting*, August 1, 2006.
13. R. Marie Griffith, "Fasting, Dieting and the Body in American Christianity," in Peter W. Williams, ed., *Perspectives on American Religion and Culture*, (Oxford: Blackwell, 1999), 222.
14. "Church of the Mighty Dollar," *BusinessWeek*, May 23, 2005.
15. "The 25 Most Influential Evangelicals in America," *Time*, February 7, 2005.

CHAPTER SEVEN: EMPIRES OF THE MIND

1. Robert Nisbet, *Conservatism: Dream and Reality*, 107.
2. John Rawls, *Political Liberalism* (New York: Columbia University Press, 1996), 1.
3. Amy Sullivan, *The Party Faithful*, 40–1.
4. Dorothy McInnis Scura, *Conversations with Tom Wolfe* (Jackson: University of Mississippi Press, 1990), 284.
5. David Brooks, "Kicking the Secularist Habit," *Atlantic Monthly*, March 2003.
6. Mike Davis, "Planet of Slums," *New Left Review*, March–April 2004.
7. Stanley Fish, "One University Under God," *Chronicle of Higher Education*, January 7, 2005.
8. Irving Kristol, "Christianity, Judaism and Socialism," in *Neoconservatism: Selected Essays: The Autobiography of an Idea* (New York: Ivan Dee, 1999).
9. Mark Gerson, *The Neoconservative Vision* (Lanham, MD: Madison Books, 1997), 154.
10. Novak, *The Spirit of Democratic Capitalism*, 14.
11. Richard John Neuhaus, *The Naked Public Square: Religion and Democracy in America* (Grand Rapids: Wm. B. Eerdmans, 1986), 37.
12. Robin Toner, "Anti-Abortion Group Maps Strategy," *New York Times*, June 27, 1993.
13. Daniel McCarthy, "Wonder-Working Power: The Roots and the Reach of the Religious Right," *Reason*, December 2006.
14. Damon Linker, *The Theocons: Secular America Under Siege* (New York: Doubleday, 2001), 221.
15. C. S. Lewis, *Mere Christianity* (New York: Macmillan, 1952), 61.
16. Lindsay, *Faith in the Halls of Power*, 78.
17. Laurie Goodstein and David Kirpatrick, "A New Breed of Evangelicals Joins U.S. Elite," *New York Times*, May 23, 2005.

18. Lillian Kwon, "Asian Americans Fast Becoming Dominant Face of Elite Campus Evangelicals," *Christian Post,* May 24, 2007.

19. Lindsay, *Faith in the Halls of Power,* 81–83.

20. Ibid., 80–81.

21. Laurie Goodstein and David Kirkpatrick, "On a Christian Mission to the Top," *New York Times,* May 22, 2005.

22. Lindsay, *Faith in the Halls of Power,* 83.

CHAPTER EIGHT: EXPORTING AMERICA'S GOD

1. Pew Forum on Religion and Public Life, "A 10-Country Survey of Pentecostals," October 2006.

2. "O Come All Ye Faithful," *The Economist,* November 1, 2007.

3. Ibid.

4. Ibid.

5. Pew, "A 10-Country Survey of Pentecostals."

6. Harvey Gallacher Cox, "Healers and Ecologists: Pentecostalism in Africa," *Christian Century,* November 1994.

7. Pew Forum on Religion and Public Life, "A 10-Country Survey of Pentecostas," October 2006.

8. Jenkins, *The Next Christendom,* 68.

9. Martin E. Marty and R. Scott Appleby, *The Fundamentalism Project, American Academy of Arts and Sciences* (Chicago: University of Chicago Press, 1991), 415–16.

10. Steve Brouwer, Paul Gifford and Susan D. Rose, with contributors Steve Brouwer and Paul Gifford, *Exporting the American Gospel: Global Christian Fundamentalism* (New York: Routledge, 1996), 20.

11. "Lighting on New Faiths or None," *The Economist,* May 3, 2007.

12. Ibid.

13. Ibid.

14. Ibid.

15. World Christian Database.

16. Robert Kagan, *Dangerous Nation: America's Place in the World from Its Earliest Days to the Dawn of the 20th Century* (New York: Knopf, 2007), 8.

17. Walter Russell Mead, *Special Providence: American Foreign Policy and How it Changed the World* (Knopf: New York, 2001), 143.

18. Michael Oren, *Power, Faith and Fantasy: America in the Middle East: 1776 to the Present* (New York: Norton, 2007), 409.

19. Nancy Gibbs and Michael Duffy, *The Preacher and the Presidents* (New York: Center Street, 2007), 65.

20. "The Battle of the Books," *The Economist,* December 23, 2007.

21. Allen Hertzke, *Freeing God's Children: The Unlikely Alliance for Global Human Rights* (New York: Rowman & Littlefield, 2004), 1.

22. Ibid., 3.

23. Dhaleen Glanton, "When T. D. Jakes Talks . . . ," *Today's Christian,* http://www.christianitytoday.com/tc/2005/001/16.42.html.

24. www.tdjakes.com.

25. www.tdjakes.com.

26. "Rick Warren Challenges South Korean Churches for a Third Wave of Revival," PR Newswire, July 16.

27. "Praying for Gain," *The Economist,* August 23, 2007.

28. Lindsay, *Faith in the Halls of Power,* 176 (see chap. 1, n. 60).

29. Hudson Institute, *Index of Global Philanthropy for 2008.*

30. Mariah Blake, "Air Jesus," *Columbia Journalism Review,* October 3, 2008.

31. Jonathan Rice, "The New Missions Generation," *Christianity Today*, January 9, 2006.

32. Paul Wiseman and Jean Chung, "South Korean Missionaries May Cut Trips," *USA Today*, August 29, 2007.

33. K. J. Guest, *God in Chinatown: Religion and Survival in New York's Evolving Immigrant Community* (New York: New York University Press, 2003).

34. The National Institute for the Renewal of the Priesthood.

35. www.foursqaurechurch.org.

36. "A New Breed of Monk Rises in Myanmar: Sitagu Sayadaw Mixes Compassion and Self-Promotion," *Wall Street Journal*, August 19, 2008.

37. Simon Elegant and Jason Tedjasukmana-Bandung, "Holy Man," *Time*, November 4, 2002.

38. "Incense, Silk and Jihad," *The Economist*, May 29, 2008.

39. Elegant and Tedjasukmana-Bandung, "Holy Man."

40. "Incense, Silk and Jihad."

41. http://www.theage.com.au/opinion/just-how-many-people-are-behind-the-polygamy-push-20080626-2xfm.html?page=-1.

42. http://insideindonesia.org/content/view/1011/47/.

43. Samantha M. Shapiro, "Ministering to the Upwardly Mobile Muslim," *New York Times*, April 30, 2006.

44. David Hardaker, "Amr Khaled: Islam's Billy Graham," *The Independent*, January 4, 2006.

CHAPTER NINE: ALL THAT IS HOLY IS PROFANED

1. Richard Tedlow, *Giants of Enterprise: Seven Business Innovators and the Empires They Built* (New York: Harper Business, 2001), 421–22.

2. The study was released on March 23, 2006.

3. Steve Coll, *The Bin Ladens: An Arabian Family in the American Century* (New York: Penguin, 2008), 380.

4. E. J. Dionne, *Souled Out: Reclaiming Faith and Politics after the Religious Right* (Princeton: Princeton University Press, 2008), 129.

5. Steve Coll, *The Bin Ladens*, 503.

6. John Thornhill, "Sarkozy Sets Out Bigger State Role," *Financial Times*, September 25, 2008.

7. Michael Elliott, "Tony Blair's Leap of Faith," *Time*, June 9, 2008.

8. Ibid.

9. Steve Coll, *The Bin Ladens*, 135.

10. Ibid., 189.

11. Ibid., 457.

12. Ibid., 560.

13. Ibid., 380.

14. Ibid., 566.

15. Claudia Deutsch, "GE: A General Store for Developing World," *International Herald Tribune*, July 18, 2005.

16. "Puritans or Pornographers," *The Economist*, February 25, 2006.

CHAPTER TEN: THE BIBLE VERSUS THE KORAN

1. Bruce Lawrence, *The Qur'an: A Biography* (New York: Atlantic Monthly Press, 2006), 1, 7.

2. Ibid.

3. William Grayam and Navid Kermani, "Recitation and Aesthetic Reception," in Jane Dammen McAuliffee, ed., *The Cambridge Companion to the Qur'an* (Cambridge: Cambridge University Press, 2006), 121.

4. John Esposito and Dalia Mogahed, *Who Speaks for Islam? What a Billion Muslims Really Think* (Washington, D.C.: Gallup Poll Press, 2008), 6.

5. C. E. Padwick, *Muslim Devotions: A Study of Prayer-Manuals in Common Use* (London: SPCK, 1961), 119.

6. Simon Henderson "Institutionalized Islam: Saudi Arabia's Islamic Policies and the Threat

They Pose," (testimony before the Senate Judiciary Committee Subcommittee on Terrorism, U.S. Senate, September 10, 2003).

7. Quoted in Coll, *The Bin Ladens*, 149.

8. David Ottoway, "U.S. Eyes Money Trails of Saudi-Backed Charities," *Washington Post*, August 19, 2004.

9. Nina Shea, "Saudi Arabia: Friend or Foe in the War on Terror?" (testimony before the Judiciary Committee, U.S. Senate, November 8, 2005).

10. Ibid., 5.

11. Simon Henderson, "Institutionalized Islam," 11.

12. Simon Henderson, "Institutionalized Islam."

13. Oren, *Power, Faith and Fantasy*, 42.

14. "Come to the Ark," *The Economist*, May 22, 2008.

15. Bernard Lewis, *The Crisis of Islam* (New York: Modern Library, 2003), 16.

16. Gallup Center for Muslim Studies, "Ordinary Muslims" (special Report on the Muslim World, March 6, 2007).

17. Timothy Savage, "Europe and Islam: Crescent Waxing, Cultures Clashing," *Washington Quarterly*, Summer 2004; "When Town Halls Turn to Mecca," *The Economist*, December 6, 2008.

18. "Incense, Silk and Jihad," *The Economist*, May 29, 2008.

19. Coll, *The Bin Ladens*, 443.

20. Ibid., 447.

21. "The Med's Moment Comes," *The Economist*, July 10, 2008.

22. "How to Spend It," *The Economist*, April 24, 2008.

23. "Will the Dam Burst?," *The Economist*, September 11, 2008.

24. Coll, *The Bin Ladens*, 442–43.

25. Melanie Phillips, *Londonistan* (New York: Encounter Books, 2006), x.

26. Pew Research Center for the People and the Press, "Views of a Changing World, 2003," June 3, 2003.

27. "Of Saints and Sinners," *The Economist*, December 20, 2008.

28. Larry Siedentop, *Democracy in Europe* (Harmondsworth: Allen Lane, 2000), 208.

29. Christopher Dickey and Owen Matthews, "The New Face of Islam," *Newsweek*, June 9, 2008.

30. Rodney Stark, *The Victory of Reason: How Christianity Led to Freedom, Capitalism and Western Success* (New York: Random House, 2005).

31. Thomas Farr, *World of Faith and Freedom: Why International Religious Liberty is Vital to American National Security* (New York: Oxford University Press, 2008), 5–6.

32. "In Death's Shadow," *The Economist*, July 24, 2008.

33. "The Moment of Truth," *The Economist*, July 24, 2008.

34. John Micklethwait is a former trustee of Policy Exchange but had no involvement with this study.

35. Pew Research Center for the People and the Press, "Middle Class and Mostly Mainstream," May 22, 2007.

36. Samuel Huntington, *The Third Wave: Democratization in the Late Twentieth Century* (Norman: University of Oklahoma Press, 1991), 77–78.

37. George Weigel, "Pope on a Mission to Surprise," *Standpoint*, October 2008.

CHAPTER ELEVEN: THE NEW WARS OF RELIGION

1. The numbers are catalogued in Shehu Sani, *The Killing Fields: Religious Violence in Northern Nigeria*, (Ibadan, Nigeria: Spectrum Books 2007).

2. "In God's Name," *The Economist*, November 1, 2007.

3. Ibid.

4. "The Muslims and Christians of Jos," *The Economist*, December 6, 2008.

5. "In God's Name," *The Economist*, November 1, 2007.

6. Thomas Donnelly, "A Question of Faith: Conflicts Driven by Religion Can Be Long and Bitter," American Enterprise Institute for Public Policy Research, December 27, 2006.

7. W. E. H. Lecky, *History of the Rise and Influence of the Spirit of Rationalism in Europe* (New York: D. Appleton, 1866), 111.

8. Eliza Griswold, "God's Country," *Atlantic Monthly*, March 2008.

9. Department of State, *International Religious Freedom Report*, 2004. Uganda.

10. Philip Jenkins, *The Next Christendom*, 155.

11. Quoted in Michael Scott Doran, "The Saudi Paradox," *Foreign Affairs* January–February 2004, 46.

12. "Does It Have to Be War?," *The Economist*, March 2, 2006.

13. Ibid.

14. Maulana Kalbe Sadiq.

15. "The widening Gulf," *The Economist*, February 1, 2007.

16. Ibid.

17. "Try to Be Nice About Each Other," *The Economist*, September 25, 2008.

18. Graham Fuller, "A World Without Islam," *Foreign Policy*, January–February 2008.

19. "Just What Are They Dreaming Of?," *The Economist*, February 9, 2008.

20. Anton La Guardia, "Special Report on al-Qaeda," *The Economist*, July 17, 2008.

21. Philip Jenkins, *The Next Christendom*, 167 (table 8.1).

22. "More Religions, More Trouble," *The Economist*, July 17, 2008.

23. Ibid.

24. Philip Jenkins, *The Next Christendom*, 178

25. "The New Wars of Religion," *The Economist*, November 1, 2007.

26. Ibid.

27. "Holy Depressing," *The Economist*, November 1, 2007.

28. Daniel Benjamin and Steven Simon, *The Age of Sacred Terror* (New York: Random House), 192.

29. "Bridging the Divide," *The Economist*, November 1, 2007.

30. Ibid.

31. Ibid.

CHAPTER TWELVE: THE CULTURE WARS GO GLOBAL

1. Richard Tomkins, "A Religion in Recession," *Financial Times* weekend magazine, July 12–13, 2008.

2. Numbers from Christian Research. Quoted in Richard Tomkins, "A Religion in Recession," *Financial Times* weekend magazine, July 12–13, 2008.

3. "Flags, Veils and Sharia," *The Economist*, July 17, 2008.

4. "Islamic Extremism: Common Concern for Muslim and Western Publics," The Pew Global Attitudes Project, July 2005.

5. "Flags, Veils and Sharia," *The Economist*, July 17, 2008.

6. "Turkey to Lift University Head Scarf Ban," *Spiegel Online International*, January 25, 2008.

7. "Pro-Lie or Pro-Berlusconi," *The Economist*, February 21, 2008.

8. "The Polish Farewell," *The Economist*, November 29, 2007.

9. Giuliano Ferrara helped to get our previous book, *The Right Nation*, published in Italy. He is also fiercely critical of *The Economist*'s attitude toward Silvio Berlusconi.

10. "The Atheist Urging Italy to Get Religion," *New York Times*, April 6, 2008.

11. "The Bishops Revolt," *The Economist*, January 10, 2008.

12. Rosie Millard, "Interview: The Rev. Gene Robinson," (London) *Sunday Times*, July 27, 2008.

13. Ayelish McGarvey, "Evangelical Elitists: The Exclusive Church Where Washington's Conservative Power Brokers Pray," *Washington Monthly*, December 2004.

14. Michael Paulson, "Consecration in Kenya Widens a Religious Rift," *Boston Globe*, August 31, 2007.

15. Laurie Goodstein, "Episcopalians Are Reaching Point of Revolt," *New York Times,* December 17, 2006.

16. World Health Organization, *Development of a Regional Position on Human Cloning,* 2004.

17. Ipsos Mori poll for BBC's *Horizon* series.

18. "A Dressing Down," *The Economist,* October 11, 2007.

19. Barbara Franz, "Europe's Mediterranean Youth," *Mediterranean Quarterly,* Winter 2007.

20. Ian Johnson and John Carreyrou, "In France 'Political Islam' Preaches Intolerance; Challenge to Secularism," *Wall Street Journal,* July 11, 2005.

21. Anthony King, "One in Four Muslims Sympathizes with Motives of Terrorists," *Daily Telegraph,* July 23, 2005.

22. See http://www.socialcohesion.co.uk /pdf/IslamonCampus.pdf.

23. See http://www.timesonline.co.uk/tol/news/world/europe/article651080.ece.

24. Andrew Higgins, "Why Islam is Unfunny for a Cartoonist," *Wall Street Journal,* July 12–13, 2008.

25. Phillips, *Londonistan,* 95.

26. Ibid., 61.

27. Jennifer Butler, *Born Again: The Christian Right Globalized* (London: Pluto Press, 2006), 2.

28. Ibid., 3.

CONCLUSION: LEARNING TO LIVE WITH RELIGION

1. Michael Luo, "In New York, Billy Graham Will Find an Evangelical Force," *New York Times,* June 21, 2005.

2. Timothy Shah and Monica Toft, "Religion's Flame Burns Brighter Than Ever," *Baltimore Sun,* August 20, 2006.

3. Harvey Cox, *Fire from Heaven: The Rise of Pentecostal Spirituality and the Reshaping of Religion in the Twenty-First Century,* 184.

4. "A Modern Prophet Goes Global," *The Economist,* January 4, 2007.

5. Olivier Roy, *The Politics of Chaos in the Middle East* (New York: Columbia University Press, 2008), 146–50.

6. Madeleine Albright, *The Mighty and the Almighty: Reflections on America, God and World Affairs* (New York: HarperCollins, 2006).

7. Ibid., 8.

8. Farr, *World of Faith and Freedom,* ix.

9. Ibid., 31.

10. Jeff Stein, "Can You Tell a Sunni from a Shiite?," *New York Times,* October 17, 2006.

11. "Mixed Blessings: US Government Engagement with Religion in Conflict-Prone Settings," Post-Conflict Reconstruction Project, Center for Strategic and International Studies, July 2007, 39.

12. Claudia Deane and Darryl Fears, "Negative Perception of Islam Increasing," *Washington Post,* March 9, 2006.

13. Pew Forum for Religion & Public Life, "Public Expresses Mixed Views of Islam, Mormonism," September 25, 2007.

14. Olivier Roy, *The Politics of Chaos in the Middle East* (New York: Columbia University Press, 2008), 49–50.

15. Ibid., 95.

16. Ibid., 73.

17. Peter Ford, "What Place for God in Europe?," *Christian Science Monitor,* February 22, 2005.

18. Stanley Sloan, "Religion and Politics: All the President's Truths," *International Herald Tribune,* May 18, 2005.

19. George Weigel, *The Cube and the Cathedral: Europe, America, and Politics Without God* (New York: Basic Books, 2005), 19, 135.

20. Farr, *World of Faith and Freedom.*

21. "When Religions Talk," *The Economist,* July 12, 2008.

22. Thomas Paine, *The Rights of Man.*

23. Quoted in Waldman, *Founding Faith,* 75.

24. Kevin Phillips, *American Theocracy: The Peril and Politics of Radical Religion, Oil, and Borrowed Money in the 21st Century,* 182.

25. Steven Waldman, *Founding Faith,* 203.

26. The Pew Forum on Religion & Public Life, *U.S. Religious Landscape Survey: Religious Beliefs and Practices: Diverse and Politically Relevant,* June 2008, 21.

27. Prothero, *Religious Literacy,* 23.

INDEX